THE BIG SORT

D0037300

THE
BIG SORT

Why the Clustering of
Like-Minded America Is
Tearing Us Apart

BILL BISHOP

with Robert G. Cushing

MARINER BOOKS
HOUGHTON MIFFLIN HARCOURT
BOSTON • NEW YORK

For Julie Ardery
and Frances Cushing

First Mariner Books edition 2009

Copyright © 2008 by Bill Bishop

ALL RIGHTS RESERVED

For information about permission to reproduce
selections from this book, write to Permissions,
Houghton Mifflin Harcourt Publishing Company,
215 Park Avenue South, New York, New York 10003.

www.hmhbooks.com

Library of Congress Cataloging-in-Publication Data
Bishop, Bill, date.
The big sort : why the clustering of like-minded America
is tearing us apart / Bill Bishop.
p. cm.
Includes bibliographical references and index.
ISBN 978-0-618-68935-4
1. Minorities — United States. 2. Political culture — United
States. 3. Group identity — Political aspects — United States.
4. Segregation — Political aspects — United States. 5. Region-
alism — Political aspects — United States. 6. Polarization
(Social sciences) 7. Social conflict — United States. 8. United
States — Politics and government — 1989– 9. United States
— Social conditions — 1980– I. Title.
E184.A1B5527 2008 005.800973 — dc22 2007043907

ISBN 978-0-547-23772-5 (PBK.)

Printed in the United States of America

Book design by Victoria Hartman

DOC 10 9 8 7 6 5 4 3 2 1

CONTENTS

THE BIG SORT

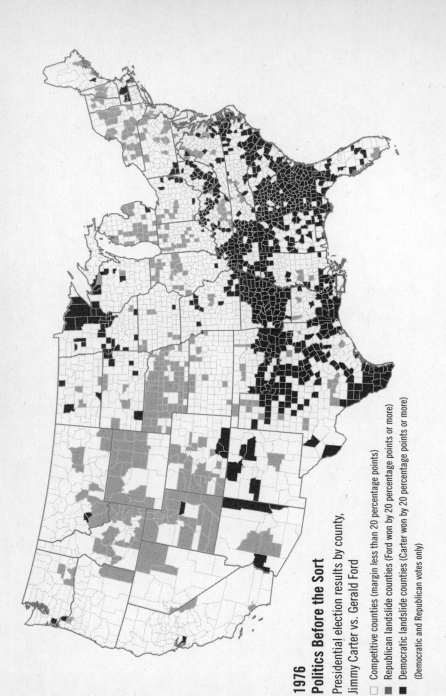

1976
Politics Before the Sort

Presidential election results by county,
Jimmy Carter vs. Gerald Ford

☐ Competitive counties (margin less than 20 percentage points)

▨ Republican landslide counties (Ford won by 20 percentage points or more)

■ Democratic landslide counties (Carter won by 20 percentage points or more)

(Democratic and Republican votes only)

2004
Politics After the Sort

Presidential election results by county,
John Kerry vs. George W. Bush

☐ Competitive counties (margin less than 20 percentage points)

▨ Republican landslide counties (Bush won by 20 percentage points or more)

■ Democratic landslide counties (Kerry won by 20 percentage points or more)

(Democratic and Republican votes only)

2008
The Sort Continues

Presidential election results by county,
Barack Obama vs. John McCain

☐ Competitive counties (margin less than 20 percentage points)

▨ Republican landslide counties (McCain won by 20 percentage points or more)

■ Democratic landslide counties (Obama won by 20 percentage points or more)

(Democratic and Republican votes only)

INTRODUCTION

> Most of us make at least three important decisions
> in our lives: where to live, what to do, and with whom
> to do it.
>
> — DANIEL GILBERT, *Stumbling on Happiness*

MY WIFE AND I made the move to Austin, Texas, in the way of middle-class American migrants. We rented a Ford Taurus at the airport, bought an Austin map at a U-Tote-Um quick stop, and toured the city in search of a place to live. We didn't have a list of necessities — granite countertops or schools with killer SATs — as much as we had a mental image of the place we belonged. We drove and when a place felt comfortable, seemed right, my wife, the daughter of one of Kentucky's last New Deal liberals, drew a smiley face on the map.

We didn't intend to move into a community filled with Democrats, but that's what we did — effortlessly and without a trace of understanding about what we were doing. We bought a house on one of those smiley-face streets, a shady neighborhood of dog walkers, Jane Jacobs–approved front porches, bright paint, bowling-ball yard art, and YOU KEEP BELIEVING; WE'LL KEEP EVOLVING bumper stickers. In 2000, George W. Bush, then the governor of Texas, took 60 percent of the state's vote. But in our patch of Austin, Bush came in third, behind both Al Gore and Ralph Nader. Four years later, eight out of ten of our neighbors voted for John Kerry.

Our neighborhood is one of the friendliest I've encountered. It is in some ways more like the rural Texas town where we lived for a time, publishing the weekly newspaper, than a community on the edge of the central city. We have potlucks in the park and movies for the kids. A woman down the street organizes outdoor concerts to raise money so the toddlers' pool in the neighborhood park stays wet and open into the torrid Texas September. We take just as much pride in our politics. Soon after the invasion of Iraq, our neighbors held a meeting and decided to print antiwar T-shirts and bumper stickers. The agreed-upon slogan promoted both place and policy. It said simply, 78704PEACE. In Austin, Zip Codes have political meaning.

I live in a place where any event holds the potential for political expression, even a neighborhood house fire. On a summer afternoon, I happened on a slew of red trucks and hoses wet and slithering across a street. Firefighters were dousing the spooky Victorian on the corner. The commotion had drawn out the neighbors and a television news crew. The owners of the smoldering house had been rehabbing the structure for years, and it was beginning to shape up. The house was big and yellow, but I remembered it mostly because it sported a large peace sign dangling from the peak of a third-story window. The sign was five feet across and wrapped with Christmas twinkle lights. I commiserated with a woman walking two dogs. She had noticed the peace sign, too. Holding the leashes in one hand, she motioned toward the TV cameraman. "I hope he gets the peace sign in the picture," she said. "After all, it's Travis Heights."

Far from avoiding politics as a topic of discussion in neighborly talks, Travis Heights encourages it. That the woman could speak comfortably to me about politics evinces the solidarity of the people who live here. It was simply understood that we agreed about the peace sign — and about all the issues and ways of life the peace sign represented. Our like-mindedness was a comfort, a shortcut to intimacy.

It can also be a shortcut to conflict. We have a neighborhood Internet listserver in South Austin that is often a source of good information about painters, plumbers, and lost animals. The e-discussion can also become a parody of liberal preciousness. One participant wrote to say that he planned to live-trap rats that had invaded his garage. The vermin-friendly homeowner wanted to know where it might be safe to "relocate" the rodents. The one Republican on the newsgroup, Stephen Mason, dared to say what most of us probably thought, volunteering that the man could release the varmints near Mason's rat terrier, Hotard, who would happily "relocate them to rat heaven." Our lone conservative correspondent, however, knew better than to make his comments overtly political. Mason, an intellectual property attorney and Texas A&M graduate, had tried to start a genuine political discussion on the list the year before. He wasn't about to try again.

It was the spring of 2004, so things were already tense when Mason called the newsgroup's attention to the election for the board of the local community college. Mason gave the names of both candidates, listed their websites, and then, after a warning that what followed was "possibly inappropriate electioneering," recommended one of the candidates. The man Mason backed was deeply conservative, a member of the Federalist Society, a former officer of the Young Conservatives of Texas, and an opponent of gay marriage and adoption. Within the day, the newsgroup reacted in a way that wasn't as much ideological as biological. Mason wasn't just someone to be argued against. For the protection of the group, he needed to be isolated, sealed off, and expelled.

First response:

Okay, as a member of this list, I'd really like to see this political discussion disappear. As a lesbian, obviously I'm not going to vote for anybody who doesn't believe I shouldn't be allowed to adopt kids . . . As a resident of Travis Heights and a member of this neighborhood list, I'm not interested in having this kind of discussion here. I have to defend myself against my government pretty much daily these days, and one place I don't want to have to do it is on this list.

And then:

A-men. Stephen, you're in the minority politically on this list and in this neighborhood, and while your opinions are your own to have, this list isn't the place for them . . . T-Hts is my home, and this list an extension of that . . . I hope we can all agree to prevent it from becoming a battleground.

Mason responded:

[The] ideological balkanization of America is dead-on true . . . Living here, especially as an "out" Republican, is a great deal of fun, and I learn a great deal from it. The most valuable thing that I learn daily is the capacity to respect people with whom I have disagreements. I hope not to be exiled to some place where the vast majority agrees with me.

Then, alas, enough with the calls for reasoned discussion:

I'm really not interested [in] being surprised by right-wing e-mail in my in box, no matter what its guise. It makes me feel bad, and I don't like it.

There were dissenting views. "I really don't want political or other uncomfortable subjects segregated into some kind of opinion ghetto where only proselytizing activists and ideologues would venture," wrote one South Austinite. Another: "I'm going to stick my neck out here. I DO want to have political discussion . . . It is a tragedy that this country is becoming more and more polarized. Neighborhoods are becoming more and more homogeneous, either Democrat or Republican. Talk about segregation!" But Mason got the picture: he was a Republican Crusoe on this Democratic island, and so he withdrew, promising never to talk politics again with his neighbors.

"Look, I know a lot about homogeneous political communities," Mason said one afternoon at a South Austin coffeehouse. He'd grown up in the Republican suburbs of Houston and attended the conservative hive of Texas A&M University. He was pugnacious about his politics, ending every e-mail message with a quote from Teddy Roosevelt: "Aggressive fighting for the right is the greatest sport in the world." Mason was also engaged to marry a feminist filmmaker, an experience that taught him that "nearly everything is political." But nothing had prepared him for the unsettling experience of being a political minority in the community where he lived — for being a minority in the age of political segregation. "I ran off that listserve when the rhetoric became so shrill that I didn't have the taste for saying about anyone the things you would need to say to win that argument," Mason continued. "I'm not going to use that listserve for politics again, and there is some shame in that." The experience had changed the way he saw himself in the neighborhood.

Knowing he was a minority, he wondered what people thought of him as he walked Hotard. "In some way after that exchange, I think I'm viewed with suspicion by my neighbors because of an act of political expression, which is a little on the bizarre side," he said. "I'm just a guy who has a dog and works a job."[1]

Discovering the Big Sort

The "red" and "blue" states shown on television maps during the past several national elections depict a country in a static standoff. On this scale, politics is a game of Risk. What will it take for Republicans to capture Michigan? For Democrats to regain Ohio? But people don't live in states. They live in communities. And those communities are not close to being in equipoise, even within solidly blue or red states. They are, most of them, becoming even more Democratic or Republican. As Americans have moved over the past three decades, they have clustered in communities of sameness, among people with similar ways of life, beliefs, and, in the end, politics. Little, if any, of this political migration was by design, a conscious effort by people to live among like-voting neighbors. When my wife and I moved to Austin, we didn't go hunting for the most Democratic neighborhood in town. But the result was the same: moving to Travis Heights, we took a side and fell into a stark geographic pattern of political belief, one that has grown more distinct in presidential elections since 1976.

Over the past thirty years, the United States has been sorting itself, sifting at the most microscopic levels of society, as people have packed children, CDs, and the family hound and moved. Between 4 and 5 percent of the population moves each year from one county to another — 100 million Americans in the past decade. They are moving to take jobs, to be close to family, or to follow the sun. When they look for a place to live, they run through a checklist of amenities: Is there the right kind of church nearby? The right kind of coffee shop? How close is the neighborhood to the center of the city? What are the rents? Is the place safe? When people move, they also make choices about who their neighbors will be and who will share their new lives. Those are now political decisions, and they are having a profound effect on the nation's public life. It

wasn't just my neighborhood that had tipped to become politically mo-
nogamous. In 1976, less than a quarter of Americans lived in places
where the presidential election was a landslide. By 2004, nearly half of
all voters lived in landslide counties.

In 2004, the press was buzzing about polarization, the inability of the
leaders of the two political parties to find even a patch of common
ground. All the measures of political ideology showed widening divisions between Democratic and Republican political leaders, and unbri-
dled partisanship in national politics became a topic for Sunday news
shows and newspaper columnists. Meanwhile, unnoticed, people had
been reshaping the way they lived. Americans were forming tribes, not
only in their neighborhoods but also in churches and volunteer groups.
That's not the way people would describe what they were doing, but in
every corner of society, people were creating new, more homogeneous
relations. Churches were filled with people who looked alike and, more
important, thought alike. So were clubs, civic organizations, and volunteer groups. Social psychologists had studied like-minded groups and
could predict how people living and worshiping in homogeneous groups
would react: as people heard their beliefs reflected and amplified, they
would become more extreme in their thinking. What had happened over
three decades wasn't a simple increase in political partisanship, but a
more fundamental kind of self-perpetuating, self-reinforcing social division. The like-minded neighborhood supported the like-minded church,
and both confirmed the image and beliefs of the tribe that lived and worshiped there. Americans were busy creating social resonators, and the
hum that filled the air was the reverberated and amplified sound of their
own voices and beliefs.

This was not an area of concern for most of those who wrote about
politics. Migration wasn't thought to be much of a factor in politics. People moved, sure, and some states gained votes while others lost. But the
effects were thought to be essentially a wash.[2] Frankly, I only stumbled
upon this trend in American politics — and that was only after I stumbled upon Robert Cushing.

I had previously worked for a small paper in the coalfields of Eastern
Kentucky, and my wife and I had owned a weekly newspaper in rural

Texas. From my experience living in small towns, I had become interested in why some communities develop vibrant economies while others stagnate, and I had written about this question as a newspaper columnist in Kentucky and then a reporter in Austin. Cushing was a sociologist and statistician who had recently retired from the University of Texas. My parents were friends with a cousin of Bob's wife, Frances. Through that tenuous connection, we met for breakfast one morning.

I remember telling Bob I had some data about Austin's economy but didn't know quite what to do with it. "I do," Bob responded. That was typical Bob, a guy who had paid his way through graduate school by working summers fighting forest fires as a Smokejumper in Montana. He did know what to do with the pile of data I had collected, and we began collaborating on projects for the *Austin American-Statesman*. We would decide on a question we wanted to answer, and Bob would begin clicking, programming, and calculating. Often in the middle of the night, a new set of charts and Excel files would arrive in my e-mail in box, and I'd see that Bob had made another remarkable discovery.

Our interest initially was why a small group of cities, Austin among them, were growing so fast and so rich. In 2002, we began working with a band of researchers, including Richard Florida and Kevin Stolarick, then at Carnegie Mellon University; Gary Gates at the Urban Institute; Joe Cortright in Portland, Oregon; and Terry Nichols Clark at the University of Chicago. What we found was that these tech-rich and innovative cities were benefiting from a special kind of migration.

There have always been patterns to migration and development. Southern blacks moved to Chicago in the 1950s. White Appalachians took the "hillbilly highway" north to booming Cleveland and Detroit after World War II. These were migrations in response to economic hardship and opportunity. The movements we saw from 1970 to 2000 were different. The flows were selective, and they varied by personal characteristics, not broad demographic descriptions. People were sorting, and the movements themselves were changing economies. Young people left old industrial towns and rural America for urban life, moving to a small group of cities. People earning higher incomes went to Austin or San Francisco. Those with lower incomes moved out of those towns. Las Vegas attracted people with less education than those who went to Seattle. Portland slurped up people with college degrees. Blacks went to Atlanta and Washington, D.C.; whites went to Austin and Orlando.

Everyone in our research group had a particular specialty. Demographer Gary Gates discovered that gay couples were congregating in particular cities — specific Zip Codes, in fact. Rich Florida and Kevin Stolarick calculated the correlation between particular types of workers — what would become Florida's "creative class" of artists, engineers, software writers, and teachers — and economic growth.[3] Joe Cortright was interested in the migration of the young. Terry Clark discovered the amenities that attracted high-wage workers. Bob Cushing and I used patents to measure economic innovation in cities. We tracked people and their incomes from county to county using Internal Revenue Service (IRS) data. We used polling data from an advertising firm to find a relationship between culture and economic growth, and we tracked various demographic groups as they moved into high-tech cities such as Austin. Everyone in our group found movements that were dizzying and profound. We could see that distinct migratory streams were reshaping regional economies. Somebody in our little ad hoc research outfit said that the zigzagging of people and money looked like "the big sort," and the name stuck.

The Politics of Place

Initially, Cushing and I were so interested in the economic effects of the Big Sort that we paid no attention to whether the phenomenon meant anything to politics. That was an oversight. After all, the movements we were tracking were enormous. More people were moving from one county to another in a single year than new population was added nationally in four years. It was clear the Big Sort wasn't random. The sorting we saw in the last decades of the twentieth century created prosperity in some places and decimated economies in others. It just made sense that this internal migration had changed the nation's politics, too. Then I received one of those magnificent midnight e-mails from Cushing.

He had access to presidential voting results for each U.S. county since 1948, collected by the web-based election data impresario David Leip. The presidential election is the only national office common to all voters. We decided to use presidential election results — instead of either voter registration or state elections — as the common measurement among the nation's more than 3,100 counties to avoid the effects of different candidates or changing voting districts. To even out the comparisons over time, we excluded third-party candidates.[4] Demographers have several ways to measure segregation, and Cushing tested them all. The formulas tell, for example, whether the proportion of blacks and whites living in Brooklyn is similar to the proportion of the races in New York City as a whole. Substitute Republican and Democrat for black and white, and these formulas provide a measure of political segregation. We ran the numbers for all the counties in the United States, and a pattern emerged.[5] From 1948 to 1976, the vote jumped around, but in the close elections, Republicans and Democrats became more evenly mixed, especially in the 1976 contest (see Table I.1). After 1976, the trend was for Republicans and Democrats to grow more geographically segregated.

The simplest way to describe this political big sort was to look across time at the proportion of voters who lived in landslide counties — counties where one party won by 20 percentage points or more. There were elections when the entire country seemed to side with one party or the other. In the electoral blowouts of 1964, 1972, and 1984, close to six out of ten voters lived in landslide counties. Landslide elections produced a lot of landslide communities.

Competitive elections provided a more accurate picture of where Republicans and Democrats were living. The 1976 election between President Gerald Ford and Jimmy Carter took place at the time after World War II when Americans were most likely to live, work, or worship with people who supported a different political party. Just over 26 percent of the nation's voters lived in landslide counties.

Then the country began segregating. In 1992, 37.7 percent of American voters lived in landslide counties. By 2000, that number had risen to 45.3 percent. There was a difference between the elections prior to 1976 and those that came after. In the polarizing, and close, 1968 election between Richard Nixon and Hubert Humphrey, 37.2 percent of voters lived in landslide counties. The last five presidential elections have all

Table I.1 Close Elections, Local Landslides

In competitive elections, more voters are living in counties with lopsided presidential votes.

	Percent of voters in landslide counties		
	Competitive elections	Uncompetitive elections	Victory margin
1948	35.8		4.7
1952		39.9	10.9
1956		46.6	15.5
1960	32.9		0.2
1964		63.5	22.7
1968	37.2		0.8
1972		59.0	23.6
1976	26.8		2.1
1980		41.8	10.6
1984		55.0	18.3
1988	41.7		7.8
1992	37.7		6.9
1996	42.1		9.5
2000	45.3		0.5
2004	48.3		2.5

Note: This table shows the proportion of voters living in counties where the local presidential election was decided by 20 or more percentage points. Competitive elections are those decided by 10 percentage points or fewer. (Third-party votes aren't included.)
Source: Dave Leip's Atlas of U.S. Presidential Elections, http://www.uselectionatlas.org.

had a higher percentage of voters living in landslide counties than in 1968. Beginning in 1992, the percentage of people living in landslide counties began an upward, stairstep progression. And by 2004, in one of the closest presidential contests in history, 48.3 percent of voters lived in communities where the election wasn't close at all.

To get a sense of the magnitude of this segregation by political party, we asked John Logan, then at the State University of New York at Albany, to measure the segregation of blacks and whites from 1980 to 2000 in all U.S. counties. In those twenty years, counties had become slightly less racially segregated. Using the same formula, however, from 1980 to 2000 the segregation of Republicans and Democrats increased by about 26 percent.[6] The trend didn't appear to be connected to the seesawing fortunes of the national parties. The increasing political segregation of

American communities continued on through the Reagan landslides, the Democratic turnaround in 1986, the Clinton resurgence, the Republican takeover of Congress in 1994 and the Bush wins in 2000 and 2004. Moreover, this trend — one that was particularly strong beginning in the 1990s — had escaped the attention of those who study and write about politics.[7]

The one political scientist who best understood the power of migration and the importance of community to politics was James Gimpel of the University of Maryland. Gimpel had written a book about the different migration paths followed by immigrants and U.S. citizens. Gimpel argued that migration was shaping communities and altering their politics. And in 2003, he wrote another book showing states to be "patchworks" of quite different and sometimes quite homogeneous communities.[8] Gimpel's work gave us confidence that migration could be shaping the complexion of a community's politics. What nobody had seen, however, was that most of America and most Americans were engaged in a thirty-year movement toward more homogeneous ways of living — that the polarization so apparent in the way political leaders talked was reflected in the way Americans lived.

Bob Cushing and I published these initial findings in a series of newspaper articles in the summer and fall of 2004. In the months after the 2004 election, we reconsidered what we had written for the paper. We knew that the pattern was clear. But was it meaningful? Did it matter that our communities were becoming more politically homogeneous? The country was polarized during the Civil War, but compared to those times, our own circumstances didn't appear dire. Furthermore, assuming that these demographic shifts *did* matter, why would they be happening now?

The last question was particularly perplexing. Certainly, in earlier years, the bonds of class, ethnicity, religion, and occupation, or the barriers of geography, had restricted movement and enforced a rough kind of segregation. But those previous periods of political polarization had come before the automobile, the interstate highway system, Social Security and other safety-net programs, commercial air transportation, widespread higher education, and laws enforcing racial equity. Americans now had unprecedented choice about where and how they wanted to live. They had incredible physical and economic mobility — but these freedoms seemed only to have increased segregation, not lessened it. Why?

These were the questions that led us to begin work on this book. We knew, however, that before we could address these larger subjects, we had to go back and reconsider the limitations of our evidence and develop ways to cross-check our findings. We were tracking both migration and political preference, something that wasn't commonly done. We knew that people moved and places changed, but we couldn't be certain that those who moved were the ones who had created the difference. So we launched another round of research. We gathered more data and delved into social theory, political history, and social psychology. We unearthed a significant amount of evidence that people's religious faith and politics helped explain where they lived. For example, we discovered that people who left counties with large numbers of Evangelicals rarely moved to counties dominated by Democrats. People who left counties with a high proportion of Evangelicals largely moved to counties of like faith. Similarly, we found that when people moved from Republican counties, they were very likely to settle in other Republican counties. We happened upon this relationship again and again. There were patterns of migration, and they were linked to culture, faith, and politics.

The more we looked, the more it became clear that migration itself wasn't driving the country's political segregation. We were seeing something more basic — a cultural shift powered by prosperity and economic security. Freed from want and worry, people were reordering their lives around their values, their tastes, and their beliefs. They were clustering in communities of like-mindedness, and not just geographically. Churches grew more politically homogeneous during this time, and so did civic clubs, volunteer organizations, and, dramatically, political parties. People weren't simply moving. The whole society was changing. Prosperity had altered what people wanted out of life and what they expected from their government, their churches, and their neighborhoods. The Big Sort was big because it constituted a social and economic reordering around values, ways of life, and communities of interest. That's why when we looked back over the thirty-year period when communities had become increasingly Democratic or Republican, we found an uncanny confluence of events. The political segregation of communities from the mid-1970s through the 2004 election coincided with a number of other social and economic transformations. Political leaders were growing more extreme during this period, as Democrats and Republicans in Congress became more ideological, less moderate, and more partisan. Churches, clubs, and the economy were all going through a very similar kind of ideological reorganization. Also, after decades when prosperity had spread more evenly throughout the nation, the U.S. economy had begun to diverge into regions of winners and losers.

The culture was changing at the top, among political and social elites, and at the bottom, among millions of Americans who were busy tailoring the ways they lived, worked, and worshiped. The polarization so apparent among political leaders was reprised and reinforced by the economy, the church, and civic institutions. And what we discovered was that all these features of contemporary life, this shift in the culture, was made manifest in the Big Sort — that is, in the nation's geography, in the places people were living. The Big Sort, then, is not simply about political partisanship, about how Americans vote every couple of years. It is a division in what they value, in how they worship, and in what they expect out of life.

It's not surprising, perhaps, that people in marketing picked up on these shifts long before political analysts did. Political writers prefer to look at demographic groupings when interpreting elections. How did young white women vote? What happened with union workers? Marketing specialists learned that these kinds of demographic features have less and less meaning. Increasingly, they see the United States sorting itself into communities of interest — enclaves defined more by similar beliefs or ways of life than by age, employment, or income. Chris Riley is a Portland, Oregon, marketing expert who has worked with Nike, Microsoft, and now Apple. At Nike and Apple, Riley said, marketing departments are giving up on traditional demographic designations because they don't fit the way people live. "I'm not allowed to use market research information, by dictate of [Apple founder] Steve Jobs," Riley told me. "They don't trust it." They don't trust it because simple demography doesn't get at the way people live today. "There is no [demographic] category for somebody who shapes his entire life around his concern for the environment," Riley explained.

Marketing analyst J. Walker Smith described the same phenomenon as extreme and widespread "self-invention," a desire to shape and control our identities and surroundings. Technology, migration, and material abundance all allow people to "wrap themselves into cocoons entirely of their own making," Smith wrote.[9] People are unwilling to live with trade-offs, he said. So they are "re-creating their environments to fit what they want in all kinds of ways, and one of the ways is they are finding communities that fit their values — where they don't have to live with neighbors or community groups that might force them to compromise their principles or their tastes."

It would be a dull country, of course, if every place were like every other. It's a joy that I can go to the Elks lodge pool in Austin to see the H2Hos, a feminist synchronized swimming troupe accompanied by a punkish band, or that I can visit the Zapalac Arena outside my old hometown of Smithville, Texas, to watch a team calf roping. Those sorts of differences are not only vital for the nation's democratic health, but they also are essential for economic growth. Monocultures die.

What's happened, however, is that ways of life now have a distinct politics and a distinct geography. Feminist synchronized swimmers belong to one political party and live over here, and calf ropers belong to another party and live over there. As people seek out the social settings they prefer — as they choose the group that makes them feel the most comfortable — the nation grows more politically segregated — and the benefit that ought to come with having a variety of opinions is lost to the righteousness that is the special entitlement of homogeneous groups. We all live with the results: balkanized communities whose inhabitants find other Americans to be culturally incomprehensible; a growing intolerance for political differences that has made national consensus impossible; and politics so polarized that Congress is stymied and elections are no longer just contests over policies, but bitter choices between ways of life.

There are no easy-as-pie remedies for this dark side of the Big Sort. Time brings change, of course. Issues will arise that cut across political divisions. Providing health care for all Americans is one of those problems with solutions that don't fit within the ideological fields fenced off by either party. A particular politician may be able to bring the country together for a time. But the Big Sort isn't primarily a political phenomenon. It is the way Americans have chosen to live, an unconscious decision to cluster in communities of like-mindedness. Maybe another generation will construct communities that look very different from these. Indeed, a generational shift is already taking place. But this fractured, discordant country is my generation's creation, so it is first ours to understand and then, perhaps, to change.

Part I

THE POWER
OF PLACE

1

THE AGE OF POLITICAL SEGREGATION

You don't know me, but you don't like me.

— HOMER JOY, "Streets of Bakersfield"

How can the polls be neck and neck when I don't know one Bush supporter?

— ARTHUR MILLER

IN THE SPRING before the 2004 election, I heard from LaHonda Jo Morgan. Jo Morgan lived in Wauconda, Washington, a one-building town (combination grocery, café, and post office) about 150 miles northwest of Spokane. She was convinced that Wauconda remained on the map "simply because mapmakers don't like to leave a lot of empty space on their products." Jo Morgan was writing about segregation — political segregation. She had seen an article I had written about the tendency of places to become politically like-minded, either increasingly Republican or Democratic. She noticed that the article came from Austin, her hometown. So she recounted that through fifty years of marriage, she had lived in a number of places across the United States and elsewhere in the world. And then she described a change she had noticed taking place in Wauconda:

This is a predominantly conservative area with most residents tied to ranching, mining and apple orchards. A few years back I began to feel somewhat disconnected in my church community, but I chalked that up to the struggle between pre– and post–Vatican II concerns. Since the strife of the 2000 election, I became increasingly uncomfortable in conversations in a variety of situations. Perhaps I had more flexible views because of having been exposed to different cultures. In fact, I felt like a second-class citizen, not entitled to have opinions. I even wondered if I [was] becoming paranoid since being widowed.

Of course, now I understand. Increasing divisiveness arising from political partisanship is giving rise to the same sort of treatment I observed growing up in racially segregated Texas, only now it is directed at people who think differently from the majority population of an area. Sort of scary, isn't it?

Jo Morgan was right about Wauconda changing. In 1976, Okanogan County in Washington had split fifty-fifty in the nearly fifty-fifty race between Jimmy Carter and Gerald Ford. That made sense. Americans in 1976 were more likely to live close to somebody who voted differently from themselves than at any time since the end of World War II. And then, like the rest of the country, Jo Morgan's community changed. Okanogan County went for Clinton in 1992 and then veered Republican, strongly so, in the next three elections. In 2000, 68 percent of Okanogan County voted for George W. Bush. No wonder Jo Morgan felt lonely.

Bonfire of the Yard Signs

But "scary"? I kept a file of the more outrageous examples of political anger in 2004. They ranged from the psychotic to the merely sad. There was the Sarasota, Florida, man who swerved his Cadillac toward Representative Katherine Harris as she campaigned on a street corner. (Harris had been the Republican secretary of state in Florida during the presidential vote recount in 2000.) "I was exercising my political expression," Barry Seltzer told police.[1] The *South Florida Sun-Sentinel* reported just a week before the election that "when an 18-year-old couldn't convince his girlfriend that George W. Bush was the right choice for president, he became enraged, put a screwdriver to her throat and threatened to kill her." The man told her that if she didn't change her vote, she wouldn't "live to see the next election."[2] Two old friends arguing about the war in Iraq at an Eastern Kentucky flea market both pulled their guns when they got tired of talking. Douglas Moore, age sixty-five, killed Harold Wayne Smith because, a witness said, "Doug was just quicker."[3]

The destruction of campaign yard signs and the vandalism of campaign headquarters was epidemic in 2004. The Lafayette, Louisiana, Democratic Party headquarters was struck twice; in the second assault, miscreants wrote "4 + GWB" on the building's front windows in a mixture of motor oil and ashes collected from burned John Kerry signs.[4] The most pathetic display of partisan havoc started at the Owens Crossroads United Methodist Church near Huntsville, Alabama. The youth minister at the church sent children on a "scavenger hunt" shortly before the election. On the list of items to be retrieved were John Kerry campaign signs. Once the kids toted the placards back to the church, the minister piled them in the parking lot and set the signs on fire.[5] The scavengers did the best they could, but in Republican Huntsville they found only eight signs, barely enough for kindling. Had the same hunt taken place in, say, Seattle, the kids could have rounded up enough fuel to signal the space shuttle.

Living as a political minority is often uncomfortable and at times frightening. In 2000, more than eight out of ten voters in the Texas Hill Country's Gillespie County cast ballots for Bush. Two years later, Democrats prepared a float for the Fourth of July parade in the county seat of Fredericksburg. "We got it all decorated," county party chairman George Keller recalled, "but nobody wanted to ride." Nobody wanted to risk the stigma of being identified as a Democrat in an overwhelmingly Republican area. "Thank goodness we got rained out," Keller said of the orphaned float.

Gerald Daugherty used to live in the hip and shady section of Austin known as Clarksville. When he became active in a campaign against a proposal to build a light rail system in town, Daugherty put NO LIGHT RAIL bumper stickers on his car and on his wife's Mercedes. That apparently didn't go over too well in Democratic and pro-rail Clarksville. Somebody "keyed" the Mercedes at the local grocery and for good measure punched out the car's turn signal lights. Was Daugherty sure the damage had been politically motivated? Not really. But then one morning he found his car coated with eggs. "There must have been two dozen eggs all over my car," he remembered. "Splattered. And then deliberately rubbed on the 'No Rail' bumper stickers. You knew where that was coming from." So Daugherty sold his house in a precinct that gave George

W. Bush only 20 percent of the vote against Al Gore. He bought a place in a precinct where two out of three people voted Republican in the same election. Two years later, Daugherty became the only Republican elected to the county governing body. His move out of Clarksville, he admits, was a political exodus. He left a place where he "stuck out like a sore thumb" and moved to a neighborhood that was more ideologically congenial. He reasoned, "You really do recognize when you aren't in step with the community you live in."[6]

People don't check voting records before deciding where to live. Why would anyone bother? In a time of political segregation, it's simple enough to tell a place's politics just by looking. Before the 2006 midterm elections, marketing firms held focus groups and fielded polls, scouring the countryside to find the giveaway to a person's political inclination. Using the most sophisticated techniques of market profiling, these firms compiled a rather unsurprising list of attributes.

Democrats want to live by their own rules. They hang out with friends at parks or other public places. They think that religion and politics shouldn't mix. Democrats watch Sunday morning news shows and late-night television. They listen to morning radio, read weekly newsmagazines, watch network television, read music and lifestyle publications, and are inclined to belong to a DVD rental service. Democrats are more likely than Republicans to own cats.

Republicans go to church. They spend more time with family, get their news from Fox News or the radio, and own guns. Republicans read sports and home magazines, attend Bible study, frequently visit relatives, and talk about politics with people at church. They believe that people should take more responsibility for their lives, and they think that overwhelming force is the best way to defeat terrorists. Republicans are more likely than Democrats to own dogs.

None of this is particularly shocking. We've all learned by now that Republicans watch Fox News and Democrats are less likely to attend church. Okay, the DVD rental clue is a surprise, and Democrats in my part of town own plenty of dogs, but basically we all know these differences. What is new is that some of us appear to be *acting* on this knowledge. An Episcopal priest told me he had moved from the reliably Republican Louisville, Kentucky, suburbs to an older city neighborhood so that he could be within walking distance of produce stands, restaurants, and coffee shops — and to be among other Democrats. A journalism professor at the University of North Carolina told me that when he retired, he moved to a more urban part of Chapel Hill to escape Republican neighbors. A new resident of a Dallas exurb told a *New York Times* reporter that she stayed away from liberal Austin when considering a move from Wisconsin, choosing the Dallas suburb of Frisco instead. "Politically, I feel a lot more at home here," she explained.[7] People don't need to check voting records to know the political flavor of a community. They can smell it.

Picking a Party, Choosing a Life

To explain how people choose which political party to join, Donald Green, a Yale political scientist, described two social events. Imagine that you are walking down a hall, Green said. Through one door is a cocktail party filled with Democrats. Through another is a party of Republicans. You look in at both, and then you ask yourself some questions: "Which one is filled with people that you most closely identify with? Not necessarily the people who would agree were you to talk policy with them. Which group most closely reflects your own sense of group self-conception? Which ones would you like to have your sons and daughters marry?"[8] You don't compare party platforms. You size up the groups, and you get a vibe. And then you pick a door and join a party. Party attachments are uniquely strong in the United States. People rarely change their affiliation once they decide they are Democrats or Republicans. No wonder. Parties represent ways of life. How do you know which party to join? Well, Green says, it *feels* right. The party is filled with your kind of people.*

---

*Sociologist Paul Lazarsfeld, working in the 1940s, saw the same kind of policy-free connection between parties and people. In his book *Voting: A Study of Opinion Formation in a Presidential Campaign* (Chicago: University of Chicago Press, 1954), Lazarsfeld wrote: "The preference for one party rather than another must be highly similar to the preference for one kind of literature or music rather than another, and the choice of the same political party every four years may be parallel to the choice of the same old standards of conduct in new social situations. In short, it appears that a sense of fitness is a more striking feature of political preference than reason and calculation" (p. 311).

How do you know which neighborhood to live in? The same way: because it feels right. It looks like the kind of place with boys and girls you'd like your children to marry. You just know when a place is filled with your kind. That's where you mentally draw a little smiley face of approval, just as my wife did as we moved from Kentucky to Austin in 1999.

Texas voted in 2005 on whether to make marriage between people of the same sex unconstitutional. Statewide, the anti–gay marriage amendment passed with ease. More than seven out of ten Texans voted for it. In my section of South Austin, however, the precincts voted more than nine to one *against* the measure. The difference between my neighborhood and Texas as a whole amounted to more than 60 percentage points. It's not coincidence that in our narrow slice of Austin, a metropolitan area of more than 1.4 million people filling five counties, the liberal writer Molly Ivins lived just five blocks from the liberal writer Jim Hightower — and at one time we lived five blocks from both of them.

During the same years that Americans were slowly sorting themselves into more ideologically homogeneous communities, elected officials polarized nationally. To measure partisan polarization among members of Congress, political scientists Howard Rosenthal, Nolan McCarty, and Keith Poole track votes of individual members, who are then placed on an ideological scale from liberal to conservative. In the 1970s, the scatter plot of the 435 members of the House of Representatives was decidedly mixed. Democrats tended toward the left and Republicans drifted right, but there was a lot of mingling. Members from the two parties overlapped on many issues. When the scholars fast-forward through the 1970s, 1980s, and 1990s, however, the votes of the 435 representatives begin to split left and right and then coalesce. The scatter plot forms two swarms on either side of the graph's moderate middle. By 2002, Democratic members of Congress were buzzing together on the left, quite apart from a tight hive of Republicans on the right.[9] In the mid-1970s, moderates filled 37 percent of the seats in the House of Representatives. By 2005, only 8 percent of the House could be found in the moderate middle.[10]

Members from the two parties used to mingle, trade votes, and swap confidences and allegiances. (In 1965, half the Republicans in the Senate voted for President Lyndon Johnson's Medicare bill.) That kind of congressional compromise and cross-pollination is now rare. More common is discord. The *Washington Post*'s Dana Milbank and David Broder reported in early 2004 that "partisans on both sides say the tone of political discourse is as bad as ever — if not worse."[11] Former Oklahoma congressman Mickey Edwards said that on a visit to Washington, D.C., he stopped at the barbershop in the Rayburn House Office Building. "And the barber told me, he said, 'It's so different, it's so different. People don't like each other; they don't talk to each other,'" Edwards recalled. "Now, when the barber in the Rayburn Building sees this, it's very, very real."

The Myth of Polarization

Some very smart people have questioned whether the American public is polarized to begin with, whether there really are vast and defining differences among Americans. Some argued that, viewed over the centuries, the increase in geographic segregation since the mid-1970s has been minor, a subtle fluctuation — and compared to the Civil War period, that is certainly the case.[12] At the same time, Stanford University political scientist Morris Fiorina proposed in the mid-2000s that Americans were *not* particularly polarized in their politics: "Americans are closely divided, but we are not deeply divided, and we are closely divided because many of us are ambivalent and uncertain, and consequently reluctant to make firm commitments to parties, politicians, or policies. We divide evenly in elections or sit them out entirely because we instinctively seek the center while the parties and candidates hang out on the extremes."[13]

Fiorina argued that the fractious politics Americans were experiencing were wholly a result of polarized political leadership and extreme issue activists. Elected officials might be polarized, the professor wrote, but people were not. Journalists miss what's really happening in the country, he contended, because "few of the journalists who cover national politics spend much of their time hanging out at big box stores, supermarket chains, or auto parts stores talking to normal people . . . When they do leave the politicized salons of Washington, New York and

Los Angeles, they do so mainly to cover important political events which are largely attended by members of the political class . . . The political class that journalists talk to and observe is polarized, but the people who comprise it are not typical."[14]

Fiorina announced that his book was needed to debunk what he described as the "new consensus" that Americans were deeply divided.[15] In the meantime, however, Fiorina's view became the new truism. Jonathan Rauch wrote in the *Atlantic* that when scholars went to look for the red and blue division, "they couldn't find it."[16] Joe Klein in *Time* blamed the "Anger-Industrial Complex" for ginning up a division that didn't exist in real life.[17] Columnist Robert Kuttner scolded a "lazy press corps" for overplaying the red and blue division when "the reality is quite different."[18] Fiorina's argument was even picked up in 2005 by the yellow pages of conventional wisdom, *Reader's Digest*.[19]

The abortion question was a favorite of those who contended that the middle was wide and the fringe narrow. Both Klein and Kuttner used abortion as such an example. Likewise, E. J. Dionne wrote in the *Atlantic* that "60 to 70 percent of us fall at some middle point" on most issues. Dionne wrote that only 37 percent of the people interviewed in a 2004 Election Day exit poll said that abortion should be "always" legal or "always" illegal.[20] Indeed, if we accepted the notion that a person who believed that abortion should be legal for victims of rape but illegal for victims of incest qualified as a moderate, then we would find nearly two-thirds of the population in the "middle" on this issue.* But a late 2005 poll from Cook/RT Strategies posed the abortion question in a slightly different way. Instead of asking if abortions should "always" be illegal or legal, Cook asked if people were "strongly pro-life" or "strongly pro-choice." In response to that question, the "middle" — those who were only "somewhat" committed to a position — shriveled to 25 percent. Those who felt "strongly" about this issue totaled 70 percent of the population, split just about evenly between the two poles.

---

*Dionne saw a much larger division in June 2007 after reviewing a poll conducted by the Pew Research Center. The Pew poll revealed that Republicans and Democrats had entirely different concerns and opinions about foreign and domestic policy. The *Washington Post* columnist wrote: "Our two political parties and their candidates are living in parallel universes. It's as if the candidates were running for president in two separate countries" (June 1, 2007, p. A15).

This kind of ideological allegiance has grown over time, as successful politicians know. Bill Bellamy has been an Oregon state representative and was a Jefferson County commissioner in the small town of Madras when we talked in 2005. Madras is on the dusty side of Mount Hood, where the Cascades flatten into fields that circle around irrigation rigs. In Bellamy's real estate office parking lot, a cowboy pulled in with a blue heeler barking and twirling on the toolbox just behind the back window of his pickup. In Portland, trailer hitches are bright chrome and virginal. Here a trailer hitch ball has seen some action. "In 1976, when I first ran and they would ask me my position on abortion, out of one hundred people, it was really important to only ten of them," Bellamy said. "By 1988, when I ran for the [state] senate, out of that one hundred people, for probably sixty of them it was very important."

Emory University political scientist Alan Abramowitz argued that Morris Fiorina "systematically understates the significance" of divisions over abortion, gay marriage, and other cultural markers. Abramowitz collected national polling data to show that differences among Americans were deep and growing deeper, increasing between 1972 and 2004, just the period when the country was segregating geographically. People who identified themselves as Democrats thought differently about issues than those who considered themselves Republicans. And those differences — on issues such as abortion, living standards, and health insurance — were growing larger. People's evaluation of George W. Bush in 2004 were more divided along party lines than at any time since the National Election Studies started asking questions about presidential approval in 1972.[21]

The sharp divisions among Americans appeared again in the results of the 2006 midterm elections. Voters split most dramatically on the war in Iraq: 85 percent of Democratic House voters said the invasion had been a mistake, compared to only 18 percent of Republican voters. But those divisions extended to most other issues. Sixty-nine percent of Democrats were strongly pro-choice, compared to 21 percent of Republicans. Only 16 percent of Democrats supported a constitutional ban on gay marriage, a position favored by 80 percent of Republicans. Nine out of ten Democrats, but less than three out of ten Republicans, felt in November 2006 that government should take some action to reduce global warming. Plotted on a graph of how they felt about the issues of the day in November 2006, American voters didn't form a nice, high-peaked bell, with most people clustered toward the happy ideological center. Instead, there was a deep, sharp V, with voters pushed hard left and right. How many voters wavered between the two parties as true independents in 2006? About 10 percent.[22]

The Origins of Division:
Gerrymandering or Conspiracy?

Typically, two reasons are given to explain our polarized politics. The most popular is gerrymandering: through years of redistricting, politicians have packed their districts to produce overwhelming majorities, creating such partisan uniformity that there is no reason or call to compromise. We elect extremists, especially for Congress, the argument goes, because politicians have drawn their districts to be extreme. And when legislators come out of these partisan districts — districts where the two parties don't compete — they push the entire country into a choice between the far left and the far right. Voters polarize not because everyday Republicans are all that different from everyday Democrats, but because political leaders are ideologues.

The second explanation — one favored by Democrats — holds that conservative activists built an interlocking structure of propaganda and money that moved the Republican Party, and the nation, to the right. The aim of the New Right after Goldwater's defeat in 1964 was to exacerbate divisions in the country and then exploit them.

Gerrymandering is a convenient — and popular* — explanation be-

---

*The *Washington Post* editorial page has assured us that "American elections are growing ever less competitive while squeezing out moderates from both parties and polarizing politics. This is in part because politicians get to choose their voters, rather than the reverse, and so they draw districts that are reliably Republican or Democratic. The system corrodes democracy" (November 15, 2005). Juliet Eilperin, who wrote *Fight Club Politics,* a fine book on Congress, claimed in the *Washington Post* that by "segregating voters according to party loyalty, redistricting has insulated incumbents of both parties and dulled competition" (November 13, 2005). Jeffrey Goldberg wrote in *The New Yorker* about the "difficulty of unseating incumbents, especially in congressional districts that, over the years, have been gerrymandered into single-party redoubts" (May 29, 2006). Elizabeth Drew, in the *New York Review of Books,* wrote that one reason for the ideological intransigence in Congress is the redistricting of the House, "in which both parties collude, and which has put more and more House seats out of contention" (Febru-

cause it does conform to an objective reality. Every ten years, legislators do, in fact, redraw districts, and an ever-increasing number of those districts are becoming more ideologically lopsided. Gerrymandering also has science behind it. Legislators use "powerful computers," which make the process nefariously exact. In addition, the gerrymandering thesis has "bad guys" — better than bad guys, really; it has politicians. Elected officials, not moderate-loving voters, have caused the problem and deserve the blame.

It's certainly true that congressional districts have grown largely uncontested. Even in the middle of an unpopular war, 90 percent of incumbent members of Congress were reelected in 2006, and although the number of competitive races increased, only 66 out of 435 House races were at all close.[23] And it's true that House districts, on average, have grown overwhelmingly either Democratic or Republican since the 1970s. By 2004, nearly half the members of Congress came from districts that had unassailable majorities. The question, however, is whether the increase in ideologically pure districts was caused by redistricting.

There are several arguments against the gerrymandering thesis. The first is that political parties aren't in the business of building supermajorities for incumbents. Parties exist to maximize their number of representatives. This imperative causes parties to spread votes around, creating more districts with, say, 10- to 15-point majorities and fewer with lopsided constituencies. Studies of redistricting have found that, indeed, "partisan redistricting often has the effect of reducing the safety of incumbents."*[24] The results of the 2006 midterm elections provided some

---

ary 12, 2004). And this is what I wrote in the *Austin American-Statesman* on October 24, 2004, before I fully understood the Big Sort: "State legislatures have drawn representative districts that are increasingly one-sided. Because so many districts are dominated by a single party, primary elections determine who will sit in most legislatures, and primaries are usually won by the most ideologically strident candidate." After not one California congressional or state legislative district changed parties in 2004, Governor Arnold Schwarzenegger proposed an end to legislative redistricting, asking, "What kind of democracy is that?" (*San Diego Union-Tribune,* January 12, 2005).

*This is exactly what former House majority leader Tom DeLay did in the infamous 2003 redistricting escapade in Texas. Confident of reelection, DeLay reduced the Republican majority in his district to bolster the fortunes of a neighbor. Jeffrey Toobin in *The New Yorker* ("The Great Election Grab," December 8, 2003) predicted that this redistricting decision could cost DeLay his seat, but we'll never know whether he was right. DeLay decided not to seek reelection in 2006. A Democrat won that seat, but only by 10 percentage points.

evidence that Republicans lost races not because they had been making seats safer, but because they had spread their majorities a wee bit thin. In Pennsylvania, Democrats targeted districts where Republican margins had been shaved through redistricting and narrowly picked up three seats. "If Republicans had been a little less aggressive (in redistricting), they could have won several of those seats," Nathaniel Persily, a redistricting specialist at the University of Pennsylvania told the *Wall Street Journal*. "If they gave the Democrats one more seat, they could have shored up by several percentage points the other seats."[25]

It doesn't appear that redistricting caused much, if any, of the increase in homogeneous districts. After all, if gerrymandering created landslide districts, you'd expect to see an increase in noncompetitive districts immediately after redistricting. Legislatures would draw new districts after the census and, bing-bang, there would be fewer competitive districts. That didn't happen. After each of the last three redistricting cycles (1980, 1990, and 2000), there were no immediate jumps in lopsided districts. When Emory University political scientist Alan Abramowitz examined the effects of redistricting in 2000, he found that the number of supersafe House seats (those with presidential vote margins of more than 20 percent) had increased by two, from 201 to 203. That's hardly a sign of much horseplay. Abramowitz found similar small effects after redistricting in the 1980s and 1990s. (After redistricting in 1980, in fact, the number of noncompetitive districts slightly decreased.) If legislative gerrymandering had caused the lopsided House, its effects certainly had been subtle, or perhaps one should say "prescient." For the districts hadn't grown more partisan at the *time* of redistricting, Abramowitz found. They had grown more partisan later, in the years between redistricting, when the districts' boundaries remained unchanged. From the first post-redistricting election in 1992 until 2000, the number of ideologically lopsided districts jumped from 156 to 201, but not a single district changed shape in those years.*[26]

---

*Redistricting may not have had much to do with why incumbents did so well in the 1990s, but money certainly did. Even in districts where Democrats and Republicans lived in near equality, incumbents had a big advantage in fundraising. Abramowitz found that from the early 1990s to 2002, median spending by incumbents in competitive districts increased from $596,000 to $910,000. Median spending by challengers in those same districts fell from $229,000 to $198,000.

Vanderbilt University's Bruce Oppenheimer looked at this phenomenon in another way. There are seven states with only one member of Congress. Five are red (Alaska, Montana, the Dakotas, and Wyoming), and two are blue (Delaware and Vermont). But none have had their legislative boundaries gerrymandered. Oppenheimer cobbled these seven districts into a single, hypothetical "state." He compared this seven-district "state-of-states" with twenty-six actual states with a similar number of districts in three very close presidential elections: 1960, 1976, and 2000. Oppenheimer checked to see which had become more lopsided, the made-up state-of-states with the static borders or the real states where politicians and their infernal computers had gerrymandered to their hearts' content.

Between 1960 and 2000, no real-life state saw partisan vote margins in its congressional districts increase more than in Oppenheimer's hypothetical state-of-states. Manipulative politicians in the twenty-six states had four chances to make their congressional districts less competitive, but even so the districts didn't match the lopsidedness that appeared naturally in the state-of-states.* "These data raise doubts about the ability of redistricting schemes to explain the decline in the underlying party competitiveness of congressional districts," Oppenheimer wrote.†[27]

If not gerrymandering, then how about conspiracy? Democrats have argued that the elections of 2000 and 2004 — and the concurrent polarization of the nation's politics — were the culmination of a forty-year effort by Republicans. The story goes like this: In the wake of the Barry Goldwater defeat in 1964, Republicans devised a grand scheme. They built a tightly wound, highly coordinated movement from the top down. Corporations and foundations paid for think tanks and advocacy groups, which supplied the movement with ideas and leaders. The right created

---

*In 1960, twenty-four of twenty-six real-life states had less competitive districts than Oppenheimer's state-of-states. By 2000, however, only four of the twenty-six similar-size states (Alabama, Maryland, Indiana, and Massachusetts) had less competitive districts on average than Oppenheimer's state-of-states.

†Others have come to similar conclusions. Keiko Ono at the University of Oklahoma found that there was little evidence that gerrymandering was responsible for the increase in noncompetitive districts. Ono wrote that there was a trend toward more like-minded districts, but it was part of a "longer, secular decline in the underlying competitiveness of House districts since the mid 1980s" ("Electoral Origins of Partisan Polarization in Congress: Debunking the Myth," *Extensions: A Journal of the Carl Albert Congressional Research and Studies Center* [Fall 2005]).

its own media — talk radio, Christian television networks, and conservative-minded college newspapers — in this centrally managed, machinelike plot to split the country ideologically and then establish a permanent majority. The result of this multigenerational effort lay in the Republicans' congressional victory in 1994 and the election of George W. Bush in 2000 and 2004.

Certainly, the conservatives wanted to take over. Winning, after all, is one goal in politics. But a conspiracy? One piece of evidence used to support the existence of this far-sighted plan is a 1971 memo written by Lewis Powell, the soon-to-be-appointed Supreme Court justice. Powell, writing to a friend with the U.S. Chamber of Commerce, warned of an "attack" on the "free enterprise system." In the early years of the George W. Bush administration, liberals unearthed this obscure manuscript and gave it nearly mythic significance. Former Democratic senator Bill Bradley described Powell's note (in what surely is an oxymoron) as a "landmark memo." The right had used the memo, Bradley wrote, as a "blueprint" to construct a "pyramid" of foundations, think tanks, and advocacy groups, all designed to support an interchangeable Republican leader.[28] Pick — or mix! — your metaphor of all-embracing power. *Harper's Magazine* editor Lewis Lapham described the "Republican propaganda mill" as "tentacles of rage." He transformed Powell's memo into a "manifesto" that held for the political right the "hope of their salvation." According to Lapham, Powell's "heavy word of warning fell upon the legions of reaction with the force of Holy Scripture."*[29] Skipping several generations, the bloggers Jerome Armstrong and Markos Moulitsas Zuniga wrote in 2006 that the Powell memo "eventually helped fuel nascent efforts to create the most sophisticated, well-funded political propaganda machine in world history," Joseph Goebbels notwithstanding.[30]

The belief on the left is that the machine (or mill or pyramid or giant squid) built of foundations, radio programs, and organizations powered the Republican comeback. The right-wing mechanism paid for scholars'

---

*Lapham quoted Powell's warning: "Survival of what we call the free enterprise system lies in organization, in careful long-range planning and implementation, in consistency of action over an indefinite period of years, in the scale of financing available only through joint effort, and in the political power available only through united action and national organizations."

sharp pencils and book contracts. Young leaders were fledged through summer camps, internships, and jobs with Republican congressional representatives until they could become self-supporting members of the movement. The right established a shadow society that built, grew, and eventually took over in the name of religion and free enterprise. And the entire operation was funded by the businesses that had suffered at the hands of Democratic government.

Mark Schmitt, the former director of policy at the liberal Open Society Institute, called this phenomenon the "legend of the Powell memo."[31] He found few historians of the conservative movement who even mention the memo. For example, John Micklethwait and Adrian Wooldridge's chronicle *The Right Nation* gives the Powell memo exactly three sentences.*[32] Moreover, Schmitt wrote, Powell was "far out of touch" with what would become the New Right.[33] The memo was given an iconic status by liberals searching for some explanation of their minority standing in national politics. (Conspiracy was a more appealing theory than a simple lack of popular support.) Best of all, this explanation was duplicable: the left could write its own Powell memo and create its own matrix of foundations, think tanks, and leadership programs. (James Pierson, executive director of the conservative, and now defunct, Olin Foundation, observed that the left had a "near-obsessive interest in conservative philanthropies."†[34]) Schmitt contended that the "reality of the right is that there was no plan, just a lot of people writing their own memos and starting their own organizations — some succeeding, some failing, false starts, mergers, lots of money well spent, and lots of money wasted."[35]

There is some truth to the conspiracy stories. Republicans schemed

---

*In explaining why beer maker Joseph Coors put up $250,000 in seed money for the Heritage Foundation in 1973, Micklethwait and Wooldridge wrote: "Coors was prodded into action in 1971 by a 5,000-word memorandum from Lewis Powell, an old-style Southern Democratic attorney (and later Nixon appointee to the Supreme Court). Powell argued that capitalism was under broad attack from some of its most pampered products — the liberal intelligentsia. He accused the business class not just of appeasing its critics, but also of financing their anticapitalist activities, and urged them to stand up more vigorously for their interests" (pp. 77–78).

†Pierson argued in the *Wall Street Journal* that the left's interest in the "supposedly nefarious strategies and tactics" used by foundations on the right ignores the ideas and policies that came out of the effort. A "particularly sinister role is ascribed to those conservative philanthropies that have helped fund thinkers, magazines and research institutions — on the assumption that no one would advance such self-evidently meretricious ideas unless paid to do so."

and conservatives talked of creating a "shadow society"; they set up alternative foundations, research groups, and media outlets. Of course, Democrats schemed, too, and the left had its own support in the foundation world. But conservatives better understood the changes taking place in the country, and that is why, for a time, Republicans were more successful politically. Republicans didn't create a movement. They recognized the cultural shifts taking place across the country — the Big Sort — and then channeled what was happening into politics, to their advantage.

What both gerrymandering and the forty-year conservative conspiracy arguments miss is that politics is a two-way street. It flows both from the top down and from the bottom up. Most explanations for our current partisanship — gerrymandering and conspiracy are two good examples — are top-down only. They assume that public opinion follows the lead of presidents, politicians, and Capitol Hill journalists. In this worldview, elites (be they elected officials, media barons, or a cabal of well-funded Republicans) use the power of money or position to push society in a particular direction. Voters are largely powerless in this process. They just choose one of the alternatives that legislative manipulation, media bias, and party propaganda provide.

But politics is bottom-up as well. Society changes and politicians follow. The Big Sort is the story of real differences in the way people think, in what they value, in how they worship, and finally in where they live. The divisions in Congress aren't simply the consequence of manipulations by left-wing interest groups or the outcome of plots hatched in a bunker deep under the Heritage Foundation. The divisions are the reflection of how — and where — people have come to reside.

A less conspiratorial explanation for why national politics has grown more partisan over the past thirty years can be found in the studies of congressional redistricting. Alan Abramowitz and Bruce Oppenheimer looked at the evidence of increasing geographic polarization we first presented in the *Austin American-Statesman* in 2002 and 2004, and they came to the same conclusion: people have been sorting. Abramowitz: "Americans are increasingly living in communities and neighborhoods whose residents share their values and they are increasingly voting for candidates who reflect those values."[36] Oppenheimer: "A final theory that I offer to explain the decline in partisan competitiveness at the congressional district level rests on the increased mobility of Americans and the corresponding growth in the freedom to select where they will reside."[37]

The Politics of Place:
What's the Matter with Ohio?

The overwhelming attention given to political celebrity — and political conspiracy — in our time has obscured the politics of place. If people simply respond to the faults, successes, and foibles of political elites, then it really doesn't matter that people are taking up residence in increasingly homogeneous neighborhoods. But politically like-minded regions practice a different kind of politics than do places with a greater mix of allegiances. Our politics are affected by our neighbors. Following is one example.

In the early 1960s, political scientist John Fenton wondered why working-class voters in Ohio supported Republicans, a political act that was against their economic interests. Fenton explained this phenomenon by looking at the shape of the state's neighborhoods. Upper-class voters lived in tightly knit, geographically compact communities. Physical proximity made it easier for them to maintain political cohesion, to move and vote in an ideological herd. In Ohio's large number of midsize cities, however, there was no corresponding critical mass of workers. Working-class voters were dispersed. "In Ohio you had a fairly even distribution of these working-class voters across the state," explained the University of Maryland's James Gimpel. "And because they lived among farmers and clerks and ditch diggers, they were not as inclined to vote so monolithically."[38] In nearby Michigan, Gimpel said, working-class voters lived close to one another, and their geographic proximity powered their ideological and political intensity. In Ohio, however, workers were spread out, and the effect of this diffusion, Fenton wrote more than forty years ago, was "profound . . . The postman did not talk the same language as his accountant neighbor, and the accountant was in a different world from the skilled workman at Timken Roller Bearing who lived across the street. Thus, conversation between them usually took the form of monosyllabic grunts about the weather . . . The disunity of unions and the Democratic party in Ohio was a faithful reflection of the social disorganization of their members."[39]

Thomas Frank recently bemoaned the failure of Great Plains residents to vote in their economic interests and asked, "What's the Matter with Kansas?"[40] Frank's answer was that manipulative Republicans who offered intelligent design rather than a living wage had duped working-class voters in his home state. In addition, thin-blooded liberals who had gotten above their populist raisings had abandoned Democratic principles. When John Fenton asked a similar question more than forty years ago — What's the matter with Ohio? — he arrived at an explanation that didn't depend on either gullibility or duplicity. Fenton found that the way people lived — and the communities they lived in — shaped their political lives.

Unlike Ohio of the early 1960s, political divisions today are as much a result of values and lifestyle as they are of income and occupation. And with those divisions has come a pervasive and growing separation. Americans segregate themselves into their own political worlds, blocking out discordant voices and surrounding themselves with reassuring news and companions. For example, it's not surprising that supporters are more likely to watch a president's speech, whereas opponents tend to change the channel. But the spread between viewers and channel changers has been expanding. The Gallup organization found that during the Clinton administration, the television audience for the yearly State of the Union address was on average 9 percentage points more Democratic than Republican. Under George W. Bush, however, the audience from 2001 to 2005 averaged 21 percentage points more Republican than Democratic. In 1995, the viewing audience for Clinton's State of the Union address was evenly split between Democrats, Republicans, and independents. By the time Bush addressed the nation in 2005, 52 percent of the audience was Republican, 25 percent was Democratic, and 22 percent was independent.[41] More and more, Americans watch and read the news that fits their political proclivities and ignore the other side. And should the choice between Fox News (on the right) and National Public Radio (on the left) seem impersonal, discriminating liberals can bob about the Caribbean on a cruise with writers from the *Na-*

tion, while conservatives can board a different ship for a trip hosted by William Kristol and Fred Barnes of the *Weekly Standard*.

The United States of "Those People"

Is the United States polarized? Maybe that's the wrong term. What's happening runs deeper than quantifiable differences in a grocery list of values. Despite the undeniable sameness of places across America — is a PetSmart in a Democratic county different from a PetSmart in a Republican county? — communities vary widely in how residents think, look, and live. And many of those differences are increasing. There are even increasing differences in the way we speak.* Over the past thirty years, communities have been busy creating new and different societies, almost in the way isolated islands foster distinct forms of life, but without a plan or an understanding of the consequences.

The first half of the twentieth century was an experiment in economic specialization, as craft production gave way to assembly lines; cabinetmakers became lathe operators or door assemblers. The second half of the century brought social specialization, the displacement of mass culture by media, organizations, and associations that were both more segmented and more homogeneous. We now worship in churches among like-minded parishioners, or we change churches, maybe even denominations, to find such persons. We join volunteer groups with like-minded companions. We read and watch news that confirms our existing opinions. Politics, markets, economies, culture, and religion have all moved along the same trajectory, from fragmentation in the nineteenth century to conglomeration in the twentieth century to segmentation today. Just as counties have grown more distant from one another politically, regional economies are also separating — some booming and vibrant, others weak and dissipating. Mainline religious denominations gained parishioners through the first half of the twentieth century, the

---

*Linguist William Labov of the University of Pennsylvania, one of the authors of *The Atlas of North American English*, told National Public Radio in February 2006 that "the regional dialects of this country are getting more and more different. So that people in Buffalo, St. Louis and Los Angeles are now speaking much more differently from each other than they ever did" (Interview, *All Things Considered*, National Public Radio, February 16, 2006, http://www.npr.org/templates/story/story.php?storyId=5220090).

age of mass markets, but lost members beginning in the mid-1960s to independent churches designed for homogeneous communities. Media, advertising, city economies — they've all segmented, specialized, and segregated.

In the mid-1970s, when counties were becoming politically integrated, most other measures of public life showed low levels of political separatism. The differences that we take for granted today were muted. For instance, how often a person went to church didn't mark him or her as a Democrat or a Republican. Women voted slightly more Republican than Democratic. The Democratic vote was slightly more rural than the Republican. Less than half the population saw important differences between the parties. The proportion of people describing themselves as true independent voters reached post–World War II highs. Fewer than half of Republicans described themselves as conservative. People often split their vote between Republicans and Democrats. Votes in the U.S. Congress were more bipartisan than at any time since World War II.

Beginning in the mid-1970s, the movement toward political mixing slammed to a halt and headed in the opposite direction. Women became more allied with the Democratic Party.* Rural areas and frequent churchgoers became more Republican. The percentage of independents and ticket splitters declined. People grew more ideological. Democrats were increasingly liberal; Republicans were increasingly conservative. Voters saw greater differences between the parties. *Congressional Quarterly* reported that 2005 was the most partisan year in Congress in the half century that the venerable publication had been keeping count.

The tale we've been told and have come to tell ourselves is that society cracked in 1968 as a result of protests, assassinations, and the melee in the streets of Chicago. Informed by the Big Sort, we can now see 1968 more as a consequence of gradual change than as a cause of the changes that followed. Old political, social, religious, and cultural relationships had begun to crumble years earlier. American culture had slowly shifted as people simultaneously grew richer and lost faith in the old institu-

---

*Pollster Anna Greenberg reports that the gender gap, which grew to a 16-percentage point Democratic advantage in the 1996 and 2000 elections, shrank to only 3 percentage points in 2004 ("Mind the Gender Gap: Why Democrats Are Losing Women at an Alarming Rate," *American Prospect,* December 2004, p. 28).

tions that had helped create that wealth: the Democratic Party, the Elks, the daily newspaper, the federal government, the institution of marriage, the Presbyterian Church. Party membership, newspaper circulation, trust in government, and the number of people in the pews of mainline churches all declined at the same time.

The old systems of order — around land, family, class, tradition, and religious denomination — gave way. They were replaced over the next thirty years with a new order based on individual choice. Today we seek our own kind in like-minded churches, like-minded neighborhoods, and like-minded sources of news and entertainment. As we will see later in this book, like-minded, homogeneous groups squelch dissent, grow more extreme in their thinking, and ignore evidence that their positions are wrong. As a result, we now live in a giant feedback loop, hearing our own thoughts about what's right and wrong bounced back to us by the television shows we watch, the newspapers and books we read, the blogs we visit online, the sermons we hear, and the neighborhoods we live in.

Politicians and parties have exploited this social evolution, and in doing so, they have exacerbated partisanship and division. Elites have always been more partisan, more extreme, and more ideological than regular voters. But today moderates on all sides are rebuffed, and those who seek consensus or compromise are squeezed out. Paul Maslin, Democratic presidential hopeful Howard Dean's pollster in 2004, explained it this way:

> If I had to say one true statement about the entire process you are describing, I think that at the national or state level, it's making life increasingly difficult for people who are trying to thread the needle, to find the swing voter. In a way Karl Rove and Howard Dean and [Dean campaign manager] Joe Trippi were all right here. It's probably one of the things that's driving our politics into a more polarized situation. While the swing vote and the classic vote in the middle still matter, you are much more willing to say now that you ignore at your peril your own base. Because as everything spreads apart, the base becomes more important because they are demographically more together. You don't have a whole bunch of 51-49 communities out there. You have more and more 60-40, 65-35, 70-30 places. Well, you better damn well be sure you

maximize your 70-30 votes, whether it's inner-city African Americans or liberal, educated Democrats or whether it's suburban, conservative Republicans or small-town, main-street, or Evangelical Republicans. We have to maximize our base, and they have to maximize their base. Ergo, polarization.

The country may be more diverse than ever coast to coast. But look around: our own streets are filled with people who live alike, think alike, and vote alike. This social transformation didn't happen by accident. We have built a country where everyone can choose the neighborhood (and church and news shows) most compatible with his or her lifestyle and beliefs. And we are living with the consequences of this segregation by way of life: pockets of like-minded citizens that have become so ideologically inbred that we don't know, can't understand, and can barely conceive of "those people" who live just a few miles away.

2

THE POLITICS OF
MIGRATION

OPPOSITES DON'T ATTRACT. Psychologists know that people seek out others like themselves for marriage and friendship. That the same phenomenon could be taking place between people and communities isn't all that surprising. "Mobility enables the sociological equivalent of 'assortative mating,'" explained social psychologist David Myers. Assortative mating — the tendency of similar types to pair up — has been studied as a cause of poverty and autism. But Myers was making a different point. Our wealth, education, and ability to move have allowed us to seek "those places and people that are comfortably akin to ourselves."[1]

The United States was shaped by migration. Explorers found their way on foot through the Cumberland Gap. Pioneers pushed west in wagon trains. Blacks left the dismal economy and deadly culture of the cotton South in the "great migration" of the first half of the twentieth century. Cubans fled to Florida after the overthrow of Batista in 1959. These mass displacements weren't what Myers was describing. He was identifying a different kind of movement, a migration of self-selection. The Big Sort included an element of personal discretion. People still moved to find good jobs, excellent schools, and safe neighborhoods. But an expanding economy, rising levels of education, and the breakdown of older social groupings had injected more personal choice into the selection of where to move and how to live. Amenities became more important as people sought out a particular kind of church or a special music or art scene. (For instance, Austin is brimming with baby boomers who moved here for the cosmic cowboy sound.) Americans could move to places that reinforced their identities, where they could find comfort among others like themselves. These weren't political choices, but they had political consequences.

Sorting the Evidence

After Bob Cushing and I discovered that Americans were segregating politically, we searched for corroborating evidence that this phenomenon was linked to larger social movements. We hoped not only to confirm the sorting we saw in elections but also to explore the nuances of what appeared to be a massive social and political reconfiguration. So we gathered what evidence was available and devised three tests of the Big Sort's influence. The first measured the voting patterns of communities over a number of presidential elections. If communities were collecting overwhelming numbers from one party or the other, majorities within communities should grow. The power of "assortative migration" would attract more Democrats to Democratic counties and more Republicans to Republican counties. By the same token, as Democrats left heavily Republican areas, those places would become even more Republican and vice versa. To be significant, this couldn't be a regional phenomenon. The sorting should be more than just the South switching from solidly Democratic to staunchly Republican. The whole nation ought to be undergoing the same kind of political separation.

Our second test would calculate the power of place. We wanted to see if geography trumped the measures normally used to designate political leanings. The most talked-about pattern of the past two presidential elections has been the overwhelming support churchgoers gave to the Republican candidate. If geography mattered, we should see a difference in churchgoers depending on the political cast of their home counties. Liberal churchgoers would live in one place and conservative churchgoers in another. If place had a special effect on people's politics, all union members wouldn't be the same either. Union members in Republican counties would have different beliefs from those in Democratic counties.

Finally, if sorting into like-minded communities had been taking place since the 1970s, we figured that we should be able to look back and see some corresponding demographic trends. We ought to be able to take advantage of the fact that hindsight is 20/20 and find the shifts in population that corresponded to the balkanized communities we live in today. Our third test searched for demographic movements that differentiated Republican places from Democratic ones over the past thirty-six years.

Test One: Does Like Attract Like?

For this test, we returned to the county-level presidential votes that had led us to our first story about political sorting and calculated how loyal each county had been to the two major political parties since World War II. Some counties (346, to be exact) had voted for the same party in every presidential election since 1948. In each election thereafter, another group of counties picked a side and stuck with it through the 2004 contest. Fifty-four more tipped in 1952; 536 tipped in 1968.

Before counties tipped, we found they were on average quite competitive. The difference between Republican and Democratic candidates over the years was just 2 or 3 percentage points in untipped counties. But here's the interesting part about the tipping phenomenon: once a county tipped, the spread kept growing. The average vote spread in presidential elections among tipped counties was huge — an overwhelming 20 percentage points in most elections. This was particularly true for Republican counties, which saw the margins for Republican presidential candidates increase over time. In addition, once these counties tipped, they grew more partisan. The trend was stronger in Republican than in Democratic counties. We surmised that this difference was caused by the tendency of Democratic counties to attract a more diverse population — more ethnic minorities, more people born outside the United States, more young people, and more people with college degrees. (I will discuss all of this later in the book.)

We found that Republican counties tended to become more politically segregated than Democratic counties.* This happened in part because Republican migrants were unusually attracted to Republican communities. Between 1995 and 2000, 79 percent of the people who left Republican counties settled in counties that would vote Republican in 2004 — and they were most likely to move to counties that would be Republican landslide counties. We don't know the politics of individual movers. We do know that when people left counties that would vote Republican in 2004, they were two and a half times more likely to move to other counties that would vote Republican than to those that would vote Democratic. By contrast, people who left counties that would vote Democratic in 2004 migrated to both Republican and Democratic counties without showing much of a preference for either — although they were unlikely to move to counties that would become Republican landslide counties.

As a result of this sorting, most counties were zooming off in partisan directions. Between 1976 and 2004, the gap between the parties increased in 2,085 counties; only 1,026 counties (33 percent) grew more competitive. California is the stereotypical "blue" state. But within California, 17 counties grew more Democratic after 1976, and 30 became more reliably Republican. Only 11 California counties (19 percent) became more closely contested. In 1976, 44 percent of San Francisco County's population voted for Republican Gerald Ford. Over the next seven presidential elections, the percentage of San Franciscans voting for the Republican presidential candidate dropped every four years. By 2004, just 15 percent of San Francisco's voters supported George W. Bush. San Francisco didn't become more Democratic because its population grew; the number of voters in San Francisco County hadn't changed since 1948. San Francisco was transformed because Democrats sorted themselves in and Republicans sorted themselves out. Orange County was always Republican. But despite a population that nearly tripled (and in a state that grew increasingly Democratic), Orange County

---

*Jacob S. Hacker and Paul Pierson wrote about "unequal polarization" in their 2005 book *Off Center: The Republican Revolution and the Erosion of American Democracy.* They contended that the primary cause of polarization in the United States was a move to the right by Republican officeholders.

voted more Republican in 2004 than in 1964, when Barry Goldwater and the John Birch Society were going strong. Literally next door, Los Angeles followed a more mixed path until 1988 and then became increasingly more Democratic (see Figure 2.1).*

This process of self-segregation would be inconsequential if only a few Americans lived in politically homogeneous counties. But the numbers, we learned, aren't small. In 2004, one-third of U.S. voters lived in counties that had remained unchanged in their presidential party preference since 1968. Just under half lived in counties that hadn't changed since 1980, 60 percent lived in counties that hadn't changed since 1988, and nearly 73 percent lived in counties that hadn't changed since 1992, voting consistently Democratic or Republican for four presidential elections in a row. National political choices were being carved into local geographies.

At the same time, we found that the number of counties with landslide majorities continued to increase. In the exceedingly close election of 1976 (Carter versus Ford), 38 percent of the nation's counties had a spread larger than 20 percentage points. In the exceedingly close election of 2004 (Bush versus Kerry), more than 60 percent of all U.S. counties produced landslide elections. As some 10 million Americans moved each year from one county to another, counties clearly were growing less competitive and more politically segregated.

The tipping phenomenon was fractal — it appeared no matter how large or how small the geography. Political commentators blame much of the nation's ideological polarization on the switch in the South from Democratic to Republican. Indeed, the South has become increasingly partisan since 1976 as it has become solidly Republican. But we found that *every* region in the country has become more segmented as it has tipped toward one party or the other. The U.S. Census Bureau divides the states into nine regions. All nine grew more segregated politically

---

*Every test of the data we devised showed increasing political segregation. For example, we measured the proportion of voters who lived in counties won by the opposing party in various presidential elections. In the elections after World War II, about half of all voters lived in places won by the opposing party. From 1976 on, however, the percentage of voters living in counties won by the other party dropped, sinking to under 40 percent by 2004. That year, when George W. Bush defeated John Kerry, only 34 percent of Democratic voters lived in counties won by Bush.

Figure 2.1 Distant Neighbors

The politics of Los Angeles and Orange Counties
are diverging, as seen in presidential voting.

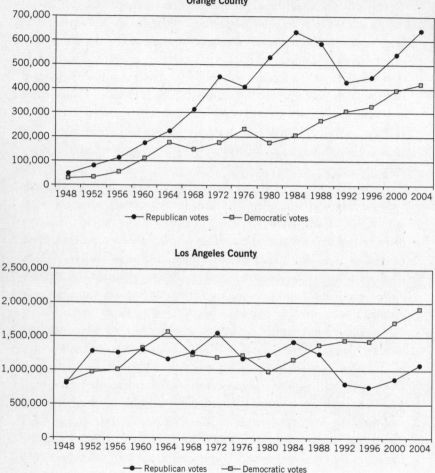

Source: Dave Leip's Atlas of U.S. Presidential Elections, http://www.uselectionatlas.org.

over the past six elections.[2] And the South is not the only region that has switched allegiance. The Pacific Coast, the Middle Atlantic States, and the North Central region were all Republican in 1948. Now these regions are strongly Democratic — and they are more politically lopsided than much of the South. Within the nine regions, there are also fewer competitive states. In the 1976 presidential contest between Carter and Ford, nineteen states had margins of 10 percentage points or more. By 2004, thirty-one states had at least a 10-point margin. In 1976, the average presidential election margin in the states was 8.9 points. In 2004, it was a bleak 14.8 points.[3]

Test Two: Does Geography Matter?

Is it just my imagination, or is Lubbock, Texas, really a very different place politically and culturally from Cambridge, Massachusetts?* Of course. (Lubbock is the Republican town, in case you didn't know.) But generally, are there significant differences in the lifestyles and beliefs of people living in solidly Republican and solidly Democratic counties? To find out, we compiled polls conducted by the Pew Research Center from 1996 through 2004 and analyzed the results by how the counties voted in the 2004 election.[4] We compared strong Republican counties (where Bush won by 10 percentage points or more) with strong Democratic counties (where Kerry won by 10 points or more). We found the following:

- In strongly partisan Republican counties, 57 percent of the people were married. In strongly Democratic counties, 47 percent of the people were married.
- Only 21 percent of the people in Republican counties earned more than $75,000 a year. In Democratic counties, 29 percent earned that.
- Republican counties were 86 percent white. Democratic counties were 70 percent white.

---

*In 2005, the Bay Area Center for Voting Research ranked cities from the most liberal to the most conservative. Lubbock was ranked the second most conservative U.S. city behind Provo, Utah. Cambridge was merely the ninth most liberal city behind, among others, Detroit, Oakland, and Berkeley.

- In Republican counties, 46 percent of the people said that they went to church at least once a week, and half described themselves as Evangelicals. In Democratic counties, only 34 percent of the people went to church at least once a week, and 32 percent were Evangelicals.

These figures are misleading, however. The standard way to calculate public opinion is to take a group — Evangelicals, the rich, the young — and then describe how this supposedly homogeneous group thinks or votes across the nation. People who go to church once a week or who describe themselves as Evangelicals are thought to be stand-up Republicans and early supporters of the war in Iraq. Nationally, that is absolutely true. But Evangelicals living in counties that voted heavily for Kerry in 2004 are an entirely different breed from those living in Republican landslide counties. According to our analysis of the Pew Research Center's polls, less than half of the weekly churchgoers and self-described Evangelicals in heavily Democratic counties supported the war in Iraq in 2004. In heavily Republican counties, however, this same demographic group supported the war three to one.

Regardless of demographic category — age, gender, religion, occupation — Pew found a difference in support for the war based on geography. Labor union members were against the war in Democratic counties but for it in Republican counties. (Nearly 30 percentage points separated union members in strong Democratic counties versus strong Republican counties.) Women were against the war in Democratic counties but for it in Republican counties (a difference of 23 percentage points). The partisanship of place overpowered the categories that researchers normally use to describe durable voting blocks.

Scott Keeter at the Pew Research Center used findings from a large poll taken in 2004 to conduct his own test of the power of geography. His unpublished report runs 136 pages.[5] Each page tells the same story: the differences between partisan counties were wide and deep. For example, 48 percent of the people living in Democratic landslide counties felt "strongly" that homosexuality "is a way of life that should be *accepted* by society." Only 21 percent of the people in Republican landslide counties agreed. In Republican counties, 49 percent believed "strongly" that homosexuality should be *"discouraged* by society," compared to 27 percent in Democratic counties. These two Americas, separated by county lines, disagreed significantly on the war in Iraq, the USA Patriot Act, and the use of military force in carrying out foreign policy. In Republican strongholds, half the people had guns in their homes; in Democratic areas, only 19 percent did.

Test Three: The 20/20 Hindsight Experiment

We began our "hindsight" experiment by dividing the nation's more than 3,100 counties into four groups based on the results of the 2004 election.* There were two groups of landslide counties — places where either George W. Bush or John Kerry won by 20 percentage points or more. That left two other groups of counties, one Democratic and the other Republican, that were competitive in the 2004 election — places where the vote totals for the two candidates differed by less than 20 percentage points. Each group contained a sizable proportion of the American population. The two groups of Democratic counties contained about 128 million people in 2000. The two groups of Republican counties were home to about 152 million people.

For this test, we examined these groups retrospectively, tracking them through time to see if and how their demographic composition changed. We knew where the groups of counties stood at the time of the highly polarized 2004 election. What we wanted to know was how they got there and whether the four groups had anything more in common than how they voted for president on the first Tuesday in November 2004.

First, we looked to see if the groups had any political coherence. From 1948 to 1960, the four groups jumped about, voting for Democrats in some years, Republicans in others. In 1976, the groups all voted at about the national average (see Figure 2.2). Beginning in 1980 with the first election of Ronald Reagan, the counties began to diverge in their political inclinations, and they continued to separate for the next quarter century.

---

*Given the unchanging nature of U.S. politics, most of these counties fell into the same categories in the 2000 election. Third-party candidates were excluded in these calculations. Including third parties changes the statistical details but not the substantive results.

This pattern appeared again and again as we evaluated other demographic measures.

Education. In 1970, the county groups were well balanced in the proportion of the population that had a college degree. After that, the percentage of college-educated people increased in every group — but the well-educated were especially attracted to Democratic counties (see Figure 2.3). People with college degrees increased the most in the Democratic landslide counties, where 29 percent of the adult population had at least a college degree in 2000. In the Republican landslide counties, 20 percent of those over twenty-five years of age had a bachelor's degree

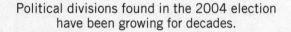

Figure 2.2 The Separation of American Communities

Political divisions found in the 2004 election have been growing for decades.

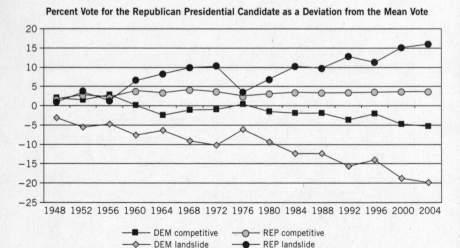

Percent Vote for the Republican Presidential Candidate as a Deviation from the Mean Vote

Note: *Republican landslide counties:* George W. Bush won by 20 percentage points or more in the 2004 presidential election. *Democratic landslide counties:* John Kerry won by 20 percentage points or more. *Republican competitive counties:* Bush won by less than 20 percentage points. *Democratic competitive counties:* Kerry won by less than 20 percentage points. 0 (zero) represents the average Republican presidential vote for the entire United States. Dropping below the 0% line means the county group is voting more Democratic than the nation as a whole. Above means the county group is more Republican.

Source: Dave Leip's Atlas of U.S. Presidential Elections, http://www.uselectionatlas.org.

or higher in 2000. According to the 2000 census, in seventeen states (including the District of Columbia), the proportion of the population with an advanced degree was higher than the national average. In 2004, John Kerry won thirteen of those states, or 76.5 percent. In thirty-four states, the proportion of people with a postgraduate degree was lower than the national average. George Bush won twenty-seven of those states, or 79.4 percent.

Religion. Church members seemed to be increasingly concentrated in Republican counties. The Glenmary Research Center collects data on the number of church members in regular surveys. According to this data, from 1971 to 2000, the number of church members increased 33.8 percent in Democratic landslide counties. In the same period, the number of church members jumped 54.4 percent in Republican landslide counties. From 1990 to 2000, Democratic counties lost churchgoers,

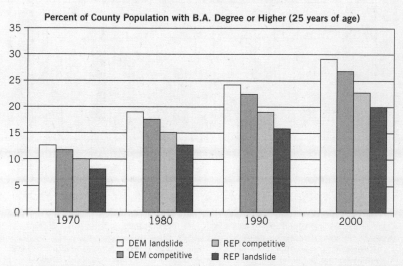

Figure 2.3 Separation by Education

Democratic landslide counties have been
gaining citizens with B.A. degrees.

Percent of County Population with B.A. Degree or Higher (25 years of age)

☐ DEM landslide   ▨ REP competitive
■ DEM competitive ■ REP landslide

Sources: Dave Leip's Atlas of U.S. Presidential Elections, http://www.uselectionatlas.org; U.S. Census of Population, http://www.census.gov.

while Republican counties continued gaining (see Figure 2.4). We even discovered a difference in migration patterns between counties with a high percentage of churchgoers and those that were more secular. Only 11 percent of the people who moved out of the counties with the most churchgoers moved to the most secular counties. The reverse was true, too: only 5 percent of those who left the most secular counties migrated to the counties with the highest percentage of churchgoers.

Immigrants. The percentage of the U.S. population that was foreign-born increased in every group of counties, but those born outside the United States favored Democratic counties. By 2000, 21 percent of the population in Democratic landslide counties was foreign-born, compared to just 5 percent in Republican landslide counties (see Figure 2.5).

Figure 2.4 The Separation of Churchgoers

Republican landslide counties have gained the most church members in the past fifty years.

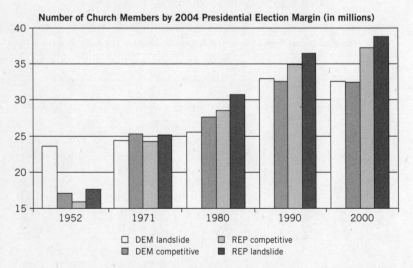

Number of Church Members by 2004 Presidential Election Margin (in millions)

☐ DEM landslide ▪ REP competitive
▪ DEM competitive ▪ REP landslide

Sources: Dave Leip's Atlas of U.S. Presidential Elections, http://www.uselectionatlas.org; Glenmary Research Center, Religious Congregations & Membership in the United States, http://glenmary.org/GRC/grc_shopping.htm.

Race. In 1970, each of the four county groups was home to about a quarter of the nation's white population — that is, whites were distributed evenly throughout the groups. (Republican landslide counties actually had a slightly *smaller* percentage of the total white population than did Democratic landslide counties.) Over the next thirty years, however, whites became more concentrated in Republican counties. Democratic counties — especially Democratic landslide counties — lost shares of white population. By the time of the 2000 census, only 18 percent of the nation's white population lived in Democratic landslide counties. By contrast, in 2000, 30 percent of America's white population lived in counties that provided Republican landslide margins in the 2004 presidential election (see Figure 2.6). The real "white flight" of the past two generations has been whites moving to communities that were becoming staunchly Republican.

Figure 2.5 The Immigration Divide

Foreign-born citizens move to Democratic counties.

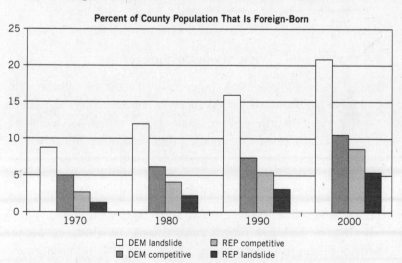

Sources: Dave Leip's Atlas of U.S. Presidential Elections, http://www.uselectionatlas.org; U.S. Census of Population, http://www.census.gov.

Figure 2.6 The New White Flight

Whites have increasingly clustered in the counties
that voted Republican in 2004.

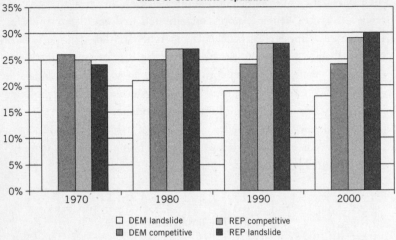

Share of U.S. White Population

Legend: □ DEM landslide ▨ REP competitive ■ DEM competitive ■ REP landslide

Sources: Dave Leip's Atlas of U.S. Presidential Elections, http://www.uselectionatlas.org;
U.S. Census of Population, http://www.census.gov.

What About the Future?

From 1980 to 2006, Republican counties gained about 50 million people,
and Democratic counties gained about 22 million people (see Figure
2.7). That means that Republican counties grew by 1 million more people a year than Democratic counties. And projections from the U.S.
Census Bureau show that this trend will continue — will even acceler-
ate — in the current century.

Birthrates are higher in Republican areas than in Democratic areas.
This phenomenon has been described as the "liberal baby bust" by *USA
Today*. In 2004, *New York Times* columnist David Brooks wrote that the
higher birthrates in Republican areas were part of a "natalism" movement. "They are having three, four or more kids," Brooks wrote of America's "natalists." "Their personal identity is defined by parenthood. They
are more spiritually, emotionally and physically invested in their homes

than in any other sphere of life, having concluded that parenthood is the most enriching and elevating thing they can do. Very often they have sacrificed pleasures like sophisticated movies, restaurant dining and foreign travel, let alone competitive careers and disposable income, for the sake of their parental calling." Some observers of the trend Brooks described predicted that the baby advantage in Republican areas would lead inevitably to larger Republican majorities.[6]

It's a plausible theory, but to this point, it isn't the primary reason red counties are gaining population faster than blue ones. People are born, it's true, but they also die. And it happens that death rates in Republican counties are also higher than in Democratic counties. When deaths are included in the calculation, it turns out that the natural increases in population — births minus deaths — account for very little of the growing difference in population between Republican and Democratic coun-

Figure 2.7 The Republican Population Shift

The greatest population increases have taken place
in counties voting Republican in 2004.

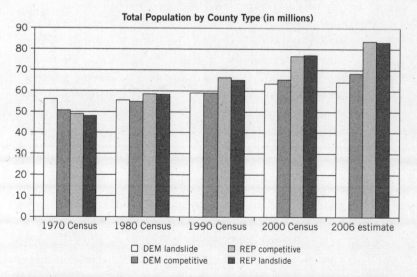

Total Population by County Type (in millions)

☐ DEM landslide   ▨ REP competitive
▪ DEM competitive   ▪ REP landslide

Sources: Dave Leip's Atlas of U.S. Presidential Elections, http://www.uselectionatlas.org;
U.S. Census of Population, U.S. Census estimates, http://www.census.gov.

ties. Republican counties gained about 28 million more people than Democratic counties between 1980 and 2006, but only 2.9 million of that increase was due to natural increases in population. (Immigrants aren't included in these calculations.)

Instead, almost all of the Republican county population jackpot was because of domestic migration. In absolute numbers, Republican counties were the winners in the Big Sort. In fact, we found that the Republican counties with the strongest majorities were the most attractive to those who moved. Meanwhile, from 1990 to 2006 alone, 13 million people moved from Democratic to Republican counties.

Many more people moved to Republican landslide counties than to Democratic landslide counties, but they were considerably poorer, earning on average only three-quarters of the income of migrants to Democratic landslide counties. In 2003, the individual income of people moving from another state into a Democratic landslide county averaged $30,492, according to IRS figures. Those moving from another state to a Republican landslide county had an average income of $22,939. And the more Republican the county, the poorer the migrant. Those moving to competitive Republican counties earned on average $25,120, almost $2,200 more than migrants to landslide counties.

Migrants with the highest incomes were those moving from a Democratic landslide county in one state to a Democratic landslide county in another state. Their incomes were 37 percent higher than the national average. Migrants with the lowest incomes were those moving between Republican landslide counties within a state. They earned 30 percent less than the national average. There is simply no telling what the consequences will be of this kind of economic sorting.

The Colorado Twist

Seen in light of the Big Sort, some puzzling dimensions of American politics begin to make sense. For example, traditionally Republican Colorado has become increasingly Democratic over the years. In 2004, Kerry cut Bush's margin of victory there to half of what it had been in 2000. A Democrat won the U.S. Senate seat in 2004, and the party swept both houses of the state legislature. Democrat Bill Ritter won the governor's race in 2006 based in large part on his promotion of alternative energy. Ronald Brownstein of the *Los Angeles Times,* writing in 2006, found that the language of politics in the state had shifted. People were more concerned with government services than with low taxes or abortion. "The whole rhetoric has changed in the past four or five years," a Democrat in Denver told Brownstein.[7]

Colorado has become more Democratic overall — but not *all* of Colorado: some parts of the state are just as Republican as at any time in the past half century. Over the past two decades, however, people from other states have flowed into Colorado. When we tracked these migrants, we learned that the Colorado counties with the highest inflows of people from other states were also the counties where support for Democratic presidential candidates was growing. The counties least affected by migration from other states had grown slightly more Republican since the 1980s. In addition, these politically opposite parts of Colorado were attracting people from entirely different places. The people moving to the fast-growing counties around Denver were three times more likely to have come from "blue" counties outside Colorado than the people moving to the slower-growing (and heavily Republican) counties along the Kansas, Oklahoma, and Nebraska borders. The county that sent the most people to Colorado between 1981 and 2004 was deeply Democratic Los Angeles County, California.[8]

The migration of people from Democratic counties elsewhere in the United States was turning Colorado into a tightly contested state. But because the Big Sort works at the community level, although the state as a whole grew more politically mixed, the divisions between Republican and Democratic areas within the state widened. Colorado's political story in the coming years will be one of expanding cultural and political division between the fast-growing Democratic counties of Denver and Boulder and the increasingly Republican counties in other parts of the state. In that sense, Colorado is a microcosm of the nation, where governments are being called on to reconcile the demands of communities that have less and less in common. It's a chore made harder by the peculiar psychology that is the special property of like-minded groups.

3

THE PSYCHOLOGY OF
THE TRIBE

Can two walk together, except they be agreed?

—AMOS 3:3

"ANTOINE KILLED A brownish snake, two feet long, in the house, at the foot of the staircase," Secretary of State John Quincy Adams wrote in his diary during the early days of Washington, D.C. Hogs nosed through trash discarded on the side of the road, and carcasses of animals putrefied in the stagnant water collecting in brickyard excavations. There were no lights and few roads that were little more than trampled-down cow paths. The city was hard to find. Abigail Adams lost her way on the trip from Baltimore back to the White House. She stumbled about Maryland for a few hours before hiring a vagrant "to extricate us out of our difficulty." Those who came to the newly built city were anxious to leave. During Washington's first three decades, nearly one in five U.S. senators resigned every two years. Better to give up public office than to live in a "cosmos of evil and immorality."[1]

Washington was, from its beginning, a politically segregated city. In his forty-year-old study, *The Washington Community*, historian James Sterling Young mapped three Washingtons, one created for each of the three branches of government. The nine members of the U.S. Supreme Court lived in the same house until 1845. Executive branch workers gathered in one section of the city, near the White House, while congressmen were bunched together nearer the Capitol. "Men whom the Constitution merely separated into different work groups separated themselves into different societies," wrote Young.[2]

Congressmen lived in boarding houses. They formed eating clubs around common tables, and they slept together, two to a room. Young tracked the membership of these new boarding house communities and found that the residential segregation that marked the entire city was repeated in the houses. Men from one state or region would board together, finding comfort in their similar cultural ties, political outlooks, and, no doubt, culinary proclivities. "Legislators had a decided aversion to sharing their mess table, their living quarters, and their leisure hours with colleagues from regions other than their own," Young wrote.[3] Washington had been created as the common ground of the nation, an intentionally heterogeneous society consisting of men gathered from across the new country. Without plan or foresight, however, the city had been transformed into an archipelago of culturally homogeneous and politically insular fraternity houses.

The homogeneity of the boarding houses crisply reflected the country, where communities were isolated by rivers, mountain ranges, and vast distances. The cultural segregation in early America was enforced by the lack of mobility, whereas today it's the ease with which Americans are able to move that has created political segregation. Even though we know much more now about the psychological effects of living in like-minded groups, the founders understood the dangers of self-segregation in ways we do not, and they sought to temper those influences. The research on the psychology of groups began more than one hundred years after the nation was formed. In scores of experiments, social psychologists learned about the power of groups to shape opinion and snuff out dissent. But without the benefit of science, the founders made an instinctual decision to embrace difference. It's not at all clear now that even with all of our knowledge, we are willing or able to make the same choice.

"He Has Betrayed Those with Whom He Broke Bread"

The residential segregation of the early-nineteenth-century boarding houses extended to the Capitol. The floor of Congress was intended to be the place where men with real cultural and regional diversity could meet, mingle, and come to a national consensus. But as Young tracked the votes in the early meetings of Congress, he found that the boarding houses and eating clubs became voting blocks. "For members who lived together, took their meals together, and spent most of their leisure hours together also voted together with a very high degree of regularity," Young discovered.[4] They were a nascent form of political parties — coalitions magnetized by regional interests and bound by residential solidarity. Young found that in three out of four House votes from 1807 to 1829, no more than one congressman would bolt from the boarding house or eating group caucuses. Members who lived in the same houses voted unanimously in just about half of the 116 roll call votes that Young analyzed over five sessions of Congress.[5] Young even found evidence that boarding house companions sat together on the floor of Congress. "They transformed a national institution into a series of sectional conclaves," he wrote.[6]

A member who voted against his tablemates risked political retribution and, worse, social exile. Representative Stephen Van Rensselaer of New York initially agreed with his eating group to support William Crawford when the 1824 presidential election had to be decided in the House of Representatives. Van Rensselaer later crossed the boarding house, however, and voted for the eventual winner, John Quincy Adams. One of Van Rensselaer's boarding house fellows wrote that he avoided Van Rensselaer on the House floor after the vote and refused to shake his hand when the tearful legislator asked for understanding back at the boarding house. "Other gentlemen of the mess" also shunned the legislator after the vote. "We let him continue with us, sit at the same table with us, but we do not speak to him," the man wrote. "He is beneath anything but contempt . . . He has betrayed those with whom he broke bread."[7]

The block voting of the boarding houses thwarted compromise or even debate. President Thomas Jefferson observed that legislators "are not yet sufficiently aware of the necessity of accommodation & mutual sacrifice of opinion for conducting a numerous assembly." Legislators came to work "in a spirit of avowed misunderstanding, without the smallest wish to agree," Jefferson wrote.[8] Far from achieving the ideal of deliberation and debate — a mixing of representatives sent by diverse communities — these legislators lived, and voted, in a segregated fashion.

Was there something of the time that caused political segregation in the first Washington community? The cultural differences between nineteenth-century Bostonians and Kentucky frontiersmen were likely greater than the social gap today between San Franciscans and southern West Virginians. Or are there psychological effects common to likeminded groups regardless of the century? These aren't questions just for historians. They are real concerns today, and not only because we live in a country where nearly half the voters live in communities where presidential elections are preordained. Two hundred years after Washington, D.C., first emerged from the coastal marshes, the ideological boarding houses are back.

In 1990, a young conservative Republican from suburban Pittsburgh named Rick Santorum challenged a seven-term Democratic incumbent, Doug Walgren. Santorum wasn't given much of a chance to defeat Walgren. In an early October poll, Walgren led 41 to 25 percent. Over the last few weeks of the campaign, however, Santorum ran a simple television ad. It showed a large white house — Walgren's house. "There's something strange about this house," an announcer said. The house was "strange" because it was located in McLean, Virginia, "the wealthiest area of Virginia," and not suburban Pittsburgh. "Maybe that's why he voted for a pay raise seven times," Santorum's ad observed. Walgren countered that he had bought a house in Virginia to "keep the family together," but the damage had been done.[9] When Santorum unseated the Democrat, the social life of Washington, D.C., changed.*

Congress is keenly attuned to survival, and members learned a lesson from Santorum's victory. "Now you don't move your family to Washington," former Republican representative Vin Weber said in late 2004. "Now you live in sort of a dormitory with members of your own party." Former Democratic congressman David Skaggs said that Newt Gingrich advised his Republican colleagues in 1994 not to appear settled in the

---

*As a U.S. senator, Santorum bought his own house in northern Virginia. That house became an issue in his 2006 reelection campaign against Democrat Bob Casey Jr., a race Santorum lost.

District, leading to the rise of what Skaggs described as "dormitory life" in the capital.[10] For example, California representative George Miller shares his house on Capitol Hill with New York senator Charles Schumer, Massachusetts representative Bill Delahunt, and Illinois senator Richard Durbin.[11] In 2006, the combined household of Democrats scored higher than 90 percent on a voting ledger kept by the liberal Americans for Democratic Action, a record more in lockstep than that of the messmates of the early 1800s. After midterm losses in 2006, the homes of former Republican House members went up for sale at 129, 131, 132, 135, and 137 D Street SE.[12]

The new boarding house norms discourage social interaction among legislators, intensifying the city's growing ideological isolation. These days, "the interactions that occurred over many decades between members, after hours . . . and on weekends and with their spouses, simply does not occur anymore," said Weber.[13] Fifty years ago, House Speaker Sam Rayburn, a Texas Democrat, served drinks at the end of the day to his Republican adversaries. Later, Republican leader Robert Michel, Democrat Dan Rostenkowski, and Republican Harold Collier shared a car on the long drive between Illinois and Washington, D.C.[14] Disputes were mediated by a culture that encouraged a kind of heterogeneous civility. Former University of Chicago Divinity School dean Martin Marty was an intern at a church in Washington in the late 1940s when a parishioner, a congressman from Illinois, scuffled with a congressman from Mississippi on the floor of the House. "The following Sunday, their two pastors had the two families together at some club," Marty told me. "Why? Because Monday they had to be talking to each other again. Well, now that doesn't happen."

Today, Weber noted, "they're on the last plane in before the first vote is cast on Tuesday, and the first plane out after the last vote on Thursday, and in between they sort of live in a dormitory, with people usually of the same party." Just as legislators brought the social segregation of their geographically isolated communities to the capital in 1800, many members of Congress today reflect the political segregation of American communities. "There is an analogue to road rage in the demeanor, the predispositions of newly elected members of Congress who are coming out of a society that is more self-isolating, more self-absorbed, less moderate in their day-to-day relationships," former congressman Skaggs said.[15]

Social psychologists began studying the effects of groups on individuals more than one hundred years ago. That people living in homogeneous groups would be loath to compromise — or would even exhibit a bit of ideological "road rage" — would not surprise these researchers in the slightest.

Judging Johnny Rocco

It was Norman Triplett's enthusiasm for bicycle racing that, in 1897, led to the first experiment in social psychology. The Indiana University professor studied times compiled by the Racing Board of the League of American Wheelman for "over 2,000 racing wheelmen, all ambitious to make records." He found that riders racing against others posted faster times than when they pedaled only against the clock. Triplett gave all sorts of possible reasons why a group might have this effect on individual riders — suction, "brain worry," hypnotic suggestion — before settling on the Jules Verne–sounding theory of "dynamogenics." He proposed that the "bodily presence of another rider is a stimulus to the racer in arousing the competitive instinct." The presence of others on the racecourse freed up "nervous energy" that a solitary wheelman could not muster; the group served as an "inspiration to greater effort." To test his theory, Triplett rigged an experiment with fishing reels to determine whether children retrieved silk thread faster alone or in competition. As with the bicyclists, the ten- and eleven-year-old children worked the reels faster in the presence of others.[16]

Triplett showed that groups change individuals in ways that individuals don't change on their own. And his results set off a century of experiments into the effects of group on individual, with results both surprising and disturbing. These studies found that people's opinions were deeply affected by groups, by notions of prestige, and by the opinions of majorities.

In an early homemade experiment, a German schoolteacher first determined who the popular and unpopular children in a school gym class were. The teacher secretly instructed the popular group to disobey clear instructions during class. When the entire class was asked to raise their right hands, the popular children disobeyed and raised their left. After the class, however, the children in the class reported that it had been the *unpopular* children who had not followed instructions.[17]

Muzafer Sherif asked Harvard and Radcliffe students to rank a list of sixteen well-known authors, including Joseph Conrad, Charles Dickens, Leo Tolstoy, and Mark Twain. The psychologist then gave the students sixteen paragraphs with the name of one of the famous authors attached to each. Sherif told them that the various authors had written the paragraphs, but in reality Robert Louis Stevenson had written them all. He asked the students to rank the paragraphs according to literary worth. The students ranked them in nearly the same way they had earlier judged the sixteen authors. When Sherif conducted the same experiment in Turkey, the Turkish students did the same thing.

The experiments conducted by the German teacher and Sherif disclosed quite a bit about the fragility of human integrity. They also showed something important in understanding politics: what we think of what we hear or see or read depends largely on who said it, did it, or wrote it, and we are likely to find evidence that confirms our preconceptions.[18]

In a 1951 study,[19] Stanley Schachter divided students enrolled in economics classes at the University of Michigan into four groups, or clubs. There was a radio club, a theater club, a movie club, and so on. Each group had three undercover members planted by the research team. One of the undercover researchers read the story of Johnny Rocco, a juvenile delinquent awaiting a court sentence on a minor crime. (Yes, Edward G. Robinson played Johnny Rocco in the 1948 movie *Key Largo.*) The reader in each group asked the members what should be done with young Johnny. The clubs were required to apply a seven-point scale of punishment, ranging from something akin to hugs to hanging. The group members talked about Johnny for forty-five minutes. One of the other two undercover researchers was the "slider." The slider began the discussion at one extreme and gradually moved to what she perceived to be the middle of the group. The slider appeared to be convinced by the group's thinking. The third undercover researcher played the "deviant." The deviant determined which way the group was leaning and then took the position at the other extreme, maintaining that opposing view throughout the discussion.

At the end of the debate, the club members were asked to make two other decisions in addition to punishment. First, they were to nominate members for an "executive committee" of clubs, clearly a position of honor. Second, they were told that the size of their club might need to be reduced. To help weed out members, they were asked to rank their preference for who should remain in the group. The deviant didn't fare well in these decisions. He wasn't picked for the executive committee and was consistently ranked low on the list of who should remain in the group. (Meanwhile, the slider was fully accepted by the group.) In all of the groups, however, rejection began long before any lists were made. As the deviant revealed himself in the discussion, group members gradually excluded him from the conversation. Eventually, they stopped talking to him altogether, effectively turning him into a nonperson. Schachter devised the test so that two of the four groups were made up of like-minded people. (Students who had a strong interest in movies or radio were placed in the same groups.) All of the groups excluded the deviant, but the more homogeneous groups were more intent on excluding the deviant than were the groups made up of a mix of students. The like-minded groups were quicker to stop talking to the person with the contrary opinion and rated him lower on the preference list for club membership.*

---

*Stanley Milgram conducted the most extreme — and most famous — conformity experiments. He asked subjects to apply electric shocks to a victim. As the charge was increased, the victim (unseen by the subjects) would moan, howl, and eventually scream. The subjects were ordered to increase the power of the charge and to administer another shock. The subjects in the tests all administered shocks well beyond the level Milgram expected. No subject stopped prior to the level where the "victim kick[ed] the wall" and could not answer questions. Of forty subjects, twenty-six administered the strongest level of shock. One of the more interesting findings was that subjects were more apt to administer higher voltages when instructed to do so by someone in person. They were less likely to do so if the instructions were phoned in. See Stanley Milgram, "Behavioral Study of Obedience," *Journal of Abnormal and Social Psychology* 67, no. 4 (1963): 371–78; Stanley Milgram, "Some Conditions of Obedience and Disobedience to Authority," *Human Relations* 18 (1965): 57–76.

Face-to-face contact is powerful. The George W. Bush campaign, especially in 2004, used face-to-face contact among culturally similar people to increase voter turnout.

A "Risky Shift" to the Extreme

There was nothing sinister in the reactions these early experiments uncovered. People were responding to an innate need: to find safety in groups. "From our earliest moments on earth, we come to associate a wide array of positive outcomes with acceptance and love from others," psychologist Robert Baron, a professor at the University of Iowa, told me. "Right from day one, you form this very generalized belief that it is always bad to disagree with others." Beginning in the 1960s, however, social psychologists came to understand that like-minded groups not only enforced conformity but also tended to grow more extreme.

The discovery began with a misdirection. In 1961, a graduate student named James Stoner asked subjects in an experiment to consider the prospects of George, a competent chess player who has the misfortune of drawing a top-ranked player in a tournament's early round. The game begins, and George sees an opportunity to attempt a risky play that could bring quick victory. If it failed, however, it would result in certain defeat. The subjects were then asked if George should attempt the risky play if there was a 10 percent chance of success, a 20 percent chance, and so on. The subjects decided individually at what odds George should try the maneuver. They were then asked to discuss as a group what George should do and arrive at a joint decision. What Stoner found — and what other researchers around the world would also find in subsequent experiments — was that the group always made a riskier recommendation than the average of the individual decisions. If, for example, the average of the individual judgments was that George should try the play if there was a 30 percent chance of success, the group would agree that George should take the risk if it paid off only 20 percent of the time.

The consistent finding in this experiment became known as the "risky shift phenomenon," and as a piece of social psychological research, it was both provocative and deceptive. When the experiment was repeated in different ways and in different countries, researchers noticed a kink in the risky shift. In the chess game situation, most people thought the overmatched George should take a risk. But what if the hypothetical game was played from the point of view of the chess champion? In this scenario, individuals in the group leaned toward a restrained approach, and the group decision was more conservative than the average of the individual answers. Although the group decision still shifted from the average, in this case it became more risk averse.

Social psychologists concluded by the end of the 1960s that what Stoner had discovered in his chess tournament experiment was the phenomenon of group polarization — that groups over time become more extreme in the direction of the average opinion of individual group members. Stoner's chess tournament advisers were inclined as individuals toward a risky play, and so their group decision was even riskier. In a different setting, where individuals were cautious, the group arrived at an even more cautious decision. Either way, the effect of discussion was to push the group and the individuals toward the extreme.[20]

In another experiment, students in their last year at a Parisian lycée were asked their feelings about the United States and General Charles de Gaulle. After discussion, the students' positive feelings toward the general increased, as did their less than favorable inclinations toward the United States. The group didn't settle on the average of what the students thought as individuals. Instead, it adopted a more extreme position. Conventional wisdom is that group discussion balances out different points of view, but these researchers found that "society not only moderates ideas [but] it radicalizes them as well."[21]

There have been hundreds of group polarization experiments, all finding that like-minded groups, over time, grow more extreme in the direction of the majority view. In one experiment, freshmen who joined fraternities were more conservative than freshmen who didn't. Senior fraternity members, however, were more conservative than freshmen. Freshmen who didn't join fraternities were more liberal, and the ideological gap between them and fraternity members widened during their years in college. In another experiment, people who were racially prejudiced became more prejudiced as they talked about race relations. In a third, intervention programs that clumped delinquents with other delinquents increased the group rate of law breaking.[22]

Even people who are impartial by training are subject to group polarization. University of Chicago law professor Cass Sunstein and University of California, San Diego, business professor David Schkade reviewed decisions of federal court of appeals panels. The panels consisted of three judges, all appointed by either Republican or Democratic presidents. Sunstein and Schkade used the difference in political sponsorship to test whether ideology mattered in the panels' decisions. It did. All-Republican panels were far more likely to side with companies in labor or environmental cases. All-Democratic panels were far more likely to find against companies in environmental, labor, and sex discrimination cases.* Perhaps it's not surprising that Republican-appointed judges have views different from Democratic-appointed judges. But Sunstein and Schkade found that the same judges would shift their positions depending on the ideological makeup of the panel. A Republican-appointed judge sitting with two other Republican appointees voted more conservatively than when the same judge sat with a mix of Democrats and Republicans. A Democratic appointee would shift to the right when sitting with Republican appointees and would vote far more liberally when sitting with two Democratic appointees.[23]

The lesson for politics and culture is pretty clear: It doesn't seem to matter if you're a frat boy, a French high school student, a petty criminal, or a federal appeals court judge. Mixed company moderates; like-minded company polarizes. Heterogeneous communities restrain group excesses; homogeneous communities march toward the extremes.†

Social psychologists have proposed several theories to explain group

---

*For example, women claiming sex discrimination won 75 percent of the time in front of an all-Democratic panel; they won only 31 percent of the time in front of an all-Republican panel. The same pattern was found in environmental and labor law cases as well.

†Gratuitous comparisons with the Nazi Party are a staple of our current political discourse. I hope not to add to that rhetorical excess by noting here that studies of the Nazi ascendance found that the party was not homogeneous across Germany, but rather was concentrated in like-minded regions. John O'Loughlin, Colin Flint, and Luc Anselin, "The Geography of the Nazi Vote: Context, Confession, and Class in the Reichstag Election of 1930," *Annals of the Association of American Geographers* (1994): 351–80.

Two geographers studying the 2004 U.S. presidential election said that they were "motivated by the striking similarity between U.S. electoral polarization and [O'Loughlin's] finding of significant geographic variations of local populations' effects on the outcome of the critical Nazi vote." Ian Sue Wing and Joan Walker, "The 2004 Presidential Election from a Spatial Perspective" (unpublished paper, 2005).

polarization. Two have survived scientific scrutiny. The first holds that people in single-minded groups are privy to a large pool of ideas and arguments supporting the dominant position of the group. If there are good arguments in favor of the group's inclination, everyone hears them, and hears them often. Moreover, as the group talks about these ideas and arguments, individuals feel more strongly about them. People are more committed to a position once they voice it. The second theory holds that people are constantly comparing their beliefs and actions to those of the group. When a person learns that others in the group share his or her general beliefs, he or she finds it socially advantageous to adopt a position slightly more extreme than the group average. It's a safe way to stand out from the crowd. It brings notice and even approbation.[24]

"It's an image maintenance kind of thing," explained social psychologist Robert Baron. Everyone wants to be a member in good standing with the dominant group position. It's counterintuitive, but people grow more extreme within homogeneous groups as a way to conform. "One way to make sure you aren't mistaken for one of those 'other people' is to be slightly ahead of the pack in terms of your Republican-ness," Baron said. "It's hard to be a moderate Republican or a moderate Democrat, in other words, because you're afraid that other people will call you whatever. In racial terms, you'd be called an Oreo if you [were] black [but went along with whites]."[25] Saint Paul knew this. Before his conversion, Paul said, "Beyond measure I persecuted the church of God, and wasted it." The disciple knew that going overboard in his pursuit of Christians served him well in the homogeneous society of the Jews. Paul explained that he "profited in the Jews' religion above many my equals in mine own nation, being more exceedingly zealous of the traditions of my fathers."[26] Or, as Holly Golightly put it in the movie Breakfast at Tiffany's, "It's useful being top banana in the shock department."

Like-minded groups create a kind of self-propelled, self-reinforcing loop. Group members send signals bolstering existing beliefs as they all vie to stand out as the most Republican or most Democratic in the group. And that sets off a new round of unspoken competition. Any successful talk radio host has realized, like Paul, that acclaim (and ratings) accrue to the most zealous. It's not enough to disagree with Bill Clinton or George W. Bush and to work for his defeat. These days, you must call for him to be impeached.

The "Constant Clashing of Opinions"

"Cato," the pseudonym of an antifederalist writer, thought that people hailing from the far reaches of the thirteen former colonies could not possibly have enough in common to bind a nation together. The "strongest principle of union" was found within the four walls of a home, Cato reasoned. He wrote that as relationships extended beyond the family to the community and then the new nation, they weakened, until "we lose the ties of acquaintance, habits, and fortunes, and thus, by degrees, we lessen in our attachments, till, at length, we no more than acknowledge a sameness of species."[27]

Cato and his allies were opposed by Alexander Hamilton, James Madison, and the federalists who sought to unite the new nation. The two sides debated qualities of human nature and the limits of democratic government. At the root of their discussions, however, was an attempt to tame the inevitable effects of group polarization and intergroup discord. In the parlance of the times, the problem was the rise of "factions," the division of people into political interest groups. Madison wrote that the "history of almost all the great councils and consultations held among mankind for reconciling their discordant opinions, assuaging their mutual jealousies and adjusting their respective interests, is a history of factions, contentions, and disappointments, and may be classed among the most dark and degrading pictures which display the infirmities and depravities of the human character."[28] Cato and his antifederalist comrades believed that the differences between the new country's isolated communities would eventually tear the nation apart. They argued that only small, like-thinking territories could be self-governing. "Brutus," the pseudonym of another antifederalist writer, explained, "In a republic, the manners, sentiments, and interests of the people should be similar. If this is not the case, there will be constant clashing of opinions; and the representatives of one part will be continually striving against those of the other."[29]

You could split the country into smaller, homogeneous enclaves, geographies of similar "manners, sentiments, and interests." That was the antifederalists' position. Madison and Hamilton made the opposite argument — that heterogeneity was a source of strength. They argued that the mixture of differing people in a large republic would both protect the new nation from factions and provide a better government. Hamilton wrote that economic diversity would "help control the problem of majority faction by diminishing the most powerful engine of faction in America — interests grounded in geographic/occupational distinctions." He predicted that as the economy expanded, it would generate a larger educated elite free from particular economic interests.[30] Madison proposed that enlarging the nation would water down local passions. The Virginian felt that a nation should be of sufficient size to contain multiple interests, large enough that no single group could gain a majority.[31] Insulation from different ideas was a danger to democracy, he wrote. Isolated groups were seedbeds of extremism — just as the law of group polarization would confirm two hundred years later. The federalists believed that the best antidote to factions was to see that communities weren't cut off from new and sometimes conflicting ideas. And the best hedge against extremism was the constant mixture of opposing opinion.[32]

Early in the constitutional debate, the framers discussed whether citizens should be guaranteed a "right to instruct" their representatives. It was a fundamental question of democracy: Should representatives be required to reflect, or "channel," the opinions of their constituents, or should elected officials vote their best judgment for the good of the country? Should legislators be a "mirror" of the people they represented, as the antifederalists urged, or should Congress be a place where representatives deliberated before they decided, as the federalists argued?[33] The men who wrote the U.S. Constitution and Bill of Rights rejected the "right to instruct" and adopted instead a government of deliberation and compromise within a heterogeneous legislature. Cass Sunstein sees the rejection of the "right to instruct" as an explicit example of the framers' realization that like-minded communities could produce extreme politics, a tendency that would be weakened by debate and understanding. Sunstein quotes founder Roger Sherman's argument:

The words [of the right to instruct amendment] are calculated to mislead the people, by conveying an idea that they have a right to control the debates of the Legislature. This cannot be admitted to be just, because it would destroy the object of their meeting. I think, when the people have chosen a representative, it is his duty to meet others from the different parts of the Union, and consult, and agree with them on such acts as are for the general benefit of the whole community. If they were to be guided by instructions, there would be no use in deliberation.[34]

Quick action by a legislature is "oftener an evil than a benefit," Hamilton claimed. It is the "jarring of parties" that "often promote deliberation and circumspection, and serve to check excesses in the majority."[35] The "constant clashing of opinions" that Brutus feared wasn't to be avoided, according to the federalists. It was to be sought after. Sunstein told me that the most profound insight of the men who framed the Constitution "was to see heterogeneity as a creative force which would enable people not to hate each other but to think more productively what might be done to solve problems. It turned this vice into a virtue. I think that was the most important theoretical contribution the framers made. And at the best moments in our history, that's what's happened."

The Consequences When the Clashing Stops

The federalists were able to impose their cooperative ideal on the new nation's government, but they couldn't repeal the laws of group polarization or the power that majorities wield over minorities. Over the past fifty years, political scientists have proved that homogeneous communities become self-propelled engines of partisanship, squelching dissent and emboldening majorities. Warren Miller used survey data to examine the 1952 presidential vote (Dwight Eisenhower versus Adlai Stevenson) in counties with overwhelming party majorities. He found that the presence of large partisan majorities had the effect of dampening turnout among citizens in the political minority. Rather than buck the majority and risk social sanction, citizens in the minority simply stayed away from the polls. They didn't vote. The minority party suffered in lopsided counties while the majority party increased its turnout — a self-reinforcing social mechanism that Miller feared could damage the country's two-party system.[36]

In communities with large political majorities, people tend to give up battling over ideas. As with the boarding houses of the early nineteenth century, a vote becomes more an affirmation of the group than an expression of a civic opinion.

A nearly even mix of Republicans and Democrats increases voter turnout, according to Notre Dame political scientist David Campbell. People are more interested in the election. They are motivated to campaign for their candidates. In landslide counties, however, there is an entirely different social dynamic.[37] Political minorities in these places vote less. Minorities in heavily majority counties not only avoid the voting booth, but they also withdraw from all forms of public life, including volunteering. People in the majority vote in large numbers — but not because they feel that their votes are important to the outcome. Instead, they want to support the community, to show allegiance to the majority. "In places where people share opinions, you are more likely to find tighter norms," Campbell told me. "And that's because, to put it bluntly, in these communities people can enforce norms. So if you haven't voted, you feel a little bit ashamed."

Furthermore, as Democrats and Republicans separate geographically, they become more distrustful of one another. Robert Huckfeldt, a political scientist at the University of California, Davis, has found that as communication between members of the parties diminishes, the two sides come to see each other as more extreme or radical. Republicans describe Democrats as more liberal than Democrats see themselves; and Democrats paint Republicans as more conservative than Republicans would describe their political preferences. "Polarized politics is not simply a matter of the actual positions adopted by Democrats and Republicans," Huckfeldt wrote in 2005. "It is also a direct consequence of the perceptions each side holds of the other, and these perceptions depend in important ways on the patterns of communication among and between citizens holding various political preferences."[38] Not knowing many real Democrats, Republicans come to believe that all Democrats are more radical than they really are. And Democrats living in homogeneous communities come to believe that all Republicans are fiendishly right-wing. Knowing a real-life Republican might settle the nerves of a Democrat. In fact, exposure to a wide array of views increases tolerance.[39] But Americans are increasingly unlikely to find themselves in mixed political company.

Not Hearing the Other Side

Even if Americans don't live among those from another party as much as they did a generation ago, they certainly have increasing access through the media and the Internet to all manner of opinions and points of view. The choice is there, but there is a media corollary to the phenomenon of assortative mating. Given unprecedented media choices, people self-segregate into their own gated media communities. In cities (most outside the United States) where a variety of newspapers reflect an array of political points of view, people don't buy several newspapers to learn what others are thinking. Instead, they buy the one that best fits their political proclivities. "They read one newspaper or the other based on what they agree with," University of Pennsylvania political scientist Diana Mutz told me. "It's one of the main problems with choice; we choose to be with people similar to ourselves."

A Stanford University professor and a *Washington Post* reporter conducted an experiment to test how Republicans and Democrats viewed news from a variety of broadcast news outlets. Professor Shanto Iyengar and Richard Morin took news stories reported by MSNBC and randomly labeled them as coming from Fox News, CNN, National Public Radio (NPR), or the BBC. Participants in the study were given a list of headlines marked by the corporate logo of the four news organizations, and then they were asked to choose which stories they would like to read. Democrats preferred CNN and NPR. Republicans flocked to the stories they thought came from Fox (even though these stories were no different from those purportedly produced by NPR, the BBC, or CNN). Having a Fox label on a story tripled the hits from Republican readers. Meanwhile, the chances that a Republican would pick a story labeled NPR or CNN were only one in ten. The polarized reading habits of American partisans were strongest when they were asked to choose stories about national politics or the war in Iraq, but Republicans even preferred to read Fox's stories about possible vacation destinations.[40] The exercise with Fox and the other news organizations is almost an exact replica of Muzafer Sherif's old experiment that asked Harvard students to judge the literary worth of passages that were labeled as being written by a variety of great authors. In this updated version, however, the test wasn't of the subjects' attachment to these literary greats but to political points of view.

The phenomenon uncovered in the news study is more insidious than readers or viewers just seeking to be soothed or reassured by a familiar point of view. People simply don't believe what they see or hear if it runs counter to their existing beliefs. "It's basic social psychology lab research," Robert Baron told me. "You show people who favor Israel and those who favor Palestine the same news coverage of the intifada. Both groups think the news media is biased against them. There is a differential evaluation. They both see the same stuff, but they draw very different conclusions."* Even if both sides of an issue are presented, people don't hear or don't remember arguments that counter their initial opinions. University of Kansas professor Diana Carlin has studied how Americans listen to presidential debates. She has found that voters watch debates in order to reinforce what they already believe. They listen for the parts of the debate that favor their candidate, she told me, and tune out the parts where their candidate does a poor job. This is especially true when people watch debates with like-minded companions.

The human inclination to find overwhelming support for an existing opinion within a speech or a news article is known as confirmation bias. Two people with opposite opinions listen to the same report, and both hear confirmation of their preexisting beliefs. The reaction seems almost automatic, and in a sense it may be. Psychologists at Emory University tested thirty men in the months before the 2004 presidential election. Half were strong Democrats, and half were strong Republicans. The men were hooked to MRI machines and then asked to listen

---

*Another example of this is a 1951 experiment in which students at Princeton and Dartmouth watched a film of a football game between the two schools. The students were asked to take note of foul play. "Dartmouth students saw mostly Princeton's offenses; Princeton students saw mostly Dartmouth's," reported the *Wall Street Journal* (Cynthia Crossen, "'Cognitive Dissonance' Became a Milestone in 1950s Psychology," *Wall Street Journal*, December 4, 2006, p. B1).

to and assess clearly contradictory statements from George W. Bush and John Kerry. The brain scans showed that as the subjects processed what the candidates said, they essentially turned off the sections of the brain associated with reasoning. Meanwhile, the scans revealed lots of activity in the parts of the brain associated with emotions, pleasure, and judgments about morality. "We did not see any increased activation of the parts of the brain normally engaged during reasoning," psychologist Drew Westen said. "What we saw instead was a network of emotion circuits lighting up . . . Essentially, it appears as if partisans twirl the cognitive kaleidoscope until they get the conclusions they want, and then they get massively reinforced for it, with the elimination of negative emotional states and [the] activation of positive ones."[41]

There is nothing new in these tendencies. "The human understanding when it has once adopted an opinion (either as being the received opinion or as being agreeable to itself) draws all things else to support and agree with it," Francis Bacon wrote in *Novum Organum* (1620). When Paul Lazarsfeld studied Erie County, Ohio, during the 1940 presidential election, he encountered all these same proclivities. Voters "somehow contrive to select out of the passing stream of stimuli those by which they are more inclined to be persuaded," he wrote. "So it is that the more they read and listen, the more convinced they become of the rightness of their own position." The more partisan the citizen, the less likely he or she was to listen to contrary arguments. Then as today, there was much public huffing and puffing about the need for free and open channels of discussion in a democracy. But, Lazarsfeld noted, "we find that consumers of ideas, if they have made a decision on the issue, themselves erect high tariff walls against alien notions."[42]

In 1940, Lazarsfeld was disturbed that half of all citizens had decided how they would vote in the fall election as soon as the candidates had been chosen in the party conventions that summer. In January 2004, however, even before the first Democratic primary, the Bush campaign figured that 92 percent of the American electorate had decided how it would vote in November.[43] (As late as 2006, true uncommitted voters hovered between 6 and 10 percent, according to University of California, San Diego, professor Gary Jacobson.)[44] Meanwhile, communities have grown more politically segregated since Lazarsfeld conducted his studies. And as people are less likely to get their news from a common source, the tremendous choice of information offered by cable television and the Internet has separated people further.

Nearly sixty years of social psychological research confirms that as political majorities grow within communities, minorities retreat from public life. Majorities have their beliefs reinforced by seeing and hearing their inclinations locally repeated and enhanced. Self-reinforcing majorities grow larger, while isolated and dispirited minorities shrink. Majorities gain confidence in their opinions, which grow more extreme over time. As a result, misunderstanding between Republicans and Democrats grows as they seclude themselves.

Americans' political lives are baffling. Reconciling the narrowness of recent national elections with the lopsidedness of local results produces mass cognitive dissonance. The facts we see on television — a nearly fifty-fifty Congress, a teetering Electoral College, and presidential elections decided by teaspoons of votes — simply don't square with the overwhelming majorities we experience in our neighborhoods.

In focus groups held in Omaha, University of Nebraska political scientist Elizabeth Theiss-Morse revealed how confused people are by the consensus they see in their neighborhoods versus the conflict they see at large in the nation. "People said many times, 'Eighty percent of us agree,'" Theiss-Morse said. "'We all want the same thing . . . It's those 20 percent who are just a bunch of extremists out there.' It didn't matter what their political views were. They really saw it as us against this fringe. The American people versus them, the fringe."

And in this age of political segregation, that "us" versus "the fringe" is often based on geography. The Nebraskans all agreed, Theiss-Morse said: "Those people in California are really weird."

Part II

THE SILENT
REVOLUTION

4

CULTURE SHIFT

The 1965 Unraveling

THE AMERICAN AFFLICTION of the 1950s wasn't partisanship. It was indifference. The country fretted about bland men in gray flannel suits, little boxes on suburban hillsides, mass marketing, and artless consumption. David Riesman wrote about the "suburban sadness," William Whyte about the "organization man." "We hope for nonconformists among you, for your sake, for the sake of the nation and for the sake of humanity," theologian Paul Tillich told a class of college graduates.[1] "By the end of the 1950s," wrote cultural historian Thomas Frank, "there could have been very few literate Americans indeed who were not familiar with the term with which these problems were summarized: 'conformity.'"[2]

Americans weren't just uninformed about politics; they were tragically indifferent. "They are not radical, not liberal, not conservative, not reactionary," C. Wright Mills wrote in 1953, "they are inactionary; they are out of it."[3] Arthur Schlesinger had observed four years earlier that most people "prefer to flee choice, to flee anxiety, to flee freedom."[4] Historian Robert Wiebe wrote that voters in the 1950s "were construed as essentially passive consumers, waiting inertly to receive messages, then choosing between more or less trivial alternatives."[5] Americans were woefully ignorant of issues and lethargic when it came to politics. In the 1958 congressional campaign, only 24 percent of voters had read or heard anything about both the Republican and Democratic candidates in their district; nearly half the voters had heard or seen nothing about either candidate. Studies in the 1950s consistently found that only one-third of voters could differentiate between the two parties on the most contentious issues of the day. People voted faithfully for a particular party, but their allegiance wasn't based on knowledge or belief. Only 11.5 percent of the population in 1960 had political beliefs that could be defined as ideological. Issues weren't linked in the minds of most voters. What one thought about labor unions had little relationship to one's opinions about Senator Joseph McCarthy's communist witch-hunt. Only half the people knew how "liberal" and "conservative" were used in contemporary politics.[6] The American ideal was to get along. The national goal was moderation and consensus. Given the trauma of the Great Depression and the horrors of World War II, these were reasonable objectives. "The dream of American consensus was conceived against a backdrop of dictatorships and death camps, paralyzing internal divisions and the devastations of war," wrote Wiebe.[7]

Contrary to today, there was no relationship between church attendance and party. Regular churchgoers voted both Democratic and Republican. Liberal churchgoers tended to vote Democratic, it's true, and conservative churchgoers tended to vote Republican. But politics weren't defined in moral terms. In 1962, a review of political ideology could conclude that "one reason for the low political tension . . . in the United States [is that] politics has not been moralized; the parties have not been invested with strong moral feeling; the issues are not seen as moral issues; the political leaders have not been made moral heroes or villains."[8]

In Congress, members visited, talked across party boundaries. They hung out at the gym, socialized at receptions, and formed friendships that had nothing to do with party or ideology. (After all, members had been elected more on their personal connections at home — what V. O. Key called "friends and neighbors" politics — than by the force of party or policy.)[9] The national calm was pervasive, and so in Congress, "this era, from roughly 1948 to the mid 1960s, was the most bi-partisan period in the history of the modern Congress."[10] Bipartisanship to this degree, some thought, had put the nation into a dangerous kind of democratic coma. (The parties were weak. They had only opened permanent national headquarters in the late 1930s and early 1940s.) Concerned about electoral torpor and meaningless political debate, the American Political Science Association in 1946 appointed a committee to examine the role of parties in the American system. Four years later, the committee published a lengthy (and alarmed) report calling for the return of ideologically distinct and powerful political parties. Parties ought to stand for distinct sets of policies, the political scientists urged. Voters should be presented with clear choices. And after an election, the winning party should be held responsible for enacting its platform. The political scientists' hope was that the parties would become more ideological, so that voters could have a "true choice in reaching public decisions." The committee of political scientists issued a list of recommendations: House terms should be longer, there should be more frequent national conventions, and party platforms and caucuses should be more powerful.[11]

A call for greater partisanship appeared to be a grand lesson in the downside of wish fulfillment during the presidential campaign of 2004. Somehow, Americans went from an indifferent society whose greatest concern was an epidemic of conformity to one with political parties so ideological that Republicans and Democrats in Congress can barely speak to one another. We've gone from lacking ideology to lacking moderation — from a period when people from different parties mixed to thirty years of increasing political segregation.

The events of the 1960s were so vivid and so dramatic (at least for those Americans who had lived through them) that they became the common explanation for everything that came after. We all like a nice narrative — a beginning, middle, and end — and chronologically the sixties provided the perfect rationale for what came after. But life doesn't always move linearly, A to B to C. Although the events of the sixties appeared to have knocked the country out of its heterogeneous complacency, underneath these events — the civil rights movement, the Vietnam War, the assassinations of John F. Kennedy, Malcolm X, Martin Luther King Jr., and Robert F. Kennedy — a slower, deeper, and largely invisible shift was changing how people went about their lives. The lasting imprint of the fifties wasn't the conformity of men in gray flannel suits, but a new and widespread economic prosperity. Abundance changed the culture in ways less evident than the upheaval of the sixties, but in a manner more profound.

The Silent Revolution

In the early 1970s, Professor Ronald Inglehart at the University of Michigan proposed a theory for why all industrialized countries appeared to be undergoing similar changes in their cultures and politics. Inglehart hypothesized that when people grew up in relative abundance, their social values — what they wanted out of life — changed. People who knew that their basic needs were satisfied would gradually adopt different values from those who lived with scarcity. Hungry people cared about survival, Inglehart said. But those who grew up in abundance would be more concerned with self-expression.[12] Those who lived in times of depression or joblessness esteemed economic growth. Those who knew plenty were more concerned about the environment and individual choice.

Inglehart's theory of social change rested on psychiatrist Abraham Maslow's theory that people act according to a "hierarchy of needs."[13] Maslow's list was specific — individuals seek to satisfy thirst before hunger, for example. In his model of human behavior, after basic physical demands are satisfied, new needs arise: survival is followed by security, then social connections, and eventually self-fulfillment. Inglehart applied Maslow's concepts about individual psychology to society and culture. He theorized that rapid economic development had produced a "new worldview" that was "gradually replacing the outlook that has dominated industrializing societies since the Industrial Revolution." The fulfillment of material needs would generally be taken for granted, and education levels would rise along with incomes, he surmised. And all that material progress, he found, "brings unforeseen changes — change in gender roles, attitudes toward authority and sexual norms; declining fertility rates; broader political participation; and less easily led publics."[14]

Inglehart's theory made predictions for these "post-materialist" societies: People would lose interest in traditional religion. They would become increasingly involved with notions of personal spirituality. Class, economic growth, and military security would decline in political importance, replaced by issues of personal freedom, abortion rights, gay rights, and the environment. Material goods would lose cachet as people sought to fill their lives with unique experiences. People would be less inclined to obey central authority and would lose trust in traditional hierarchical institutions — the big organizations that had created America's modern, industrial society: the federal government, broad-based civic groups, and traditional church denominations.

Furthermore, people wouldn't participate in politics in the same old ways, Inglehart hypothesized. Instead of being "elite-directed," they would engage in "elite-challenging" activities. They would vote less but be more likely to join a boycott or sign a petition. People wouldn't become disengaged from politics, even though voting percentages would decline. Rather, they would adopt a politics of self-expression. Post-materialists wouldn't settle for picking between two candidates. They would want to make decisions themselves, acting more directly on their political choices instead of following the orders of leaders.[15]

Inglehart predicted one more aspect of this post-materialist phenomenon: since the cultural transformation would happen at a generational pace, it would be in a sense a "silent revolution."[16] People would assume that the "erosion of confidence" in government, religion, and social institutions was because these institutions were singularly corrupt or inefficient. But the decline of trust wouldn't be peculiar to a place or government, Inglehart wrote. "We are witnessing a downward trend in trust in government and confidence in leaders across most industrial societies."[17]

Inglehart then tested his theory. Beginning in 1970, he conducted surveys around the globe, looking for signs of a culture shift. His first poll studied a half-dozen countries. Now his World Values Survey includes eighty societies that encompass more than 75 percent of the world's population. Inglehart has found that not all cultures change as fast or as much as others. The Nordic cultures are the most "post-materialist," while Americans are stubbornly traditional. (Here Inglehart diverges somewhat from Maslow, who proposed that his hierarchy of needs would operate cross-culturally. Inglehart has found that local culture alters the order of importance of social needs — a fact, as we will see, that is particularly evident in the United States.) But Inglehart's post-materialist trend has been true for every country: the higher the level of economic development, the more widespread the values of self-expression. In 2005, Inglehart wrote, "One rarely finds such a consistent pattern in social science data: there are no exceptions to this pattern among the eighty societies for which we have data."[18]

The politics of industrialized countries demonstrate Inglehart's post-materialist shift. For American voters, concerns over economic growth have been equaled (sometimes surpassed) by issues of self-expression, such as abortion, gay rights, and a personal concern for the environment. People have sought to take control of political systems directly, through recalls and ballot initiatives. Abortion, divorce, and gay relationships are more accepted, especially among younger people.[19] In 2007, fewer than half of Americans under age thirty believed it was their "duty as a citizen" always to vote.[20] In the United States, participation in traditional religious denominations declined even as nondenominational churches boomed and people explored every back road to individual spirituality. And, as Inglehart predicted more than thirty years ago, trust in government has continued to decline.[21] Inglehart contended that the change to a post-materialist culture would become more entrenched with each generation. Just as he predicted in the 1970s, each succeeding generation of Americans has been more accepting of homosexuality, more secular, and less likely to want women to play traditional roles.*[22] But the post-materialist culture shift has also been filtered through America's unusually strong religious traditions. So while some Americans have adopted more European styles of self-expression, others have found new meaning — what has eventually become political meaning — in fundamentalist or Evangelical Christianity. Once free from the discipline demanded by economic scarcity, people began to define

---

*In early 2007, when the Pew Research Center charted views of "traditional values" championed by the Republican Party, the polls showed an increasing number of Americans holding more liberal views on abortion and sexual orientation, for example. If Republicans have found their traditional base to be eroding, it may have something to do with the failures of George W. Bush or the war in Iraq. But the change is also the result of a post-materialist shift in American culture.

themselves by their values, and that altered what it meant to be either a Democrat or a Republican.

Looking back, we can see when post-materialist politics in the United States reached a point of no return. It was in the summer of 1965, when the silent revolution made quite a bit of noise.

1965: The Unraveling

Philip Converse, the grand political scientist at the University of Michigan, long puzzled over a curiosity of public opinion, an unexplained shift in the way Americans thought about themselves and political parties — all happening suddenly in 1965. Converse knew that beginning in 1945, American politics had entered an almost steady state of partisanship. People were loyal to their political party, even if neither party was particularly ideological. (Both Democrats and Republicans, after all, tried to recruit Eisenhower as a presidential candidate in 1952.) But the percentage of people saying they were Republicans or Democrats, not independents, remained high and stable. A Gallup poll taken in January and February 1965 showed levels of party loyalty among the highest since the question was first asked in 1945. Party allegiance was slightly lower in a poll taken in June 1965. But when Gallup published its poll in October 1965, the percentage of Americans who identified themselves as Republican or Democrat had "moved sharply downward."[23] More accurately, it had dropped like a rock. Many Americans were abandoning political allegiances that had remained steady for two decades. And it had all happened over that summer. There's often talk about realignment of political parties. In 1965, there was a sudden *dealignment*, a mass withdrawal of support for *both* parties.

Converse hunted for demographic clues for why Americans were suddenly abandoning their old allegiances. Were new, younger voters accounting for the shift away from party identification? No, the change appeared in all generations. In fact, even if all the young people new to the voting rolls had declared themselves to be independents, it wouldn't explain the drop. The Democrats were losing control of the previously solid South, but the abandonment of party affiliation was a national phenomenon. The decline was marginally worse among Democrats, but both Democrats and Republicans were declaring themselves free of party attachment. Nor was this political shift a fad. The number of self-declared independents increased in 1966, and the trend "proceeded almost majestically" through the mid-1970s.[24]

Converse focused on party allegiance, but he could have easily expanded his examination. Scholars found the disruption Converse discovered in politics occurring across American society. The mid-1960s were a time when society began to unwind and fall about in loose coils, like fishing line spilled from a broken reel. Institutions that had been gaining members for hundreds of years suddenly stopped their advance and began to decline. Relationships and attitudes that had remained unchanged for generations became unhinged. And it all happened at the same time.

Harvard University's Robert Putnam wrote about the shrinking of longtime civic organizations in his 2000 book *Bowling Alone*. Putnam averaged the membership in thirty-two national groups, from the Moose to the League of Women Voters. He determined that the "two decades following 1945 witnessed one of the most vital periods of community involvement in American history." Then society swerved. The rates of membership in these groups "peaked in the early 1960s, and began the period of sustained decline by 1969." Putnam's iconic example of civic engagement was the bowling league, the communal beer and tenpin contests that mixed people from different neighborhoods and of different political leanings. In 1964, 8 percent of all American men and 5 percent of women were bowling league members. After the mid-1960s, people began to bowl alone.[25] A daily newspaper was the most common source of information for eight out of ten households in 1964, a degree of market penetration that newspapers would never see again.[26] At the same time, crime rates and divorce rates started to rise. "Beginning in about 1965," Francis Fukuyama wrote in *The Great Disruption*, "a large number of indicators that can serve as negative measures of social capital all started moving upward rapidly at the same time."[27]

Most mainline religious denominations had grown uninterrupted from colonial times, a two-hundred-year record of orderly expansion. That growth ended in 1965. Martin Marty, former dean of the University of Chicago Divinity School, described the year as the epicenter of a "seismic shift" in religious life. "From the birth of the republic until around 1965, as is well known, the churches now called mainline Protestant* tended to grow with every census or survey," Marty wrote.[28] After 1965, the mainline denominations stopped growing or began to shrink as people turned to independent or Evangelical congregations. The six largest Protestant denominations together lost 5.6 million members between 1965 and 1990.[29] "At least ten of the largest (and theologically more liberal) denominations have had membership losses in every year after 1966," religious historians David Roozen and Jackson Carroll wrote in 1979.[30]

The decline of traditional mainline denominations wasn't the result of a political movement. There was no "religious right" in 1965 that called people out of these churches. Evangelical ministers concentrated on "otherworldly" concerns. In 1965, the Reverend Jerry Falwell was a Virginia preacher who professed to "have few ties to this earth . . . Believing in the Bible as I do, I would find it impossible to stop preaching the pure saving Gospel of Jesus Christ and begin doing anything else, including fighting communism or participating in civil rights reforms . . . Preachers are not called upon to be politicians but to be soul winners. Nowhere are we commissioned to reform the externals."[31] Nobody led Americans out of mainline churches. They left on their own, and they began their decampment in 1965.

Everywhere, it seemed, Americans were abandoning traditional institutions. Polling firms soon discovered that underlying this social disruption was a concomitant decline in trust: 1965 was the year Americans lost their faith. In the two decades after World War II, people maintained a remarkable trust in government. Maybe this confidence was a defensive reaction to the pressures of the cold war or psychic residue from Great Depression solidarity and World War II success.[32] In the late 1950s, eight out of ten Americans said that they could trust government to do the right thing most of the time, a level of faith maintained through 1964.[33] By 1966, however, Americans' faith in government had been replaced with doubt. "From 1964 to 1970, there was a virtual explosion of

---

*Mainline Protestant denominations would include, among others, Episcopalians, Methodists, Lutherans, Presbyterians, United Church of Christ members, Disciples of Christ, and American Baptists.

anti-government feeling," Seymour Martin Lipset and William Schneider wrote. The 80 percent of Americans who had approved of government in the late 1950s had dropped to 33 percent by 1976.[34] The lack of confidence spread beyond government. Faith in universities, medicine, major companies, and journalism all dropped during this period. People came to believe that government was run by the few. The percentage of Americans who trusted the federal government to do the right thing most of the time dropped from 75 percent of the population in 1964 to 25 percent just a few years later.[35] The sense that government had gotten out of hand was entirely bipartisan. In 1964, a quarter of self-described liberals and three-quarters of conservatives said that government was too large. By 1972, however, a majority of both liberals and conservatives said that government was overgrown. They may have disagreed about other things, but on the question of whether government was thick and stupid, left and right found common ground.[36]

The Sound of Music and *Repulsion;* Selma and Watts

When Philip Converse had exhausted all the possible demographic reasons for America's sudden rejection of political party affiliation in 1965, he turned to the historical causes. Converse was skeptical that the events of the spring and summer of 1965 were "epochal" enough to cause such a massive shift in public opinion, but when he began reviewing the year, he was "somewhat mollified." He discovered the "density of events surrounding both Vietnam and race relations which was indeed almost overwhelming, and which I suspect might be shown more objectively to have stood out on the record even against the backdrop of a generally troubled time."[37]

Nineteen sixty-five was a hell of a year, and Vietnam and race relations were just part of it. The front pages chronicle a year that began with incredible ambition and triumph, only to end with riots, war, and the beginnings of deep cultural discord. At the movies, people could see both *The Sound of Music* and Roman Polanski's *Repulsion*. In short, the year held all the good that government could achieve as well as all the ways that American society had sundered.

President Lyndon Johnson's reach was unlimited. A compliant Congress followed his instructions to remake the country, from filling symphony halls to rebuilding broken highways in Appalachia. On January 8, Johnson considered the creation of a new health care program for the aged and for poor children of the "utmost urgency." The bill creating Medicare and Medicaid passed both houses of Congress by July, with half of the Republican senators voting for it. On January 9, Johnson announced he was "determined to eliminate barriers to the right to vote . . ." (At the time, the percentage of blacks registered to vote in Mississippi was smaller than it had been in 1899.) He signed the 1965 Voting Rights Act in August and immediately dispatched forty-five federal agents to the South to register black voters.

Earlier that year, in March, Johnson's Justice Department ordered all schools to desegregate, threatening to withhold federal funds from any district that didn't integrate its schools by the fall of 1967. On the first day of school in the fall of 1965, Gene Roberts of the *New York Times* reported that southern educators "said it was the biggest day of integration in the South's history."[38]

On January 25, LBJ proposed a budget containing what the *New York Times* described as the "biggest expansion of domestic welfare and educational programs since the New Deal of the nineteen thirties."[39] Two months later, Johnson signed the bill creating the Appalachian Regional Commission, the first, but certainly not the last, War on Poverty bill to reach the president that year. The first children entered Head Start in May. In 1965, "for the first time since the Great Depression, the federal government began to exert a strong and direct influence on the arts," wrote Julia Ardery, as Congress created both the National Endowment for the Arts and the National Endowment for the Humanities.[40]

Johnson could control Congress, but he couldn't contain the conflict in Vietnam or the American South. At the beginning of the year, fewer than 20,000 American troops were in South Vietnam. Every month brought an escalation in the war. In February 1965, U.S. planes attacked North Vietnam, and in June B-52s based in Guam began to carpet-bomb Vietcong positions. (In the first raid of the war, two B-52s collided in midair and crashed.) Johnson called up U.S. Army reserves in July and told the country it would assume the "main burden" of the war.[41]

Opposition to the escalating conflict stirred in 1965. The first "teach-in" on college campuses took place that May. Poet Robert Lowell refused an invitation to the White House in June because of his "dismay and distrust" of U.S. foreign policy.[42] In August, the *New York Times* reported "the burning of village huts at the hands of United States marines."[43] Antiwar protests flared across the country in October; 10,000 people paraded in New York City. Attorney General Nicholas Katzenbach said that the Justice Department would investigate the march because "there are some Communists involved in it."[44] (William F. Buckley, running for mayor of New York, called the protesters "young slobs," mocking "their epicene resentment over a gallant national effort to keep an entire section of the globe from sinking into the subhuman wretchedness of Asiatic Communism." The *New York Times* helpfully turned to *Webster's* to inform readers that "epicene" was defined as "sexless" or "effeminate."[45]) A few days later, twenty-two-year-old David J. Miller became the first person to be arrested for burning a draft card. A draft counselor at Yale University told the *New York Times* in November that he had had appointments booked "every 20 minutes every day for the last month."[46] During one week in late November, 240 American GIs died in Vietnam, and 25,000 people — "more babies than beatniks," according to the *New York Times* — demonstrated in the "March on Washington for Peace in Vietnam."[47] The December military draft enrolled more than 45,000 men, the largest monthly total since the Korean War. By the end of 1965, more than 200,000 American troops were fighting in Vietnam.*

The civil rights movement was both brutal and triumphant in March 1965, as Alabama state police assaulted protesters crossing Selma's Edmund Pettus Bridge on what became known as Bloody Sunday. Three days later, Martin Luther King Jr. led a larger march across Alabama to the state capital in Montgomery. There were dozens of marches across the country made in concert with King's trek; for instance, 10,000 people joined Governor George Romney in a demonstration in Detroit. At the

---

*Converse considered the rapid increase in U.S. involvement in Vietnam a potential cause of the sudden disaffection with political parties. He noted, however, that public support for the war didn't decline during 1965. "Public enthusiasm about the war actually increased in tune with the mobilization, and reached its all-time peak late in the fall of 1965," Converse wrote (*The Dynamics of Party Support*, p. 108). The real shocks to the American system, he concluded, had to do with race.

end of the month, Johnson "declared war on the Ku Klux Klan."[48] In August, however, the shoulder-to-shoulder success of the Selma-to-Montgomery march was lost in the anarchy of the Watts riots. South Los Angeles was ablaze for days. The *New York Times* carried headlines about "gangs of negroes" and "youths run wild."[49] There were more riots in Chicago and Long Beach, California. In November, Gene Roberts wrote a story headlined "Negroes Still Angry and Jobless Three Months After Watts Riot."[50]

That was 1965. Within every event were the beginnings of political alignments that would extend for the next forty years. Days after troops subdued the Watts rioters, the *New York Times* reported that "California candidates of both parties, openly or warily, viewed the Los Angeles riots today as providing a ready-made issue for next year's important campaign for Governor." Ronald Reagan was considered the front-runner and the primary beneficiary of the riots.[51] Earlier, in June, the U.S. Supreme Court struck down a Connecticut law that officials had used to close and fine a Planned Parenthood birth control clinic. In *Griswold v. Connecticut,* the Court ruled for the first time that there was a limited constitutional "right to privacy." (It would base its 1973 *Roe v. Wade* decision legalizing abortion on reasoning used in the earlier decision.) The American Catholic Church was still debating its stand on birth control in 1965. By the end of the year, however, Pope Paul VI had reaffirmed the church's prohibition against all chemical or mechanical methods of birth control.

The religious news of 1965 was largely about ecumenicism and reform. In March, U.S. Catholic churches began changing their services to conform to the calls from the Second Vatican Council for more active participation by congregants. The World Council of Churches and Pope Paul VI called for greater Christian unity. Also in March, the World Council asked the United States to pull out of Vietnam, and ministers led the civil rights march from Selma to Montgomery. We know in retrospect that just as Catholics and the traditional Protestant denominations were promoting racial reform and world religious cooperation, members of most of these churches had begun to leave. They were headed to independent Evangelical and fundamentalist churches that distrusted ecumenical religious organizations.

Malcolm X was assassinated at the Audubon Ballroom in New York City on February 21. Bob Dylan drew a huge crowd to the Newport Folk Festival in July, but he enraged the folkie faithful when he plugged in his electric guitar and ripped into "Maggie's Farm." Sociologist Todd Gitlin called the Selma-to-Montgomery march the "high water mark of integrationism" and noted that by the fall of 1965, the Student Nonviolent Coordinating Committee (SNCC) had begun forcing out all its white staff members.[52] On the same day in November that a blackout cut power to nine northeastern states, stranding 800,000 people in subways, a twenty-two-year-old Vietnam War protester named Roger Allen LaPorte, a member of the Catholic Worker movement, sat down in front of the United Nations and set himself on fire.

When Change Is Not a Noun

Vietnam, the civil rights movement, and the Watts riots were powerful enough shocks to Americans' sense of themselves that they could well explain the decline in trust that began in the mid-1960s — a decline that political scientist Walter Dean Burnham described as "among the largest ever recorded in opinion surveys."[53] But there's a post-materialist catch. Measures of trust declined for almost *all* professions and institutions, not just politicians and government. And such a widespread, near universal change in attitude raises some questions. Why would a riot in Watts cause trust in doctors to decline? And how would a war in Southeast Asia lead to increasing distrust in educators? And why would a bloody confrontation between police and demonstrators at the end of a bridge in Selma, Alabama, lead to a decline in trust in businessmen among the Japanese?

In 1981, Gallup took the questions about trust and confidence that had been part of its polls in the United States and asked them simultaneously in eleven advanced industrial societies. The polling firm found that levels of institutional trust were low everywhere. Compared with the other ten nations, in fact, trust levels in the United States were fairly robust. Gallup found the highest levels of trust in Ireland. U.S. citizens ranked second behind the Irish in their confidence in their country's leadership, followed by people in Britain, Denmark, Spain, West Germany, Belgium, Holland, France, Japan, and Italy.[54] Political scientist Russell Dalton compiled polls for sixteen economically advanced countries between 1971 and 1994 and found that measures of trust had declined in all of them. (The sturdy Dutch were an aberration, showing here and there some increases in trust.)[55]

Americans have normally explained the decline in trust in this country with American experiences. Scholars have compared levels of trust with U.S. crime rates, U.S. inflation statistics, U.S. child poverty numbers, and U.S. measures of unemployment. One thing they have found is that Americans' trust was related to national political scandals.[56] (Trust levels dipped sharply after Watergate in the mid-1970s, for example.) Also, if the economy hit a bad patch or if government seemed overly prone to bungle, trust declined. One political scientist declared that the country wasn't suffering from a crisis in confidence, but a "crisis of competence."*[57] The problem with these particularized explanations, however, was that they failed to account for the universality of the phenomenon. Researchers were asking similar questions around the world — and coming up with similar findings. After World War II, trust in the political systems of Japan and Italy soared, then, after peaking in the 1970s, began to fall. Just as in the United States, people in West Germany grew more allegiant to their political parties and more trusting of their leaders during the 1950s. Then the Germans detached from their parties and lost faith in their government, on roughly the same schedule as the Americans.[58]

The decline in public trust spread across the industrialized world. The response to it was similarly uniform. President Jimmy Carter warned of "a fundamental threat to American democracy," which was a "crisis of confidence . . . a growing disrespect for government and for churches and for schools, the news media and other institutions."[59] Carter continues to be mocked for his televised speech about Americans' malaise, but

---

*The question of individual competence seems a permanent part of our political critique and an ever-ready explanation for our politics — from the sweater-wearing (and supposedly incompetent) Jimmy Carter to the bumbling Ronald Reagan to the dallying Bill Clinton to the Katrina- and WMD-surprised George W. Bush.

other countries were reacting the same way to the same malady.* After a series of government scandals, the British Parliament formed the Committee on Standards in Public Life in the mid-1990s. Professor Ivor Crewe was Carteresque when he testified that "there is no doubt that distrust and alienation has risen to a higher level than ever before."[60]

When Americans looked within their own history to explain this change in the national psyche, they latched on to nouns: Watts, My Lai, Watergate, Stagflation, Monica, Enron, Katrina. But, as Dalton explained, nouns don't tell the story. People, places, and events familiar to Americans wouldn't cause trust to decline in countries with wildly different political histories.

Why Bill Clinton Didn't Declare a War on Poverty

The loss of faith in public institutions has been the "key change in American public opinion over the last 40 years," Vanderbilt University political scientist Marc Hetherington concludes. The decline in trust placed Democrats at a permanent disadvantage, one that both diminished their chances for winning elections and hogtied their efforts to govern.[61] President John Kennedy had been able to proclaim a "New Frontier" and President Lyndon Johnson could declare a "Great Society" because Americans trusted government. After 1965, however, Democrats were forced to become ideological contortionists. In the new political climate, they proposed solutions to public problems that were to be carried out by a government that most people — even Democrats — no longer trusted to act in society's best interest. Hetherington points out that Bill Clinton was not so different from Johnson in his background or his politics. Both had grown up poor in the South. Both were presidents during economic expansions. Both had partisan advantages in Congress. But whereas Johnson declared the War on Poverty, Clinton announced that the "era of big government is over." What separated Johnson's administration from Clinton's wasn't the power of the right wing, the reticence of business, or Democratic perfidy, Hetherington argues. The

---

*For the record, Carter never used the word "malaise" in his July 15, 1979, speech.

difference was that people trusted government in 1965 and they didn't in 1993.[62]

Hetherington found the perfect example of the Democrats' dilemma. In 1964, 41 percent of Americans wanted the federal government to integrate schools. The demand for integrated schools was nearly universal by the early 1990s — 95 percent of Americans wanted their schools integrated — but the support for federal intervention to enforce desegregation laws had dropped to 34 percent. It's possible, of course, that Americans felt there was no longer a need for the government to desegregate schools — a reasonable response if schools were already integrated. But by the early 2000s, America's public schools were resegregating; they were less integrated than they had been in the 1970s.[63] Something more fundamental had changed in the way Americans thought about government.

What happened? It's simple, according to Hetherington, even if Democrats have been painfully slow to catch on. The plummeting levels of trust changed what's possible for politicians to say and for government to do. The incredible national ambitions of the early 1960s were built on a consensus cemented by overwhelming trust in government. As trust declined, the reach of the federal government shortened, and its potential was reined in. Americans found it hard to reach a consensus — on anything. The reason Bill Clinton didn't declare his own "war on poverty" was that so few people trusted government to engage in such an ambitious campaign — fewer than in the era before 1965, when Americans would lose their trust in government to do much of anything at all.[64]

Where Are All the "Good" Men?

Ron Inglehart's theory of post-materialism has engendered surprisingly little interest among observers of American politics.* Harold Wilensky,

---

*In a 1997 paper, political scientists Geoffrey C. Layman and Edward G. Carmines ("Cultural Conflict in American Politics: Religious Traditionalism, Postmaterialism, and U.S. Political Behavior," *Journal of Politics* 59, no. 3 [August 1997]: 751–77) noted that even as "recent trends indicate that American politics is becoming more 'cultural' or 'value-based' . . . the leading account of cultural conflict in advanced industrial democracies — Ronald Inglehart's theory of Postmaterialism — has received little attention from students of American politics" (p. 751). It

an esteemed political scientist at the University of California, Berkeley, has called the post-materialist culture shift a "myth." Wilensky has written that the surveys Inglehart used have technical problems and their results show little significant change. Besides, Wilensky has argued, most of the trends identified by the post-materialists (women's rights, environmentalism) were in motion during the heyday of the industrial economy. Wilensky suggests that we "drop" terms such as "post-materialism" "from our vocabulary."[65]

Other scholars, however, acknowledge that society has changed focus. Daniel Bell announced the "coming of post-industrial society" in the title of his 1973 book. Working with Ronald Inglehart, the University of Chicago's Terry Nichols Clark has described a "new political culture" born of economic prosperity and a more democratic workplace.*[66] Market researchers Paul Ray and Sherry Ruth Anderson have described a growing number of "cultural creatives," people who have many of the same interests and sociabilities as Inglehart's post-materialists and those Clark has identified in his new political culture.[67] Ruy Teixeira and John Judis have predicted a new constituency for the Democratic Party in the fast-growing tech cities. These new Democrats, they wrote, will be highly educated and affluent, "products of a new postindustrial capitalism, rooted in diversity and social equality, and emphasizing the production of ideas and services rather than goods."[68]

All of these researchers were fishing in the same pond, and what they found explains much about the cultural shift in the United States. Paul Ray and Sherry Ruth Anderson, for example, have an answer for that common question among young, single women: "Where are all the 'good' men?" Ray's polling has shown that his "cultural creatives" are seeking new experiences and deep relationships. The issues that are most important to them come straight from the post-materialist grocery list: individual rights, alternative medicine, and the environment. Ray and

---

appears that explanations for political change that don't depend on leaders or political elites sell as poorly in the academy as they do in the press.

*This "new political culture" is fiscally conservative and socially liberal, Clark wrote. It rejects centralized authority and seeks personal freedom. "The main conflicts today are not about socialism versus capitalism or more versus less government, but about hierarchy versus egalitarianism," Clark wrote in his 1998 book *The New Political Culture* (p. ix).

Anderson also have found that among the core group of "creatives," two-thirds are women.[69] So where *are* all the "good" men? Well, there are as many men as there have always been, just fewer "cultural creatives" and more guys dropping out of college, watching mixed martial arts cage matches on television, and voting Republican.*

Consider the following news items, which make more sense when viewed not as consequences of events that happened in the 1960s, but rather as the results of a long-term shift in the culture of industrialized societies.

- A fifth of all Americans say that they've read Rick Warren's book *The Purpose-Driven Life,* and Warren's Saddleback Church is one of the largest in the country. But how many people know that Warren and Saddleback are affiliated with the Southern Baptist Convention?[70] The connection just isn't mentioned. Post-materialists prefer local, nonhierarchical institutions, so churches now downplay their national affiliations. "Denominations just don't mean the same thing to people that they did in the past," Baylor University sociologist Kevin Dougherty told the *Austin American-Statesman.* "People don't think of themselves as a good Southern Baptist. They think of themselves as a good member of their congregation."[71]

- The Netherlands and Belgium rank among the countries with the largest percentage of postmodern citizenry, according to Inglehart's polls. They were also the first two countries to legalize gay marriage.[72]

- U.S. college students show little interest in voting, but true to post-materialist form, they seek out ways to change the world in person. Nearly three-quarters of U.S. college students said that they did volunteer work; only a quarter said that they would consider entering politics.[73]

---

*In 2004, unmarried women voted for John Kerry by a 25-point margin (62 to 37 percent), according to a report issued by Greenberg Quinlan Rosner Research ("Unmarried Women in 2004 Presidential Election," January 2005, p. 3, http://www.wvwv.org/docs/WVWV_2004_post-election_memo.pdf). Married women, meanwhile, voted for Bush 55 to 44 percent, leading the polling firm to conclude that the "marriage gap is one of the most important cleavages in electoral politics."

- Divorce rates in Japan have more than doubled since the 1970s. Japanese women are earning more and taking increasing control over their lives.[74]
- By the turn of the twenty-first century, Americans were spending $4 billion a year on herbal remedies. "People are not turning to health professionals," a professor at the University of North Carolina observed.[75] Why? Because post-materialists are less trusting of established authorities, including doctors and scientists.
- In November 2005, the Swiss voted to support a five-year ban on genetically modified crops, reflecting the rejection of some kinds of scientific innovations by the increasingly post-materialist Europeans.[76]
- Canada ranks higher on Inglehart's measures of post-materialism than the United States. Little wonder that a *New York Times* headline read, "Canada's Views on Social Issues Is Opening Rifts with the U.S."[77]

There is also a post-materialist geography in the United States. The *Washington Post* reported in early 2006 that "Democratic-leaning states increasingly are regulating energy use and emissions," typical post-materialist environmental issues.[78] Judges in Massachusetts and New Jersey have okayed gay marriage, and the list of states funding stem cell research is largely colored blue. Meanwhile, school districts in West Texas offer courses in the Bible, Kansas fights over whether to teach evolution, and solidly red states vote wholesale to ban gay marriage. Fulton, Missouri, has forbidden high school theater students to stage *The Crucible* and *Grease,* while in my little neighborhood in Austin, the Netherlands of Texas, parents have helped their kids construct a "peace garden" at the elementary school.[79]

Abandoned Parties and Split Tickets

By 1966, an increasing number of Americans thought the game of government was unfair and the realm of public life dishonest. There was no economic reason for people to lose faith. Nineteen sixty-five had been an exceptionally prosperous year. Companies were making huge profits, the number of factory jobs hit a twenty-one-year high in the spring, and unemployment was down to 4.6 percent by the beginning of the summer. The nation was enjoying its longest peacetime economic expansion in history. And with Johnson's Great Society, government was providing more benefits and services than ever before.

Good times weren't enough, though. People who were doing well grew distrustful of government, as did those who were earning the least and working the most thankless jobs. In fact, those at the bottom of the economic ladder were more distrustful, even as government programs for the poor and for minorities greatly expanded. In polls taken in 1964, at the beginning of the Great Society, blacks were more trusting than whites, manual workers were more trusting than businesspeople, and poor people were more trusting than those who were better off. By 1970, all of these relationships had reversed.[80] The "negative swings against government power and away from trust in government [were] particularly concentrated among just those elements in society that could have been expected to benefit from and support government the most," wrote Walter Dean Burnham.[81]

There was no discernible pressure from political leaders or the press to lose faith in government, to quit the mainline churches, or to stow the bowling ball bag. Republicans were still hoping to pick up votes from blacks in 1965. In July, Republican congressional leaders chided Johnson for being "Lyndon-come-lately" in his support for new civil rights legislation. House Republicans opposed a buildup in troops in Vietnam, even as Senate Republicans supported Johnson. In April, newspaper publishers reported "widespread support" for Johnson's Vietnam policy, and "media coverage was quite supportive of official policy on Vietnam and shifted toward a more critical view only after the public grew unhappy."[82]

The political and journalistic elite was the last to know what was happening in the country. In late November 1965, the New York Times's David Broder wrote a story headlined "Victory Doubted by G.O.P. Leaders." The Republicans Broder had interviewed had concluded that "their party has no realistic prospect of regaining control of either house of Congress in the 1966 election."[83] Yet in November of 1966, Republicans gained forty-seven seats in the House and three in the Senate. In one sense, Republicans were right: They hadn't gained control of either the House or the Senate. But the country had turned. Johnson's approval rating dropped to 44 percent in 1966. It had been 66 percent in 1965. "Suddenly, the Great Society had run its course," wrote political scientist James Sundquist.[84]

There were further dips in trust and party attachment in the late 1960s, then more after the Watergate scandal and Richard Nixon's impeachment in the early 1970s. The percentage of voters who called themselves independents peaked in the early 1970s, and then the parties came roaring back. But trust in government did not return. Over the past forty years, there have been ups and downs in Americans' attitudes toward public institutions, but trust in government has never come close to its pre-1965 highs. Even after the attacks on September 11, 2001, trust in government rebounded only to the levels during the Nixon administration.[85]

The dealignment of voters was almost entirely a white phenomenon. During the 1960s, black voters' affiliation with the Democratic Party solidified, just as whites grew increasingly independent, and Americans' attention increasingly shifted to race. In 1962, the most important issues to voters were the high cost of living, international tensions, and unemployment. In 1963, racial tensions rose to the top of the list and stayed there for a decade. Until the Watts riots in August 1965, a majority of northern whites said that Democrats were pushing integration "about right." By September 1966, the proportion who said that integration was proceeding "too fast" nearly doubled, jumping from 28 percent to 52 percent. Similarly, in 1965 street crime appeared just behind public education on the list of most important issues. Street crime had never before been of much concern. By 1968, 81 percent of Americans agreed that "law and order has broken down in this country."[86]

Ronald Reagan did not lead white men out of the Democratic Party with his 1980 campaign. Rather, the switch can be traced to 1964, when "men's support for the Democratic Party dropped precipitously from 51 percent to the high 30s throughout the seventies to a low of 28 percent in 1994." The gap in the party preferences of white men and women that became so pronounced in the 1990s and has continued into this century resulted from white men leaving the Democratic Party beginning in the mid-1960s.[87]

The Decline of Polarization

The collapse of social institutions, the dropping levels of trust, and the abandonment of political parties beginning in 1965 all contributed to a decline in partisan political behavior. White people continued to leave both the Republican and Democratic parties. Ambivalent, they split their vote. In 1960, 73 percent of voters cast a straight ticket, voting for the same party in all elections. By 1966, the percentage of straight-ticket voters had dropped to 50 percent, and by 1972 it was 42 percent. In 1904, only 2 percent of the country's congressional districts voted for a House candidate from one party and a presidential candidate from the other. By 1968, a third of the districts did so. Walter Dean Burnham wrote of a "secular trend toward the gradual disappearance of the political party in the United States."[88] In *The Changing American Voter*, Norman Nie, Sidney Verba, and John Petrocik found signs that voters were becoming more ideological by the early 1970s.*[89] The parties were ideologically ambidextrous, and the low levels of polarization in Congress that emerged after World War II continued well into the mid-1970s. Party elites in Washington were content with a politics of compromise and tempered ideology.[90] And, we know now, American communities were integrating politically. In the 1976 presidential election, Democrats and Republicans were more geographically blended than at any time since the end of World War II.

With few people's knowledge and with nobody's permission, a new kind of politics was forming. Society had shattered in the mid-1960s,

---

*In 1956, 41 percent of the population counted themselves as political "centrists," based on answers to questions about five issues. The shape of public opinion looked like the classic bell curve: a steep plurality in the center that quickly fell off as ideology became more extreme. By 1973, however, only 27 percent had opinions that placed them in the ideological middle. The bell curve turned into more of a flat concrete block. Only 25 percent of the public was either "leftist" or "rightist" in 1956. By 1973, 44 percent of the public had migrated to the extremes. ("Leftists" increased from 12 percent to 21 percent; "rightists" increased from 13 percent to 23 percent.) *The Changing American Voter* was later criticized for failing to take into account changes in the way some questions were asked.

and the forces that pulled it together again, piece by piece, created the world we know today. The new politics was molded by post-materialist realities. Tradition, economic class and occupation, religious denomination, civic structures, and party politics — the ways of life that had molded the country over the previous century — were losing significance. The new society was more about personal taste and worldview than public policy. It was as much or more concerned with self-expression and belief as with social class and economics. And it appeared suddenly, with a flash of anger and violence, in the coalfields of West Virginia in the summer of 1974.

5

THE BEGINNING OF DIVISION

Beauty and Salvation in 1974

THE REVEREND MARVIN Horan left the high school up Campbells Creek in the tenth grade. "Back then, the big thing was going to work," Horan said, remembering 1955. Most kids left West Virginia for the upper Midwest in the 1950s. ("If you made it to Cleveland, you had a job," he recalled.) Horan "always wanted to be a truck driver," and that's what he's always been — except for the two years he spent in federal prison, sent up on a charge that in 1974 he conspired to dynamite an elementary school.

Marvin Horan was twenty-five years old and newly married when four women from the Campbells Creek community church came to call in 1964. "I was sitting at home one night watching television," he remembered. "Four women stopped, and they were talking with me about the church. And when these four women left, my whole life changed. It was a *miraculous* change. I have never been the same since that night, and that's been forty-one years. I have never had the same desires that I had prior to that experience. You cannot come in contact with the Creator and be the same. You just can't. It's impossible."

Horan was called to the ministry that night. To prepare for his work, he "acquired a small library" and began to study. He read for the next three years, until, he said, "I had come to the place where I could address a congregation and do it with some sense and reasoning behind it." Then, as is the way with the independent churches in rural West Virginia, he proclaimed himself a minister. He drove a truck six days a week and preached on Sundays. Reverend Horan led revivals and traveled the circuit among the small fundamentalist churches dotted up the creeks that carve through the southern mountains. In 1969, he was filling the pulpit of a church that was between ministers when he had what he called a "vision." He told the congregation he saw a time when he would be "preaching to thousands of people." He had the premonition again early in 1974, and then, in September of that year, the vision came to pass.

Marvin Horan became the leader of the nation's most violent conflict over school textbooks. In 1974, thousands of people in Kanawha County, West Virginia, believed that some of the new books adopted by the local school board were anti-American, antireligious, "trashy, filthy and one-sided."[1] Objections to the books first voiced in the late spring escalated into meetings, and meetings evolved into mass rallies and marches by late summer. Soon after the children returned to their classrooms in the fall, Horan and others called on parents to keep their children out of school. Coal miners and truck drivers went out on strike in sympathy with the textbook protesters, and by the fall of 1974, most of Kanawha County's commercial life snapped closed. Ten thousand coal miners left their jobs. Parents kept children home, and dozens of schools were emptied. On the first Sunday in September, Horan spoke from the pulpit of his Two-Mile Mountain Mission church. He urged his congregation to continue the boycott of the Kanawha County schools, promising that they would prevail over the school board and the books. He also told his flock that he had received a "vision . . . God has revealed to me a victory speech."[2]

Partisanship Returns — and So Does Religion

Ten years after the Kanawha County textbook controversy, Don J. Goode, a doctoral student at Michigan State University, contacted people who had been on both sides of the textbook war. Goode hoped to learn if opinions about school textbooks were "reflective of more general values."[3] He wanted to know if a stand in the textbook war could be considered a proxy for a larger constellation of beliefs — a worldview of society, religion, and politics. Goode convinced the former textbook combatants to answer several questionnaires. In the first, he asked participants what they thought of the nation's courts. The anti-textbook group strongly disagreed with the Supreme Court's decision to ban teacher-led school prayer. The pro-textbook group strongly agreed with this decision. The anti-textbook group thought that the courts gave criminals too many rights and failed to preserve traditional values and that judges too often "made" laws rather than interpreted those on the books. The pro-textbook group thought the opposite.

In another set of questions, Goode asked whether county services would improve if the people of Kanawha County could afford to pay more in taxes. The pro-textbook group strongly agreed that the county could make good use of increased revenues. The anti-textbook group strongly disagreed. The anti-textbook group, Goode concluded, simply "did not have confidence" in government.

Not surprisingly, Goode found a "wide schism" between the groups when he asked about education. The textbook opponents favored prayer in schools, discipline, and the teaching of "traditional Christian and American values." They also thought that extracurricular activities didn't provide "valuable learning experiences" and that schools shouldn't provide "special services (such as hot meals and daycare centers) that some families can't provide" for themselves. The textbook supporters were generally in favor of afterschool activities and the use of schools to provide social services; this group was significantly less enthusiastic about a curriculum that emphasized discipline, school prayer, and the teaching of Christian values.

Finally, Goode prepared a list of eighteen values — such as equality, self-respect, and national security — and asked that individuals rank them in order of importance. The two sides judged many of the values similarly. Both pro- and anti-textbook activists placed a "comfortable life" relatively low on the scale; both sides thought that health and "freedom" were important. The anti-textbook group ranked "national security" significantly higher than the pro-textbook group and "equality" (defined as "brotherhood, equal opportunity for all") significantly lower. The pro-textbook group ranked a "world of beauty in nature and the arts" significantly higher than the anti-textbook group.

The most severe difference between the two groups — people who initially had divided only over which textbooks they thought should be used in the Kanawha County schools in the fall of 1974 — came to light in how they judged the importance of a "saved, eternal life." The group that had favored the introduction of the new textbooks placed "salvation" last in their hierarchy of values. Those who opposed the new books ranked a saved, eternal life first.

Political scientists Geoffrey Layman and Edward Carmines gathered survey results from the 1980 through 1992 presidential elections. They compared the effects of race, age, education, religion, and a desire for personal freedom on voting behavior.* They found that measures of traditional faith appeared to have the strongest impact on presidential votes. Voters cared about issues affecting self-expression — they wanted freedom of speech protected, for example — but traditional religious values mattered the most.[4] The political division in this country wasn't between regions or classes, Layman and Carmines found. It was between people with liberal notions of religion and those with traditional beliefs.

This was the new politics that appeared in 1974 in Kanawha County. The divide there was about religion and values — and it was expressed geographically. The textbook opponents came largely from the small towns in rural Kanawha County; those who supported the textbooks and the board lived mainly in Charleston, the state capital. There were class differences, too. Opponents were working people who earned less and had less formal education than those living in the city. The mainline religious denominations and the establishment organizations in Charleston — civic clubs and the daily newspaper — supported the school board's choice of books. Opponents worshiped at the Open Door Apostolic Church, the Spradling Gospel Tabernacle, and Reverend Horan's Two-Mile Mountain Mission. This wasn't simply a conflict between clubs

---

*They used a survey that asked people to rank as national goals maintaining order, giving people more say in decisions, fighting inflation, or protecting free speech.

or institutions, however. Kanawha County residents were divided over their way of life.

Religion, Public and Private

Social scientists have been predicting for the past three centuries that religion would soon run its course and disappear. Sociologist Rodney Stark found the first forecast of religion's demise in 1710, when Thomas Woolston calmly calculated that Christianity would no longer be with us in 1900. Voltaire (1694–1778) figured that religion would last only another fifty years. In 1822, Thomas Jefferson surmised, "There is not a young man now living in the United States who will not die a Unitarian."[5] Max Weber, Sigmund Freud, Herbert Spencer, and Karl Marx all predicted that ascendant industrialism would eventually render religion meaningless. Society would simply "outgrow" the need for organized faith, and humans would be rid of ritual, superstition, and sacred traditions. More bluntly, sociologist Peter Berger announced in 1968 that "by the 21st century, religious believers are likely to be found only in small sects, huddled together to resist a worldwide secular culture." Indeed, Berger wrote, "the predicament of the believer is increasingly like that of a Tibetan astrologer on a prolonged visit to an American university."[6]

The promise that religion would fall victim to modernization "has been regarded as *the* master model of sociological inquiry," one of the "key historical revolutions transforming medieval agrarian societies into modern industrial nations," wrote political scientists Pippa Norris and Ronald Inglehart.[7] Which means, of course, that a central tenet of the social sciences over the past three hundred years has been proved spectacularly wrong. (Berger had the good sense to recant in 1997.) But a modernizing, industrial society did have an impact on faith in America. The economic panics of the late nineteenth century, the influx of immigrants, and the contradictions between scientific discoveries (say, evolution) and religious faith led to a split in the Protestant church. The division that appeared at the turn of the twentieth century was not so much between denominations; it was more about how people viewed the world. On one side was what Martin Marty has called "Private Protestantism."[8] Private Protestants promoted individual salvation and promised that personal morality would be rewarded in the next life. On the other side of that great divide was "Public Protestantism," a conviction that the way to God required the transformation of society. The latter laid the foundation for Democratic liberalism. The former provided the moral footing and rationale for Republican conservatism.

Private Protestantism considered the consumption of alcohol a personal failing; Public Protestantism looked at drunkenness as a social ill. Private Protestants supported "blue laws" (closing places of business on Sundays); Public Protestants promoted the minimum wage and the eight-hour day. Dwight Moody, a Private Protestant revivalist, witnessed the Haymarket labor riot in 1886 and concluded that either "these people are to be evangelized or the leaven of communism and infidelity will assume such enormous proportions that it will break out in a reign of terror such as this country has never known." Public Protestants, Marty wrote, saw the Chicago labor strife and reasoned, "either the people were to be evangelized and their needs were to be met and their rights faced, or the Kingdom of God would not come." At the World's Columbian Exposition in 1893, both a session on the Social Gospel (the name given to Public Protestantism) and a revival conducted by Reverend Moody were held. While the Social Gospel ministers confronted industrial life and sought human perfection through political reform, Moody defined his task differently: "I look upon this world as a wrecked vessel. God has given me a lifeboat and said to me, 'Moody, save all you can.'"[9]

Josiah Strong, a turn-of-the-century Congregationalist minister, described "two types of Christianity" alive in the country. The division was "not to be distinguished by any of the old lines of doctrinal or denominational cleavage," Strong wrote in 1913. "Their difference is one of spirit, aim, point of view, comprehensiveness. The one is individualist; the other is social." The one staged revivals; the other sought to reform the world.*[10]

---

*James Davison Hunter made this same distinction in two insightful books, *American Evangelism* and *Culture Wars: The Struggle to Define America*. In the former, Hunter wrote that the advocates of the Social Gospel "repudiated an individuated conception of moral and social ills in favor of an interpretation of such phenomena as resulting from social, political, and economic

Walter Rauschenbusch was the most well-known proponent of the Social Gospel. Rauschenbusch pastored a church in New York's Hell's Kitchen neighborhood, and from that vantage point in the new urban slum, he watched the modern industrial order rub raw against humanity. He was an optimist, believing in the "immense latent perfectibility of human nature."[11] Perfection, however, required social intervention. Rauschenbusch wrote in 1908 that a "sense of equality is the basis for Christian morality." And to reach that equality, the Social Gospel theologian promoted legislation: a minimum wage, shorter workdays, better food, and cleaner air. The Social Gospel was a moral crusade against the cruelty of the industrial city. Western civilization was at a "decisive point in its development," Rauschenbusch wrote. "Either society confronted social injustice or society would fall: It is either a revival of social religion or the deluge."[12]

The country — or at least a majority of its citizens — followed Rauschenbusch. In 1908, the Methodist Church adopted its Social Creed, a list of social reforms, including "equal rights and complete justice for all men," the end of sweatshops, the prohibition of child labor, the protection of workers from dangerous machinery, and the "abatement of poverty." The title of Charles M. Sheldon's 1896 novel, *In His Steps: What Would Jesus Do?*, would become the inspiration for w.w.j.d. bumper stickers and woven bracelets sported by Evangelicals in the 1990s. But the original book was a call for Christian socialism. Ecumenicism was the organizational form of the Social Gospel. Thirty-three denominations were represented when the Federal Council of Churches was formed in 1908. The combined representation of Protestant faiths quickly adopted the Methodist Social Creed.[13]

There was a period of intradenominational conflict, but the Social Gospel crowd won most of these organizational disputes. (For instance, modernist Baptists took over the denomination's theological schools and missionary boards, steering them in the direction of the Social Gospel.)

realities over which the individual had little or no control." Reform wasn't a revival, but "the modification of the structural conditions precipitating these social maladies" (*American Evangelism* [New Brunswick, NJ: Rutgers University Press, 1983], p. 28). *Culture Wars* portrays the current political divisions in light of these earlier disputes.

The so-called Fundamentalists "lost in their efforts to gain control of any of the denominations" in the early twentieth century, Marty wrote. So the traditionalists responded by setting up institutions parallel to those dominated by practitioners of the Social Gospel.[14] Left out by the mainline denominations, Private Protestant pastors established councils of Fundamentalist preachers, printing houses, and seminaries.*[15] The traditionalists published their own manifesto, twelve booklets printed between 1910 and 1915 titled *The Fundamentals: A Testimony to the Truth*. These scholarly works fenced off the theological boundaries of Private Protestantism: the Virgin Birth of Christ, the inerrancy of the Bible, Christ's death on behalf of sinners, his Resurrection, and the Second Coming. Three million copies of these booklets were distributed; this was the birth of Fundamentalism.[16]

But after the humiliation of the 1925 Scopes "monkey trial" in Dayton, Tennessee, where a public school teacher was found guilty of violating the state law that prohibited the teaching of evolution, the contest was over. The Fundamentalist movement was brought to an "abrupt halt" by the ridicule resulting from the trial, according to the Reverend Jerry Falwell. *Christian Century* magazine predicted in 1926 that Fundamentalism would be a "disappearing quantity in American religious life." There was a "noticeable drop in attendance" at the 1926 meeting of the World's Christian Fundamentals Association. What followed was the "Great Exodus," Falwell's description of the mass movement of Fundamentalists out of mainline denominations and public life.[17] Evangelicals didn't disappear, of course; they separated. Conservatives organized the National Association of Evangelicals in 1942. They experimented with radio and television. (Between 1967 and 1972, membership in the National Religious Broadcasters increased fourfold.[18]) Occasionally, religious conservatives poked their heads out and showed some political force, supporting, for example, the inclusion of "under God" in the

---

*Readers may note the similarity here with the approach conservatives took after their defeat in 1964. Much has been made of the separate foundations, professional organizations, radio stations, publishing houses, think tanks, and schools that conservatives have established since the mid-1960s. The history of American fundamentalism shows there is nothing unusual in these tactics. It's what groups do when they lose control of society's established institutions.

Pledge of Allegiance in 1954. But the purpose of the church was saving souls, not saving society.[19]

For much of the 1960s and 1970s, the people who would become the Republican religious right were pre-political. They were either un-aligned or stuck in political formations established by the Civil War or the New Deal. In 1960, 60 percent of Evangelical Protestants identified themselves as Democrats.[20]

"Is God Dead?"

In the mid-twentieth century, the strands of what we would recognize as modern conservatism were mostly unconnected. There were libertari-ans, business conservatives, religious fundamentalists, and conservative intellectuals. But they didn't have a party, and they didn't have each other. After World War II, there occurred what historian Sara Diamond has called a "conservative transformation." The various threads of con-servative thought and faith began to intertwine, and social, religious, and ideological movements slowly braided together.[21]

The groups found they had things in common. Libertarians saw as primary the conflict between the individual and the state. They distrusted a government that substituted programs for personal respon-sibility and freedom. Christian traditionalists also thought that the country lacked discipline and distrusted a government that substituted programs for salvation. (James Dobson sold more than 2 million copies of his 1971 book *Dare to Discipline,* which encouraged parents to spank children who were disrespectful. The conservative movement simply hoped to extend family discipline to the nation.)[22] New York neoconser-vatives, libertarians, and southern fundamentalists distrusted "social en-gineering" by the state, whether it was Stalin's Five-Year Plan, Johnson's Great Society, or textbooks recommended by English teachers in West Virginia. Finally, libertarians and fundamentalists found ready allies in the business wing of the Republican Party, those pressing for smaller, cheaper, and less intrusive government.

Historian Lisa McGirr has described the shift in conservative politics in the 1960s from stiff anticommunism to a tossed salad of libertarianism, racial homogeneity, social conservatism, and fundamentalist Christianity. She found the formation of the "New Right" a continent away from Kanawha County, in Orange County, California. The people in Orange County in the 1960s "embraced a set of beliefs whose cornerstone element was opposition to the liberal leviathan that was, in their eyes, the postwar federal government . . . Many Orange County conservatives, then, drank a heady and muddled cocktail of traditional and libertarian ideas, linking a Christian view of the world with libertarian rhetoric and libertarian economics." The new conservative movement didn't grow just in the rural South or in coal country. Fundamentalist churches and right-wing politics also thrived among a "modern, young, and affluent population" in California.*[23]

During the late 1960s and early 1970s, this impromptu conservative movement in Orange County steered toward the public schools.† Anaheim fought over sex education from 1968 to 1970. In 1969, Orange County parents protested and eventually shut down a sex education program in the public schools. Parents warned that "secular humanists" were worming their way into the classrooms.[24] The John Birch Society in Orange County reprinted and distributed copies of the nineteenth-century McGuffey Readers. By the time the textbook fight began in West Virginia, Orange County conservatives' "concerns about 'morality' and permissiveness would become the driving force behind a full-fledged battle over schools."[25]

The New Right was starting to coalesce. Religious traditionalists melded with anticommunists. Advocates of traditional morality and personal responsibility found themselves in sympathy with laissez-faire capitalists and Private Protestants. They all had a common enemy in government.[26] Free markets, small government, anticommunism, and

---

*Liberals, as is their wont, were dismissive of the Orange County conservative movement. One explanation for the emerging New Right was that the movement was a reaction against modernization. Another was that the people were "paranoid." Even *Fortune* magazine described Orange County in 1968 as "nut country" (McGirr, *Suburban Warriors,* p. 6).

†America has a tradition of using the schools to work out its religious, ethnic, and class conflicts. One of the early school wars broke out in New York City in the 1840s. Catholic leaders saw the school system as one designed to socialize children into a Protestant world. They asked why the schools used the King James Version for Bible readings instead of the Catholic Douay Version. When officials refused to include the Douay Version, the church established a separate system of Catholic schools.

traditional values, Martin Marty wrote, were all deemed by Private Prot estants to be part of "the mission of Christ to the world."[27] The "enemy of my enemy" connections could be bizarre. Intellectual conservatives and religious conservatives, for example, found common cause in their distrust of international law and the United Nations. The hardheaded neoconservatives who emerged from New York University thought that the UN was a "charade kept alive by liberal piety about international co-operation and world peace."[28] Similarly, in Tim LaHaye and Jerry B. Jenkins's Left Behind series of "end of time" novels, the Antichrist takes power in the world by first gaining control of the UN. Nicolae Carpathia (the Antichrist) becomes secretary-general of the UN, promoting disar-mament and "global community."[29] (In the early 1960s, the Magnolia School District in Orange County banned the UN as an "unfit" topic for the schools.[30]) Intellectuals who opposed the supremacy of interna-tional law would gradually join those who had millennialist fears of world government — and fundamentalist Christians living in West Vir-ginia coal camps would eventually find common ground with neocon-servative urban Jews and suburban Californians.

The Social Gospel, meanwhile, became the equivalent of a state reli-gion, its policies enacted by Progressives, New Dealers, and purveyors of the New Frontier and Great Society.[31] Public Protestantism domi-nated most of the mainline churches, denominations that all grew at a steady clip through the 1950s. There was a surge of interest in ecumeni-cism. *Time* magazine placed Eugene Carson Blake on its cover after he gave a sermon in 1960 at Grace Cathedral in San Francisco proposing to merge four major Protestant denominations. (Blake was later named the head of the World Council of Churches.) Mainline denominations were prominent in the early civil rights movement. Blake was arrested along with other religious leaders when they tried to integrate a Baltimore amusement park on July 4, 1963.[32] The National Council of Churches (formerly the Federal Council of Churches) called for a "mass meeting of this country's religious leaders to demonstrate their concern over ra-cial tensions in Selma" in 1965.[33]

There was talk of a "new reformation" in the mid-1960s, and it was a religious movement designed by Public Protestants. The future lay with the "servant church," announced a *Time* cover story in 1964.[34] Theologians found in the Bible ample teachings that Christianity was a life in service, that the "purpose of the church is mission," not worship or revival.[35] *Time* reported that "modern church thinkers" questioned the need for an organized church at all, believing that "God may well be more apparent in a purely nonreligious organization or movement — such as the civil rights revolution or the fight against poverty and hunger in the world — than in the actions of the churches."[36]

In May 1966, *Time* asked what was a very reasonable question in a country dominated — or so it seemed — by Public Protestantism. In large red letters against a pitch-black background, the magazine invited Americans to consider "Is God Dead?"[37]

"Even Hillbillies Have Constitutional Rights"

Kanawha County was contemplating new textbooks in the spring of 1974 because it had been ordered to. The West Virginia Board of Education had passed a resolution directing local districts to adopt books that "accurately portray minority and ethnic group contributions" to American history and culture.[38] The Kanawha County school superintendent recommended 325 books and then put the volumes on shelves in the county's main public library. The board didn't comment on the books; the local press didn't report that new books were on the way. For nearly a month in March and April, the books sat and few people bothered to crack a cover. In mid-April, however, Kanawha County school board member Alice Moore — "Sweet Alice," as she would come to be known — piped up.

Moore was the wife of a fundamentalist preacher in St. Albans, West Virginia. She had run for a seat on the Kanawha County school board in 1970, beating an incumbent in a campaign that was dominated by debate about the propriety of including sex education as a classroom subject. In 1969, the school board had adopted a sex education curriculum recommended by the state and written under a grant from the U.S. Office of Education. In good Social Gospel style, the school board announced that the "public school system should assume responsibility for instruction in any important area of community or family living which is not being adequately assumed by home or other agency or institution."[39]

Moore disagreed. She considered sex education a descent into moral relativism, a "denial of absolutes." Moore argued that the classes represented "the humanistic approach of reasoning out right and wrong on the basis of circumstances," which was "a denial of God." And to Moore, "God's law is absolute!" Her opponent, Dr. Carl Tully, didn't curl up in his confrontation with Sweet Alice. He charged that the John Birch Society supported Moore's campaign. ("Lies Inspired by Birchers Hit Campaign, Tully Says," blared one headline in the *Charleston Gazette*.) Moore and her supporters wouldn't be happy simply to scrub the schools clean of sex education, Tully warned; they intended to "gain control of the school board and in turn dictate what textbooks will be used, what books to have in the library, and what subjects can be taught and who will teach them."[40] Rumor spread around Kanawha County that Texas oilman H. L. Hunt had given $100,000 to Moore's 1970 school board campaign. Moore denied it. She also denied a connection with any "Birchers." Moore obviously didn't need much outside help. A week before the election, she appeared on television holding two Bibles she claimed a janitor had retrieved from a school incinerator. "And they [Tully's supporters] have the nerve to call me a book burner," Moore said, holding the crispy sacred texts, fresh from the fiery furnace.[41] Moore defeated Tully in May 1970, and sex education classes were soon banished from Kanawha County schools.[42]

Moore's initial questions about the 1974 books concerned the use of an African American dialect in some of the language arts texts. "My main objection is that they simply attack traditional philosophy of good grammar and English," Moore said at a May meeting. A week later, Moore's objections were more strenuous. She told the board she represented "a wide constituency of people who don't want this trash." The books presented a view of America from the black perspective, she argued, but they didn't convey the point of view of middle-class whites. "I'm not asking for something anti-black, but we have got to have something from both sides," Moore said. "I want to see something patriotic in those books."[43]

In the summer of 1974, Marvin Horan was hauling rock used to construct the interstate highway running through Charleston. One of the road job superintendents gave the minister a pamphlet and asked him to read it. Horan said that he glanced at the pamphlet and saw that it was about books in the county schools, "and then I forgot about it." But in August, Horan came home one evening to find a crowd gathered at his neighborhood church, the Point Lick Gospel Tabernacle. His wife told him that the group was examining a set of textbooks, and she suggested that they take a look, too. Alice Moore was there. So were the books. The crowd grew, overflowing the building, so Horan recommended that the group move to a nearby park. Horan mounted the stage. He said a prayer to open the meeting. "And I never did get off that stage because people were insistent that I speak for them," Horan said. "It just happened. Nothing was preplanned. There were no meetings. Nobody talked it over and said this was the way to do it and this would be our approach. None of that was done. It all happened just instantly."

Parents were meeting all over rural Kanawha County. At one rally, protesters passed empty Kentucky Fried Chicken buckets, collecting $719.75, enough to purchase a full-page newspaper ad in the Charleston newspaper criticizing the textbooks. The next meeting on Campbells Creek was larger, Horan recalled more than thirty years later. Thousands came. Police had to close the road entering the park. Horan led that meeting and another at a school gym. Meetings at the park on Campbells Creek ripened into mass marches in Charleston. Horan urged parents to keep their children out of school, and they did, at least in the rural areas of Kanawha County where the movement was centered. "The common man don't know what to do except what he's done, and that's to go home and sit down," Horan said, explaining his strategy. On the first day of school after Labor Day, attendance in Kanawha County schools was off by 20 percent. Protesters appeared in front of school buildings, one carrying a sign saying EVEN HILLBILLIES HAVE CONSTITUTIONAL RIGHTS. United Mine Workers of America (UMWA) members honored pickets thrown up by parents, and soon every coal mine in Kanawha County and several in neighboring counties closed.[44]

There was a rural/urban divide in the textbook strike. The *Charleston Daily Mail* surveyed parents in thirty elementary schools on the use of one group of health textbooks. Only six schools had a majority of parents who would allow their children to use the books. Four of those six were in the city of Charleston. In one rural school that November, only 9 of

922 students attended classes.[45] Also divided were the independent churches in rural Kanawha County and the mainline denominations in Charleston. And underlying that divide was an increasingly popular belief among Private Protestants in the imminent Second Coming of Christ. Carol Mason, a women's studies professor at the University of Nevada, Las Vegas, interviewed participants in the controversy. Several told her that one of the most read books in the region in 1974 was Hal Lindsey's *The Late Great Planet Earth*.[46] Lindsey's book was a precursor of the Left Behind publishing phenomenon. It presented a meticulously detailed prediction that the world was approaching the end of time and that the Second Coming of Christ would take place in 1988.* (Carol Mason observed that the book sold more than 10 million copies and, unintentionally perhaps, served as the religious right's equivalent of the Port Huron Statement, Tom Hayden's 1962 manifesto founding Students for a Democratic Society.)[47] The religious milieu of Kanawha County was a volatile one, where a good number of people were reading about the decline of American civilization and the end of the world, a descent that could be forestalled only by what Lindsey described as a "widespread spiritual awakening."[48]

Class Warfare Inverted

To political leftists of the early 1970s, the Kanawha County textbook dispute was a clear case of "class warfare," the description Calvin Trillin used in *The New Yorker*.[49] It was a fight pitting the rich folks on "the hill" in Charleston against those up the creeks out in the county. When UMWA miners joined the strike, the class credentials of the protesters were complete. These were the same coal miners, after all, who had just led a union revolution, deposing a corrupt president and electing rank-and-file miners to high office. The story had a neat, working-class symmetry. The new president of the UMWA, Arnold Miller, was a miner with black lung from Cabin Creek in Kanawha County.† It was a com-

---

*The Late Great Planet Earth wasn't just a book for the rural or the uneducated. Orson Welles made a movie based on Lindsey's book in 1979.

†Miller had defeated Tony Boyle for the UMWA presidency in 1972. Boyle was later convicted of the 1969 murders of union activist Jock Yablonski and his wife and daughter. I worked for UMWA secretary-treasurer Harry Patrick when he ran to replace Miller as union president in 1977.

pelling story (and one that explained away radically conservative behavior by the white working class), but it missed another change that had taken place. Since the end of World War II, class had been diminishing as a marker of political division. Actually, the traditional order of class voting was being inverted. Under the familiar New Deal alignment, working-class voters had supported Democrats and liberal government. (In 1936, Franklin Roosevelt had won 73 percent of voters Gallup identified as of "low socioeconomic standing.") Beginning in the mid-1960s, however, white working-class Americans had begun voting Republican.[50]

This is a disputed area of research, but the academic arguments over class voting have more to do with definition than fact. Princeton University political scientist Larry Bartels has correctly reported that the poorest whites, those in the lowest third of the income strata, are still reliable Democratic voters, a pattern that has remained unchanged for the past thirty years. Others also have found that low-income whites have an increasing allegiance to Democrats and that Republicans have gained most of their new votes from middle- and upper-class Americans.[51] If "working class" were defined strictly by income, the discussion would be over. But what about Horan? He drove a truck during the week and often worked a second job pouring concrete at night or on Saturday. He lived in a nice home on a large lot; he wasn't poor, but his labor was manual. Other scholars have defined "working class" to include people like Horan. They consider not only income but also occupation and education. When "working class" is defined using all of those measures, we see a dramatic shift in voting patterns, one that began after the mid-1960s' unraveling.

In the late 1970s, polling expert Everett Carll Ladd Jr. compared white voters of high, medium, and low socioeconomic status (SES). High-SES voters were managers or white-collar workers with some college training. Low-SES voters worked as farm laborers, in service jobs, or in other semiskilled occupations. In 1960, Ladd found, 38 percent of high-SES white workers voted for John F. Kennedy, but 61 percent of low-SES white workers did so. The configuration was straight out of the New Deal handbook. Bosses, managers, and white-collar workers voted Republican. Laborers, field hands, and truck drivers voted Democratic. When Ladd looked at the behavior of white voters by occupation and education from 1948 to 1972, he saw that the New Deal coalition was flipping. Low-SES workers — the white working class in his definition — were voting Republican at increasingly higher rates. High-SES workers, however, were voting more Democratic. In particular, whites who had graduated from college or graduate school were becoming more Democratic. A 1974 Gallup poll found "among graduate students, an almost unbelievably low proportion of 9 percent identified with the GOP."[52]

The perceptive southern writer John Egerton went to Kanawha County for the *Progressive* magazine to report on the "battle of the books." What he found was a conflict based on something more than income. The division was a clash between the "hillers" in Charleston and the "creekers" in rural Kanawha County: "Charleston is Episcopalian, Methodist, Presbyterian; the churches in the narrow hollows are Free-Will Baptist, Pentecostal, Church of God in Prophesy. Charleston is double-knit suits, sports cars, cocktail parties; rural Kanawha is khakis, coal trucks, white lightning and abstention. Charleston aspires to a modern, affluent future; Cabin Creek struggles against heavy odds to preserve a hard but often heroic past."[53]

The divide in West Virginia wasn't between Republicans and Democrats or rich and poor. While Ladd was finding a new division in the broad numbers of the electorate — a New Deal turned upside down — Egerton was seeing the same divide on the ground in West Virginia. That division — of rural and urban, college-educated and working-class, Public and Private Protestant — defines our politics today. In 2004, poor white people continued to vote Democratic. According to Bartels's figures, John Kerry won half his votes from white families earning less than $35,000 a year, a percentage that hasn't changed in thirty years.[54] But when political analyst Ruy Teixeira looked at whites without a college education in families with a total income between $30,000 and $50,000 a year, George W. Bush beat Kerry by 23 percentage points. The important difference wasn't income, however, but education. Among white college graduates in the *same* income level ($30,000 to $50,000 per family), Bush and Kerry split the vote evenly. Teixeira found that in 2004, Democrats did worst among working-class whites.[55]

The Organization of a "Political Revolution"

As the Kanawha boycott continued, shots were fired, and one man was beaten. The *Charleston Gazette* castigated "religious fanatics who encouraged their venomous followers." A minister prayed for the deaths of the three school board members who had voted for the books. "I am asking Christian people to pray that God will kill the giants who have mocked and made fun of dumb fundamentalists," implored the Reverend Charles Quigley. An elementary school on Campbells Creek was firebombed; another on Cabin Creek was dynamited. Shotgun blasts raked school buses. In a strange episode, a constable from Witchers Creek arrested the county school superintendent and three school board members for contributing to the delinquency of minors, a charge brought by the Upper Kanawha Valley Mayors Association. (The officials were arrested at a Methodist church where they were talking with textbook opponents at a meeting arranged by the local bishop.) The charges were dismissed. Protesters attacked some board members at a meeting in early December. Eventually, the Ku Klux Klan marched in support of the textbook opponents.[56]

The violence peaked, and then, as winter came, it ended. The Kanawha County textbook war just petered out. The school board promised to review the textbooks, and in December several men were arrested for the school bombings. The schools gradually refilled with students. In mid-January 1975, a federal grand jury indicted Marvin Horan for conspiring to blow up two elementary schools. According to the indictment, Horan had told a group that he had "paid enough taxes" to own one of the schools and that they "had his permission to do anything they wanted" with the building.[57] Horan was eventually found guilty of one charge of conspiracy. He appealed the verdict and ran for the state senate, losing to the incumbent. (The political factions of the strike had yet to find a home in the two parties, so Horan ran as a Democrat.) After his appeals were denied, Horan took up residence at a federal prison in Pennsylvania. The warden allowed him to hold prayer services on Sunday evenings and to baptize convicts at a church in a nearby town. "You might find this strange," Horan said, "but if I had been a single man, I wouldn't have cared if they ever let me out. The ministry was so rewarding then."

When Horan left prison after two years, just before Christmas 1978, he moved "right back to Campbells Creek, right back into the ministry." But Horan's life wasn't the same there after the strike and his time in prison. Churches across the Midwest asked him to speak, but in Kanawha County the ministers who had supported the strike now shunned the movement's leader. He stayed on Campbells Creek for fourteen years before moving to North Carolina in 1993, when he was fifty-three years old. Horan still drives a truck and preaches, and he is more convinced than ever that the 1974 textbook war was worth fighting. "The books were teaching our children to do things that went against everything we stood for," Horan told me in 2005. "I mean, it took . . . the pride of the children away from them. It destroyed the children." Still fond of prophecy, the preacher envisioned the inevitable downfall of the United States, a victim of its moral failings. "Make a mental note of this," Horan said. "Within ten years or twenty years from this day, there'll be another country ruling this one. Another country will be running this one."

In the fall of 1974, after the strike was well under way, the Heritage Foundation sent a lawyer to consult with some of the movement's stalwarts. The newly formed foundation brought leaders of the strike to Washington, D.C., to meet with education commissioner Terrel Bell and an aide to President Gerald Ford.[58] Conservative activists in Washington hadn't created the movement in West Virginia; Horan and the people in the coal camps of Kanawha County had done that themselves. But the Heritage Foundation and other conservative groups recognized within the uprising a potent and, as it turned out, enduring combination of Private Protestant values, distrust of an intrusive government, racial insecurity, and a millennialist belief that America was losing its moral authority and world standing. While liberals either romanticized the textbook strike as "class warfare" or labeled strikers "religious fanatics," conservatives got busy channeling Horan and others into the New Right coalition and the Republican Party. The New Right movement wasn't created as a result of a conspiracy. It was emerging from places like Campbells Creek. The ingredients of conservative ideology were scattered across the country. They just needed to be gathered, organized, and put together using the right recipe. In 1975, the Heritage Foundation formed a group to help coordinate some two hundred textbook protests that had cropped up nationwide.[59] It asked donors to "help Heritage stop forcing pornography and other objectionable subjects into schools all over America."[60]

The West Virginia textbook strike flipped a switch and illuminated the way the Republican Party could form a coalition of working-class voters; religious conservatives; and small-government, free-market capitalists. Emerging Republican leaders adopted the Kanawha County strikers. Robert Dornan traveled from California to West Virginia to speak at a few rallies.[61] Two years later, he won his first term in Congress. Representative Philip Crane, an Illinois Republican and a founder of the new conservative movement, sent out letters in December 1974 charging that textbook protesters had been subjected to "police brutality."[62] The Reverend Charles Secrest, a representative of Billy James Hargis's Church of the Christian Crusade, visited Alice Moore, and Moore went to Tulsa to speak to a Christian Crusade audience. The organization sold a tape of her speech for five dollars.[63] "It would be a mistake to consider the textbooks the sole point of protest," said Elmer Fike, a businessman and supporter of the strike. "The textbooks were a last straw. Parents here as well as nationwide are calling for a return to fundamental and basic education." After the strike ended, more than seventy Kanawha County residents drove to Washington, D.C., to join Boston antibusing protesters in a rally against federal education policies. "This is the first time the two big struggles against busing and dirty textbooks have stood side by side," said the Reverend Avis Hill. "This is the beginning of a political revolution."[64]

West Virginia–style protests spread, as this new conservative concoction found a purpose and a public voice. "Since the battle of the books in Kanawha County in 1974, incidents of censorship or attempts at censorship have increased markedly," wrote education professor Edward B. Jenkinson. "During the 1977–78 school year, more incidents of removing or censoring books occurred nationally than at any other time in the last twenty-five years."[65] In 1979, Richard Viguerie, the direct-mail impresario of the conservative movement, complained that during "the 25 years that I've been active in politics, the major religious leaders in America have been liberals who were in bed politically with the Democratic Party."[66] Viguerie led a group of conservative activists (including Paul Weyrich and Ed McAteer of the Conservative Caucus) away from the cities and the centers of Public Protestantism to Lynchburg, Virginia. They visited with a relatively unknown preacher by the name of Jerry Falwell, a man the conservatives thought had a message that ran counter to the mainline churches' tenets of the Social Gospel and ecumenicism. The New Right leaders urged Falwell to use his church, his weekly television broadcast, and his contacts among other conservative preachers as the foundation of a national political and religious network. Viguerie would help raise funds through direct mail. They said Falwell could call the new organization something like the "moral majority."[67]

Kanawha County, USA: 1974–2004

Political scientist Peter Francia and his coworkers at East Carolina University divided voters in the 2004 presidential election into three groups based on their beliefs about the Bible.[68] *Fundamentalists* believed in biblical inerrancy. (Fundamentalists accounted for roughly half of the voters in Republican states, but only 28 percent of the voters in Democratic states.) *Biblical Minimalists* believed that the Bible was the work of men, not God. (They were 12 percent of the voters in red states, 18 percent in blue states.) *Moderates* believed that the Bible was the Word of God but shouldn't be taken literally. (This middling group accounted for 38 percent of voters in red states and 53 percent in blue states.)

The geographic division of people by biblical belief and political leaning is further evidence of the Big Sort. But Francia's more interesting finding is that voters' assessment of the Bible could predict how they felt about a range of other issues. Nearly eight out of ten Fundamentalists in *red* states *opposed* any government spending for abortions. Three-quarters of the biblical Minimalists in *blue* states *favored* government spending for abortions. Nine out of ten Fundamentalists in both blue and red states *opposed* gay marriage. Nearly three-quarters of the biblical Minimalists *favored* gay marriage.

Abortion and gay marriage are issues affected by faith. But the divisions between the two religious camps reappeared even with questions that had no discernible connection with faith — and aligned neatly with Republican and Democratic Party positions. Fundamentalists favored increasing the budget deficit in order to cut taxes; biblical Minimalists did not. Fundamentalists supported issues such as a strong military, jobs over the environment, and George W. Bush. Biblical Minimalists were less inclined to believe that it was extremely important to have a strong military, favored the environment over jobs, and didn't support George W. Bush. "It is not a culture war between red states and blue states," Francia wrote, "but rather a war between Fundamentalists and biblical Minimalists within both the red and the blue states."[69]

When graduate student Don Goode questioned West Virginia textbook warriors in the 1980s, he found two cultural tribes. When Goode asked them what they thought about government, the courts, salvation, and welfare, the two camps disagreed about all of these issues. People held remarkably coherent beliefs, so that what a person thought about the power of the courts predicted what he or she believed about school lunch programs. What someone believed about religion, national defense, and the importance of beauty lined up with what he or she thought about the content of school textbooks. Francia discovered that by the 2004 election, Kanawha County politics had gone national.

Democrats tend to blame the division on Jerry Falwell, Rush Limbaugh, the Heritage Foundation, Barry Goldwater, Ronald Reagan, George W. Bush, and Karl Rove. Republicans tend to blame it on the 1960s, welfare, drugs, Jimmy Carter, and Bill and Hillary Clinton. Looking back at the split between Public and Private Protestants and the Kanawha County textbook strike, one can see that the divide Francia uncovered wasn't foisted on Americans in a conspiracy of the right or the left. The conservative movement of the 1980s and 1990s was successful because it orchestrated — and then amplified — the politics emerging from communities as different as Orange County, California, and Kanawha County, West Virginia. Polarization did not come from politicians or the media. Indeed, according to Francia, "elites may be responding to the polarization that exists within the electorate rather than the other way around."*[70] It's just that in the past three decades, Republicans responded better than Democrats.

As with the decline in trust, however, the alignment of right-leaning political parties with churchgoing wasn't something made only in America. It happened everywhere. The most religious people in every industrialized country have come to support the political party on the right. It seemed to come as a surprise to Americans after the 2000 election that those who attended church once a week were overwhelmingly Republican. But there wasn't anything unusual about that relationship. A survey of thirty-two countries in the late 1990s found that seven out of ten of those who attended church once a week voted for the political party on the right. In fact, church attendance in all industrialized societies is the best predictor of right-leaning political ideology.†[71]

The United States is peculiar among these nations only in that there are so many churchgoers. Pippa Norris and Ronald Inglehart combined different polls to find that the percentage of people who expressed a belief in God has declined in seventeen of nineteen countries over the past half century. Typically, Scandinavian nations have had the largest percentage of people drifting away from the pews. The two countries that haven't experienced a significant diminishment in belief are Brazil and the United States. When it comes to the number of people who believe in God and attend church regularly, Norris and Inglehart wrote, the United States is, statistically speaking, "a striking deviant case."[72]

Over time, the ties between churchgoers and the party on the right have weakened in most industrialized countries, but not in the United

---

*The Institute for Studies of Religion at Baylor University reported similar findings in a poll released in October 2006. Bible literalists were less likely to want government to end the death penalty, for example. Evangelicals and Bible literalists also were against the redistribution of wealth, further regulation of business, and increased protection of the environment. "American Piety in the 21st Century: New Insight to the Depth and Complexity of Religion in the U.S." (selected findings, Baylor Religion Survey, September 2006), p. 24, http://www.baylor.edu/content/services/document.php/33304.pdf.

†The relationship between church attendance and ideology is reversed in agrarian societies: the parties on the left are supported by the most religious citizens, a relationship we can see in American history (see Norris and Inglehart, *Sacred and Secular: Religion and Politics Worldwide*, p. 207). In *What's the Matter with Kansas?* Thomas Frank wonders what became of this combination of faith and politics. The social science answer would be, simply, time. It's no longer the 1890s, and Kansas is no longer an agrarian state.

States. The unusual thing about this country has been the stubborn and quite strong connection between religious belief and political party — a cultural peculiarity that, in the post-materialist politics of values, has allowed computer technicians in Orange County to find common cause with West Virginia coal miners and truck drivers.[73]

6

THE ECONOMICS OF
THE BIG SORT

Culture and Growth in the 1990s

Opportunity, not necessity, is the mother of invention.

—JANE JACOBS

"An Inexplicable Sort of Mass Migration"

THE *Baton Rouge Advocate* ran a series of stories in 2002 titled "Leaving Louisiana" — and people were. They were hoofing it from Louisiana by the hundreds of thousands long before Hurricane Katrina washed, rinsed, and tumbled out those who remained. In the flow of people back and forth across the state line, Texas cities alone had a net gain of 121,000 Louisianans between 1992 and 2000. Most went to Houston or Dallas, but a good number migrated to Austin. There were enough Louisiana expatriates to turn the Shoal Creek Saloon into home away from bayou home — gumbo on the menu, a huge Saints football helmet on the roof, and the hated Cowboys banned from the television.

The migration of people and money throughout the United States in the 1990s created a stark pattern. Some cities were sucking up people and income. Others were flinging them out with what appeared to be centrifugal force. Portland (I'm talking about Oregon throughout this chapter), Seattle, Dallas, and Austin gained at the same time the *Cleveland Plain Dealer* described the depopulation of its city as a "quiet crisis" and the *Baton Rouge Advocate* published its series. Dave Eggers, in his 2000 autobiographical book *A Heartbreaking Work of Staggering Genius*, called the movement of his educated and young midwestern friends to San Francisco "an inexplicable sort of mass migration."[1] Actually, it was perfectly explicable. Eggers and his heartland buddies weren't the only ones switching addresses. As many as 100 million Americans resettled across a county border in the 1990s. People didn't scatter like ants from a kicked-over hill. There was an order and a flow to the movement — more like the migration of different species of birds. Eggers and his flock landed in San Francisco. A larger group of people — with a very different view of the promised land — migrated to Las Vegas. Economies, lifestyles, and politics merged in the Big Sort. Choices about lifestyle changed regional economies. And those differences in local development were reflected in a place's politics. The Big Sort wasn't happening at the state level. Rather, communities within the same state showed entirely different patterns of development and growth. The U.S. economy, its culture, and its politics were changing town to town, city to city.[*2]

The picture the United States had of itself in the 1950s, 1960s, and 1970s was of a nation that was increasingly becoming one — religiously, racially, politically, and economically. From the 1950s through the mid-1970s, communities did grow more politically integrated. There was an economic convergence, too. The South — once "the nation's number one economic problem," according to Franklin D. Roosevelt — had become the beaming Sun Belt. Wages in different parts of the country began to converge. People with college degrees were "remarkably evenly distributed" among America's cities, according to Harvard University economist Edward Glaeser.[3]

If such economic, partisan, and educational balance was the Ameri-

---

*"City" here and elsewhere in this book refers to a metropolitan area. Technically, "city" is a political designation. Washington, D.C., for example, is limited to the District of Columbia. The U.S. Office of Management and Budget, however, determines regions that effectively work as one economic unit. The "city" of Austin falls almost entirely within one county. The Austin metropolitan area includes five counties — a far more accurate description of the Austin economy than the antiquated and more arbitrary political designation.

can way, by 1980 a decidedly un-American trend began. Places stopped becoming more alike and began to diverge. The economic landscape stopped growing flatter, and, in Richard Florida's description, it got spikier.[4] The country got particularly spiky after 1980 as Americans segregated by education. In the last thirty years of the twentieth century, education levels surged nationally. In 1970, 11.2 percent of the population had at least a college degree. That figure increased to 16.4 percent in 1980, nearly 19 percent in 1990, and 27 percent in 2004. But as the national totals of college-educated people grew, education differentials between cities widened with each decade. The variance among cities was astounding. The percentage of adults with a college education increased in Austin from 17 percent in 1970 to 45 percent in 2004. In Cleveland, the change was only from 4 percent to 14 percent. Not only was Cleveland behind, but it was falling further behind. Schooling attracted schooling, as people with degrees moved to live among others with the same level of education. By 2000, according to Glaeser, there were sixty-two metropolitan areas where less than 17 percent of adults had college degrees and thirty-two cities where more than 34 percent had finished college.[5] The differences were even more dramatic among the young. More than 45 percent of twenty-five- to thirty-four-year-olds in Raleigh-Durham, North Carolina, had a college degree in 2000; that figure was only 16 percent in Las Vegas.[6]

Education had always predicted city growth, but beginning in the 1970s, that relationship strengthened.[7] The cities that grew the fastest and the richest were the ones where people with college degrees congregated. (Fast-growing Las Vegas was obviously an exception.) As people with different levels of education sorted themselves into particular cities, the migration pattern set off segregation by income. Average city wages, which were converging in the 1970s, grew more unequal throughout the 1990s.*[8] The per capita income of the ten metro areas with the best-educated residents rose 1.8 percent a year in the 1990s. The per

---

*Income inequality increased not only regionally but also among individuals. Beginning in 1969, the most common measure of family income inequality increased steadily. Nolan McCarty, Keith T. Poole, and Howard Rosenthal, *Polarized America: The Dance of Ideology and Unequal Riches* (Cambridge, MA: MIT Press, 2006), p. 6.

capita income of the ten cities with the least educated population grew only 0.8 percent a year.[9] Segregation by education was particularly apparent in rural areas. By 2000, the percentage of young adults with a college degree in rural areas was only half that of the average city.[10]

This was the Big Sort of the 1990s. Every action produced a self-reinforcing reaction: educated people congregated, creating regional wage disparities, which attracted more educated people to the richer cities — which further increased the disparity in regional economies.* The Big Sort was just beginning with education. Or was it *ending* with education? It was hard to tell. By the turn of the twenty-first century, it seemed as though the country was separating in every way conceivable.

Race

An astounding 40 percent of the country's 320 metropolitan areas lost white population in the 1990s. The common notion of "white flight" is as a Caucasian escape from the central cities to the suburbs. In the Big Sort, however, there was a wholesale shift of white residents from one set of cities to another. Whites fled two kinds of cities. They abandoned older factory towns in the North and Midwest. Pittsburgh, Detroit, Buffalo, Hartford, Providence, Cleveland, Milwaukee, Jersey City, and Newark all lost tens of thousands of white residents. Whites also left the nation's largest cities, some of which were growing increasingly expensive: Los Angeles, New York, San Jose, Chicago, and Philadelphia (as well as Orange County, California).

Whites went to high-tech cities: Atlanta, Phoenix, Denver, Portland, Austin, Dallas, Raleigh-Durham, Seattle, Minneapolis, and Boise. And they filled retirement or recreational cities: Las Vegas, West Palm Beach,

---

*There are wheels within wheels in the Big Sort. Dora Costa, an MIT economist, argues that since college-educated people increasingly marry others with similar levels of education, they tend to congregate in larger cities where both husband and wife have a better chance of finding fulfilling work. In 1970, 29 percent of what Costa calls "power couples" lived in cities of more than 2 million people. By 1990, 50 percent of these highly educated pairs lived in large cities. The "bundling" of educated people has further exacerbated regional disparities in income. See Dora Costa and Matthew E. Kahn, "Power Couples: Changes in the Locational Choice of the College Educated, 1940–1990," *Quarterly Journal of Economics* 115, no. 4 (November 2000): 1287–1315. Also available at http://web.mit.edu/costa/www/bindqje8.pdf.

Orlando, and Tampa. Blacks, meanwhile, moved to cities with strong black communities: Atlanta, Washington, New York, Chicago, Houston, Dallas, Fort Lauderdale, Baltimore, and Philadelphia. Only 9 out of 320 cities lost black residents.

Age

In 1990, young people were evenly distributed among the nation's 320 cities. By 2000, twenty- to thirty-four-year-olds were concentrated in just a score of cities. Some 124 American cities had a net loss of Generation Xers in the 1990s, and more than 700,000 young adults left rural America.* If Hispanics are excluded, 170 U.S. cities — more than half — lost young people in the 1990s. (Young Hispanics increased by 8 percent nationally, decreasing in only seven metro areas.) Eighty percent of the non-Hispanic whites ages twenty to thirty-four who moved during the 1990s relocated to the twenty-one cities highest in technology and patent production.†

Young people are more likely than old people to move. And young, educated people are more likely to move farther and more often than are young, less educated people. According to one longitudinal study covering most of the 1980s and 1990s, only 19 percent of young people with only a high school degree moved between states, but 45 percent of those with more than a college education migrated to a new state.[11] Young people moved disproportionately to central cities. The likelihood that a twenty-five- to thirty-four-year-old would live within three miles of a city center increased significantly in each of the fifty largest metro areas during the 1990s.[12] Older people, meanwhile, clustered in the country's least dynamic (economically and technologically, at least) cities. The 119 cities producing the fewest patents had the highest proportion of people age sixty-five or older.

---

*We compared the number of people who were ten to twenty-four years of age in 1990 with the number of those twenty to thirty-four years of age in 2000.

†In 2003, twenty-one cities had above-average output in technology-related industries and produced patents at above the national per capita rate. They were San Diego, Chicago, Los Angeles, Philadelphia, San Jose, Phoenix, Denver, Boston, New York, Seattle, San Francisco, Albuquerque, Washington, Rochester (Minnesota), Boise, Portland, Raleigh-Durham, Austin, Atlanta, Houston, and Dallas.

Ideas

It's not easy to trace ideas as they arise and then become economically useful. (Education is one surrogate measure.) In the Unites States, however, you can track patents. From the 1970s to the 1990s, the average number of patents granted each year rose nearly 50 percent. But the distribution of those patents was vastly unequal, and that lopsidedness contributed to the growing regional wage inequality. In the 1990s, people who lived in the places that produced the most patents earned higher wages than those who lived in the places that produced the fewest patents — not so surprising. Harvard University's Michael Porter calculated that 30 percent of the variation in wages across regions could be statistically related to differences in patent production.[13] Between 1975 and 2001, San Francisco's yearly patent production increased nearly 170 percent. Patents in Minneapolis rose 116 percent. Atlanta was up well over 200 percent, Portland 175 percent, and Seattle 169 percent. Little Boise, Idaho, increased its patent production by a factor of ten. In the 1970s, Austin produced fewer patents each year than Greenville, South Carolina; Davenport, Iowa; Elmira, New York; and Lancaster, Pennsylvania. The yearly production of patents in Austin jumped from 75 a year in 1975 to more than 2,000 by 2001 — a twenty-seven-fold increase in twenty-seven years. In 1999, Austin produced more patents per capita than all but Rochester, New York, and Minneapolis. Meanwhile, other cities lagged: patents in Cleveland were down 13 percent and in Pittsburgh 27 percent.

Wages

This sorting and clustering of highly educated people had an inevitable effect on wages. By 2000, Michael Porter found "striking variation in average wages" across economic regions, with average pay ranging from just over $19,000 a year in western Nebraska to over $52,000 in San Francisco.[14] Wages during the 1990s increased 7.1 percent a year in Austin, but only 1.8 percent a year in Wheeling, West Virginia.[15] Growing wage inequality tracked increasing political polarization, according to political scientists Nolan McCarty, Keith Poole, and Howard Rosenthal. The nation's income distribution grew more unequal in parallel with the rising partisanship in Congress.[16]

Occupation

Richard Florida was a professor of regional development at Carnegie Mellon University when he noticed a switch in the way businesses went about hiring new workers. Instead of people moving to corporations, corporations had begun moving to where pools of talent were deepening. Florida, Kevin Stolarick, and a group of researchers at Carnegie Mellon identified a new class of workers. They called them "creatives." These were top managers, artists, writers, engineers, and teachers. They thought for a living. Florida tracked the increasing numbers of these workers over time, and then he tracked them across space.*

Creative-class workers were sorting themselves into the same cities that, according to our analysis, were also producing most of the country's patents. The top five cities in percentage of creative-class workers were Washington, Raleigh-Durham, Seattle, San Francisco, and Austin. Las Vegas had the lowest percentage of creatives, followed by Miami, Memphis, and Louisville. Florida found that the cities teeming with creative-class workers had fewer working-class jobs — the assembly-line, mechanical, construction, and production jobs traditionally called blue-collar work. The cities with the most service jobs (Las Vegas being at the top) also lacked creative-class workers. There simply wasn't much overlap. Few cities had both a sizable working class and a large creative class. The same kind of segregation was happening at work. Older firms — General Motors and U.S. Steel — hired people with all manner of skills. In the economy being created, there were high-skilled firms and low-skilled firms — Google and McDonald's. People with skills and education were less likely to work for a business that hired employees without a college degree.[17] Florida concluded that the American "working population is re-sorting itself geographically along class lines." The sorting had little to do with region. There were creative cities in the Sun Belt (Atlanta and Raleigh-Durham), the Frost Belt (Minneapolis and Rochester, New York), and the heartland (Chicago, Dallas, and Denver).

---

*For details, see Florida's 2002 book, *The Rise of the Creative Class*. From the middle of 2001 through the middle of 2002, Florida, Gary Gates, and Kevin Stolarick worked with Robert Cushing on a series of studies. Those studies resulted in a series of newspaper articles I wrote with Mark Lisheron for the *Austin American-Statesman* in 2002. See Bill Bishop and Mark Lisheron, "Cities of Ideas," *Austin American-Statesman*, http://www.statesman.com/specialreports/content/specialreports/citiesofideas/.

But cities increasingly differed in the types of workers they attracted. And this differentiation, Florida warned, would lead to a "new form of segregation."[18]

That is exactly what happened.

The FedEx Truck Doesn't Stop Here Anymore: The Other Side of the Big Sort

The cast of Harlan County, Kentucky's community play *Higher Ground* consisted of retired coal miners, teachers, bluegrass musicians, and members of church choirs. They had assembled in the late summer of 2005 in a darkened auditorium at the community college to work through some scenes. This night they were to begin work on what would come to be known as the "drug zombie dance." In the scene, a doctor sat in a chair as the chorus stumbled and staggered onstage. They were the drug zombies who had come to the doctor for pain pill prescriptions. As the doctor wrote on little slips of paper, the zombies sang — chanted, really — "I've got a pain; I've got a pain; I've got a pain in my back. And I'm searching for a cure to take my pain away." The zombies passed money to the doctor, who tossed dollar bills in the air as police sirens began to whine.

Most small towns put on community plays to celebrate their founding by brave pioneers or a battle won by stalwart local soldiers. They commemorate "little engine that could" determination that leads to inevitable civic success. In 2005, however, Harlan County was producing a community play about civic failure — about the county's battle with drug addiction, primarily the painkiller OxyContin. It was a struggle the county had so far lost.

Harlan County sits in the extreme southeast corner of Kentucky and is perhaps the most infamous coal community in the country. For most of the last century, Harlan County was an outpost of industrial America. Ford, U.S. Steel, and International Harvester all had mines there. In the 1930s, "Bloody Harlan" became the center of union organizing efforts by both the Communist Party and the United Mine Workers of America. And in the 1970s, it was the scene of another mine strike chronicled in the Academy Award–winning film *Harlan County U.S.A.* Fortune, however, has not accompanied fame. Close to 80,000 people lived there in the 1940s. Now the population is roughly one-third that size and dropping with each census.

Traveling the eastern coalfields is a reminder that the most abundant product of the Big Sort has been inequality. Sixty years ago, the proud city of Welch, in southern West Virginia's McDowell County, was a "little San Francisco," local historian Jean Battlo told me. Guy Lombardo and Glenn Miller played Welch, and on a Saturday afternoon, the city was crowded with pedestrians and Packards. McDowell County was at the core of industrial America's economy. Then it wasn't. Three-quarters of McDowell's people left between 1950 and 2000. It lost nearly 10 percent of its population in the first four years of the twenty-first century. "Rational people leave, if they can," Jerry Beasley, president of nearby Concord College, told me. There's always been an economic and cultural distance between the small towns in the coalfields and urban America. But the gap has been growing, and it's now almost unimaginable that Welch and Austin are part of the same country.

It's not just Harlan County and Welch that have lost ground. The Big Sort has left much of rural America behind. The realities of rural life come to light in the list of Americans killed in Iraq and Afghanistan. Bob Cushing and I began tracking the hometowns of those killed in the war when the conflict began, and our very first tallies revealed that the U.S. military was disproportionately filled with young men and women from rural counties. The bigger the city, the smaller the percentage of its young people were likely to die in the war. By late 2006, rural counties had casualty rates 60 percent higher than cities and suburbs.[19] By early 2007, Bismarck, North Dakota, had a casualty rate among its military-age citizens that was almost ten times that of San Francisco. The Pentagon is straightforward in its recruiting strategy. The military finds the highest proportion of its recruits among good kids who have few prospects for decent jobs or further education. Or, as a Department of Defense study put it in reverse, "propensity to enlist is lower for high-quality youth, youth with better-educated parents, and youth planning to attend college."[20] There has been a form of economic conscription at work in the wars in Iraq and Afghanistan. The death rate among military-age residents living in the nation's high-tech cities has been half that of military-age people from rural America.

The speeding economic collapse in the southern mountains has produced a kind of civic dysfunction. In McDowell County, the state took over the school system in 2001 after an audit found failing students and a school board preoccupied with politics. (Kentucky had ousted the Harlan County school board a few years before for similar transgressions.) In Harlan County, a former sheriff running for his old office was shot and killed in 2002 after he collected a pouch of money from a drug dealer. Just over the mountain, a Wise County, Virginia, grand jury found 1,000 violations of voting laws in one 2004 election — two crimes for every vote cast. The mayor of the town of Appalachia allegedly bought votes with sacks of fried pork rinds. The zombies in the play *Higher Ground* weren't fictional creations. They were neighbors. In 2005, Federal Express stopped making deliveries of prescription drugs in many Eastern Kentucky counties. Drivers had complained that their trucks had been surrounded by staggering, stumbling people anxious for the deliveries. "If a driver goes up one of these hollows and comes up on six or eight people who know he has drugs on there, they may decide to take them," said one Eastern Kentucky sheriff. "There's a legitimate concern."[21]

Struggles with addiction are part of everyone's daily life in Harlan County. Just off the wonderful main square in the county seat, a large Christian church has strung a banner over its front door promoting "Recovery Night." Every Thursday, two hundred to three hundred people gather at the church for inspiration and smaller twelve-step meetings. Up the Clover Fork in the coal camp of Evarts, the medical clinic quietly opened a drug treatment program; it quickly filled twenty-two openings and had a dozen people on a waiting list, according to clinic director Dr. J. D. Miller. This in a town of just 1,000 people. "It's been said that every family here is touched," Miller told me early one morning in 2005 at a breakfast joint filled with dust-covered miners just off the hoot owl shift. "Everybody here has a close personal friend or a relative who is on OxyContin. That's true." A few years ago, the local mental health agency needed several vans to transport pregnant women from Harlan County to a methadone clinic in Corbin, a nearly two-hour drive over sixty-three miles of mountain roads. Although Harlan County had a population of only 32,000 at the time, Miller said that forty young mothers were in the methadone program.

The "drug zombie" scene in *Higher Ground,* with the actors holding aching backs, zeroed in on how Harlan County's uniquely pervasive drug problem began. "In the past, coal miners spent hours each day crouched in narrow mine shafts," concluded a report issued in 2002 by the U.S. Department of Justice. "Painkillers were dispensed by coal mine camp doctors in an attempt to keep the miners working. Self-medicating became a way of life for miners."[22] In the fall of 2005, a disability attorney's come-on could be seen on a large billboard at the entrance to town. It showed an old, bent, and particularly grizzled miner and asked, "Broke Down?" OxyContin came to Harlan County because people here have pains — in hips, backs, and shoulders — resulting from working underground. The country wanted the coal, and the miners needed the work. Pain pills were an unstated part of the arrangement — and it probably lowered the cost that the unsavory bargain was struck in a place so far out of sight, a piece of America that is literally at the end of the tracks.

The OxyContin sales force targeted Appalachian doctors. Reports in the *Lexington Herald-Leader* found that Purdue Pharma's marketing plan for its new medicine was to seek out physicians who were already prescribing large amounts of painkilling drugs. In 1998, according to the newspaper, Purdue shipped more OxyContin per capita to portions of southern West Virginia and Eastern Kentucky than to any other region or city in the nation.[23] (In 2007, Purdue Pharma and three of its executives agreed to pay more than $650 million in fines for the misleading ways it had promoted OxyContin.)[24] Richard Clayton, an addiction expert who heads the University of Kentucky's Center for Prevention Research, told the Lexington newspaper, "This may be the first epidemic — if it is an epidemic — that started in rural areas."[25]

Joan Robinett now lives in a brick house perched on a hill above the town of Harlan. She led a decade-long effort in the Dayhoit coal camp that eventually won more than $20 million from a firm that had polluted the town's ground water. The fight changed Robinett from country girl to

Kentucky's Erin Brockovich. You have to climb seventy-five steps to get to her house, which also served as headquarters for the Harlan County "listening project." In 2005, Robinett and her coworkers conducted more than 450 interviews with residents about drug abuse and their hopes for Harlan County. The stories are a mixture of hopelessness and horror. A young divorced woman said:

> The quality of life is so low. People look ahead and see the mountains blown off and the water ruined. And the drugs come around. When you deal with what people have to deal with here. I don't know how to say it . . . Me and my son were on our own and everywhere I went I began to feel like a failure. I never dreamed I would turn to drugs but it seemed to be the easy way out. The Xanax at first I used it to help me cope and later found if you took two you would feel good and later realized if I drank on it I felt really good. Before you know it I began to sell my home interior and then my furniture. Before you know it, I thought I couldn't live without it.

A middle-aged woman with four years of college education said:

> Doctors and drug companies feed us drugs just like giving a baby candy . . . It's so bad that I can no longer trust some people in my own family. They steal from you — lie. You never know who is on drugs — people drooling — taking from their parents and children. It's awful.

Living has never been particularly easy in Harlan County, but it had always maintained a connection with the rest of the country. The Big Sort has cut many of those ties. Now the county has fallen away and staggers about in a haze. FedEx drivers are afraid to deliver, and the life expectancy for men is no better than in Ecuador, Turkey, or Colombia.[26]

Eugene Goss is a Republican, a lawyer on the main square in the town of Harlan, and one of the grand men of Kentucky. To get to Harlan County from Virginia, you drive the smooth Gene Goss Highway. He's lived through the Depression, strikes, and coal mine disasters. Now this, the zombie dance. "We're at the end of the line," Goss told me while munching a biscuit his secretary had made for a midmorning snack. He described Harlan County as a "storage tank" for the rest of the country, a place tapped for its energy and then forgotten. Goss stayed in Harlan

County because he saw a future there, but now even hope is gone. He said, "There's a whole lot of feeling that we are the way we're going to be and there isn't anything to be done about it. We are what we are, and that's how it's going to continue."

The Culture of Prosperity

In 2000, Robert Putnam commissioned a survey of 30,000 people in forty American communities. Putnam is the author of *Bowling Alone,* the book documenting the decline in civic organizations that began in the mid-1960s. His 2000 survey was designed to measure the nation's civic well-being, so he asked people if they went to church, voted, volunteered, donated to charities, belonged to clubs, or attended discussion groups. Putnam asked how often people socialized and how much they trusted others. People living in different places gave widely varying responses. Those living in places such as Bismarck, North Dakota; Birmingham, Alabama; and Kalamazoo, Michigan, exhibited strong social ties; they volunteered, went to church, stayed close to their families, and voted. Based on his earlier research in both the United States and Italy, Putnam assumed that the stronger the social connections, the healthier the community.*

As Bob Cushing and I looked at how the Big Sort was creating greater inequality among cities — in patents, incomes, and levels of education — we wondered whether there was a relationship between culture and economic success. Putnam's groundbreaking analysis gave us the data, and we set to work examining our high-tech cities with his measures of civic health. In fact, there was a relationship between the health of the local civic culture and the well-being of the economy. It was negative. The tighter the social ties, the fewer the patents, the lower the wages, and the slower the rates of growth. Bismarck, Baton Rouge,

---

*In *Making Democracy Work: Civic Traditions in Modern Italy* (1993), Putnam explored the differences between thriving northern Italy and the dragging south. He concluded that the stronger economy and more efficient government in the north were results of the region's strong civic traditions. In speeches, I heard Putnam say that the number of choral societies in a city predicted how quickly the local government would answer the phone. The greater number of civic organizations (such as choral societies) made northern Italy's economy more vibrant and its government more efficient than those in the less connected south.

and Cincinnati all had whopping numbers of civic connections (social and volunteer groups, high rates of voter participation), but they had relatively few patents and showed slow (if any) growth. Cities such as San Diego, Houston, Los Angeles, and Atlanta (as well as Silicon Valley) all had bottom-of-the-barrel social connections but high rates of innovation and growth and high incomes.[27] The high-tech, fast-growing cities scored high on only two of Putnam's eleven gauges of social well-being: their residents registered a high degree of interracial trust and were more inclined to engage in "protest politics." They voted less than those in more traditional cities but signed more petitions and joined more demonstrations and boycotts — in other words, they acted politically as post-materialists.

Some cities boasted strong social ties, while others appeared to be flying apart — volunteers diminishing, church attendance declining, voting rates dropping. Our American sense of right and wrong would tell us that the cities with vibrant clubs, full pews, abundant volunteers, and eager voters should be more economically successful than the civic wastelands. They would be the places with strong businesses and high wages. People would be flocking to these good communities. But they weren't.

We examined another database Putnam had used. The DDB Needham Life Style survey[28] asked 87,000 Americans dozens of questions from 1975 through 1998 about how they spent their free time — whether they volunteered, visited museums, or worked in a political campaign. Again we found that the cities that needed civic respirators were the most prosperous. These regions were filled with people filing patents and businesses paying higher wages. They were the places where young people were migrating. The civic-minded cities — those with crowded clubs and churches and abundant volunteers — had lower rates of innovation and lower average pay. We compared the 21 cities that had produced the most patents and had the most activity in technology-related businesses with the 138 cities that had the lowest rates of patent and high-tech production. We found that people in the high-tech cities had significantly different answers to the DDB surveys than those in the low-tech cities. The economic differences between these two groups were reflected in the agency's polling.

High-Tech Cities (Compared to Low-Tech Cities)
    More interested in other cultures and places
    More likely to "try anything once"
    More likely to engage in individualistic activities
    More optimistic
    More interested in politics
    Volunteering increasing, but less than in low-tech cities
    Church attendance decreasing
    Community projects decreasing
    Club membership decreasing

Low-Tech Cities (Compared to High-Tech Cities)
    More likely to attend church
    Club membership decreasing, but less than in high-tech cities
    Community projects increasing
    Volunteering increasing
    More active participation in clubs, churches, volunteer services, and
        civic projects
    More supportive of traditional authority
    More family oriented
    More feelings of isolation
    More feelings of economic vulnerability
    More sedentary
    Higher levels of stress
    Political interest decreasing
    More social activities with other people

Within the United States, groups of cities seemed to be developing in radically different ways, moving along diverging trajectories. There were obvious distinctions in the basic ways people were going about their lives, and these social distinctions seemed to have economic consequences.

Birmingham, Alabama, scored high in Putnam's survey on church attendance, civic leadership, volunteering, and club membership, but below the national average on interracial friendships and protest politics. On Putnam's measures of civic vitality, Boulder, Colorado, scored above the national average *only* on protest politics and interracial friendships — and the per capita rate of patent production in Boulder was *four times* that of Birmingham. Young people were particularly attracted to places with low levels of social capital. (Perhaps the massive inflow itself created problems in maintaining close social ties.) The number of Generation Xers (ages twenty to thirty-five) increased by 9 percent in Birmingham in the 1990s (well below the national average); the number in the Denver/Boulder metro area increased by more than 50 percent.

The calculations that Bob Cushing's computer was churning out backed up Richard Florida's argument that there was a link between talent, technology, and tolerance — that educated young people in the "creative class" would flock to places where they would not be bound by old ideas or tight social ties. (Florida used our analysis in his book *The Rise of the Creative Class*.)[29] Certainly, none of the old explanations seemed to apply to these socially fragmented but economically thriving cities. Indeed, this wasn't the way economies were supposed to work at all.

In the 1970s, cities were dying — at the same time mainline churches, civic organizations, and political parties also were dying. People were moving out. Most cities had their lowest population growth in the 1970s. For the ten largest cities (except Houston), each showed a decline in per capita income relative to the rest of the country. In four of the five largest cities, housing prices plummeted. (Only Los Angeles escaped the 1970s house price slump.) Crime rose in the 1970s, and metro areas bled people.[30] Everyone pretty much concluded that cities were dead, murdered by the automobile; phones, faxes, and computers; and the rush to the Sun Belt suburbs. People didn't have to cluster in one place. There simply wasn't much need for cities or for people to be close to one another. People could scatter; they could live anywhere because distance no longer mattered.

Or did it?

A New Theory of Growth

Paul Romer, a Stanford University economist, delights in using everyday items to construct mathematic formulas that end in inconceivably large numbers. In a favorite example, Romer presents a child's chemistry set stocked with 100 substances. If someone set out to test all the possible combinations of these items, that would be a very time-consuming chore. There are 10^{30} possible compounds in the box (and that's without changing proportions). "If every living person on earth (about 5 billion) had tried a different mixture each second since the universe began (no more than 20 billion years ago)," Romer wrote, "we would still have tested less than 1 percent of all the possible combinations."[31]

Romer's point isn't just to show the power of exponential multiplication. The chemistry set is a metaphor for the story he has to tell about the sources of economic growth. If one looks at each possible formula from a child's simple chemistry set as the equivalent of a new idea — a potentially economy-changing compound — it becomes clear that the stock of potentially valuable knowledge in the world is quite literally infinite. Only a small percentage of those "ideas" have economic value, but a small percentage of such a large number means that the potential for growth and wealth from those new ideas is still limitless.

Until 1957, the prevailing theory was that increasing the application of labor and capital — more coal, ore, machines, and workers — made economies grow. That year, economist Robert Solow wrote a paper arguing that labor and capital alone couldn't account for the continuing expansion of the economy. Solow argued that a third factor, technical knowledge, combined with labor and capital to increase economic productivity.[*32] In the 1980s, Romer refined that concept. "We now know that the classical suggestion that we can grow rich by accumulating more and more pieces of physical capital like forklifts is simply wrong," he wrote.[33] Economic growth wasn't a function of forklifts. Nor, to the disbelief of several generations of southern governors, was prosperity a function of the accumulation of Yankee smokestacks lured by low taxes. Counting physical assets missed what development was all about, Romer said. Using a Betty Crocker analogy, Romer insisted that an abundance of great ingredients — lots of oil, deep ports, or fertile ground — didn't make a place rich. The source of wealth was having the right

---

*Solow's paper "Technical Change and the Aggregate Production Function" led to his being awarded the 1987 Nobel Prize in economics.

recipe. The places that grew wealthy were those whose people learned to arrange their ingredients in ever new and economically useful ways.

According to Romer, not every idea (or new recipe) was big or even based on scientific discovery. Economies grew because people were constantly incorporating new ideas into all aspects of work. If a guy on a loading dock figured out a better way to pack a truck, that idea could increase profits throughout a firm. And once an economically useful idea was hatched, it could be used and reused without wear and tear. An idea, unlike a forklift, also could be put to work simultaneously by a limitless number of people. Eventually, other companies would pick up the idea about packing a truck. Then it would be modified for use in warehouses. Everyone using the truck-packing idea would benefit. The entire society would be more productive and richer because of one person's new way of arranging a limited set of ingredients.[34] "No amount of savings and investment, no policy of macroeconomic fine-tuning, no set of tax and spending incentives can generate sustained economic growth unless it is accompanied by the countless large and small discoveries that are required to create more value from a fixed set of natural resources," Romer wrote.[35] According to Romer-inspired "new growth theory," ideas were the essential factor in increasing economic returns.

City life was key for such economies of ideas to flourish, because cities sped both the creation and the spread of useful knowledge. That insight came from a woman who never graduated from college and was best known for her observations about city planning. In 1969, Jane Jacobs published the first edition of *The Economy of Cities,* a book that described how ideas scattered through urban areas, creating new industries and new wealth.* Jacobs wrote that new wealth and businesses didn't stem from isolated discoveries or unique inventions. Innovations sprang from older lines of work — "parent work," she called it. Consider, for example, the brassiere. Ida Rosenthal was a custom seamstress in early-twentieth-century New York, as Jacobs told the story. In trying to find ways to make her goods better fit her customers, Rosenthal be-

---

*Jane Jacobs is best known for her book on urban design, *The Death and Life of Great American Cities* (1961), a work that undergirds today's New Urbanist movement. But most of Jacobs's time was spent producing her trilogy about economic growth: *The Economy of Cities* (1969), *Cities and the Wealth of Nations* (1984), and *The Nature of Economies* (2000).

gan experimenting with different garments to be worn underneath her dresses. A result of her innovations was the brassiere. Her customers liked the new undergarment so much that in time, Rosenthal stopped making dresses altogether and went into the business of sewing undergarments full-time. She called her company Maidenform Brassiere.[36]

The Economy of Cities is filled with examples of how a series of small innovations can spawn entirely new industries. The Minnesota Mining and Manufacturing Company (3M) was a small firm founded in 1902 to produce the sand used as an abrasive in the production of metal casings. To find other uses for its primary product, 3M tried making its own sandpaper (a product already invented). The adhesives the company was using failed, so 3M experimented with sticky substances. That's where the new work began to appear. In a series of innovations, 3M first produced a gummed paper that house painters found useful (masking tape), then electrical tape, Scotch tape, plastic tape, and sound recording tape.[37]

Sure, there had been significant scientific discoveries, Romer said. Penicillin, for example, hadn't been cobbled together on the shop floor. But great advances didn't often stem from fundamental scientific research. If that were the case, Romer wrote (echoing Jacobs), the study of thermodynamics would have led to the development of the steam engine. The reverse happened instead: the people who solved the practical problems of making steam engines uncovered the basic principles that led to the science of thermodynamics.*[38]

Cities were essential in the work of innovation not because they were efficient or practical, because they certainly were neither. They were essential because economic development was the *social* process of problem solving, discovery, and innovation. Henry Ford failed twice in his single-handed attempts to manufacture an entire automobile. He succeeded when he pieced together parts from other small businesses around Detroit. This process of making connections and sharing ideas worked best when people involved in related kinds of work could meet face-to-face and share new ideas.[39] Almost twenty years after Jacobs wrote *The Economy of Cities,* academic economists developing new

---

*More recently, MIT president Susan Hockfield noted that in semiconductor electronics, "the applied work transformed the fundamental research — not just the other way around" (speech, Brookings Institution, April 28, 2006).

growth theory adopted her observations. If cities were simply accumulated sets of production factors (capital, people, and land), economist Robert Lucas wrote, they would "fly apart." Land was always cheaper outside cities. Cities were crowded and inefficient, crazily so. By any ration of common sense, everyone should move out. But they didn't. In fact, the opposite happened. Firms paid higher rents to be in cities than elsewhere. What could these businesses be paying for, Lucas reasoned, "if not for being near other people?"*40

Research in the 1970s and 1980s explored how economies were social enterprises. A grad student in sociology in the early 1970s was curious about how people found out about new information. Mark Granovetter read a study of a southern textile mill swept by a "hysterical contagion." The first people to report being bitten by a mysterious insect were workers at the mill who had few close friends. (The biting critter was, in fact, imaginary.) The "disease" started at the social margins of the mill and then moved into the more conformist social center of the factory's workforce. Granovetter theorized from this case that new ideas (good and bad) didn't start where there were a lot of strong, stable social ties. New behaviors and ideas were transmitted first and fastest through weak, peripheral relationships. Granovetter wanted to discover how people learned about new job openings. Based on the example of the southern textile mill, he predicted that finding a new job wasn't a function of having *strong* friendships. The best bet for hearing of a new opening was to have a slew of *weak* relationships. Strong ties between people bottled up information, Granovetter theorized. That made sense. Your friends know what you know. That's why they're your friends. "Weak ties" tapped new pools of information — and weak ties allowed that information to flow.

To test his hypothesis, Granovetter went to a Boston suburb and in-

---

*Smart companies realized the need for face-to-face contact among workers. Businesses feared becoming the next Xerox, whose scientists developed pieces of the personal computer in the 1970s at the company's Palo Alto Research Center but failed to transmit that knowledge to the developmental engineers in Dallas or Xerox management in Stamford, Connecticut. As a result, BMW opened its Research and Engineering Centre north of Munich, where it commingled its research, design, development, and production engineering staffs — and designed the office so that nobody would have to walk more than 50 meters (164 feet) to meet a coworker. So much for the triumph of technology over distance.

terviewed people who had recently found new jobs through personal contacts. Granovetter asked his subjects how often they saw the person who had told them about the job. Only 17 percent of those newly employed people said they were often in contact with their source, 56 percent said they occasionally saw their source, and 28 percent said they saw their source rarely. Granovetter described this phenomenon as the "strength of weak ties." The more bridges connecting a person to others, no matter how tenuous or seldom used, the better his or her chances for employment. The same would hold true for a community, Granovetter proposed. Communities with lots of internal bridges, even if they were flimsy ones, would be better off than places with social groups that were tightly knit internally but unconnected to other groups in the community.[41]

Historian Peter Hall examined the dynamic cities in history — Manchester, England, in the late eighteenth and early nineteenth centuries, San Francisco in the second half of the twentieth century, Berlin from 1840 to 1930 — and found that they were constructed on the strength of weak ties. "Most of these places seem to have had egalitarian social structures: they were unstuffy, un-classbound, non-hierarchical places," Hall wrote.[42] At the turn of the twentieth century, all the newly discovered technology in the entertainment industry — pictures that both moved and talked — was located in New York, along with most of the country's acting talent. If the economy of motion pictures depended on the accumulation of valuable stuff, the industry should have flourished in New York. Instead, the movie business took root in a no-place town called Hollywood. The reason wasn't just because of southern California's sunny weather, according to Hall. After all, there was sun aplenty much closer to New York in Florida or Cuba, where filmmakers first traveled to escape New York winters. Hollywood was a good place for a new industry to grow — especially a new industry headed largely by immigrant Jews — because it lacked an established hierarchy or social aristocracy. Los Angeles wasn't balled up with those strong social connections that can kill gumption, trap new ideas, and suffocate innovation.[43]

Why, in the early 1990s, did Silicon Valley add more jobs and create more new businesses than the high-tech cluster along Route 128 in Boston? Thinking more like an anthropologist than an economist, AnnaLee

Saxenian found the answer in the Wagon Wheel restaurant in Mountain View, California, where people from different firms would meet, mingle, and trade information. She noticed that people switched jobs in Silicon Valley often and with impunity. As they flitted from one office to another, they pollinated their new firms with ideas they'd gathered along the way. In Boston, Saxenian observed firms that were more cylindrical, hardened, and isolated. People tended not to change jobs. Firms preferred employees who were "in for the long haul." There weren't many bridges between businesses. There were few natural meeting places for people from different firms to mix, no Wagon Wheel restaurant. There were fewer weak ties.[44]

Cities Come Back — with Weak Ties

After the disastrous 1970s, when the future of cities seemed bleak, people returned. In the 1980s, housing prices began to rise in the same cities that had experienced drops in the previous decade. New York City gained population. Personal income in cities increased, too, reversing declines in the 1970s. Not all cities added people and income. Edward Glaeser discovered that there was a complete switch in the types of cities that grew. In 1950, seven of the eight largest cities had a higher percentage of people employed in manufacturing than the nation as a whole. By 1990, six of the eight largest cities had proportionally *less* manufacturing than the country as a whole. The urban revival wasn't led by places that made things, but by cities that produced ideas.

When Glaeser examined the urban resurgence of the 1990s, he could see that falling crime rates helped spur a return to the cities. But safe streets alone didn't cause the urban renaissance. Glaeser found an increased demand for what cities created in abundance, and that was human interaction. The demand was economic. Face-to-face discussions may not have been important in a Henry Ford–style assembly line, but they were essential to an economy based on the development and rapid spread of new ideas. The tightly wound mass production economy that shaped American society through the 1950s was shrinking, replaced by firms specializing in knowledge. A certain group of cities had a culture and a way of life that supported this kind of economy.

Cities mattered again. Glaeser found that there had been both a "remarkable increase in the importance of knowledge" in the 1990s and an increasing economic demand for cities that "facilitate social interactions."[45] Other researchers had discovered that inventors tended to cite patents produced by other inventors who worked nearby. Patent citations decreased as physical distance between inventors widened. By the late 1990s, the tendency of inventors to cite others from the same city in their patent applications was increasing. Proximity was becoming more important in the creation and transmission of ideas.[46] In late 2006, a Silicon Valley business professor named Randall Stross wrote about the "twenty-minute rule" adopted by several venture capital firms. "If a start-up company seeking venture capital is not within a 20-minute drive of the venture firm's offices, it will not be funded," wrote Stross. Proximity translated into convenience, of course, but the venture capital firms also knew that frequent face-to-face contact was essential. And despite world-flattening technology, there was something magical about place. Craig Johnson, managing director of a Silicon Valley venture capital firm, told Stross that having all the entrepreneurial ingredients nearby created an intensity that was missing from more spread-out geographies. Los Angeles, after all, had great universities and talent and boatloads of money. "But in Los Angeles, people are scattered across a wide area; everything is spread out," Johnson explained. "Like a gas, entrepreneurship is hotter when compressed."[47]

The busting of the tech bubble in the early 2000s slowed the growth in these cities, but only temporarily. By early 2007, demographer William Frey was telling a "tale of two kinds of cities." Those producing patents and technology were expanding again; the older cities that made things — Buffalo, Cleveland, Toledo, Detroit — were reporting continuing declines.[48]

The Rise of the Superstar Cities

People migrate to maximize their economic returns. At least that's been the most common explanation for why people move. They pull up stakes to make or save money. Economic utility seemed to be motivating both employers and workers in the 1970s; then, big-city businesses were paying higher wages to keep and attract workers. But by 1990, there was no wage advantage to living in one of the twenty-six largest metro areas. By 2000, it cost more to live in those places than any premium received in wages.[49] According to traditional economics, when this kind of imbalance occurs, either wages rise or people stop moving to such overpriced areas. But the opposite was happening. People were moving to places that cost more and where, in comparison to other cities, they would be earning less. Additionally, defying every economic precept, six out of ten well-educated young adults moved to places with slower job growth than the cities they left.[50] Weird things were going on in urban America. Cities were no longer places whites fled. Instead of people jamming the roads from homes in the suburbs to jobs in the central city, people were reversing the direction, commuting from downtown homes to workplaces outside the city. By 2007, the number of whites living in Washington, D.C., was increasing, while the number of blacks was decreasing.[51] There was a surge of people who wanted to live in cities for what could only be social — or even aesthetic — reasons.[52]

Economist Joseph Gyourko compiled a list of metro areas so attractive, so in demand over the past two decades, that housing prices had far outstripped any wage advantages the cities might offer. Housing prices in much of America rose modestly during this time. In the sought-after cities, however, they shot out of sight. In 1940, for example, the average house in Cincinnati cost more than a home in San Francisco. Over the next sixty years, the price of a Cincinnati house increased from $65,000 to $145,000. The total population of San Francisco had changed little in that time, but the average house price rose by a factor of nine, from $60,162 to nearly $550,000. Gyourko dubbed these places "superstar cities," metro areas where residence had become, in essence, a luxury good.[53] People paid for the privilege of being in cities such as San Francisco, Seattle, San Jose, Portland, Los Angeles, New York, Austin, and Raleigh-Durham because they wanted to live there, not because they expected an economic return.

The function of cities had changed. Their reason for being — and their residents' reason for living within them — was no longer to produce salable goods and services. The city's new product was lifestyle. Glaeser called these metro areas "consumer cities" — metro areas that catered to the well-paid, well-educated people who moved there.[54] Richard Florida found that these cities attracted "creative-class" workers.[55] The University of Chicago's Terry Nichols Clark proposed that cities had become "entertainment machines."[56] To attract the people who would power their economies, cities had first to produce the sounds, sights, tastes, and experiences desired by post-materialists engaged in their part of the Big Sort. These new social and economic arrangements had changed a fundamental American assumption: that citizens have the right to live in whatever city they choose. Just as not everyone could own a Mercedes-Benz, Gyourko wrote, Americans no longer had the right to live in San Francisco, central Austin, or northwest Washington, D.C. Both the car and the cities were extravagances.[57]

Meanwhile, the way Americans sorted themselves created a new kind of cultural separation. People living in different cities literally had different ways of relating to family, to government, to strangers, and to religion. This gave people another choice. There were places where they could enjoy the comfort of strong families, bustling civic groups, near universal political participation, and abundant volunteering. And there were cities that offered anonymity, the opportunity for self-invention, and the economic benefits of loose ties.

Using Putnam's data, we discovered that high-tech cities had cultures that differed from manufacturing towns. The high-tech towns had fewer volunteers, lower church attendance, and weaker family connections. We then found that these differences extended to politics. High-tech cities were slightly more liberal than the nation as a whole prior to 1990, but since then they have become more liberal.* Before 1990, people living in low-tech cities described themselves as slightly more liberal than the national average, but after 1990 an increasing number labeled their politics as conservative. Prior to 1990, high-tech cities were at the national average in terms of party identification. After 1990, these places were Democratic strongholds. Manufacturing cities and rural areas moved in the reverse direction, growing more Republican.

---

*We compared the twenty-one metropolitan areas with the most technology to the nation as a whole, using surveys conducted by the National Opinion Research Center at the University of Chicago. The center's General Social Survey asked people whether they thought of themselves as liberal or conservative.

These shifting political cultures emerged over time in presidential elections. Bob Cushing and I divided U.S. metro areas into five groups with descending levels of high-tech and patent production and then compared how these groups of cities voted in the six presidential elections from 1980 to 2000. In the earliest election, all the city groups voted much the same. The twenty-one high-tech areas were slightly more Democratic than the nation as a whole. Suburban cities adjacent to these high-tech areas (places such as Boulder outside Denver, Orange County outside Los Angeles, and Galveston outside Houston) were slightly more Republican than the national average. But in 1980, the vote in all these areas approximated how the nation voted as a whole.

As time passed, voting patterns in the city groups diverged. The high-tech group tilted increasingly Democratic, so that by 2000, these twenty-one cities were voting Democratic at a rate 17 percent above the national average. (Take out the Texas tech cities — Austin, Houston, and Dallas — and the remaining eighteen metro areas were voting Democratic at a rate 21 percent above the national average.) The cities adjacent to the high-tech hubs flipped altogether, turning strongly Democratic as a group. (This was true even with the inclusion of still-Republican Orange County.) The low-tech cities and rural America grew increasingly Republican. The exceedingly close 2000 election ended with Democrats leading by a half million votes nationally. With the vote broken down city by city, however, the election was a series of local landslides that aligned with local economies. Al Gore was the winner in the high-tech cities. He led George W. Bush in these metro areas by more than 5.3 million votes. Bush made up this deficit in low-tech cities and rural America. This pattern reappeared in 2004, when John Kerry outpolled Bush by more than 5 million votes in the high-tech cities, in an election the Republican won by more than 3 million votes.

The near fifty-fifty results in presidential politics belied the divisions appearing locally. Young voters in rural eastern Oregon abandoned the Democratic Party. In Pendleton, home of one of the country's best rodeos, only 21 percent of voters twenty-one to thirty-five years of age were registered as Democrats in 2004. Among Pendleton residents a generation older, from forty-five to sixty-five years of age, 35 percent were registered Democrats. In Portland, however, young voters were going in exactly the opposite direction, and fast. In two typical inner Portland precincts in 2005, the percentage of young people (ages eighteen to thirty-five) registered as Republicans dipped to 5.4 and 7 percent.[58]

An economic/social/political chain reaction was taking place. Over three decades, people separated by education, income, race, and way of life. The best-educated abandoned old manufacturing cities such as Cleveland — and rural communities such as Harlan — and moved to new high-tech cities. Regions such as southern West Virginia and northern Virginia diverged according to income. Blacks favored some cities (Atlanta, Houston, Dallas), while whites preferred others (Phoenix, Las Vegas, Austin). Finally, people segregated by the way they wanted to live. Young college graduates moved to a select group of urban "entertainment machines," such as Chicago and San Francisco, willing to pay a premium for the lifestyle found there; others thought of a city as someplace best to flee. Prospects for prosperity deviated wildly, as innovations sprang from some cities but not others.

And all of this migration created political imbalances that grew more pronounced by the year.

Part III

THE WAY WE LIVE TODAY

7

RELIGION

The Missionary and the Megachurch

The Homogeneous Unit Principle

AMERICAN CHURCHES TODAY are more culturally and politically segregated than our neighborhoods. This happened partially because we prefer to worship in like-minded congregations. But churches also grew more homogeneous because ministers took what was learned nearly a century ago by Christian missionaries trying to overcome the caste system and language barriers in India and applied those lessons to the new American villages appearing on the subdivided plains outside the central cities — neighborhoods where the castes consisted of taste, culture, lifestyle, and, in the end, political belief.

The strategy was as simple as like attracts like. The new and crowded megachurches were built on the most fundamental of human needs: finding safety within the tribe. The method worked so well that now these techniques for creating group cohesion through like-mindedness are employed in most churches. And the same power of building communities with "people like us" is used in subdivision development, advertising, college dormitories, volunteer groups, and political campaigns. It's the way we live today. In the welter of choices provided by our post-materialist culture, people are choosing the comfort of agreement. When new technologies give people fresh ways to meet and form communities, they seek out people like themselves. By early 2007, the social communities found on MySpace and Facebook looked dated to software developers. The trouble with these massive social networks, according to a *New York Times* report, was that "big Web sites attract masses of people who have dissimilar interests and, ultimately, little in common." By 2007, it seems, gathering people who had little in common was an endeavor that was transparently foolish. The *New York Times* touted new sites that would quickly and easily move people into like-minded online groups. One of the first to use this strategy was aptly named Tribe.net.[1]

Rick Warren, the author of *The Purpose-Driven Life* and pastor of the 22,000-strong (and rising) Saddleback Church, recounted that he came to understand how to create what became the megachurch when he was a student missionary in Japan in 1974. He found an old copy of *HIS*, a Christian magazine, and discovered an article with the provocative title "Why Is This Man Dangerous?" There was a photograph of an elderly gentleman "with a goatee and sparkly eyes." His name was Donald McGavran, a missionary with what the mainline denominations considered revolutionary ideas about how and why churches grow. "As I sat there and read the article on Donald McGavran," Warren wrote, "I had no idea that it would dramatically impact the direction of my ministry."[2]

Rick Warren's generation of ministers snatched McGavran from obscurity. Two decades earlier, McGavran had concluded that his life's work had been passed over. In 1955, McGavran believed that he had learned why churches grow, and he wrote a book that laid out a new vision of missionary work and evangelism. That book, *The Bridges of God,* was a flop. It gained little notice in the missionary community and was shunned by mainline church leaders in the United States. If anything, those leaders considered McGavran a "dangerous man." In 1959, when McGavran and his wife were traveling through the Eola Hills just west of Salem, Oregon, he later recalled, "I said to my wife, . . . 'Mary, let's settle down here. Nobody's been listening to what I've been saying. My life is ended. There's nothing more that I can do.'"[3]

McGavran was the son and grandson of missionaries. His grandparents had sailed around Africa to reach their missions in India. Born in Damoh, India, in 1897, he was "saved" fourteen years later at a church meeting in Oklahoma. He went to school in the States, joined the military during World War I, and decided to take up the family trade when he returned from the war. He finished school, married, and moved back to India. He spent most of his life as a workingman's missionary. He founded churches and managed a leper colony. He scaled the Himalayas and stanched a cholera epidemic. In his travels about India, he shot an attacking tiger and battled a wild boar. Having trudged and pedaled along footpaths between villages for nearly three decades, McGavran thought the most useful degree a rural missionary could hope to obtain would be a DC, a doctor of cycling.

The Yale- and Columbia-educated missionary gradually worked his way up the church hierarchy, and as he did, he became increasingly appalled at the stunning ineffectiveness of his calling. While secretary-treasurer of the India mission of the United Christian Missionary Society, McGavran reviewed the books one year to find that his organization had spent $125,000 but had added only fifty-two members to the church rolls.[4] The plain futility of his church's efforts led McGavran to rethink how missionaries went about their work. The strategy at the time was built around the central "mission station." White Christians would establish a foreign mission that simulated Western ways of life. Missionaries would construct schools, hospitals, orphanages, and leprosy homes, all in Western style and affect. The mission station became a Christian colony, a transplanted white world from which missionaries would set off for surrounding villages.

As an institutional feat, the missions were marvels of will and faith. But McGavran realized that they didn't save many souls. The stations stood isolated from the people they were built to save. "Separated by colour, standard of living, prestige, literacy, mode of travel, place of residence, and many other factors, the missionary was, indeed, isolated from those to whom he brought the message of salvation," McGavran concluded. How could missionaries save people when they didn't eat the same food as the men and women they were trying to convert? Meanwhile, the costs and effort of providing medicine, teachers, doctors, and orphanages dominated the missionary board's concerns. Inevitably, McGavran wrote, "the mission station becomes an end in itself, instead of a means to the discipling of peoples."[5]

McGavran could see that the old system, created in a century of white colonization, had run its course. Rising nationalism in former colonies had changed the relationship between people and the church. "The temper of these days in the East is not that of humbly sitting at the feet of missionary tutors," McGavran noted.[6] As countries built their own hospitals and schools, what good, exactly, were the mission stations providing? The missionaries had come to India, Africa, and Asia to save souls, to bring people to Christ. They found themselves panhandling among U.S. congregations to maintain the physical infrastructure of outdated and unwanted colonial outposts. McGavran set out to find the evangelism that converted the most people. He wasn't looking for who ran the most efficient hospital or who sent the most students to universities — the old concerns of Public Protestantism. Instead, he wanted to discover the person who was saving the greatest number of souls, who was fulfilling the Private Protestant goal of bringing the most lost sheep to Christ. That search led him to Bishop J. Waskom Pickett.

Pickett had been a Methodist missionary in India since 1910, and unlike many of his colleagues, he filled his churches. He had written a book in the early 1930s titled *Christian Mass Movements in India* that explored which missionary churches had been successful. Pickett found in his research that the soul-saving church benefited most from a "mass movement" of people. Converts didn't come to the church one by one, he discovered. They came in groups. And those groups were socially and culturally coherent. They were tribes, castes, or villages. Yet the practice of missionaries at the time was exactly contrary to the strategy. Rather than stimulating mass movements into the church, missionaries took individual Christian converts from their villages and sequestered them within the central mission. Separated from their people, few of the new converts prospered. Pickett wrote, "They became too dependent — socially, economically, and religiously — upon the missionaries, and learned to think of themselves as a people apart, not only from the groups to which they had belonged but from the whole body of their fellow Indians."[7]

Learning from Ditt

Pickett told the story of Ditt, a member of the untouchable caste of Chuhras in the Punjab. Ditt was a "dark, lame, little man," a leather-worker by trade. In the 1870s, Ditt converted to Christianity at the central mission, and, against the advice of the missionaries, he returned to his tribe intending to spread what he had learned. Three months later, Ditt reappeared at the mission with his wife and daughter and two neighbors. They had walked thirty miles to the mission to be baptized — and after they had received the rites, they immediately walked back to their village. Six months later, Ditt brought four others from his village. He had instructed his converts in the rudiments of the Christian faith, and they, too, were baptized. Ditt traded hides for his living, and this work took him to other Chuhra villages, where he also preached the Christian Gospel. Eleven years after Ditt left the mission, there were five hundred Christian Chuhras. By 1900, more than half of the Chuhras were Christians. By 1915, only a few hundred Chuhras *weren't* baptized members of the church.[8]

The story of Ditt and the lessons learned in his own missionary work led Pickett to insights about how knowledge of goods, technologies, and religions traveled through society. What Pickett observed in the strict castes of India was that when Christianity spread in "mass movements," it circulated within a tight-knit group, a discrete social network. Ditt didn't convert Indians willy-nilly. He moved within the society where he was known and had credibility. Since Ditt evangelized only among the Chuhras, he avoided the barriers of caste, tribe, and language. He didn't start a movement of *all* Indians to Christianity; rather, he started a movement of a particular social group. Ditt converted the Chuhras.[9] McGavran described Pickett's work as an "epochal book," and he spent parts of a year learning from the Methodist missionary. When people later praised McGavran as the father of what would become known as the "church growth movement" in the United States, he invariably said, "I lit my candle at Bishop Pickett's fire."[10]

"The individual does not think of himself as a self-sufficient unit, but as a part of the group," McGavran wrote in *The Bridges of God*. "His business deals, his children's marriages, his personal problems, or the difficulties he has with his wife are properly settled by group thinking. Peoples become Christian as this group-mind is brought into a life-giving relationship to Jesus as Lord." Missionaries needed to build bridges between the culture of the village and Christianity. The bridges were anthropological — language, culture, music, even the food offered at a service. Ditt was successful because he knew what to cook. He was a Chuhra. People would come to Christ, McGavran wrote, when they saw that "the messenger of the Christian religion is one of my own family, my own people, one of us."[11]

Good works wouldn't bring people to Christ, McGavran told his fellow missionaries. Hospitals, schools, and orphanages didn't save people's souls, despite the teachings of the Social Gospel. Missionaries needed to get out of the central stations and "work the villages," McGavran wrote. They needed to speak the same language, eat the same food, and sleep in the same kinds of beds as those they were trying to convert. They needed to understand local marriage customs in South America, and they had to know the seventy-five words used to describe human relationships in China. "The Christian missionary who believes that in Jesus Christ God has revealed a way of life rewarding for all men, also uses anthropology for directed change," McGavran wrote in 1970.[12]

His visits with Bishop Pickett and his study of successful church movements around the world led McGavran to conclude that a church grows when it is based within a "homogeneous unit." People live in groups, and they develop group solidarity and awareness, a "people consciousness," as "members think of themselves as a separate tribe, caste or class." McGavran believed that any church — any religion — that asked people to abandon their tribe, caste, or class would fail. "It is foolish to add racial and linguistic barriers to the essential religious and moral hurdles which converts must surmount," McGavran wrote. "Men do not join churches where services are conducted in a language they do not understand, or where members have a noticeably higher degree of education, wear better clothes, and are obviously of a different sort." In speech after speech all over the world, McGavran promoted his "homogeneous unit principle" of church growth and soul saving. He told generations of pastors, "Men like to become Christians without crossing racial, linguistic, or class barriers."[13]

McGavran's message landed in the United States smack-dab in the middle of Public Protestantism's dominance. When McGavran's first book, *The Bridges of God,* appeared in the mid-1950s, America was undergoing a revival of interest in mainline religious denominations. The generation back from the war was a group of inveterate joiners, and they flocked, in Ozzie and Harriet boxed sets, to the mainline denominations. Church membership and church attendance reached all-time highs. Donations to churches filled offertory plates.[14] Mainline denominations didn't need an elderly man who had spent the past three decades saving lepers and shooting tigers to tell them how to attract people to church. They were filling the pews doing things the same old way. All the mainline churches needed in 1955 were architects and carpenters to build new sanctuaries.

McGavran's ideas weren't really rejected or reviled; that would come later. They were ignored. McGavran couldn't find a publisher in the United States for *The Bridges of God.*[15] When he moved back to the States, he opened the Institute for Church Growth at the out-of-the-way Northwest Christian College, an unaccredited school in Eugene, Oregon. He held small classes for missionaries — very small: the "institute" consisted of McGavran and two or three students sitting around a table. McGavran was ready to shutter his institute when he received a call from the president of Fuller Theological Seminary.[16] The Evangelical school in southern California wanted him to move his operation to Pasadena. It was the spring of 1965 — ten years after publication of *The Bridges of God* and ground zero for the shifts that would alter American political and religious life.

The Great Commission

There is nothing remotely reminiscent of colonial India at the Second Baptist Church in Houston. American churches the size of Second Baptist — 40,000 members and growing — have a Starbucks quality. The furniture may be arranged differently place to place, but the pieces are all the same. The big-church prototype isn't the heavenly aspiration of Chartres or the Zen contemplation of the Rothko Chapel. Its model is the cruise ship. Second Baptist — "Exciting Second," the church's phone operators answer — has a fitness center, a school, pool tables, football and soccer fields, daycare, a stadium-style worship hall, and a food court (offering chicken with sun-dried tomatoes and Asiago cheese, when I was there, to be served in the adjacent "Walking on Water" room). There is a well-appointed bookstore where one can buy a biography of Charles Colson, Karen Hughes, or Clay Aiken.

And there's parking. Goodness knows, they have parking. (The one time Rick Warren's Saddleback Church in Orange County, California, paused in its growth was a period in the late 1990s when traffic around the 118-acre campus began to clot. Saddleback spent $4.5 million on a mini–highway project, and the people returned.)[17] For a time, Second Baptist named sections of its parking lot after locations in the Holy Land. (Second Baptist's pastors picked up this idea at a seminar that the Walt Disney Company held for churches.) A driver just needed to remember whether he or she parked in Bethlehem or Gethsemane. It was purifying for Jesus to wander forty days and nights in the desert, but in the planned-by-the-minute world of the megachurch, you don't want stragglers from the nine o'clock service blocking pilgrims arriving at eleven.

Second Baptist was "founded by 171 Christians" in 1927, according to a plaque on the church grounds, and had only two hundred or three hundred members when Dr. H. Edwin Young arrived in 1978. Young targeted an audience in the growing middle-class suburbs west of Houston. He sped up the service, added music, and, as the church grew, began to attach members of his larger church to smaller groups. The danger of a church this big is that people will have no personal relationships tying them to the larger group. How can a person be "found" in a crowd that would fill an NBA stadium? The solution adopted by large churches is a system of cells, or, at Second Baptist, "shepherd groups." ("Cells" sounds a bit Maoist.) Every organization at Second Baptist — from Sunday school class to choir — is divided again (and again), so that each person is a member of a group of no more than ten. For example, there are some five hundred people in the Second Baptist choir. The altos form one group within the choir, but within the altos there are a dozen shepherd groups of altos.

Sunday school classes also are divided by age, sex, and, most important, attitude. Twentysomethings at Second Baptist have the MTV-sounding "Real World" class. There's also the Greatest Generation–sounding "Boot Camp," "Basic Training" for the over-fifty set, and "Fresh Start" for single parents. The list of classes reads like a satellite radio channel guide. Parishioners are encouraged to shop for the group most like themselves. "If I go to the upper-forties group and it seems like they are fuddy-duddies because I'm in my younger forties, I may want to go to a younger group," the Reverend Gary Moore told me. "You just kind of go in and see the content of who's in there and if you like those folks or not . . . By and large, people tend to herd up according to people they identify with."

Nine out of ten megachurches establish a cell structure of small groups.[18] Malcolm Gladwell, writing for *The New Yorker,* described Warren's Saddleback Church as "the cellular church."[19] Gladwell attributed Saddleback's success to the "stickiness" of small groups. Cells have a tendency to bind people together within a larger institution. But church "shepherd groups" weren't a 1970s innovation devised in the American suburbs. They came from a Korean minister named David Yonggi Cho. Pastor Cho created the largest church in the history of Christianity in Seoul. His Yoido Full Gospel Church (a Pentecostal congregation) grew to more than 8,000 members in the 1960s. As Pastor Cho tried to care for such a massive flock, he was hospitalized for exhaustion. To save himself and his church, he began the cell system. He trained mostly women (men were reluctant to make home visits to organize the cells) to link groups of ten to sixteen parishioners to the larger church. The cells met weekly and still do. They minister to the day-to-day needs of cell members and recruit converts to the church. The Yoido Full Gospel Church now has more than 800,000 members, a congregation knit together by tens of thousands of cell groups. Pastor Cho believes that the cell groups are the primary reason his church has grown so large. The idea of the cell group, he has said, was a revelation from God. For American ministers, the "cellular church" was certainly a revelation from Pastor Cho.[20]

Attendance at mainline Protestant churches began to fall in 1965, reversing a two-hundred-year record of growth. At the same time, however, Evangelical denominations and independent churches started to pick up members. By the early 1970s, church leaders and scholars noticed two distinct trends: (1) people were leaving mainline Protestantism — Methodists, Presbyterians, Episcopalians — and (2) people were joining Evangelical and conservative churches that were often independent of any denomination. A debate ensued about why conservative churches were growing while the sanctuaries at mainline denominations were emptying. Some argued that the 1960s counterculture led baby boomers out of their parents' churches. Others said that churches would naturally decline as society became richer — the old secularization argument that as societies grow more educated, people become less likely to be formally religious. Dean Kelley, author of *Why Conservative Churches Are Growing,* argued that mainline denominations had gotten flabby. They no longer provided much leadership or discipline. Liberal churches were declining, wrote Kelley, because they had lost, or abandoned, their ancient purpose "to respond to the basic human search for meaning."[21] The old American denominations had loosened their grip — a relaxation long in coming, perhaps. Wednesday and Sunday evening services had been thinning out over the past several decades. The churches had become less strict. Before World War I, Presbyterians had rules against worldly amusements and immodest dress. Those strictures had faded, as had all the customs and laws that limited activity on the Sabbath.

The mistake made by the mainline denominations, said the conservatives, was that they had placed their concerns for society — civil rights, the environment, women's rights, the Vietnam War — ahead of saving souls. Mainline church leaders in the 1960s had preached that the "purpose of church is mission." Evangelicals were saying that the purpose of church was to fulfill the Great Commission.

According to the Gospels, Jesus issued the Great Commission after his Crucifixion. After he rose from the dead, he sent word to his disciples to meet him in Galilee. As instructed, the eleven came to a mountain, and Jesus appeared. He told them: "Therefore go and make disciples of all nations, baptizing them in the name of the Father and of the Son and of the Holy Spirit, and teaching them to obey everything I have commanded you" (Matthew 28:16–20). The Great Commission was the animating force behind Donald McGavran's work — to discover how churches grow. It was — and still is — the primary directive of Evangelicalism. Here is a fundamental difference between Public and Private Protestantism. While liberal denominations profess their faith by trying to make the world a better place, Evangelicals believe that the world would be a better place if more people became Christian disciples. From Donald McGavran's perspective, the church could build hospitals or gather God's lost sheep. The Great Commission told McGavran it was more important to gather the sheep.*

"Due to the social upheavals of the decade, church leaders who were deeply involved caused their denominations to put a ministry of social concern in a higher priority position than evangelism," wrote C. Peter Wagner, a former missionary and one of McGavran's colleagues at Fuller Theological Seminary. "This produced a wave of dissatisfied customers, so to speak, who deserted their churches in droves."[22] (Wagner promoted homogeneous church congregations in his book, brazenly titled *Our Kind of People*.) The 1960s and 1970s brought a "collapse of the middle" in American church life, according to Martin Marty, then the dean of the University of Chicago Divinity School. The survivors in this religious transformation, according to Marty, "were polarized into right-wing churches" (a term Marty said that he did not use "invidiously") and "secular humanist culture, which could not have cared less what was going on in the subculture of conservative religion." The "middle" that was disappearing consisted of Marty's Public Protestants, the tradition of socially involved, liberal Christianity that extended from Walter Rauschenbusch's outpost in Hell's Kitchen to Eugene Carson Blake's stand on the frontlines of the civil rights movement.[23] The middle has kept dwindling to this day. As late as 2004, a longtime student of church membership trends found that "oldline Protestantism only leads the Judeo-Christian tradition in the United States in the physical condition of its buildings."[24] Marty wrote of the Evangelical churches, "After about 1968 their inning came."[25] And they had a surprise cleanup man in Donald McGavran.

---

*In Mark 16:15–18, the Great Commission supplies the basis for a more fundamentalist Christianity. In this Gospel, Jesus orders his disciples to "proclaim the Good News to all creation." And then, "He who believes and is baptized will be saved; he who does not believe will be condemned." How will believers be identified? Jesus says that they will "cast out devils; they will have the gift of tongues; they will pick up snakes in their hands and be unharmed."

The Church Growth Movement

Nobody approached the Great Commission quite like Donald McGavran. Newly arrived at Fuller Theological Seminary in Pasadena, California, he began by displaying graphs and charts, business school–type data on how and why churches grow. Charles Fuller, the school's founder, was cool toward McGavran, whom he considered more a technician than an evangelist. After McGavran finished with his first statistics-chocked presentation at the seminary, Fuller made no comment, only asking the audience to join in a chorus of "Heavenly Sunshine," the confection of a song that always ended his enormously popular radio show, the *Old Fashioned Revival Hour.*[*26]

The emptying pews at the mainline denominations had spurred an interest in theories of church growth in the United States. Unlike the 1950s, McGavran now had an audience — preachers hungry for ways to bring Americans back to church. Students interested in domestic ministry took McGavran's classes, and then working pastors began attending. His message to American preachers was the same advice he gave missionaries in *The Bridges of God:* culture matters. (The first person McGavran hired at his Fuller church growth institute was an anthropologist.) Ministers everywhere should design their churches for a culturally defined "homogeneous unit," he advised.

The cultural tribes developing in suburbia were more apparent to others than to McGavran. In *The Bridges of God,* he wrote, "Western nations are homogeneous and there are few exclusive sub-societies."[27] But American ministers consumed by the Great Commission and the ideal of "church growth" soon came to understand that McGavran's stories about evangelizing "peoples" in the Third World could be applied to the United States, particularly to the "homogeneous units" that were developing in American society. The ministers who formed the vanguard of what became known as the church growth movement studied the Old Testament and the census. They conducted market research. They took

---

*Heavenly sunshine, heavenly sunshine,
  Flooding my soul with glory divine.
  Heavenly sunshine, heavenly sunshine,
  Hallelujah! Jesus is mine.

an anthropological interest in their communities, noting the kinds of music people who lived there listened to and the kinds of clothes they wore. They designed their churches to appeal to targeted groups, demographic types. People wouldn't be attracted to a church filled with a diverse membership, these ministers learned from McGavran. But they would come to a church custom-built for people like themselves. The megachurch's ample parking, kicking sound system, and casual dress were the bridges these ministers built to Dockers-clad tribes. McGavran's legacy wasn't a missionary reform. Instead, the bewhiskered gentleman with the sparkling eyes changed how a new generation of American ministers thought about the relationship between the community and the church.

Members of the "disappearing middle" objected to McGavran's tactics. To some, the goal of the church was diversity (a Public Protestant virtue), not growth (Private Protestantism as defined by the Great Commission). "The church is called by Christ to be a transformer of culture," wrote Robert Evans, a theologian at the Hartford Seminary Foundation. "I can find no emphasis in the New Testament on a self-conscious strategy for growth." Jesus' kingdom was a feast, and those "at the table would be Samaritans and Jerusalemites, Pharisees and slaves, harlots and the holy," Evans continued, taking dead aim at McGavran. "It is, if I understood the image correctly, the greatest breaking down of homogeneous units we will ever know."[28] The World Council of Churches issued a warning against ministers finding safety in "the power of their race, class or nation."[29] The magazine Rick Warren picked up in 1974 warned that McGavran could be "dangerous." These were words from the listing ship of liberal Christianity, however, and the warning was lost in the waves of ministers clamoring for their churches to grow.

Filling Churches with "People Like Us"

Rick Warren's account of how he founded Saddleback Church is a set piece of megachurch lore.[30] Warren wrote that in the summer of 1979, he "practically lived in university libraries doing research on the United States census data." Concentrating on four counties in California, he eventually "discovered" that the Saddleback region of Orange County was the fastest-growing end of the nation's fastest-growing county. "This fact grabbed me by the throat and made my heart start racing," Warren wrote. He would plant his church in the Saddleback Valley — and he would start it using the church growth techniques pioneered by Donald McGavran.

Warren and his wife moved to Orange County in December 1979. He studied maps and realized that the county "already had many strong, Bible-believing churches." (This was, after all, the home of Robert Schuller's massive Crystal Cathedral and had been a conservative Evangelical refuge for more than a generation.) Warren spent his first twelve weeks going door-to-door, listening. His seat-of-the-pants market survey helped the young minister, as he described the process, "build a bridge to the unchurched." This was McGavran's metaphor, of course, taken straight from his 1955 book. Warren was out to bring the "peoples" of the Saddleback Valley into the faith. To do that, the young minister needed to break down the cultural barriers between this group and his church.

Warren practiced what he called "targeted evangelism." Based on his research into what sorts of people were moving to this booming area, he composed a composite portrait of the "unchurched" person he expected to attract to his church. And he named him: Saddleback Sam. Saddleback Sam was in his thirties or forties. He was college educated, married (to Saddleback Samantha, naturally), liked contemporary music, preferred casual dress, and had little free time. The picture of Saddleback Sam in Warren's book is of a white guy on a cell phone wearing a middle-age-baggy pair of pleated pants. Having identified his tribesman, Warren went to work breaking down the barriers between his church and Sam. He made the services shorter and tighter. He invested in the best sound system and musicians. He built the best daycare center and made sure there was plenty of parking. Warren didn't wear a suit or a turned-around collar. Formal dress made Saddleback Sam antsy. So Warren filled his closet with a collection of floral shirts.

Warren doesn't claim that any of what he did at Saddleback was new. All of these techniques — including the use of small groups — were there for anyone to see in the church growth literature. What *was* new, however, was the application of techniques used to overcome cultural barriers in the Third World to the new world of American suburbia. Like those on the political right who discovered the new politics bubbling up in places like Kanawha County, West Virginia, Warren didn't start a movement. Nobody tricked millions of people into attending churches like Saddleback and Second Baptist in Houston. The genius of Rick Warren and Edwin Young was in understanding the people filling the new neighborhoods being created by the Big Sort and in designing a church just for them.

"A Choice of a Way of Life"

A few months before the 2004 election, I asked Martin Marty what was distinctive about church life today, forty years after the "collapse of the middle." In Marty's view, the hugely successful church growth movement had undermined the church's older purpose — that of building community. Churches were once built around a geographic community, Marty said. Now they are constructed around similar lifestyles. "A huge element in retention of loyalty and acquisition of new church members can be summarized in a very simple phrase: a choice of a way of life," Marty said. "The great tragedy of it all is that. I've always argued that what society needs are town meeting places where people with very different commitments can meet and interact. Churches have been that. If you're a Methodist and you move to Des Moines, Iowa, and you get to the nearest Methodist church, thirty or forty years ago you would have an open encounter. People who were pro-Bush or pro-Kerry would talk. Fertilization would go on. Now it simply doesn't happen."

The two United Methodist churches in central Austin are a twelve-minute drive apart. Tarrytown United Methodist is your rich uncle's church. People at Tarrytown still dress up on Sunday. When the service started the Sunday morning I visited, the music was Handel, and it rumbled out of a gut-shaking pipe organ. Tarrytown counts among its members the Republican governor of Texas, Rick Perry. Tarrytown, it so happens, was also the home of the previous Republican governor of Texas, President George W. Bush. Just a few miles away at Trinity United Methodist, the service kicked off with the congregation singing and swaying to Sting's mystical anthem "Love Is the Seventh Wave." Trinity made a point of welcoming worshipers regardless of "sexual orientation" or "sexual identity." The Sunday I visited, the Reverend Sid Hall was continuing a series of talks on medieval female mystics.

Not everyone at Tarrytown is a Republican. (A minister there told me that Tarrytown was the church home of a few Jesse Jackson supporters.) Nor are all the members of Trinity Democrats. But it's hard to imagine Rick Perry or George W. Bush going to Trinity, a church that identifies itself in its literature as being of the "cultural left," a church that promotes "social and ecological justice." And there is about a zero chance that any member of Trinity would trade Sting for Handel or talks about mystical Christianity for the straight-pew formality and by-the-book liturgy at Tarrytown. These are two different "peoples" in the McGavran sense, and both are quite homogeneous.

Trinity is an older church, closer to the center of town than to Austin's procreating suburbs. When Hall arrived in 1989, the membership was aging, the services were traditional, and few new people were coming in the door. Trinity was a textbook example of the disappearing middle in American religion. Hall told me that he began to "reach out" to the neighborhood. He opened the church for public meetings about the redevelopment of an abandoned airport nearby. He started a parents' night out. Hall attended these evening events, sticking around afterward to talk with the people who wandered in from the neighborhood. He noticed that the people he was meeting didn't look like those in Trinity's pews on Sunday. The neighborhood, just north of the University of Texas, was changing, and, Hall observed, the new people moving in "tended to be cultural left." Trinity changed "almost by accident," Hall said, because it began to reflect the cultural transformation of the neighborhood. Hall, who describes himself as "left leaning," welcomed the politically liberal folks who were attracted to central Austin. Eventually, some of these folks joined the church. These new members wanted Trinity to openly embrace gays and lesbians. At the time, a "reconciling" movement had begun in the Methodist Church. Some congregations were voting to support "full participation" of gay and lesbian church members — which included marriage. In 1992, Trinity voted to become a "reconciling" church, only the fifty-eighth Methodist church in the country to do so.

Like does attract like, just as McGavran and his Fuller colleague Peter Wagner said. After Hall changed the political and cultural tenor of Trinity, it began attracting the left-leaning people moving into the neighborhood. Trinity tipped from standard Methodism to something else. Like Rick Warren's Saddleback Church, Trinity now breaks down into smaller groups, but they are geared toward the kind of people who go to that church. There is a "social justice initiative" (the church is filled with activists) and the "Trinity Triangle," for gay and transgendered members. Trinity has even held weeknight courses on the meaning of the tarot. "We have some Wiccans who are part of the congregation, and that works," Hall said. "When I take the Beliefnet.com test, I always come out 'neo-pagan,' so who knows."

Trinity changed because the old-style church — the delivery of a standardized denominational liturgy to all comers — no longer worked. By 2004, Trinity had only eight members who were with the church when Hall arrived. "The church would be dead if we hadn't redefined ourselves," Hall told me. "It wasn't a lack of caring or anything else. But if we had stayed a kind of general Methodist church, then why would you go? Our parents would have gone [to the closest] . . . Episcopal or Methodist or Presbyterian [church], . . . but those of us who came after, we're more discriminating. Denominational labels don't mean that much."

There is no longer national "brand loyalty" in regard to religion. There are, however, local micro-brands. Ministers "try to market their church, to find a niche, whether it's being open to gays or lesbians or being strong as a pro-life church," Henry Brinton, an author and Presbyterian minister in northern Virginia, told me. "It's really finding a niche in the religious marketplace and then exploiting it." A minister's job these days entails more than transforming the spiritual lives of congregants. A minister keeps his pulpit by providing the type of services expected by his particular niche market. Trinity became a "reconciling" church, the name Methodists use to describe gay-and-lesbian-friendly congregations. Lutheran churches of the same persuasion are "reconciling-in-Christ." Presbyterians have "more light" congregations. The United Church of Christ has "open and affirming" churches. Some Unitarian churches call themselves "welcoming." And there is an "Evergreen" association within the Baptist Church. What tells more about a church these days, its denomination or whether there's a little rainbow flag attached to its welcome sign? The answer is the flag. Just as the political differences among states are not as great as the political differences among communities, the greatest political disparities are among individual churches, not denominations. Forget whether the church is Baptist or Episcopalian. The important question is whether the service begins with praise music, Handel, or Sting.

Sunday Morning's Big Sort

The discussion going into and coming out of the 2004 presidential election was about the relationship between church attendance and voting. Sixty percent of those who attended church once a week voted Republican in both 2000 and 2004. But that rough statistic misses what's happening within communities and within churches. Trinity's members go to church once a week, and they vote Democratic. Tarrytown's members also go to church every Sunday, and that home to Texas Republican governors, the minister told me, "tends to steer to the right." The Reverend Martin Luther King Jr. wrote in the late 1950s, "The most segregated hour of Christian America is 11 o'clock on Sunday morning." King was referring to racial segregation, and his observation may be as true now as it was then. But today eleven o'clock on Sunday morning is *politically* segregated, too. In the late 1990s, Diana Mutz, a University of Pennsylvania political scientist, surveyed people about their partners in political discussions. "Overwhelmingly, people said the people they met in church were extremely homogenous with them politically," Mutz reported. Church congregations, she wrote, exhibit "strong, extreme homogeneity." There is political discussion within churches, Mutz found, but because it takes place among like-minded people, the discussion tends to reinforce the beliefs of the group. Thus, the result of political discussion in a church built around homogeneous units is greater homogeneity in attitudes.[31]

The University of Akron's John Green has conducted polls about religion and politics since the early 1990s. Rates of church attendance have been a crude way to measure faith and politics; Green has dug deeper.

He asks about the nature of personal beliefs — for example, is the Bible inerrant? — and uses this information to classify respondents as traditionalist, centrist, or modernist.[32] A traditionalist Protestant church member would attend church often and believe that the Bible is the inerrant Word of God. A traditional Catholic would fully accept the authority of the pope. The Second Baptist Church in Houston is a traditionalist church. In 1999, for example, during the festival of Divali, the church distributed a booklet warning that Hindus were under the "power of Satan."[33] The church is "famous for its extensive program of (conservative) political activity," and a picture of George W. Bush hangs on the wall in the church's office.[34] By contrast, Trinity United Methodist's exploration of "creation spirituality . . . an eclectic tradition that honors women's wisdom and the cosmologies of indigenous cultures around the planet" might resonate with a modernist mainline church member.

When Green used those designations of belief to examine voters, he found the real religious divide. Thirty-two percent of modernist Evangelicals were Republican in 2004, compared to 70 percent of traditionalist Evangelicals. Similarly, 26 percent of modernist mainline church members were Republican, compared to 59 percent of traditionalist mainline church members. The categories formed a straight-line trend: the more traditional a person's religious beliefs, the more Republican his or her political beliefs.* Voters who considered the Bible the inerrant Word of God were odds-on members in good standing of the Republican Party. Put a candidate in place of a generic party label, and the divide becomes even deeper. In the spring of 2004, Green found that among likely voters, a whopping 81 percent of traditionalist Evangelicals planned to vote for George W. Bush. Modernist evangelicals, however, favored John Kerry by more than 8 percentage points. Traditionalist mainline churchgoers favored Bush by 34 points. Modernist mainliners favored Kerry by 41.6 points.[35]

As Americans have sorted themselves geographically, they've sorted

---

*Race trumped religion in Green's polling. Black Protestants were the most Democratic of the groups, followed closely by Jews and Latino Catholics.

themselves religiously, too — and just as unconsciously. "People don't say, 'What's the most Republican church in town?'" Green explained to me. "They say, 'Where is the church that is most like me?' Which means that nine out of ten people in the church are going to be Republican. And it happens with liberals as well." The large churches, most of which follow McGavran's church growth techniques, are almost invariably traditionalist. Only 7 percent of the 1,210 megachurches counted in 2005 described themselves as "moderate." (That's as far to the left as the designations went.) Eight out of ten fell into traditionalist categories — charismatic, Pentecostal, fundamentalist.[36] By Rick Warren's estimation, 85 percent of the Saddleback Sams and Samanthas in his church voted for Bush in 2004.*[37]

These days, people are unlikely to meet many at church whose politics differ from their own, so the forces of group polarization are at work within the sanctuary, too. "To the extent that people receive information from congregations, they are likely to have that information reinforced by the people they worship with," Green told me. "It's like having a big filter. You get some kinds of messages, and those messages are reinforced . . . There has been a lot of emphasis on this happening with conservative Christians, but of course it happens across the board. This kind of filtering happens in liberal churches, too." The lesson learned in scores of group polarization experiments is that like-minded groups grow more extreme over time. And that is exactly what Green has found. "Overall, particularly among the large white religious communities, there does seem to be that hardening," Green said in 2004. Since his first polls in 1992, traditionalist Evangelicals "have experienced a steady Republican shift." Meanwhile, the political makeup of modernist mainline churches also has changed drastically — "from 50 percent Republican to 26 percent."[38]

Are Green's religious types also segregating themselves geographically, with traditionalists settling in some communities and modernists in others? Bob Cushing and I have discovered that men and women of

---

*Warren explained the overwhelming support for Bush at Saddleback by saying, "It's Orange County." But Bush received only 60 percent of the vote in that county in 2004.

every faith (Evangelical, Catholic, Jewish) are more politically conservative in heavily Republican counties than are those of the same religious description in Democratic landslide counties. That's because there are more religious *traditionalists* in Republican counties. For example, 45 percent of the population in heavily Republican counties attends regular Bible study or group prayer meetings. By contrast, only 28.7 percent of the population in heavily Democratic counties participates in such activities.[39]

It's Not About You — Except When It Is

Rick Warren's wildly popular book *The Purpose-Driven Life* begins with a challenge to Americans' post-materialist self-centeredness: "It's not about you." In the sense of the Great Commission, that is exactly right. Life and the church are about finding salvation in Christ. The imperative of "like attracts like" evangelism, however, caters to the individual from the time the convert first answers the call to worship. Whenever the evangelist Billy Graham issued his altar call, inspired people would stream to the foot of the stage to pledge their lives to the church. At that first moment of their new faith, Graham made sure the freshly converted were met by volunteers of the same age, sex, and race.[40] The shepherding of people into their proper "homogeneous units" begins at the beginning. Which raises a question: in this world of segmented Sunday school classes, stopwatch-timed sermons, "people like us" altar calls, and preachers in market-tested cruise ship attire, isn't there something very pervasive that's *all* about you?

"My contention is that McGavran was never really heard in North America," said Eddie Gibbs, the Donald A. McGavran Professor of Church Growth at Fuller Theological Seminary. McGavran came to his strategy because of his commitment to the Great Commission. Warren repeatedly makes the same point — that the homogeneous unit principle is simply a way to make it easier for people to become Christians. Whereas McGavran was a missionary building bridges from castes or villages to Christ, today's churches define tribes in the same way people are attracted to different sections of a shopping mall. McGavran hired an anthropologist to understand the multiple meanings of human affinity in China. Megachurches today consult with Disney about how to design parking lots.*

The successful North Coast Church in Vista, California, follows a fundamentalist doctrine: the inerrancy of the Bible, water baptism, and the "imminent" Second Coming of Christ. North Coast has found an innovative way to grow through the homogeneous unit principle, beaming a central service to video screens in different meeting places. Everyone hears the same sermon, but everyone listens in a place with its own special "ambiance." The venues in 2007 were described on the church's website in terms that almost parody brand-defined, music-segmented, American mall-speak. In the central church, North Coast offered "a full worship band, Starbucks coffee, and a 'Barnes & Noble' style bookstore in the lobby." At the "Country Gospel" venue, North Coast adopted *Hee Haw* informality, encouraging just-folks, "Y'all come on over and . . . join us for some bluegrass/country gospel." The "Traditions" hall provided "an intimate and nostalgic worship experience led from a baby grand piano." At "The Edge," churchgoers could count on "Starbucks coffee, Mountain Dew, big subwoofers and teaching via big-screen video."

The goal of the church in other times was to transfigure the social tenets of those who came through the door. Now people go to a church not for how it might change their beliefs, but for how their precepts will be reconfirmed. "I find very little evidence that churches are really transforming their congregations," University of Maryland political scientist James Gimpel told me. "It's rather quite the reverse. Ministers depend on pleasing a particular congregation for their longevity. The last thing they want to do is offend those people or try to transform their viewpoint . . . . It's conformity all the way." We have more choices than ever before in the hundreds of religious niche markets. But given a choice, we select sameness. This was hardly Donald McGavran's intention when he came upon a church community that was losing members and introduced a

---

*Disney shared many tricks of the trade in training sessions held for church leaders, Second Baptist Church minister Gary Moore told me. For instance, the entertainment company talked to trainees from megachurches about how popcorn and cotton candy smells are pumped onto Disney's "main streets" as a way to attract people into stores. Ministers have adopted this technique to lure people into church dinners or religious dinner theaters.

young generation of ministers to missionary techniques discovered in India.

"The church needed to be birthed within . . . indigenous cultures and take on that indigenous expression," Eddie Gibbs told me. "It was a missional principle, and when it came to the U.S., it became a marketing principle: how to gather more people like us. [Churches] picked up the tactical parts, but I'm not too sure they understood the deeper mission implications. And they didn't really address the cultural implications, because mission morphed into marketing."

8

ADVERTISING

Grace Slick, Tricia Nixon, and You

If everyone agrees with you, where's the fun?

— GUY BARNETT, founder of
Brooklyn Brothers advertising agency

A NEW YORK adman began an article in a 1973 issue of the *Journal of Advertising* with an odd question: "Are Grace Slick and Tricia Nixon Cox the Same Person?" Traditional advertising research in the early 1970s would have taken this question, plugged in demographic data, and answered, with quantifiable certainty, "Yes, they are." Both were white, rich, educated, urban, from upper-income homes, and between the ages of twenty-five and thirty-five. They had even attended the same college.

But conventional marketing research was blind, wrote John E. O'Toole, president of Foote, Cone & Belding Communications. Wasn't it obvious? "Go ask Alice, I think she'll know." As would anyone. The lead singer for the psychedelic rock group Jefferson Airplane was nothing like the blond-haired daughter of President Richard Nixon. Grace Slick originally wanted to name her daughter god but settled for China. Tricia Nixon married a Republican presidential aide on the White House lawn. In 1970, when Slick was invited to a White House reception for Nixon's fellow Finch College alums, the Secret Service stopped the singer when she tried to bring along her "bodyguard," Yippie founder and Chicago Seven defendant Abbie Hoffman. (The two said they intended to spike the president's iced tea with LSD.) Unless advertisers could learn to distinguish the composer of "White Rabbit" from the president's daughter, O'Toole wrote, marketing research was useless.

O'Toole argued that statistics on income, age, and education had lost relevance because there had been a "Revolution of the Individual" in the United States. The advertising executive didn't acknowledge having read about Abraham Maslow's hierarchy of needs or Ronald Inglehart's silent revolution. But he was describing the same phenomenon — the explosion of self-expression in a post-materialist economy. People were no longer willing to be treated as part of a mass because they didn't think of themselves that way, O'Toole told his fellow marketing executives. They were growing their hair long and "forming liberation groups: black, feminist, gay, consumer, anything." O'Toole wrote that marketers had snoozed through the revolution and insulted customers by discounting "their intelligence in favor of some vast common denominator." It was 1973, but advertisers continued to "shout at a crowd rather than talk to persons."[1]

O'Toole's manifesto appeared just three years after Donald McGavran published his 1970 masterwork on religion and homogeneous units, *Understanding Church Growth*. Although the two were writing for radically different audiences on wildly different subjects, McGavran and O'Toole reached remarkably similar conclusions: people lived, bought, and worshiped in groups "united by common attitudes or lifestyles or perceptions of themselves." Those were O'Toole's words, but they could have been McGavran's. The ministers who listened to McGavran, such as Rick Warren (see chapter 7), created the megachurch. Those in the commercial world who followed O'Toole devised the kind of target marketing that transformed modern business — and in 2004 helped win the presidency for George W. Bush. Both movements reinforced and deepened the segmented and segregated lives Americans live today.

From Torch Lights to Image Tribes

Most of the language Americans use today to describe politics can be traced to the decades just after the Civil War. In the late nineteenth century, political races became "campaigns." Politicians referred to "precinct captains," "old warhorses," "rank-and-file voters," "last-ditch efforts," and "battleground states." Political campaigns mimicked the tactics as well as the language of the battlefield. They were mass endeavors: people rallied; they turned out for speeches and marched in torch-light parades; they literally donned the uniforms of their parties. In the 1870s, the Republican glee club in one Indiana county put forty singers and an organ on a wagon drawn by six horses.

Although we've retained the language of post–Civil War politics, we long ago lost the style. By the summer of 2006, politics had turned from a mass undertaking into a calculated exercise of social segmentation and niche marketing. Both parties had pollsters in the field asking questions they hoped would help identify likely Democrats or Republicans so that the parties could isolate and target individual voters. Democrats were startled when Republicans in 2004 plucked out likely supporters by their choices in magazines and liquor. These were advertising strategies that businesses had used for decades, and to catch up, Democrats quickly hired their own marketing firms. By the time of the 2006 midterm elections, both parties were segregating, slicing, and separating voters.

Political marketing has always lagged behind commercial merchandizing. Politicians adopt new techniques long after they are proven in the commercial world. The parades and horse-drawn choirs of the late nineteenth century were abandoned in part on the advice of John Wanamaker, President William Henry Harrison's postmaster general and the originator of the department store.[2] Wanamaker and others realized that the military style of campaigning was good at turning out voters, but the turnout was indiscriminate. Campaigns of the late nineteenth century energized friend and foe alike. Wanamaker argued that people shouldn't be whipped into a fury or paraded down the street. Voters ought to be approached as individuals, as consumers. Instead of spangly party uniforms and pipe organs pulled to mass rallies by horses, Wanamaker advised, politicians should use a new weapon to contact voters individually: advertising. A politics of mass movements would become a politics of mass marketing.

The parties began printing millions of newspapers. They dispatched speakers to thousands of clubs to discuss the issues of the day. The candidates spent money on postage, not torches. Illinois Democrats in 1892 distributed 1.9 million pamphlets in twelve languages and mailed 2 million pieces of literature across the Midwest. Instead of ginning up crowds of party supporters with marches and rallies, the new merchandising style of political campaigning focused on the undecided voter.[3] Political advertising was coming from the world of the department store, and it was all about mass marketing to individual consumers.

Consuming the Vote and Segmenting the Market

Business at the beginning of the twentieth century was all about getting big. Between 1898 and 1902, in a massive wave of mergers, 2,653 firms consolidated into just 269. "With remarkable swiftness," historian Daniel Pope wrote, "large-scale corporate capitalism had appeared."[4] Mass production, with its heavy capital investments, demanded mass markets. "The essence of manufacture," wrote a DuPont executive at the beginning of the twentieth century, "is steady and full product."[5] Marketing was geared to encourage allegiance to the new national brand names: Coca-Cola, Quaker Oats, Kodak. By 1930, the fifty biggest American corporations accounted for half of the nation's industrial production.[6]

National advertising and mass merchandising worked for ketchup, cigarettes, and sweet, brown-colored water, and it was soon employed for political candidates as well. No parades, just facts. No brass bands, just pamphlets to be read by atomized voters. The merchandising technique elected candidates, but it devastated democratic participation. Turnouts in national elections dropped from 80 percent of eligible voters in 1896 to under 50 percent in 1924.[7] Democracy was no longer a craft skill; it was a commodity of mass production. Voters weren't owners of a process; they consumed a product, democracy, designed by department store moguls. *Nation's Business,* the publication of the U.S. Chamber of Commerce, eagerly anticipated the 1956 presidential campaign, when "both parties will merchandise their candidates and issues by the same methods that business has developed to sell goods."[8] Those methods, however, were about to change, both in business and in politics.

One year after Donald McGavran's *The Bridges of God* appeared in 1955, adman Wendell Smith introduced the idea of "market segmentation." Smith described the old mass-marketing strategy as "bending . . .

demand to the will of supply." In this model, Smith wrote, manufacturers looked upon the national market as a large cake and worked to take a full layer. Smith suggested that firms slice in a different direction. Manufacturers should consider tailoring products to the specific needs of a smaller number of consumers. Companies could charge higher prices to more loyal customers if they gave fewer people exactly what they wanted. Instead of taking a thin horizontal layer of the national market, business should consider taking a deep, vertical, wedge-shaped slice.[9]

Smith's article was about a marketing strategy, but it was also an insight into how Americans were changing — the "Revolution of the Individual" O'Toole would write about in 1973. In the 1950s, a time of unprecedented prosperity, consumers were willing (and able) to pay more to buy just the item they desired. At the same time, manufacturers had learned to gain economies of scale in shorter production runs. (A factory didn't need to make every car a black Model T to be profitable. Manufacturers had learned to add variety without losing income.) These new, more flexible manufacturing techniques, Smith announced, could be used to meet "the desires of consumers or users for more precise satisfaction of their varying wants."[10] It was a shift in perspective, away from trying to generate sales for what manufacturers could make in volume to producing exactly what groups of consumers were willing to buy.

When advertisers thought grandly about their profession early in the twentieth century, when the mass market ruled, they saw their work as a thick strap that pulled the nation together. Taking the ideals of Progressive politics and the Social Gospel into the commercial world, Albert Lasker, president of the Lord & Thomas agency, told his employees in the 1920s that "we are making a homogeneous" people out of a nation of immigrants.[11] Marketing research in the 1950s and 1960s, however, discovered that commerce would be more profitable if the nation were divvied up into smaller, segmented groups. Moreover, the melting pot turned out to be a flop. People, classes, and races didn't "melt" as expected. The *Chicago Tribune* conducted a survey in the late 1950s to see whether economic class made a difference in the way people thought about buying, saving, and shopping. The assumption at the time was that a rich person was simply a poor person with money. That's not what the *Tribune*'s research found. A "Lower-Status person is profoundly different in his mode of thinking and his way of handling the world from the Middle-Class individual," Pierre Martineau wrote in 1958. "Where he buys and what he buys will differ not only by economics but in symbolic value."[12]

People of different classes shopped in different stores not simply to find a particular style and price but also to be safely among those who were like themselves. "The shopper is not going to take a chance feeling out of place by going to a store where she might not fit," Martineau wrote. The most important function of advertising wasn't to boast of prices or quality. It was to "permit the shopper to make social-class identification."[13] The role of advertising was to help shoppers sort themselves into the social group where they felt the most comfortable. Martineau urged retailers to develop "personalities" in their stores, arguing that it was a mistake "to be all things to all people."*[14] McGavran found that people wouldn't cross class boundaries to go to church. Martineau was simply applying the same "homogeneous unit principle" to shopping. It worked in both realms.

By the early 1960s, market segmentation was the norm. In 1966, the *Journal of Marketing* quoted an advertising executive as saying, "It has become practically impossible to enter the national market on a broad, undifferentiated basis with any real hope of success."[15] The business of marketing became the science of defining market segments, the art of division. For this purpose, Daniel Yankelovich announced in 1964, quantifiable traits such as age and income were useless. More crucial were qualitative characteristics such as "attitudes, motivations, [and] values."[16]

The transformation of marketing was evident in Pepsi's battle with Coca-Cola. In the 1930s, Pepsi advertised cost: you got "twelve full ounces" of cola with a Pepsi instead of six and a half ounces in the thick, green glass of a Coke bottle. In the 1950s, however, Pepsi began appealing to customers "on the basis of who they were rather than what the

---

*Martineau's article definitely fails any twenty-first-century measure of political correctness. But the adman foresaw that the market was getting more complicated. Although all classes of people liked accumulating things, Martineau wrote, the growing middle class was most interested in buying experiences, "spending where one is left typically with only a memory" ("Social Class and Spending Behavior," p. 129). Forty-one years later, B. Joseph Pine II and James H. Gilmore would write *The Experience Economy: Work Is Theater and Every Business a Stage.*

product was."[17] In the late 1950s, the slogan was "Be Sociable, Have a Pepsi." By 1961, Pepsi was for "Those Who Think Young." And then, in 1963, soda pop drinkers were urged to join the "Pepsi Generation."[18] Marketers learned that they could not only find segments, but they could also create them. And in the new post-materialist world, those segments would be less about the cost of a product and more about the values it represented.*

One Nation, Many "Image Tribes"

The divisions grew finer. The Pepsi Generation had to be divided again between LSD-laced rock singers and blond daughters of Republican presidents, and again between hockey players and golfers, between environmentalists and Evangelicals. Researchers parsed consumers into ever-smaller homogeneous groups. In the early 1990s, marketing consultants Don Peppers and Martha Rogers announced the ultimate in market segmentation, the "one to one future." Computing power allowed producers to develop relationships with individual customers. Firms were told to "manage your customers, not just your products," and to produce specific goods for specific people. Peppers and Rogers described a nation of consumer "hunters and gatherers," traveling in groups "held together by a sense of common purpose, not confined by any sense of place. This is the 1:1 future . . . It will be a tribal society at light speed. Individuals will congregate in wandering, venturesome image tribes, held together by their pursuit of common ideas, common icons, common entertainment — linked, in other words, by nothing more than a sense of belonging. It will not be a geographic community."[19]

Peppers and Rogers summed up the early 1990s, as mass media disassembled and production batches shrank. (The average assembly run for a set of identical automobiles was only fifty cars; the manufacturing system was no longer geared for mass production but for mass customization.)[20] The job of marketers (and pastors and politicians) was to find

---

*In 2004, 34 percent of those buying Toyota Prius hybrid cars said that they purchased the vehicle because it "makes a statement about me." By 2007, that number had risen to 57 percent. Micheline Maynard, "Say 'Hybrid' and Many People Will Hear 'Prius,'" *New York Times,* July 4, 2007, p. A1.

ways to manage the fractious society being created. Marketers used computers to track individual customers. Peppers and Rogers were right about the return to tribes — McGavran's homogeneous units. But they were wrong about another thing: the tribes were geographic, too. They were sequestered in neighborhoods and in churches.

When John O'Toole posed his question about Tricia Nixon and Grace Slick, he was telling fellow marketers that they had better be able to tell one woman from another, because any advertising that seduced Nixon types was sure to turn off Grace Slick fans. "Marketing and media executives are sure that people gravitate to materials that most closely zero in on their likes and dislikes, their sense of themselves," wrote historian Joseph Turow. "But marketers also believe the converse: that people prefer not to confront materials that cause them discomfort."[21] People had grown intolerant of advertising's intrusiveness,* but that impatience was just part of a deeper distress. Americans were developing a generalized discomfort with differing points of view. It was a deepening anger that encompassed politics, culture, entertainment, religion, and commerce. In the summer of 2004, J. Walker Smith told me that his polling for Yankelovich Partners detected this rancorous turn in public opinion beginning in the 1990s. People became "increasingly uncomfortable with tolerating trade-offs," Smith said. "So it makes it difficult for people to compromise or to listen to other people's opinions."† Smith ran a poll asking whether people identified more with integrity or success. It was a false choice, in theory, since the two aren't mutually exclusive. But Smith figured that the question was a way of determining which term resonated more with people — whether means mattered more than ends. Beginning in the 1990s, Smith said, he found a big jump in the sa-

---

*Eight out of ten Americans told Yankelovich Partners in 2003 that they felt inundated by advertisements and, when given a chance, they reacted against unwanted commercial messages. Ten million Americans signed up for a national no-call list in the first four days the service was offered in 2003. See J. Walker Smith, Ann Clurman, and Craig Wood, *Coming to Concurrence: Addressable Attitudes and the New Model for Marketing Productivity* (Evanston, IL: Racom Communications, 2005), pp. 17–18.

†A Public Agenda poll released in January 2005 found sharp decreases in the percentage of Americans who said that "deeply religious" public officials might at times need to "make compromises" in their convictions in order to "get results while in government." "Religion and Public Life, 2000–2004: Survey Shows Religious Americans Less Likely to Support Compromise," January 23, 2005, http://www.publicagenda.org/research/research_reports_details.cfm?list=1.

lience of means (integrity) over ends (success). Principles were paramount. "Nobody is willing to live with trade-offs anymore," Smith said. "We're in this no-compromise world."

The Geography of Influence

Market segmentation and psychographic market research roused the same fears as McGavran's homogeneous units. Vance Packard warned in his 1957 book *The Hidden Persuaders* that advertising employed "mass psychoanalysis" to manipulate consumers. This was *The Manchurian Candidate* fear that advertisers had managed to "invade the privacy of our minds" to manipulate both sales and political opinion.*[22] Other social critics said that beyond exploiting consumers, advertising and marketing were actually making national consensus impossible. Joseph Turow argued that marketing tactics aimed at segmenting society instead of making society whole was causing the "breaking up" of America. Beginning in the 1970s, there was, he wrote, a "profound movement by advertisers away from society-making media." Marketers created the electronic version of gated communities, encouraging "small slices of society to talk to themselves." For example, Cubans in Miami had a relatively low opinion of Mexicans, who were commonly used in Hispanic-oriented commercials, Turow reported. So Saturn produced a new set of car ads for South Florida using Cubans. Marketers were "surrounding individuals with mirrors of themselves, their values, and their activities."[23] Historian Robert Wiebe wrote in his book *The Segmented Society* that the "major casualty of the 1960s was a dream of moderation, accommodation, and cohesion, and its passing brought acute feelings of loss and betrayal." The country adopted a new "national style," one that was "sectarian, not pragmatic. When Americans encountered problems, they looked not for the common ground but for the boundary dividing it . . . Americans appeared automatically to know that security and comfort could only be found inside a fortress."[24]

Advertisers, however, were, like pastors in the church growth move-

---

*The fear that people could use psychological techniques to gain control of the political system was described in Eugene Burdick's cold and eerie 1956 novel *The Ninth Wave*.

ment, simply following their customers — and Americans were sorting themselves into more homogeneous groups without any help from Madison Avenue. Marketers didn't make these groups, but they did take advantage of them. Advertising firms soon realized that people were linked most strongly to others who had similar interests or beliefs. Environmentalists talked to other environmentalists; swimmers hung out with other swimmers. Once identified, these "peoples" (in McGavran's sense) could be either sold a new kind of deep-dish pizza or recruited to a megachurch. The makers of the first PowerBars, for example, were triathletes, and they found their initial market among fellow long-distance runners, swimmers, and cyclists. To generate sales among golfers or mountain bikers, they had to "plant separate seeds" in each sports network. Back in nineteenth-century India, Bishop J. Waskom Pickett realized it was essential that a convert named Ditt plant Christianity among his Chuhra tribe (see chapter 7). When the makers of PowerBars wanted to introduce their product within a new "tribe" — say, tennis players — they hired a tennis player, somebody who knew the language of the court — a Ditt with a crisp crosscourt backhand.[25]

The whole concept of markets was changing as business came to understand the social psychology of groups. "People speak about the 'mass market,'" William H. Whyte wrote in *Fortune* magazine in 1954. In reality, the market "breaks down into a series of groups," and these groups "exert a great power, sometimes of frightening intensity, over their members." To prove his point, Whyte conducted an early experiment examining the power of groups in the marketplace. He decided to test the power of "word of mouth" by mapping how air conditioners, then a relatively new appliance, spread through city neighborhoods. He snapped aerial photographs of row houses in an outwardly homogeneous Philadelphia development. (All the houses were the same style, the same size, and approximately the same price.) If a house had an air conditioner, it was easily seen on the photograph. Overall, about 20 percent of the houses had air conditioners. But the percentage for the neighborhood as a whole was misleading when Whyte looked block by block. In one block of fifty-two houses, there would be three air conditioners. In another, there would be eighteen. Whyte marked the air-conditioned houses on his aerial photographs with a grease pencil. When he looked at the clusters of air conditioners, he saw clear "symbols of a powerful communication network." Individuals didn't buy air conditioners as much as "peoples" bought air conditioners.[26]

This experiment has since been replicated with far more sophistication than Whyte's ad hoc aerial photographs. Finnish economists recently examined automobile purchases in two of that country's provinces over two years. Their findings matched Whyte's discovery of fifty years earlier. People who lived close to one another tended to buy the same kind of car. They weren't buying out of envy or in competition, the Finnish economist discovered. The most reasonable explanation was that neighbors were making group decisions from shared information.[27] Whyte proposed that there was some leadership involved in these group-influenced purchases. It wasn't necessarily a good or virtuous person who was a group leader. ("Sometimes the leader is a bitch," Whyte wrote.) But it was the "catalytic influence of a leader" that connected people and helped transfer information.[28] Whyte's hypothesis matched other research. Elmo Roper was conducting polls in the 1950s to try to find "influential" Americans. Roper proposed that a small group of people ("influentials") swayed the opinions (and purchasing decisions) of many others. All of this research would later be systematized into "buzz" or "viral" marketing and described in Malcolm Gladwell's 2000 book on social "epidemics," *The Tipping Point.* But in the 1930s, J. Waskom Pickett, a lone Methodist bishop living in India, had described the same movement of ideas and faith through an interconnected group. And when church growth advocates in the 1980s wrote about Pickett's research, they said that Christianity moved "contagiously" — just as "buzz" strategists would rediscover a decade later.[29]

Marketers also discovered geographies of culture or lifestyle. Chris Riley is a Portland, Oregon, marketing expert who worked with Nike in the 1990s. The sporting goods company was unique, Riley told me, because it had largely abandoned standard demographic market research. The company had found that "people [were] clustering around their interests" and those clusters had little to do with standard demographic categories. Nike also had recognized a "geography of influence" in the market. Depending on the subject, belief, or product involved, each interest, Riley explained, had its own map. "If you go down to Mount

Hood [outside Portland] and have a look at the snowboarders, I challenge you to find a [Nike] swoosh," Riley said. Snowboarders avoided Nike "like it was the bubonic plague." Riley said that the company had tried to do a market study with snowboarders around Boulder, Colorado, but couldn't even recruit people for the research. Riley explained, "You go to Boulder and you're wearing the swoosh, and it's like, 'What the hell are you doing here? You've obviously come from New York. You're not one of us. You're about the urban experience. You're about basketball. You're about a giant corporation. We don't want you here.'"

When Riley thinks about markets now, he envisions local communities of special interests. What happens within these homogeneous clusters *is* the market. So instead of spending money on demographic research, Riley tries to tap into these lifestyle communities. When I met Riley in the fall of 2005, he was working at Apple. He said that he planned to take his Apple marketing staff to Marfa, Texas, because the little town on the edge of the Big Bend section of the Rio Grande appeared to be an emerging center of cultural influence. The minimalist sculptor Donald Judd had moved to the West Texas town decades ago, and Marfa had since become a most unlikely boomtown of art galleries, espresso cafés, Prada shops, French restaurants, and cool hotels. People were aggregating around communities of interest, Riley said, and those communities had an address. Riley said that he could learn more about hip culture by spending a weekend in Marfa than by buying reams of Zip Code research.

Place matters, and so does proximity. An MIT researcher tracked the communication patterns among employees in seven research and development firms. The closer people were to one another, the more they talked.[30] William Whyte showed with his study of air conditioners in Philadelphia that we buy what those close to us buy. The purveyors of "buzz" marketing schemes count on the word about their products traveling through networks that are created, in part, by physical proximity.

Like Sells to Like

In the early 1960s, F. B. Evans studied the links between the sellers and the buyers of life insurance. Evans proposed that the "more similar the parties" in the relationship, the more likely the salesman would be to make a deal. In a study of 125 salesmen and 500 prospects, he found that sales were more likely between people of the same height and similar education, but that sales dropped if the salesman earned less than the prospect. Sales were *highest* when the salesman belonged to the same political party as the client. Sales were *lowest* when the salesman and prospect had different political allegiances.*[31]

The Hartford Institute's David Roozen searched for the secret of church growth in a survey of more than 11,000 Protestant congregations in 2000. He found that churches with a defined "niche" grew faster than those with broader, more general missions. (Segmenting worked with religion as well as with Tide detergent.) Churches with a variety of programs (mass customization) grew faster, too. But the most important feature of growing churches, Roozen found, was an absence of conflict.[32] Marketers, ministers, and, soon, politicians learned that people wanted both conformity in interests and agreement in opinions. They wanted the society they lived in to be just like the cars they bought — customized.

In 2003, historian Lizabeth Cohen wrote that at one time, politicians tried to "convince voters of some common good, as Roosevelt, Truman, and Eisenhower all struggled to do." But a new political strategy that applied techniques of market segmentation to politics led the nation away from these ideals, requiring candidates to "at best construct a composite vision out of the specialized interests of their distinct constituencies, and at worst avoid discussing any common good at all." Old-style campaigns with parades, uniforms, and choirs in horse-drawn wagons may have aimed at the lowest common social denominator, but, as Cohen noted, at least they enhanced the democratic notion of commonweal.[33]

When politicians began to apply one-to-one marketing methods to elections, they abandoned the possibility of a common good. Breaking the country into tiny market segments resulted in the death of consensus — and the possibility that Americans could agree at times to split the difference. "I've been struck in this election," marketer J. Walker

---

*There are product equivalents to the research on insurance sales. Emanuel Rosen wrote in *The Anatomy of Buzz* that Birkenstocks made such a strong political statement that it "took the company years to convince mainstream customers to wear the sandals" (p. 64).

Smith told me in the summer of 2004, "in the way that . . . this one-to-one business philosophy characterizes what the Democratic and Republican parties are doing." The presidential campaign that year was both loud and omnipresent, but there was little evidence of persuasion. There were no attempts to turn Republicans into Democrats, or Democrats into Republicans. Early on, it seemed, both parties determined that what they cared most about was loyalty. The campaigns cultivated the cocksureness that arises within all like-minded groups. This was going to be an election based on turnout, and confident people vote in higher percentages than do those who feel conflicted. Besides, in this world, who likes, wants, or needs conflict — especially conflicting ideas?

"We're going to market to our own party," Smith said, explaining the strategy. "We're not going to worry about a message that would be broadly inclusive. We're only going to tell Republicans or only tell Democrats what they want to hear. We aren't going to talk to them about things they might not want to hear. And we are going to try to ensure that they feel so loyal that they'll get out and vote. What we're trying to do is drive customer loyalty — and, in marketing terms, drive the average transaction size or improve the likelihood that a registered Republican will get out and vote Republican. That's a business philosophy applied to politics that I think is really dangerous, because it's not about trying to form a consensus, to get people to think about the greater good. That is a business philosophy applied to politics that is all about polarization."

9

LIFESTYLE

"Books, Beer, Bikes, and Birkenstocks"

Specialization is for insects.

— ROBERT A. HEINLEIN, *Time Enough for Love*

PAUL GUINAN EXPLAINED the unlikely happenstance that brought Superman, Wonder Woman, Batman, Conan the Barbarian, Catwoman, and the Fantastic Four together in a one-room office on the third floor of a building on SW Fifth Street in downtown Portland, Oregon. "It's like an immigrant finds out a place is okay and then brings his family," Guinan said as he worked away in the middle of Mercury Studio, the office that houses thirteen of the nation's best comic book artists. (At one time or another, these artists have drawn or inked nearly every superhero.) "We're like that. We're like the Irish." Well, not *exactly* like the Irish. The comic book artists and writers who moved to Portland over the past twenty years weren't fleeing potato blight. They weren't southern field hands or Appalachian coal miners gone to Detroit, Chicago, or Cleveland after being displaced by automated cotton pickers or continuous mining machines. Rather, they came to Portland because this was where they wanted to be, where they could live among their own kind.

The English economist Alfred Marshall examined the agglomeration of industries in nineteenth-century England — textile manufacturers in Manchester and cutlery makers in Sheffield — and observed the economic advantages when industry clustered. Textile manufacturers in

Manchester shared knowledge about the latest weaving techniques and markets. Skilled spinners were ready for hire because the business of mills and textiles was part of Manchester. "Great are the advantages which people following the same skilled trade get from near neighborhood to one another," Marshall wrote. "The mysteries of the trade become no mysteries, but are, as it were, in the air, and children learn many of them unconsciously."[1] Jeff Parker channeled Marshall when he explained why he had moved to Portland and Mercury Studio from Chapel Hill, North Carolina. "It's the whole idea of why you send your kid to Harvard," Parker told me as he rewrote the story line for a Fantastic Four book. "You see people around here doing it, and it just seems normal. It becomes more normal for you. Seeing the possibilities is important."

The comics business has flourished in Portland partly because of Mike Richardson. Richardson opened a chain of comic book stores in the early 1980s, first in Bend, Oregon, and then in Portland. His stores did well, and before long he wasn't just selling comic books; he was publishing them.[2] Richardson hired comic book writers, editors, and artists — so many of them that his Dark Horse Comics became the third-largest comic book publisher in the country, home of *Star Wars, Alien, Predator, Buffy the Vampire Slayer,* and *The Terminator.*[3] The first comic book migrants who found their way to Portland worked for Dark Horse. Others followed.

The same economic forces that Marshall had described in Manchester's cluster of textile mills were at work in the Portland comic book scene — and, in particular, in the warren of artists at Mercury Studio. Mercury serves as a loosely formed business partnership. When an artist at Mercury is up against an impossible deadline, others in the group pitch in, drawing backgrounds or inking. They share ideas and leads on jobs. For publishers, the cluster of Portland artists makes it easier to find workers. (New York executives from big comic book houses such as DC Comics and Marvel make trips to Portland.) The artists at Mercury save money by sharing space, and they keep up a steady rap about industry gossip, current events, and comic book lore as they sketch and ink. When I was there, Drew Johnson claimed that when he drew Wonder Woman, he was "the first guy who actually shrank her boobs." The "mysteries of the trade" were certainly in the air.

An economic magnetism was pulling those interested in the comics business to Portland, but something else was at work, too. The city's way of life was uniquely hospitable to artists, writers, and book publishers. Portland was (and is) a city of books and readers. In the 1990s, it was one of 17 cities, out of 211 media markets, that had both a low rate of television watching and a high rate of reading. The city ranked 5th in the absolute number of used bookstores (after New York, Chicago, San Francisco, and Seattle). It ranked 11th in the sale of science fiction. Portland was a good home for comics because the people who lived there read books and bought books.[4]

Portland also was where these comic book artists and writers wanted to be.

The Tiebout Theory of Migration; or "Books, Beer, Bikes, and Birkenstocks"

Comic book people moved to Portland with no particular plan. "They didn't have a job lined up, they didn't have a place to stay, but they had somebody to crash with for a while, and they figured it would work out," explained comic book editor and writer Anina Bennett. The Portland comic book community is filled with those who got there through a lack of planning. Randy Jarrell, one of the founders of the independent Oni Press, was married and hanging around Austin when, "literally, on a Sunday we said, 'Lets move to Portland; I have some friends there.' On Wednesday, we hit the road."

Portland economist Joe Cortright explained that the Portland economy is built on "books, beer, bikes, and Birkenstocks." Sockless footwear is code for liberal politics (Portland's Multnomah County voted seven to three for Kerry in 2004), which means that artists come to Portland for a cultural constellation that includes comics, microbrews, lifestyle, and a Democratic majority. "The reason I moved here wasn't because of comics," said Randy Jarrell. "The reason I moved here is probably the reason everyone else moved here. A lot of it had to do with politics, you know. Portland [has] all the amenities your typical liberal-type person would want. You have a great library system, one of the best in the country. You have great parks. You get public transportation, affordable universities. A lot of that had to do with it."

The three guys who run Oni Press all were raised in the Republican suburbs of the Southwest. They moved to a Democratic city where they didn't always have to drive a car. Jeff Parker, the Fantastic Four writer, said he moved to Portland because it was a "place I could ride my bike. It's like a little Amsterdam." As David Hahn puttered away on a Bite Club book (with a vampire mafia motif) for DC Comics, he explained that he used Portland's many bookstores — particularly the mammoth Powell's Books — as a giant reference library. Steve Lieber (Batman and Swamp Thing) said that his wife is a librarian, whose "life revolves around books." They moved to Portland so that she could work in "the best library system in the country."

In 1956, economist Charles Tiebout theorized that people would pick and choose among communities to find a desirable array of local services at an acceptable level of taxes. People would look for the best deal and then move. There would be millions of "elections," as people cast their votes for communities with moving vans and apartment leases. According to Tiebout, the sorting would mostly be based on economics, as people sought their own balance between services provided and taxes charged. But he also imagined people making their decisions about where to live based on who would be their neighbors. In a footnote to his classic article "A Pure Theory of Local Expenditures," the economist allowed, "Not only is the consumer-voter concerned with economic patterns, but he desires, for example, to associate with 'nice' people." Whether for low taxes or the right kind of neighbors, people would cast their ballots for a community. They would vote with their feet.[5]

The Big Sort has been a national manifestation of the economist's theory — a post-materialist Tiebout migration based on these non-economic goods, as people have sought out places that best fit their ways of life, their values, and their politics. Because I've been concentrating on a group of comic book artists who moved to a high-tech city that tipped solidly Democratic in the 1990s, it might be easy to think of the Big Sort as a liberal phenomenon. That would be incorrect. The Big Sort has traveled in several political directions. Not everyone who moved in the

1990s was a liberal trying to escape the suburbs for a city of bikes, dark beer, and a Democratic majority. Many more people were moving in another cultural direction, toward Bible studies, big backyards, and Bass Weejuns.

People even took their segregated communities with them on vacation. The Catskills resorts in Sullivan County, New York, displayed a special kind of sorting by lifestyle and religion. Beginning in the late 1800s, Jewish immigrants vacationed in the hotels upstate from New York City.* As that market diminished, in the 1970s the old hotels attracted a more mixed group of patrons: Jews, Italians, and Irish. The resorts integrated socially and ethnically. In the 1980s and 1990s, however, the Sullivan County tourist trade segregated again, only this time into communities of interests and values. The Foundation for *A Course in Miracles* occupied one lake house. There were Hasidic retreats, Hindu retreats, and Christian retreats. One Sullivan County resident told the *New York Times* that the community had come "full circle." Exclusively Jewish resorts had been replaced by a mixture of people, and now, with the faith-based resorts, "it seems like we're back to segregation."[6]

Living in the Niche

Bicyclists and public transportation have an extremely strong political constituency in Portland. A new mayor met with an organization of riders before he sat down with the local business establishment.[7] More than 10,000 bikes cross the four Willamette River bridges each workday, and when REI held a grand opening for a new store downtown, the outdoor equipment company provided valet parking . . . for bicycles.[8] The word got out, and because of Portland's policy decision to promote bicycle riding and public transportation as alternatives to automobiles, the city began attracting a certain type of citizen. Portland's public transportation authority found in a survey that, unlike the situation in most cit-

---

*Similarly, Jewish migrants were attracted to the small village of Bethlehem in northern New Hampshire. The old resort town now has a Jewish film festival in the summer, and two of the five members of the town's board of selectmen are Jewish. See Sarah Schweitzer, "In N.H. Town, a Cultural Widening," *Boston Globe*, June 11, 2007, p. A1.

ies, young, college-educated people in Portland are more likely to ride the city's trains or buses than were their peers with less schooling. In Portland, the probability that a young resident will hop aboard a bus or train rises with years of education. Those who have recently moved to Portland, regardless of age, are more likely to take the train or bus than are natives. Portland economist Joe Cortright's conclusion is that "people who value transit are much more likely to move here than, say, to Phoenix." In Portland, Cortright found, young people with a college degree are more apt to live downtown than in the suburbs. In Phoenix, they have exactly the opposite way of life: they buy houses outside the city and drive in.*

That is the Big Sort. People who move to Portland want good public transportation and city life. People who don't give a hoot about those things migrate to Phoenix, suburban Dallas, south of Minneapolis, or north of Austin. But people don't move to Portland just because of bike trails and metro stops. They are looking for an array of things that make them feel at home. They want to be able to buy certain books, see certain kinds of movies, and listen to particular styles of live music.

Of course, in a strict sense, place no longer limits the availability of goods. People can rent obscure movies through Netflix and buy books at Amazon.com that their local stores can't afford to stock.† Digital technology and cheap transportation have given everyone access to nearly everything, no matter where they live. In the geography of niche markets, however, people can best fill their lives with the stuff or experiences they want only if they live around others with the same tastes.

---

*In Portland, according to Cortright, young people living within three miles of the center of town are more than twice as likely to have a college degree as those living in the suburbs. The same is true in Chicago and New York. In Phoenix, San Antonio, and Las Vegas, the distribution is reversed, with suburban young people being twice as likely to be college educated as their peers in the central city.

†Journalist Chris Anderson described this phenomenon, which he called "the long tail," from the producer's point of view in an article he wrote for *Wired* magazine in 2004. Anderson's metaphor was based on the statistical bell curve. His point was that digital technology, cheap transportation, and the Internet have made it possible and profitable to sell to the smaller markets found on the long tails of the bell curve. Anderson contended that there are huge volumes of sales within these smaller markets. From a consumer's point of view, however, it still makes sense to live around those with similar tastes. See Chris Anderson, "The Long Tail," *Wired*, October 2004, http://www.wired.com/wired/archive/12.10/tail.html.

Those interested in seeing a recently released foreign film or the new documentary on Townes Van Zandt on the big screen need to live in a community that can fill the theater. Similarly, someone who wants to participate in a specialized sport, worship in a less than mainstream church, or catch the latest alt-country acts will be drawn to certain locations. The appeal of the Big Sort is powerful because consumers, believers, and citizens all benefit from living in homogeneous communities.

In an economy of extreme niche markets, location itself becomes a commodity. "There [is] more cultural stuff [in Portland] that I [like] than in Houston, the fourth-largest city in the U.S.," explained Randy Jarrell. "I have access to more bands coming through town, better movie theaters, better bookstores, all that cultural stuff. We get way more limited-release films than if we lived in a comparable-size city in the Midwest." There are also political components to these consumer choices. If a person wants a public job in a town that provides health benefits to domestic partners or schools that teach creation science, he or she will move to a jurisdiction where a majority of the residents favor those kinds of public expenditures. Given these consumer/political demands, Charles Tiebout wouldn't have been at all surprised by the migration of the Big Sort. In the 1990s, people began moving to the places where they could find the amenities — and the politics — that they wanted.

The Density of Division

The picture of exurban America most of us conjure is sunny, hot, and southern. The only thing southern about Scott County, Minnesota, however, is its relationship to Minneapolis. The Sun Belt doesn't have a monopoly on the combination of fast-growing counties and Republican politics. Scott County grew 55 percent in the 1990s. In the first four years of the new century, it was the twelfth-fastest-growing county in the United States and one of seven counties around the Twin Cities that were among the nation's top 100 in growth. After the 2004 presidential election, Ronald Brownstein and Richard Rainey of the *Los Angeles Times* reported that 97 of those counties voted for George W. Bush.[9] Robert Thibodeaux is a young Republican leader in the Scott County town of Savage. Thibodeaux joked that the Bush campaign would ask its volunteers in Savage to identify voters as Republican or Democrat. The flow of people into Scott County was so politically one-sided, the task seemed silly: if you moved to Scott, you were a Republican. Thibodeaux told me, "We'd say, 'Okay, if you live in Scott County, I'm through with voter I.D.'"

People weren't deliberately moving to Scott County or to the exurban counties west of Houston or north of Atlanta because these places had Republican majorities. When you talk to people in Scott County, they describe a kind of longing for space, for countryside, for something manifestly not urban. No one says it — and probably few think about it so starkly — but they also were looking for a white community. Since the 1970s, white people have been moving in disproportionate numbers to the counties that in 2004 voted overwhelmingly for Bush. Scott is whiter than most. Tom Gillespie, Minnesota's state demographer, ticked through the ethnic backgrounds claimed by Scott County residents — Irish, German, Norwegian, English — and before long he tallied 94 percent of the population claiming to have come from Caucasian stock. Even in white Minnesota, Gillespie said, "those are overwhelming numbers."

Robert Thibodeaux grew up in Grapevine, Texas, a small town between Dallas and Fort Worth. He was shocked by a rape and a rash of pregnancies at his high school. He blamed Dallas, which he felt was reaching out to touch his hometown. "There was this creeping big-cityness," Thibodeaux said. When he moved north for work, he decided to distance himself from all things citified.

Those active in the Scott County Republican Party have an anti-urban idealization of rural America. Barbara Lerschen was Scott County Republican Party chair in the 1980s. She moved from the Twin Cities because, she said, you can "breathe the freedom [in this exurban county]. South of here, there are still fields. You can get out, and you're not crowded. In St. Paul, you have people telling you what to do." Ben Adams runs a car stereo shop in Minneapolis but lives in Scott County. He moved there with his wife, a schoolteacher, because "we loved the fact that once you drove south of the [Minnesota] River, you had ten minutes of driving where you had fields on both sides of the road. It was the separation from the Twin Cities . . . that we liked. We're not urban people."

One Republican I met at a GOP get-together in Savage grimaced when he talked about "places you go [in the Twin Cities] where there are a lot of gray, pasty-faced people. I like it here." I brought up the trendy city neighborhood of Uptown in Minneapolis, a place brimming with young people. Nobody was much impressed. "I have real good liberal friends, and that's where they want to be, right there in Uptown," one Scott County Republican said. Wes Mader, a Bush campaign organizer, told me, "A lot of us are fed up with the urban lifestyle. I would not want to see my grandchildren raised in downtown Minneapolis in an environment that is different from the one out here. I want to split my own wood and be less dependent on government." Randy Penrod, a 285-pound rugby player and Scott County's Republican Party chair, said that Republicans and Democrats have a basic difference: "I have a theory that the farther away you are from another human being, the more likely you are to be a Republican."

New York Times columnist David Brooks described the exurbs in his impressionistic 2004 book *On Paradise Drive*. After these fast-growing counties appeared to have reelected Bush that year, there was a mini-burst of research into what the exurbs were all about. The research was never particularly rewarding because nobody could agree on how an exurb differed from a suburb or a rural community. But anyone who has visited the outskirts of a U.S. city recently has seen these communities clinging to the hull of the city, just outside the older suburbs. Bob Cushing and I discovered that in counties where populations were growing fast and where a high percentage of people commuted across county lines to work (two-thirds of Scott County's workers leave the county for their jobs), the 2004 presidential vote was heavily Republican. But it was difficult to single out places that were purely exurban. The best study found that a whopping 6 percent of the people living in large metro areas could be found in an exurb — hardly enough of a vote to be changing the dynamics of presidential elections.[10]

To understand who voted for Bush — and to see how the country was sorting — a more useful calculation is the one proposed by Randy

Penrod: population density. Republicans were moving into places where people lived farther apart; Democrats were clustering in places where people lived closer together. According to political scientist Michael Harrington, the average population density for counties voting for Bush was 108 people per square mile in 2000 and 110 people per square mile in 2004. Counties voting for Al Gore in 2000 averaged 739 people per square mile. Those voting for John Kerry in 2004 averaged 836 people per square mile. "As population density steadily decreases from the urban core to the rural periphery, Mr. Bush's share of the vote increases from 24 percent to more than 60 percent," Harrington wrote.[11] Robert Lang and Thomas Sanchez saw a straight-line relationship between population density and the 2004 vote. "At each greater increment of urban intensity, Democrat John Kerry received a higher proportion of the vote," the two Virginia Tech demographers wrote. "There is a metropolitan political gradient in the big US metro areas: the center tilts to Democrats and the fringe to Republicans."[12] The phenomenon occurred in staunchly blue and red states alike. In Bush's former hometown of Dallas, Kerry came within a percentage point of winning Dallas County, which voted in a Hispanic lesbian as sheriff in the same election. Bush won all of Dallas's suburban counties by at least 40 percentage points. Republicans didn't spend much time looking for votes in downtown Portland, however. The Bush campaign sent workers to precincts in the "farthest reaches of Multnomah County," one Bush organizer told me. They targeted the neighborhoods with the newest mortgages — and the largest expanses of lawn.

Thirty years ago, before the Big Sort, the spatial arrangement of voters was more balanced. In 1976, the average Democratic county in the presidential election had a slightly smaller population than the average Republican county. Over the next two generations, however, people made choices about how and where they wanted to live. Democrats gravitated toward cities. Republicans moved where there was a bit more grass to be mowed. It wasn't the suburban turf that transformed people into Republicans; nor did the city streets turn people Democratic. Instead, the cheek-by-jowl existence of the city attracted a different kind of person than the wide expanses of the exurbs. The change in geography was really a sorting by lifestyle and, ultimately, by political party.

Ideology Comes to Rural America

Doug Breese ranches land his grandfather began piecing together in 1905. Homesteaders who had come to central Oregon realized that they weren't making any money and likely never would, so Breese's granddad was able to pick up land in Crook County at fifty cents an acre. Ranching is a make-do occupation, and ranchers are some of the world's best recyclers. The pipe running water from a spring to the Breese homestead was recovered from San Francisco after the 1906 earthquake. The ranch is now a model of flexible production operating in a world market. Breese points from his pickup window to the pasture where he's experimenting with grass-fed beef. He grew peppermint until the Russians and Brazilians undercut his price by a third. He produced garlic seed one year, sold it for twelve cents a pound, and made money. The Chinese then put garlic seed on the market for two cents a pound. "It's okay," he said, in the best manner of a former president of the Oregon Farm Bureau. "They're learning to produce just like we learned to produce."

We drove down a road between Breese's ranch and the town of Prineville, the county seat. Doug pointed to the spot where the Democrats lost Crook County. Over there, Breeze said, the owner of the county's last sawmill went out of business. "He finally gave up because he couldn't get any wood," Breese explained, pushing back his ANIMAL PHARMACEUTICALS gimme cap. In the mid-1970s, no matter where you went in Oregon, people had good feelings about environmentalists. But after a decade or so of fighting about old-growth forests, spotted owls, and endangered species, rural Oregonians concluded that environmentalists were the enemy — the people who wanted to do away with jobs in counties such as Crook. Some people — in fact, quite a lot of people — argued that Oregon's milling operations were hurt more by markets than by the Endangered Species Act — a bill, Oregon Democrats like to point out, that was signed by Richard Nixon. But there were once six sawmills in Prineville, and now there are none. The perception here is that those environmentalists were people from the city. They wanted to tell rural people how to live — where they could build, what they could cut, and how many guns they could own. And those people doing all the telling were Democrats.

This isn't just the way rural Republicans view Democrats. At the Sandwich Factory in Prineville, Crook Democratic Party chair Steve Bucknum smoothes out a sheet of paper and draws a diagram of a wagon wheel that he says explains the Democrats' troubles in rural America. There are issues that cause problems for rural Democrats, Bucknum says, such as gun control and the Endangered Species Act. These are the spokes in the wheel. Spokes can be replaced, he said. The real difficulty the party has is the hub. "At the center of the wheel is elitism," Bucknum said. "The reason rural people become resentful is that they feel like in every one of these issues, they are being told what to do by someone who claims to know better. And that elitism is seen as Democratic, no matter where it comes from."

Back in Portland, it's easy to see how rural Oregonians might come to think poorly of the city and the Democrats who live there. At the too-cool Jupiter Motel — one of the manifestations of hipness in the new century is the transformation of 1950s and 1960s flophouses into hard-to-book accommodations with concrete floors, low beds, and minimalist decorations — a wonderfully nice woman with two-tone hair and tattoos that began on her fingers and disappeared up her shirtsleeve directed me to the Doug Fir Room. Young people ate off tables made of thick planks of Douglas fir and bought drinks at a sculpted Doug fir bar. They soaked in the romance of Oregon as a timber state while listening to whatever indie surfer rock band was making the rounds. Around Prineville, nobody cuts Doug fir for a living anymore, and there's nothing romantic about ranch work. Doug Breese and his son have spent the past three years pulling rocks from one field. The stones filled a dump truck and rested in piles, and the field still wasn't planted. That's ranching. The Breeses cut juniper and medusahead to keep the pastures clear, and when the stuff grows back, they cut it again. Breese sees endangered species laws protecting trees and birds, but there's no law promising that his ranch will be around for his kids.

Democrat Steve Bucknum is the only registered property appraiser in Crook County, so he meets most of the new people moving in.

Bucknum told me that the old-timers in the County, such as Doug Breese, are different from those who have come here in the past decade. In the early 1990s, good old boys ran the courthouse. The county judge was a rodeo veteran who told ranch stories. Longtime Crook County residents, Bucknum said, were pragmatic about life and politics. After all, there's no such thing as ideological ranching. Between 1995 and 2004, however, the number of Crook County voters registered as Democrats or Republicans jumped by 28 percent. Eight out of ten of those new voters registered as Republicans. In the 1976 presidential election, Crook County cast 55 percent of its votes for Democrat Jimmy Carter, compared to 53 percent of the votes in Portland's Multnomah County. In 2004, however, whereas 73 percent of Multnomah County voted for Kerry, 69 percent of Crook County supported Bush.

These newcomer Republicans are people who wanted out of the city — more by-the-book conservatives rather than brogan Republicans. "The people who grew up here sort of have a laid-back way of talking, and they like things the way they are — they aren't fearful about the world," Bucknum said. "The people who have recently come here, from the Willamette Valley in particular — from Salem, Portland, and Eugene — [who] self-selected to leave those areas, talk about their fears. It's just very concrete. The people who are new to the area are, by and large, motivated by fear. Wrapped up with that are Christian fundamentalism, property rights, and economic theory, and it's more pervasive than political party. It's a worldview."

Chet Peterson runs an insurance office on Prineville's Main Street and helped organize the Bush campaign here in 2004. He's in good shape and sits up straight. He told me the story of Les Schwab, an ambitious kid from the Crook County logging camps who bought a tire-recapping business with borrowed money and became the largest independent tire distributor in the country. Peterson moved here in 1996 and does business with a lot of the newcomers. I asked him where these people are coming from. "They are coming from big cities," he answered. "Big cities are dangerous." They are also debilitating. People who live in cities, Peterson said, "become dependent on what government offers, all the way from mass transit to food stamps." Cities coddle. They make people weak and get them hooked on government. Rural places are filled with pioneers and capitalists, do-it-yourselfers like Les Schwab.

Ted Robinson moved to Crook County from the city and became Republican Party chair. In the Democratic Party, Robinson told me, "anything goes. It's the sixties. But people want to live in a community where they have values, where they aren't going to force gay marriage down your throat. Where you live within your means and people expect you to live up to what you can do."

The Strict Father/Nurturant Parent Divide

Linguist George Lakoff described American society as divided between "two different forms of family-based morality": the "strict father" and the "nurturant parent."[13] The strict father sets rules and exerts authority. Children obey, and by obeying they build character, gain respect for authority, and grow self-reliant. This is Chet Peterson's and Ted Robinson's vision of Crook County and the Scott County Republicans' conception of their almost-rural community. The other moral system, the "nurturant parent," sees love and empathy as paramount in raising a child. Children are to be supported and protected; obedience stems from love and respect, not from fear. The goal of children is to be happy and fulfilled. Welcome to Portland and Austin (Travis Heights). Lakoff argued that these two moral systems essentially distinguished political conservatives (strict fathers) from liberals (nurturant parents).

After the 2004 election, there was a great deal of discussion about whether "moral values" — gay rights, abortion, religious beliefs — drove voters' decisions. Two political scientists, Marc Hetherington and Jonathan Weiler, took another approach. They decided to apply Lakoff's theory and determine whether, at root, the United States was divided by a difference in worldview, one revealed in two styles of child rearing.[14] Hetherington and Weiler looked at data on children's issues gathered by the National Election Studies (NES). In 1992, 2000, and 2004, the large survey conducted through the University of Michigan presented voters with pairs of attributes and asked which of the two were more important for a child to have. Was it better for a child to demonstrate independence or respect for elders? Obedience or self-reliance? Curiosity or good manners? To be considerate or well behaved? Hetherington and Weiler realized that the answers to these four questions fell on either side of Lakoff's strict father/nurturant parent division. Moreover, unlike gay marriage, abortion, gun control, and other issues used to identify values, these questions had some distance from the news of the day. They didn't carry any ideological baggage. The NES's questions asked about traits that were all admirable. Presumably, parents would want their children to be both considerate and well behaved, so these questions elicited more discerning — and revealing — answers. Hetherington and Weiler surmised that the questions exposed underlying views of authority — whether people favored the strict father or the nurturant parent.

Hetherington and Weiler constructed a scale based on the answers to these four questions. Those who picked respect, obedience, good manners, and being well behaved were the most authoritarian, and the researchers counted them as strict fathers. Those who favored independence, self-reliance, curiosity, and being considerate were nurturant parents. Then Hetherington and Weiler tested to see if opinions about child rearing were correlated with political beliefs. They were, and to a striking degree. Republicans favored respect, obedience, good manners, and being well behaved. They were strict fathers. Democrats were nurturant parents.

This splitting of moral perspectives, and its connection to political affiliations, seemed to be something new. Hetherington and Weiler pointed out that before the 1960s, there was little real difference in how Americans raised their children. During the cold war, the political scientists wrote, authoritarian types could be found aplenty in both parties. In the 1960s, there were plenty of strict father Democrats. Over the last generation, however, these two moral syndromes emerged in families and then sorted into Republican and Democrat. In 1992, there was little difference between the parties on the child-rearing scale. By 2000, the differences were distinct, and by 2004 the gap had grown wide and deep. Answers to questions about child rearing, in fact, provided a better gauge of party affiliation than did income.* The parenting scale was also more closely aligned with "moral issues" than political orientation. Knowing whether a person was a nurturant parent or a strict father provided a better guide to his or her thinking about gay rights than knowing whether he or she was a liberal or a conservative, a Republican or a Democrat.

Hetherington and Weiler found that the two parties differed on a cluster of issues revolving around "muscularity." How tough should the nation be in battling terrorists? (When a foreign leader violates international law, Hetherington and Weiler asked, what is our response? Do we send him to "time-out" or do we spank?) Should laws be passed to protect the traditional family, to prosecute flag burners, and to tap the phones of suspected terrorists? The answers to these questions divided strict fathers from nurturant parents. The child-rearing scale also helped explain the steady migration of the white working class away from the Democratic Party. It showed that Evangelicals were largely strict fathers. And in 2004, voters who had attended graduate school had a strict father score on the four-question survey that was only half that of voters who hadn't graduated from high school. "Little wonder our politics today are polarized," Hetherington and Weiler concluded. "The values of Republicans and Democrats are very much at odds. We do not agree about the most fundamental of issues."[15]

In 1974, the division in the Kanawha County school textbook fight (see chapter 5) was between those who believed that salvation was the most important value and those who sought beauty. In the mid-1990s, George Lakoff defined strict fathers and nurturant parents. On the first Tuesday in November, these divisions are given another set of labels: Republicans and Democrats.

Living on Islands

Political scientist Daniel Elazar traced the political development of the United States by the early flows of migrants moving east to west. As peo-

---

*Minorities were an exception to this alignment; they were likely to be both strict fathers and Democrats.

ple migrated, they brought their politics with them, setting down their beliefs with their trunks and suitcases. In the early days of the frontier, like-minded people traveled together, and when they settled, they created political cultures that spread across regions of the country. A few years before his death in 1999, however, Elazar noticed the emergence of "lifestyle" communities. He suspected that these communities heralded a "new sectionalism." The aging political scientist optimistically believed that the emergence of like-minded communities would "encourage recrudescence of the kind of territorial democracy that potentially allows different lifestyles to flourish in different places without clashing."[16] Elazar was referring to life in nineteenth-century America, when communities were narrowly defined and isolated. At that time, the rich in one city intermarried, according to historian Robert Wiebe, never knowing, or caring to know, their contemporaries in other urban areas. "Within the city limits yet detached from its core, neighborhoods provided fairly cloistered way stations between urban and rural living," Wiebe wrote. Farm communities were "usually homogeneous, usually Protestant . . . In all, it was a nation of loosely connected islands, similar in kind, whose restless natives often moved only to settle down again as part of another island."[17]

The physical barriers of frontier life may have helped create these nineteenth-century islands, but the segmentation of community life in the last quarter of the twentieth-century was manmade, a reaction, perhaps, to the fast-paced, wild, and woolly changes taking place in the nation and the world. "When people find themselves unable to control the world, they simply shrink the world to the size of their community," observed sociologist Manuel Castells.[18] Sociologist Craig Calhoun described the growth of "enclaves of people who have made similar lifestyle choices. These life-style enclaves — especially suburban and exurban ones — are characterized by an extraordinary homophilia (primarily in non-sexual senses)."[19]

There is a market demand now for "lifestyle" communities. Before developers built the Ladera Ranch subdivision in Orange County, California, they surveyed likely residents about their beliefs and values. The surveys asked how strongly people agreed with statements such as "We need to treat the planet as a living system" and "I have been born again in Jesus Christ." People fell into distinct groups — and that's the way the development was built. There is "Covenant Hills" for the faithful (big family rooms and traditional suburban architecture) and "Terramor" for what the developers call the "cultural creatives" (bamboo floors and instead of a family room, a "culture room").*20 (Cultural creatives? Yes, Paul Ray, one of the authors of the 2000 book *The Cultural Creatives,* was a consultant for Ladera Ranch.) There is a Christian school for the believers in Covenant Hills and a Montessori school for the "cultural creatives" in Terramor. More than 16,000 people live in the subdivision now, and what's vaguely creepy (well, maybe not so vaguely) is that people drive in the same entrance and then split off into neighborhoods designed for different lifestyles and values — the twenty-first-century version of nineteenth-century "island communities."

We have come to expect living arrangements that don't challenge our cultural expectations. Responding to the demands of students, colleges offer "thematic housing." Two residence halls at Brandeis University are set aside for those interested in "Justice, Service & Change." Colgate has a foreign film dorm. Union College has a residence based on recycling and the environment. Wesleyan University has twenty-eight thematic dorms, including one for "eclectic" students. Kids have grown up in neighborhoods of like-mindedness, so homogeneous groups are considered normal. "The guys on my floor were respectful, but they weren't the kind of people I hang around with — they were jocks," one Brandeis student told the *Boston Globe.* Then he added, "It was hard to find balance."†21

It's not just lifestyle that differs by subdivision. There's now a geography of family structures and mores as the meaning of family changes from place to place. Beginning in the 1960s, there was a shift in how some people formed households and raised families. Women married

---

*The names of these lifestyle subdivisions leave nothing to doubt. The *Washington Post* reported similar lifestyle subdivisions in northern Virginia. "Dominion Valley" has golf and white columns; "Brambleton" has high-speed Internet connections and a patchouli-scented slogan, "Connect with life" (McCrummen, "Redefining Property Values," p. A1).

†Some colleges refuse to allow these kinds of segregated living arrangements. Williams College permits "no special interest housing." A Williams spokesman said, "The belief is that students will interact more with people who are different from them if their residence hall isn't segregated" (Schweitzer, "Like Recycling?").

when they were older, and if they had children, they had them later. The link between marriage and procreation shattered as more people lived together without getting married and more children were born out of wedlock. Reproduction fell well below the level of replacement. An increasing number of people lived as singles, and when a spouse died or a couple divorced, fewer people married again. The Belgian demographer Ron Lesthaeghe saw that this new demographic combination was tied to changing attitudes about life.* The people in these changing, more fluid families were less concerned with traditional institutions, such as old-line church denominations (Episcopalian, Catholic) and civic clubs (Masons, Rotary). Gender roles were getting squishy, and people forgot to get married. They were less interested in material success and more interested in experiences and individual freedoms.[22]

Lesthaeghe and his colleagues discovered Ronald Inglehart's post-materialism manifested in how people formed families (or not) and had children (or not). Moreover, this new kind of family had a geography. Lesthaeghe could see that nontraditional families were most prevalent in western Europe, particularly in the Low Countries. (The Dutch had the largest percentage of people in this demographic group.)

When Lesthaeghe mapped these trends in the United States, he saw that by 2000, white women in Massachusetts, Connecticut, and New Jersey were marrying and having children in ways that matched their cohort in western Europe. White women in New York, Rhode Island, California, Maryland, Illinois, Minnesota, New Hampshire, and Delaware weren't far behind. In these states, a greater proportion of people were living together without marrying than in the rest of the United States. Women had babies later, if they had children at all. People married later,

---

*Lesthaeghe and those working in this field called the change in families that took place as the economy switched from farms to factories in the late nineteenth and early twentieth centuries the "first demographic transition." The change he saw beginning in the 1960s was tied to the gradual decline of industry and the rise of service employment. Lesthaeghe called this the "second demographic transition." The change was gradual, of course, but it is interesting that in the unraveling year of 1965, the *New York Times* announced in a front-page story that the "shift in the nation's employment from goods manufacturing to services has become so pronounced that it is no longer correct to call the United States economy an 'industrial economy.' It is a 'service economy.'" The number of people making tangible goods had begun declining in 1953. By 1965, fewer than half of the nation's workers (45 percent) were employed making, mining, or harvesting (*New York Times*, June 28, 1965, p. A1).

and if they divorced, they often didn't remarry. It struck Lesthaeghe that the states that were the most like western Europe in terms of family formation were also the most Democratic in recent U.S. presidential elections. Comparing his measures of family formation and the 2004 presidential results, Lesthaeghe said that he "could find no better way to predict the vote for Bush" in 2004 than these demographic measures. Then Lesthaeghe checked at the county level. The effect lessened slightly, but again western European, Dutch-like family styles essentially predicted a hefty Democratic vote. In counties where people voted in waves for Bush, fewer couples had ever lived together before marriage, and women married and had children at a younger age.

By 2004, Americans had divided into communities with different family structures and, even more basic, with different understandings of the phases of life: At what age did people marry, if they married at all? How old were they when they had children, if they bore children at all? Family types had segregated in the same way the country's politics had segregated. Lesthaeghe would say in *exactly* the same way.

Back to the Horde

One of the fundamental questions of sociology asks how societies are held together. Émile Durkheim, a founder of modern sociology, wrote near the end of the nineteenth century about a change in the way societies were glued together. Preindustrial peoples were united in "mechanical solidarity," according to Durkheim. Everyone did the same work and had the same beliefs. They were interchangeable. Durkheim described the members of these traditional societies as "repetitions . . . rather like the rings of an earthworm," and called this grouping a "horde."[23] In television parlance, these societies were somewhat like the Borg, the race flying about in cube-shaped spacecraft in the series *Star Trek: The Next Generation*. The Borg's power is that every individual member contains all the knowledge, skills, and morality of the whole. New members are "assimilated" into the Borg collective with brutal and total efficacy. (As the Borg say, "Resistance is futile.")

Mechanical solidarity is complete with the Borg in a way that could never be found outside television. But recall that Americans lived on

Borg-like "islands" in the nineteenth century, the isolated towns circumscribed by shared work, a common church, and traditional families. Industrial society flooded these islands, and the division of labor in modern mass production systems separated people. They no longer lived according to tradition or lineage, but by their place in the labor market. According to Durkheim, industrial society was held together through "organic solidarity," the interdependence of people through an economic system based on the division of labor. The glue that would bond society, he predicted, would be an industrial economy built on workplace specialization that demanded connection and cooperation among occupations.[24]

The new system uprooted a way of life that had existed for centuries. Industrial society stripped away old boundaries and gave people unprecedented freedom from tradition. The problem with this new mode of life, Durkheim wrote, was that "unlimited desires are insatiable by definition and insatiability is rightly considered a sign of morbidity."[25] Durkheim called the sense of emptiness and disorientation brought on by industrial life "anomie" and he traced its effects in rising rates of suicide. Durkheim believed that anomie would be quelled as modern workplace structures took the place of the Borg-like village. The corporation would be the institutional structure that would provide people with a common purpose, what Daniel Bell described as a "sense of kindredness" through work.[26] The interdependence required in the modern workplace would replace the sense of place and belonging found in the totality of the village.

The past half century tells a different story. As we've lost trust in traditional institutions, the tenuous bonds of the workplace have proved insufficient to satisfy people's need for belonging. In response, we have found ways to re-create Durkheim's "mechanical solidarity" in increasingly like-minded neighborhoods, churches, social clubs, and voluntary organizations. "People want to associate or form communities with others who share the same values," J. Walker Smith, president of the market research firm Yankelovich Partners, told me. "The reassurance that people find in more homogeneous, like-minded communities may be one sort of psychological response to the anxiety of living in a broader social and political environment that is increasingly riven with scandals and betrayals of faith." Americans lost their sense of a nation by accident in the sweeping economic and cultural shifts that took place after the mid-1960s. And by instinct they have sought out modern-day recreations of the nineteenth-century "island communities" in where and how they live. "Do people fundamentally end up going to live where people who look like them live?" asked G. Evans Witt, CEO of Princeton Survey Research Associates. "Yes, pretty much. But it's not look, it's act like them, think like them."

Americans still depend on organic solidarity in their economic lives, in their mixed and mixed-up workplaces. But in their social, religious, and political lives, they are seeking ways to rejoin the horde.

Part IV

THE POLITICS
OF PEOPLE
LIKE US

10

CHOOSING A SIDE

THE RIGHT WING may or may not be conspiratorial, but it is certainly vast. The ballroom at the Gaylord Texan hotel, a continent-size resort near the Dallas airport, holds just over 7,000, and in the summer of 2005, it was packed with mostly Republican state legislators, staff, lobbyists, and representatives from the Fortune 500, the Russell 1000, and, it seemed, half the businesses found in the Dallas yellow pages, all trampling over the gold and maroon carpet decorated with massive woven belt buckles, Stetsons as big as Pontiacs, and longhorns that stretched twenty yards tip to tip — a rug clearly ordered from the J. R. Ewing Collection.

At that time, there were about 7,500 state legislators in the United States. Some 2,000 of them were there for the thirty-second annual meeting of the American Legislative Exchange Council (ALEC). President George W. Bush addressed the crowd from a riser set between jumbo screens that later listed the event's sponsors: Boone Pickens, Exxon, Peabody Energy, Pfizer, R. J. Reynolds, and the National Association of Home Builders. Nothing is really hidden about this joint venture of legislators and industry. The organization's budget ($6 million in 2003) is funded primarily by corporations who "pay to play" on ALEC's committees. And the committees, made up of legislators and representatives of business, write "model" legislation for state governments.[1] Former House Speaker Newt Gingrich was a featured speaker at this convention, and so was a representative of the association of shopping mall owners.

ALEC might be considered a trade association for conservative state legislators. There was a more nonideological association of state legislators before ALEC was formed in 1973, but a small number of conservatives thought the National Conference of State Legislatures (NCSL, that organization's name today) was a prop for big government, an association for "bureaucrats" rather than lawmakers and their partners in business. Representative Harold Brubaker, former Speaker of the North Carolina assembly, said that he attended one NCSL meeting in 1980 but never went back. "I just felt more at home at ALEC," Brubaker told me. "I was around legislators who had the same philosophy as I had on running government." There may have been Democrats there at the Gaylord, but they were scarce. Tax-cutting conservative activist Grover Norquist asked during his talk if anyone in the crowd was from Massachusetts. The question elicited some chuckles but no raised hands. (In contrast, forty-six of forty-nine members of the Nebraska legislature were ALEC members in 2003.)[2]

ALEC is the new way of doing politics — new, at least, in the past three decades. It's the politics of people like us, of segmentation, of the Big Sort, and it's changed the nature of American public life. In homogeneous voting districts, politicians have drifted to extremes, changing the nature of elections and even the type of person who will run for office. With a dwindling number of moderates, Congress has balkanized, enduring nearly four decades of what one legislative scholar described as "stalemate," with little new in policy or government action.[3] Meanwhile, in states and cities where the Big Sort has resulted in increasingly large majorities, there has been an explosion of innovation and legislation. Federal leadership has been replaced by a wild display of federalism, as like-minded communities put their beliefs into law.

"Advocacy Funding" — Left and Right

An ALEC convention is conservatism presented with the variety of the dessert table at a chamber of commerce banquet. In one room at the

2005 convention, delegates discussed how American conservatives can work with flat-tax, small-government activists in the states emerging from the old Soviet Union. In another, a Wal-Mart representative spoke about the union-funded campaign against his company. One PowerPoint slide advised the assembled legislators, "The target is WMT [Wal-Mart] for now. The real target is you." Representative Tom Feeney, a Florida Republican, warned of U.S. Supreme Court justices who were "importing foreign laws and social mores" by citing statutes from other countries. These judges "fancy themselves as participants in some kind of international elite," Feeney said. Elsewhere, Thomas Borelli of Action Fund Management announced "the left has begun to take over corporations." It was, in fact, a "liberal dream" to sever the corporation from policy debates, Borelli said, and to "have a company lobby for [their] social agenda."

ALEC is a character in the story liberals tell about the synchronized, centrally planned effort to bring conservatives to power. A Democratic-leaning report called ALEC corporate America's "Trojan horse," referring to the way business has bought its way into fifty statehouses.[4] Right-wing impresario Paul Weyrich (the man who came up with the "moral majority") founded ALEC, according to investigations by the People for the American Way, the Defenders of Wildlife, and the Natural Resources Defense Council. That Weyrich had conceived ALEC was further proof of the alleged conspiracy's encompassing genius. By the 1990s, ALEC had become the "voice of corporate America in the states."[5]

The story ALEC members tell of the organization's founding is somewhat less awe-inspiring. Mark Rhoads was working for a member of the Illinois senate in 1973 when he proposed a "caucus for conservative lawmakers with a conservative staff." Rhoads called this new outfit the Conservative Caucus of State Legislators, switching to the American Legislative Exchange Council after consulting with other activists. "Times were different in 1973," Rhoads told me. The word "conservative" wasn't a particularly good draw. Conservatives at the time felt powerless. In the late 1960s and early 1970s, every institution appeared to be under the dominion of big-government types — the foundations, the mainline denominations, Congress, the existing organization of state legislators. Even a Republican president seemed against them. Much of the impetus to create ALEC came from the right's disappointment with Richard Nixon. The size of the federal government had exploded under Johnson, and then it continued to expand under Nixon, said Duane Parde, ALEC's executive director. Nixon created the Environmental Protection Agency and instituted wage and price controls. "ALEC was really started to counter that, at least on the state level," Parde told me during the 2005 convention. The original founders weren't movement conservatives based in Washington, D.C. Weyrich provided a room for an early meeting, Rhoads and Parde said, but not much more. ALEC was the creation of a patched-together cadre of midwestern state legislators who discovered their mutual distrust of Washington.

ALEC is one of several conservative organizations that evolved in the early 1970s. The Heritage Foundation opened in 1973, supported by the John M. Olin Foundation.[6] Other foundations joined the fun — Scaife and Bradley. Associations sprang up: the Federalist Society and the Manhattan Institute for Policy Research. The only thing surprising about this growth of conservative organizations is that anyone would be surprised that it happened. The strategy followed by political conservatives in the 1960s and 1970s — after Barry Goldwater's defeat in 1964, the Great Society, and Watergate — was the same as that adopted by Christian conservatives after the humiliation of the Scopes trial in 1925. Shut out of the mainline denominations and the established divinity schools, fundamentalists built their own social institutions: schools, printing presses, church organizations, and broadcasting outlets. Political conservatives felt that they were adrift, ignored by what they perceived as liberal foundations (Ford, Rockefeller, Carnegie), by established think tanks (the Brookings Institution), and by their own president (Nixon).

Conservatives weren't the first to fund ideological organizations. Liberal foundations were "pioneers in social movement and advocacy funding" in the 1960s and 1970s, according to sociologist Theda Skocpol.[7] McGeorge Bundy at the Ford Foundation promoted philanthropy to support social activism, and grants from foundations helped create the infrastructure of the American left, the Environmental Defense Fund, the Natural Resources Defense Council, and the Mexican American

Legal Defense and Education Fund.[8] In response to these initiatives from the left — and to the backsliding of Republican leaders in Washington — conservatives organized their own foundations and think tanks, and they nurtured their own organizations and leaders. Mark Rhoads said there was talk at the time of building a "shadow society." But what else were they supposed to do? Conservatives were literally starting from scratch after World War II.*

But conservatives were rebuilding just when America's civic life was about to shift.

From the Eastern Star to Common Cause

America in the 1950s was brimming with broadly based, locally rooted civic organizations. There was the AFL-CIO, the nation's largest membership organization, and the Free Masons, PTA, American Legion, United Methodist Women, Farm Bureau, and Order of the Eastern Star. Many of these organizations were segregated by race or gender, but they were all rooted in local chapters, and they all included people across lines of class, occupation, and political party. Civic organizations at the time copied the federal system, with chapters and members who elected local, state, and national officers. The kind women of the Eastern Star learned the fundamentals of self-government, and they held dinners, as they did in my former hometown of Smithville, Texas. The bank president would attend those dinners; so would the women from the school lunchroom and the guys from the volunteer fire department. Organizations such as the Eastern Star were political in that they represented their members in state and national capitals. They were democratic training grounds, where people learned to hold meetings, run for office, stage elections, give speeches, and wield power. Mass membership organizations that cut across lines of class, occupation, and religion occasionally produced unpredictable political results. Theda Skocpol, in

---

*In his history of the conservative movement, George H. Nash wrote, "In 1945 no articulate, coordinated, self-consciously conservative intellectual force existed in the United States" (*The Conservative Intellectual Movement in America Since 1945* [New York: Basic Books, 1976], p. xiii).

Diminished Democracy, her study of civic life, pointed out that the normally conservative American Legion lobbied in the 1940s for the GI Bill, one of the most successful big-government social programs of the last century.

Skocpol discovered how these American civic organizations changed, starting at the time of the 1965 unraveling. Quite suddenly in the mid-1960s, Skocpol wrote, "old-line membership federations were no longer where the action was." Membership in broad-based, cross-class, fraternal and veterans groups plummeted in the late 1960s and early 1970s and "civic life was abruptly and fundamentally reorganized."[9] The Elks, Masons, and Eastern Star were replaced by an avalanche of advocacy. The new groups weren't broad based, and they weren't democratically controlled. They were run from the top and organized around policies or issues. They weren't for fraternization; these new groups had agendas. John Gardner started Common Cause in 1970, and the organization has been lobbying for campaign finance reform and open government since. Marian Wright Edelman moved to Washington, D.C., in the late 1960s to lobby for Mississippi's Head Start program. By 1973 — the same year conservative midwestern legislators met to begin ALEC — she had raised the money to begin the Children's Defense Fund.

There wasn't a conspiracy by the left or the right. The breakdown of broad-based organizations was taking place throughout American society. Political parties and mainline religious denominations both lost membership at the same time people quit the Free Masons and the Eastern Star, the United Methodist Women and the Lions.* Broad-based groups declined and were replaced by associations of narrow ideological intents. This shift fit the Big Sort pattern. As Americans divided physically and spiritually into communities of interest, they divided into civic groups of interest, too. It wasn't a plot. Americans were simply constructing organizations in their own images.

---

*The shift wasn't due entirely to a change in generations. Philip Converse found that the decline in partisanship spanned all age groups (*The Dynamics of Party Support,* p. 59). Skocpol wrote that the "great civic transformation of our time happened too abruptly to be attributable primarily to incremental processes of generational replacement" (*Diminished Democracy,* p. 175).

"Their Own Echo Chambers"

In 2001, Katrina vanden Heuvel, editor of the liberal magazine the *Nation,* wrote, "We need to build an ALEC for our side."[10] Michelle Goldberg traced how conservative groups created their own reality through self-reinforcing reports and radio broadcasts in *Kingdom Coming,* her book on the religious right. As the antidote, Goldberg wrote, "liberals need to create their own echo chambers to refute these kinds of distortions."[11] Internet bloggers Jerome Armstrong and Markos Moulitsas Zuniga wrote admiringly about the "network of conservative organizations promoting and coordinating their efforts." That strategy was brilliant, according to Zuniga and Armstrong. Liberals shouldn't condemn what the Republicans had done. These founders of the websites Daily Kos and MyDD suggested that Democrats should create something just like it — a "vast left-wing conspiracy." Democrats needed candidates adept at "market segmentation," "micro-targeting," and "data mining."[12] Writer Bill McKibben wrote that Armstrong, Kos, and the people of the "Net Left" were "all about winning. That's what animates the on-line activists . . . The issues aren't secondary, exactly, but there's a clear consensus that worrying about the fine points of policy is an empty exercise without real power, and that power comes from party unity."[13]

Party unity brings with it other things. Conformity, secrecy, and obedience spring to mind, as does the segregated politics now at large in the country. But nobody stopped to think through the consequences of what was happening. Everyone was too busy setting up parallel institutions in an arms race of political organization building. In 2003, liberals created ALICE, the anti-ALEC American Legislative Issue Campaign Exchange; now every state legislator could meet with lawmakers from other states and be ideologically "at home." Liberals created think tanks in states to match white papers with think tanks established by the conservative State Policy Network. Pro–stem cell research groups battled anti–stem cell groups. The National Center for Science Education, founded in 1981, set out to defend "the teaching of evolution in public schools." Its conservative doppelganger was the Discovery Institute, founded in 1990 to promote the teaching of "intelligent design" as an alternative to evolution.* Republican lawyers had the Federalist Society; Democrats had the American Constitution Society. The American Civil Liberties Union (ACLU) was countered by the anti-ACLU American Center for Law and Justice. EMILY's List raised money for pro-choice women candidates; the Susan B. Anthony List did the same for anti-abortion women candidates. The Club for Growth doused conservative candidates with contributions, so unions and left-leaning bloggers created They Work for Us in early 2007. There are liberal summer camps and conservative summer camps to prepare the next generation of ideological warriors — and now even Conservapedia for those who find Wikipedia too liberal.[14]

In 2003, Rob Stein began showing his PowerPoint presentation "The Conservative Message Machine's Money Matrix." The former Clinton administration official's slide show was a history of modern conservatism, an architectural diagram of the social and political infrastructure conservatives had created beginning in the 1970s.[15] In mid-2005, at least eighty rich liberals inspired by Stein's presentation pledged $1 million each to pay for a Democratic mirror of the conservative system. The Democracy Alliance set a goal of raising $200 million to develop left-leaning institutions to counterbalance the think tanks and leadership groups on the other end of the ideological seesaw.[16]

And so the circle was complete. The left raised money to create a political infrastructure to counter foundations on the right that created a political infrastructure to counter a political infrastructure created by foundations on the left. The left scrambled to match a conspiracy by the right, which began when the right attempted to better a strategy of "advocacy philanthropy" that liberals had pioneered.

Politics of the Centrifuge

In the spring of 2005, I wandered to a downtown Austin hotel to attend the Southwest Landowner Conference. This was a rancher crowd. The men's footwear was heavy on dogger heels and exotic hides: ostrich,

---

*The Discovery Institute funded $3.6 million in research between 1996 and 2005. See Jodi Wilgoren, "Politicized Scholars Put Evolution on the Defensive," *New York Times*, August 21, 2005.

snake, and gator. The median facial hair was the handlebar mustache. The women worked their needlepoint while the men adjusted their hearing aids and squinted at maps projected at the front of the room. The spirit was western friendly and bighearted. These people came from Sonora, Fort Davis, and Cortez because they wanted to learn, as one speaker put it, "how private property is being abolished in America."

Many rural landowners worry about the effects of laws such as the Endangered Species Act and federal regulations preserving wetlands. The landowner conference went beyond a simple mistrust of an intrusive government, however. Perceived threats were coming from all over — the United Nations, the Kyoto Protocol, activist judges, advocates of "sustainable development," and the Nature Conservancy. The environmentalists' demand for "open space," said a speaker, was "one small step toward a larger agenda," which was, we learned, the end of private property. "They will eventually take your land," said Michael Coffman, a former manager for a paper company. The aim was socialism, he said, and the force driving the anti-landowner movement was theological. The UN protocols and the environmentalists' agenda, Coffman said, sprang from a "pantheistic" faith, "the belief that nature is God . . . and must be protected from the use and abuse of man."*

After Coffman's speech, a man from Oregon stood up and told the crowd that in his state, "we have linked the Christian movement with the property rights movement." I later asked the gentleman what he meant, and he pulled out the voting results from two referenda on the Oregon ballot in November 2004. One prohibited gay unions. The other extended the rights of property owners against certain types of zoning. He spread out sheaves of county-by-county voting totals and pointed to the "yes" votes for the two proposals. "Those people and those people," he said, stubbing a finger at those who voted for both measures, "are the same."

This isn't a story about paranoia among western cattlemen. (When these landowners fret about the end of private property, they sound positively carefree compared to those on the left who believe that the attacks on 9/11 were coordinated by the federal government and that the collapse of the World Trade Center towers was caused by explosives set by

*One bumper sticker I see in my neighborhood actually states, NATURE IS GOD.

order of the president.) The ranchers represent a general American phenomenon. Over the past thirty years, Democrats and Republicans have
come to disagree about more and more issues. In the 1970s, there was
little difference between Democrats and Republicans on issues such
as abortion, school prayer, and women's rights, according to Thomas
Carsey and Geoffrey Layman, the two political scientists who have done
the most work in this area.[17] Now the two parties differ on everything —
not only abortion and school prayer but also the war in Iraq, who should
be on the Supreme Court, even Wal-Mart's business practices.

In traditional political science theory, as parties take opposing sides
on new issues, older disagreements tend to disappear. Fresh conflicts
take the place of older, staler divisions. According to this theory, the rise
of cultural issues in the 1970s should have displaced the economic differences that divided the parties in the 1930s or the civil rights and social
welfare divisions that emerged in the 1960s. But these long-standing issues didn't go away. Republicans and Democrats still cling to the opposite sides of economic matters (such as the minimum wage) and civil
rights, differences that have existed for generations. Instead of displac-
ing the old issues, the new cultural issues were added on. The differences between the parties now include economics (tax cuts, health
care), race (social welfare), the environment (global warming), and the
array of issues that fall under the general heading of "culture": abortion,
gay rights, women's rights, and school prayer. Layman and Carsey have
shown through their analysis of survey data that the conflict between
the parties has been extended. The differences between the parties are
particularly acute among party activists. Carsey and Layman have found
that Republican Party activists have grown more conservative than Democratic activists have grown more liberal, a discovery in line with Jacob
Hacker and Paul Pierson's findings in *Off Center: The Republican Revolution and the Erosion of American Democracy*. Hacker and Pierson argued that while both parties have become less moderate, polarization
has been "unequal," that Republicans have moved more to the right
than Democrats have edged to the left.*[18] That advantage, if one can

---

*It's important to note the timing of these political changes. Hacker and Pierson marked the
change in the Republican Party as taking off in 1975 (*Off Center*, p. 26) — the same time Americans began to sort racially, educationally, religiously, and politically.

call it that, in Republican extremism may be temporary. Layman and Carsey have found that newer activists from both parties are more polarized than older party stalwarts.

People certainly change parties when their beliefs conflict with party platforms or leaders. But Layman and Carsey have found the opposite happening as well. People are changing their minds to align with their parties' positions. "Even on issues as divisive and emotion-laden as abortion and racial equality," they wrote, "there is evidence of individuals bringing their attitudes into line with their party ties."[19] People don't methodically take an inventory of their political beliefs and then cast about for the political party that best matches their ideology. Carsey and Layman have found that people at times change their beliefs to conform to the positions of their party. "When party leaders, candidates, and platforms take distinct stands on these issues, it signals to citizens which views on these issues go with each party," Layman and Carsey wrote. "This creates pressure for citizens to bring their party identification and views on these issues closer together."[20] Party membership is not simply an affiliation. It's a screen that filters and shapes the way people perceive the world. Again, politics is working both top-down, as people pick up and follow signals from party activists, and bottom-up, as growing majorities in legislative districts push elected officials to the extremes.

In the early 1990s, Bill Bellamy, a Republican county commissioner in Jefferson County, Oregon, began to see a change in the way his constituents posed questions. They were linking issues. People would ask Bellamy about property rights, and once he'd answered, they would then assume that they knew his views on abortion, taxes, and gun control. "The interesting thing is because of my position on land use, they didn't have to ask me about the others," Bellamy told me. "The religious right has gotten very good about asking questions other than the direct one. If they ask[ed] you about land use and property rights, they would walk away feeling very comfortable about what your position was about abortion and gun control, without you having to say what it is."

No wonder the ranchers at the Southwest Landowner Conference saw a connection between the United Nations, private property rights, gay marriage, and party politics. They *were* connected. Over the past thirty years, the parties have cultivated more areas of disagreement, and people

have allied themselves more tightly with their parties, either by changing parties or by changing their minds. As new issues have cropped up
— the war in Iraq, telephone spying by the government, a Spanish version of the national anthem — Americans have divided neatly by party.
And all this has taken place as people have sorted themselves into more
like-minded churches and communities, all social networks that tend to
enforce uniformity of beliefs. In 1972, the democratic theorist Robert A.
Dahl warned that a sign of extreme political polarization was when two
sides "posed two alternative ways of life, two kinds of society, two visions
of man's fate and man's hope."[21] Today the division in the country isn't
about party allegiance. It's about how we choose to live. And as the parties have come to represent lifestyle — and as lifestyle has defined communities — everything seems divisible, Republican or Democratic.

- The top-ten-grossing theaters for Michael Moore's film *Fahrenheit
9/11* were all in heavily Democratic cities: Los Angeles, New York,
Seattle, and San Francisco. The best theaters for Mel Gibson's *The
Passion of the Christ* were in deeply Republican Mesquite, Texas;
Houston; Morrow, Georgia; and Orange, California.*[22]
- Republicans withdrew from a thirty-seven-year-old Capitol Hill
softball league for Senate and House staff members in 2006 because they claimed that the Democratic commissioner of the league
had introduced a "socialist" playoff system. Republicans charged
that the new system favored teams with poor records. One Republican staffer wrote in an e-mail message: "The commissioner has a
long-standing policy of punishing success and rewarding failure.
He's a Democrat. Waddya' expect?"[23]
- Seven out of ten conservative Republicans think Wal-Mart has a
good effect on the country, but only four out of ten liberal Democrats agree.[24] By August 2006, six Democratic presidential candidates had appeared at anti–Wal-Mart rallies.[25]
- Democrats flock to taverns in local chapters of Drinking Liberally,
an organization that "gives like-minded, left-leaning individuals a

---

*The best theater for both films, however, was the Empire 25 venue in New York City's Times
Square.

place to talk politics." On the other hand, there is a "Christian alternative to yoga." Scores of people have been trained to teach PraiseMoves, a combination of "deep stretching, gentle movement and *strong* Scripture."

- Democrats are more protective of plant life than Republicans (who are more apt to restrict their environmental concerns to the impact on fur-bearing creatures). Democrats more than Republicans say that laws ought to be passed to limit consumption of natural resources — especially by the rich.[26]

- In a poll taken eight days after Hurricane Katrina hit the Gulf Coast, three-quarters of Democrats said that the reaction by federal authorities had been fair or poor. Nearly two-thirds of Republicans said that the federal response had been good or excellent.[27]

- In the spring of 2006, just days after *USA Today* revealed that the National Security Agency had been collecting phone records of U.S. citizens, 73 percent of Democrats said that this was an invasion of people's privacy, while 69 percent of Republicans said that it was a necessary tool to fight terrorism.[28]

- The Cook County, Illinois, Republican Party felt the need to take a position on junk food. In 2006, it sent out a news release asking the media to attend a book signing by *Fast Food Nation* author Eric Schlosser and to "ask a challenging question or two."[29]

- Just days before the 2006 midterm elections, the Pew Research Center released a poll finding a "vast divide" between Democrats and Republicans. The poll confirmed that only 10 percent of the public was truly independent. Seven out of ten Republicans said that the economy was doing just fine. Three-quarters of Democrats said the opposite. Six out of ten Republicans said that the war in Iraq was going at least fairly well. Eight out of ten Democrats thought that the war was going poorly. Democrats and Republicans, Pew found, "see the world quite differently."[30]

Minnesota Not-So-Nice

"Hey, Sheila, it's time for you to be a true independent." With that, Minnesota senate minority leader Dick Day told state senator Sheila Kiscaden that she would have to vacate her office, the one she had shared for twelve years with other Republican state senators. Day called a sergeant at arms, and Kiscaden was escorted out of her office and out of the Republican Party.

Kiscaden recounted the story as she slid a pan of bran muffins from the oven at her house in Rochester, Minnesota. There's butter, thick coffee, and a conversation about how a three-term state senator could be ushered from her office because she failed to color within the lines prescribed by the Republican Party. In today's politics, Kiscaden is an unlikely Republican. She's a former board member of Planned Parenthood. A book by liberal theologian Jim Wallis rests under her reading lamp. In 1994, she voted to protect gay, lesbian, and transsexual state employees from discrimination. She is pro-choice and is open to the idea of gun control.

Kiscaden ran as a Republican for the state senate in 1992 for what is now an old-fashioned reason. Democrats "weren't being fiscally responsible," she said. But Republican Party ideology was narrowing, soon to the exclusion of mere fiscal conservatives. In Minnesota, where local conventions make party endorsements, several right-wing groups banded together against Kiscaden. After ten years of her moderate partisanship, they'd had enough. In 2002, the National Rifle Association (NRA) and a conservative education organization jammed the local nominating caucus in Rochester. "I went to the endorsing convention, and the gun guys were out," Kiscaden recalled. "Some came up and said, 'We gotcha. We've got rid of you.'"

They nearly did. The Republican Party successfully denied Kiscaden an endorsement and an automatic place on the ballot. She acknowledged that she wasn't alone; these purges had been taking place all over the state. The party had rejected moderate Republican state senator Martha Robertson two years earlier, replacing her with a conservative football coach. Twice censured by his local party for supporting gay rights and statewide education standards, state senator Dean Johnson, a Lutheran minister and National Guard chaplain, left the Republican Party in 2000 after two decades in office.[31] It wasn't simply district-level extremists who were eager to purify the Minnesota GOP. It was the state party's leaders. The Republican executive committee said that it would withhold funds from the local party organizations if they nomi-nated either Kiscaden or Robertson. Kiscaden ran in 2002 as a member of the Independence Party and won. She caucused with Republicans until 2004, when the minority leader grew convinced that Kiscaden had disclosed the party's secret strategy on a spending bill to some people in Rochester. Basically, Kiscaden just didn't fit in. Dick Day told her to move her office and promised to spend $200,000 to beat her if she ran again in 2006.[32]

Kiscaden was born just after World War II in St. Paul. Her father was a house painter, and her mother was a nurse's aide. She was the oldest of four children growing up in a two-bedroom house. She paid her way through college, married, worked, and volunteered with an international development group. She drove a battered Mercury Sable around her district, and the bran muffin recipe was her grandmother's. Her troubles began when the Republican Party concluded, Kiscaden said, that "I wasn't pure enough." She didn't mean that in a Joan of Arc kind of way. "It's not about Sheila Kiscaden. It's not about me," she explained. "It's about big political forces that are going on in our country. And I just got caught up in it."

Extreme Districts, Partisan Candidates

Sandy Maisel, chair of the government department at Colby College, studies Congress. In the 1990s, Maisel set out to understand why some people decide to become candidates for political office and others don't. He picked a random set of congressional districts and asked prominent residents of these communities — labor leaders, party officials, cham-ber of commerce presidents — to name people who would be good members of Congress. Maisel and his colleagues then interviewed 1,500 of these prominent, well-thought-of citizens about the pros and cons of running for the U.S. House of Representatives. Most of the objections to entering politics were expected. Running meant interrupting careers, leaving families, and losing free time. Few of these good citizens wanted to raise money. They weren't naive, however, and most said that they could put up with the fundraising calls and the time on the road, even if the process was hard and, at times, distasteful. There was something more fundamental that bothered these potential candidates, however: the politically lopsided nature of most congressional districts.

Single-minded districts deterred those in the minority party, which made sense. These potential candidates had slim chances of winning. But one-sided districts put off people in the majority party, too. They simply "didn't like the kind of campaigns they would have to run to get the nomination," Maisel told me. The prospective candidates understood that a primary campaign in a homogeneous district would likely be "bitter and acerbic," Maisel found. They sensed the campaign "would be extreme, and most of the issues these people were concerned with were not at the extreme."

The prominent citizens Maisel interviewed were right about the narrow limits of what the parties will accept in a candidate. Back in Oregon, Bill Bellamy calculated the ideological boundaries of today's politics. "On a scale of one to ten from conservative to liberal, the Republican Party starts at one and stops at three," Bellamy told me. "There is just no such thing as a liberal Republican. Now, if you get to three or four, then the ones and twos start claiming you're a liberal." As a Republican, either you get back to three (or, better, two) or you don't run.

When Sheila Kiscaden went to her party caucus in 2002, she expected to see twenty or so constituents and neighbors. She was greeted by more than two hundred people rounded up by the NRA and a conservative education group. To win the nomination, Kiscaden had to please those "ones and twos" — something she was not willing to do. As Maisel said, "you get people who are interested in issues at the extreme." Those are your candidates.

Steroidal Federalism

Congress had given up governing by the summer of 2006. And not a whole lot had been happening before. Nelson Polsby, a congressional scholar, calculated that the federal government had been largely deadlocked since the late 1960s. It was as if Americans had lost the ability to speak a common civic tongue. Polsby wrote, "In important respects the U.S. population resembles the population that attempted to build the Tower of Babel."[33] By 2006, even the slow-moving wheels of government had seized up. In June, Charles Babington wrote in the *Washington Post,* "Congress seems to be struggling lately to carry out its most basic mission: passing legislation."[34] Whatever the issue — the minimum wage, immigration reform, bankrupt pensions, global warming, energy policy, stem cell research, inquiries into domestic surveillance, resolutions on the war in Iraq — it slipped under the surface of Congress's deepening pool of discord. In early July, former House Republican leader Dick Armey said bluntly, "I'm not sure what this Congress has accomplished."[35] So Congress quit pretending and just stopped meeting. In 2006, the House met nine fewer days than it had in 1948, the year President Harry Truman dubbed the legislature the "do-nothing Congress."

In the past, when the nation had failed to reach a consensus, the custom was for local governments to strike out on their own. In the early part of the twentieth century, Progressive majorities in the Midwest bypassed a polarized Congress and enacted laws governing railroad rates, limiting corruption, and promoting conservation.[36] The same thing is happening now. With Congress more polarized than at any time since the end of World War II, people see no sense waiting for the national fifty-fifty division to resolve itself. After all, one of the advantages of living in a like-minded community is that you can live under the laws you and your neighbors want. The federal stalemate has touched off an eruption of activity by state and local governments — federalism that doesn't sleep.

Abortion. South Dakota's legislature made it a felony for a doctor to perform an abortion for any reason except to save the life of a pregnant woman. (This stark law was defeated in a 2006 statewide referendum; 56 percent of South Dakota's voters cast ballots against the bill.)

Birth Control. In early 2006, while the federal Food and Drug Administration dithered over the legality of the "morning-after" birth control pill, more than sixty bills were filed in state legislatures to settle the issue locally. "The resulting tug of war is creating an availability map for the pill that looks increasingly similar to the map of 'red states' and 'blue states' in the past two presidential elections," reported Marc Kaufman in the *Washington Post,* "with increased access in the blue states and greater restrictions in the red ones."[37]

Gay Unions. Very blue Massachusetts legalized same-sex marriage, and (also blue) Connecticut, Vermont, New Jersey, and California allow some form of same-sex unions. Meanwhile, half of the states have banned them.

Guns. Florida passed the "Stand Your Ground" act in 2005, which allows citizens of that red state to kill in self-defense without first attempting to flee. By mid-2006, fifteen states had enacted similar laws. Nearly all were Republican-leaning states in the South and Midwest.[38]

Education.

- California governor Arnold Schwarzenegger vetoed a bill passed by the California legislature that would have prohibited textbooks or school instruction that "reflect adversely" on gays and lesbians.
- After 6,000 people signed a petition asking for an elective high school course on the Bible, the Odessa, Texas, board of education added the course to the curriculum.[39]
- Meanwhile, students in Philadelphia's public schools are required to take a course in black history.[40]
- In 2007, the Federal Way school district in exurban Seattle banned the showing of Al Gore's global warming documentary, *An Inconvenient Truth.*[41]

The Environment. After the Bush administration decided it had no authority to regulate greenhouse gases, blue America sued. A coalition of twelve states — all but one of which voted Democratic in the last two presidential elections — two bright blue cities, and thirteen environmental groups asked the courts to intervene. In April 2007, the U.S. Supreme Court sided with the states and ordered the federal government to begin regulating the gases that are warming the planet. Meanwhile, in mid-2006, ten northeastern states were negotiating caps for greenhouse gases. California, Oregon, and Washington were setting up similar ceilings on the Democratic Pacific Coast.[42] And cities — the urban voters who largely supported Al Gore and John Kerry — are "racing ahead of the federal government in setting carbon emission targets and developing strategies to deal with climate change," according to a story in the *Washington Post.* By June 2007, 522 U.S. mayors had agreed to meet the goals set out in the Kyoto Protocol, including those from deeply Democratic Boston, New York, Boulder (Colorado), Seattle, Portland (Oregon), and Austin.[43]

The most popular tactic in the age of political segregation is to start locally, with overwhelming majorities, and work your way up. Andrew McDonald, the Connecticut state senator who sponsored a successful gay union bill, said that the state's action sent "a powerful message to the rest of the country . . . Everybody understood that this was not just a Connecticut issue, that this was going to serve as a platform for many other discussions and debates around the country." One of the ironies of political segregation is that it's turned Democrats into the party of states' rights, while Republicans, when they still had their congressional majorities, were more inclined toward federal mandates. "State sovereignty, once the discredited viewpoint of segregationists, is now becoming the battle cry of mainstream liberals," wrote political scientist James Gimpel. "Conservatives, for their part, are now citing the constitutional views of government centralizers they once despised."[44]

After the federal government allowed only limited kinds of stem cell research and Congress was unable to resolve the dispute between researchers and the religious right, the states stepped in. California voted $3 billion for stem cell research, and other blue states — Illinois, New Jersey, Maryland, and Connecticut — provided funding, too. Stem cell research is now clearly a Democratic cause, but that seems more a consequence of divided politics than of either ideology or biomedical research. After all, the first town to place limits on DNA research was Cambridge, Massachusetts. One of the most liberal cities in the United States nearly outlawed genetic research in 1977. "Originally, you evaluated recombinant DNA technology the same way you would evaluate a new kind of pesticide or a large dam," Marcy Darnovsky, associate executive director of the Center for Genetics and Society in San Francisco, told me in 2005. When the religious right came out against embryonic stem cell research, however, it created "this reflexive response to that religious point of view. What's happened is fascinating."

The opposition of the religious right and President George W. Bush turned stem cell research into a Democratic bugle call, but the sides could have been reversed. After all, without the opposition of the religious right, isn't it possible that the $3 billion California stem cell initiative would have been couched as a giveaway to the pharmaceutical industry and Frankenstein research? Instead, the stem cell initiative became a surrogate for the presidential contest between Bush and Kerry. In August 2004, a Field poll found that two-thirds of the people who supported Kerry also supported the stem cell initiative. Two-thirds of those who said they favored Bush said they would vote against the proposition.*[45]

California's position on stem cell research also sent a broader signal about the state's culture and the kind of people who would find comfort within its borders. It said that California is not dominated by Bush Republicans or the religious right. Those kinds of signals affect decisions about migration, which in turn increase social homogeneity. People want to live in places where their work and their point of view are respected.

In 2005, the Texas legislature was considering a bill to limit stem cell research in the state. One medical school dean told legislators that if they passed the bill, Texas would hear a "giant sucking sound" as scientists from Houston decamped to California. I drove to the huge medical research complex that fills blocks of downtown Houston, and the researchers I talked with there were naturally worried that Texas would outlaw their work. But that wasn't their greatest concern. More than the money or the law was a sense that the scientists didn't want to live where they weren't wanted. "If your state is going to make it miserable for you not just in the absence of support but in the presence of political disdain, people are going to leave," said Michael Mancini, a research scientist at the Baylor College of Medicine. "If science is seen as evil, with monsters, it means we'll have to go elsewhere."

In 2002, researchers at the School of Public Health at the University of Michigan surveyed scientists about constraints on their work. The

---

*That division held in the 2006 midterm elections. Three-quarters of Missouri voters who supported Democrat Claire McCaskill for the U.S. Senate also voted for a constitutional amendment that would protect stem cell research, according to exit polls. Three-quarters of those who voted for Republican incumbent Jim Talent voted against the measure. A person's position on stem cell research told almost as much about his or her vote as whether the person saw himself or herself as liberal or conservative.

scientists were concerned, of course, that new laws could end entire lines of research. But the survey found that they were most affected by "informal constraints," the sense that society disapproved of what they were doing. The researchers realized there was such a thing as "forbidden knowledge" in some societies. They were less concerned about laws and more worried about what the press would say about them or how the community where they lived would react to their research. They were much more concerned about social sanctions than legal ones. "I would like to lunatic-proof my life as much as possible," one scientist said.[46]

So would we all. But these days, one town's lunatic is another town's civic leader.

Eating in Mixed Company

Sheila Kiscaden took me to an Italian restaurant across from the Mayo Clinic where we had an unusual lunch for the year 2005. We ate in mixed company. There were two Republican politicians, one Democrat turned independent, and Kiscaden, who by this time was a Republican turned independent thinking about turning Democrat. They had all lived through the transition from a more congenial kind of Minnesota politics to what they had in 2005 — and none was pleased with the change. Tim Penny was a pro-life Democratic congressman who eventually ran for governor as an independent and lost. Duane Benson and Dave Bishop were Republican legislators, both more moderate than the current party average. (Benson was pro-choice, which earned him the Kiscaden treatment; his local party refused to endorse him in 1988.) The four poked at a spaghetti bar lunch and listed the ways they thought they had been shunted out of the political process.

Tim Penny summed up the situation this way: "Here's what's happening. You have districts that are self-selecting. More and more liberal-leaning and Democratic-leaning people want to live in this neighborhood or this city, and similarly the suburbs are being populated by people who are leaning more conservative. But a small percentage of these people are dominating the party and determining the candidates in these districts. The nature of the town is that they still vote for the

Republican candidate, but it's not the Republican who broadly represents the more moderate constituency. As long as you keep the red-hot base happy, everybody thinks everything is fine."

"And if you want to buck that red-hot base," chimed in Duane Benson, "you've got work. It's much easier to vote your way back in by taking care of that red-hot base and then work [to the middle] from there."

Piece by piece, what the four described didn't sound so bad. What's wrong with living around people you like? And isn't the essence of democracy to be involved, to be passionate about politics and policy? But it was the cumulative effect that was so sinister. They portrayed a self-reinforcing cycle that squeezed people out of politics — people like themselves. The Big Sort was making places more ideologically homogeneous, and in the process, it was making people more extreme. There were fewer voters with mixed, nonpartisan relationships. Organizations with membership based on fellowship and community had been disappearing since the mid-1960s, replaced by those angry good old boys rounded up by the NRA who had greeted Kiscaden at her party caucus. And not only were communities more like-minded, but Republicans and Democrats also were more internally aligned: to be a member of a party meant agreeing up and down the line on a grocery list of issues. Politics had become so tribal that people were changing their minds about fundamental issues in order to conform to what it meant to be a Republican or a Democrat. So politicians found that if they didn't satisfy one "red-hot" portion of the party, they risked losing the votes of all who considered themselves good and true Democrats or loyal Republicans.

These four politicians looked tired, survivors whose talents for politics had become obsolete. They found themselves living in a political ice age. Benson recalled how he and a Democratic legislator had put together the rarest of laws, a compromise on abortion. "The bill would have reduced the number of abortions, but it would have also guaranteed rights," Benson said. "We thought naively that we had the formula. It was a wonderful experience, and we went through the whole process and we got two votes. His and mine. Because everybody else was pushed to their base." Penny, suddenly excited, said, "Now *get* this.

Their proposal would have measurably decreased the number of abortions in Minnesota, *and* it would have not made abortion illegal. But they couldn't get support from either extreme." There was a bit of silence, and then Benson said, "What we have today is idea segregation."

Dave Bishop said that he used to get much of his best work done at receptions, where he could talk with Democrats and form cross-party coalitions. But legislators don't mix much anymore, he said. Ethics laws have cut down on the number of social gatherings, and besides, the two sides don't have much to talk about. They don't like each other. Kiscaden agreed. "The legislative system was designed for deliberation, to take people away from their homes and put them in one place to talk to each other and work it out," she said. "But that only works as long as people really trust their representatives." And people don't trust anymore, said Bishop. Legislation in St. Paul is "just pounded through" by the majority, he said. "It's a perversion of the strength of the legislative process."

Kiscaden and I walked across the street and into the Mayo Clinic. Massive swirling blue and gold glass constellations by artist Dale Chihuly dangled over one staircase. We roamed about the clinic, and Kiscaden told me about the "coffee and conversation" meetings she had organized in Rochester. More than one hundred people would turn out on a Saturday morning just to talk about their town and state. One January, she held a "Beyond Bickering" seminar for state legislators. About 75 out of 201 showed up.

Kiscaden eventually joined the Democratic-Farmer-Labor Party and in early 2006 agreed to run for lieutenant governor on a ticket with a moderate Democrat, Kelly Doran. The campaign never gained traction; Doran and Kiscaden dropped out before the primary. Kiscaden said that she wouldn't run for her old seat in the state senate, and so, for the time being, she is out of politics — not because she wanted out, but because she really doesn't have a place. Her situation isn't that unusual.

In 2004, a rancher and former school board president from Waco, Texas, entered the Republican primary for a newly redrawn U.S. House district in central Texas. Dot Snyder ran against Arlene Wohlgemuth, who billed herself as "one of the most conservative members of the

[Texas] legislature."* The winner would take on Democratic incumbent Chet Edwards in a district that was 60 percent Republican. Edwards, a conservative, had been elected seven times, and everybody expected the general election to be a doozy. But the real fight ended up being the primary between Snyder and Wohlgemuth.

Wohlgemuth attacked Snyder for what in a less polarized time would be considered good citizenship. Snyder had served on the board of Waco's chapter of Planned Parenthood. (She had resigned when Planned Parenthood began to offer abortions.) And while serving on the school board, she had voted for some tax increases. (The state legislature at the time was systematically reducing its share of funds for public schools, so every Texas school board was raising local tax rates.) The conservative Club for Growth labeled Snyder a "Republican-in-name-only" (RINO) and pushed $400,000 into the Republican primary to support her opponent. Wohlgemuth was a "taxpayer superstar," the Club for Growth said, and the little primary in the blackland prairie of central Texas became the club's "highest priority" House race in the spring of 2004.

Snyder's ranch is near Crawford. Her husband was one of George W. Bush's fraternity brothers. Snyder was a volunteer worker on the Bush campaign the week before the 2000 and 2004 elections. When I spoke with her in 2004, she described herself as a "rock-solid, 100 percent Republican." But she wasn't conservative enough for the Club for Growth. Overwhelmed by the Club's money, she lost in a primary runoff.† "The process was an awakening for me," Snyder said. "I did not expect to be misrepresented. And I think that the process perhaps forces that to happen . . . Voters in the primaries are certainly not representative of those who vote in November. They skew to the edges." Would she run again? "No," she answered, laughing. "That's easy."

Incumbent Arlen Specter received only 52 percent of the vote in the Republican primary for his U.S. Senate in Pennsylvania in 2004. His opponent, Representative Patrick Toomey, a conservative, labeled Specter

---

*This district was gerrymandered in an unusual special session of the Texas legislature in 2003 — the bizarre summer session orchestrated by former Senate majority leader Tom DeLay. This was the second redistricting in Texas since the 2000 census. Democratic legislators hid for several weeks at a Holiday Inn in Ardmore, Oklahoma, to protest what they considered a legislative heist.

†Wohlgemuth lost to Edwards in the fall of 2004.

a "Ted Kennedy" liberal, and the Club for Growth spent $2.3 million to broadcast that message. Toomey didn't win, but the Club for Growth didn't give up. The conservative group turned its attention to the Pennsylvania statehouse, targeting a dozen moderate Republicans. When Pennsylvania conservatives in the 2006 primary defeated twelve Republican state legislators they considered insufficiently doctrinaire, the Club for Growth announced, "Toomey Beats Specter." (These folks certainly can hold a grudge.)

St. Paul mayor Randy Kelly, a Democrat, endorsed Bush in 2004 and was defeated one year later as punishment. After a few Republicans on the Houston city council supported the Democratic majority's proposal that stalled cars be towed immediately off the city's notoriously clotted freeways, local Republican officials promised retribution.* "We're not looking for council members who are going to go along and get along," said Jared Woodfill, chairman of the Harris County Republican Party. "We're looking for council members who are going to stand up for conservative values."[47] Surely, political ideology has teetered over some high cliff when towing can be described as a "value." What's next, a doctrine of potholes, the water pressure credo?

The One-Way Street of Polarization

Over the past thirty years, most U.S. House districts haven't flipped back and forth in their political allegiance, or even in the ideology of their representatives. There's little ebb and flow in results because the composition of the districts isn't ebbing and flowing. Congressional districts are, as a rule, growing more politically homogeneous. When older officials leave office, they are inexorably replaced by someone further to the left or the right. Nolan McCarty, Keith Poole, and Howard Rosenthal have charted the increasing polarization of Congress. From the end of World War II until the mid-1970s, the political scientists found, the mix of the two parties in the U.S. House was fairly stable. Republicans tended to be conservative, and Democrats were largely liberal. But poli-

---

*Council seats in Houston are nonpartisan, but everyone knows the party affiliations of members.

ticians of different parties overlapped in their ideology. After the mid-1970s, the two parties began to move apart. Democrats got more liberal and Republicans got more conservative.[48] In the 95th Congress (1977–1979), 40 percent of the 435 members were moderates on the McCarty/Poole/Rosenthal scale. By the 108th Congress (2003–2005), this moderate bloc had been whittled down to 10 percent. The U.S. Senate has seen a parallel decrease in overlap between the two parties (see Figure 10.1). The middle has dropped out of Congress altogether.[49] Some of that polarization was due to conservative southern Democrats being weeded out of the party (by either conversion to Republicanism or retirement). But members of Congress from *every* region in the country had moved away from the political center. The South has its peculiarities — country ham, Bob Wills, and Dr Pepper — but polarization is the product of a nation.*[50]

McCarty, Poole, and Rosenthal observed that polarization has consequences. Without a sizable group of moderates, Congress has a harder time passing major legislation. The parties engage in the horseplay Americans see daily in Congress — the endless efforts to blame the other side for failures and the mountainous debate over trivial legislation — while significant issues are sidelined. Moreover, these political scientists found that when Congress is gummed up, the president and the courts are encouraged to act unilaterally.†[51] "It's calcifying our politics," Democratic pollster Paul Maslin told me. "Where is the common ground if I as a Republican legislator in the Central Valley of California never have to worry one damn bit about ever losing an election to a Democrat?" The same is true for a Democrat in Los Angeles, of course, and so both steer to the extremes, conceded Maslin, who was Howard Dean's pollster in 2004 and joined Bill Richardson's campaign in 2007.

---

*Moreover, women in Congress are more polarized than their male colleagues. Brian Frederick at Northern Illinois University compared Democratic and Republican women members of Congress in the first two years of Bush's second term and found them further apart ideologically than their male colleagues. See Brian Frederick, "The Feminine Side of Polarization in the U.S. House" (paper prepared for the annual meeting of the American Political Science Association, August 30–September 3, 2006).

†In *Polarized America,* McCarty, Poole, and Rosenthal contended that polarization has its strongest impact on poorer Americans. The failure of Congress to raise the minimum wage for so long was typical. (It was finally raised in 2007 after ten years.) Polarization tends to work to the advantage of conservatives, especially regarding social spending.

"So now if you have legislative bodies that can't act anymore, they either go lurching from one side to another, which means we have no continuity, or they are immobilized. If they are immobilized, that breeds cynicism: 'I hate the politicians.'" Maslin described a perpetual motion machine of polarization. "It means the middle starts opting out. Now you are creating a real snowball effect. The middle is opting out because they're furious. This whole thing is a mess."

The most effective sessions of Congress were from 1963 to 1966, just before the midsixties social and civic collapse. From that point on, the House and Senate grew more ideologically balkanized and, at the same time, less productive. The percentage of important issues ending in deadlock has increased since.[52] "The moderates have been washed out of both parties," lamented former Republican congressman Mickey Edwards of Oklahoma. "There's just a homogeneity there" in the districts and among politicians, Edwards continued. Is the polarization of Con-

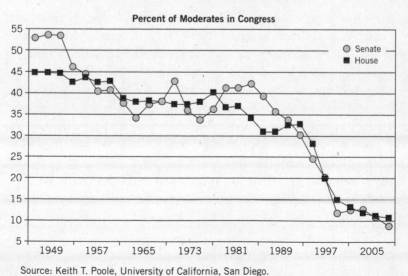

Figure 10.1 The Decline of the Political Center, 1949–2005

Moderates have been disappearing
from the U.S. House and Senate.

Percent of Moderates in Congress

Senate
House

Source: Keith T. Poole, University of California, San Diego.

gress led by elites or by partisans back home? It's both, said Edwards. "It's who they are *and* who they represent."

Thomas Jefferson circumvented the boarding house factions during his presidency by inviting legislators to the White House for dinner, no more than a dozen at a time. He sat them at a large, round table, both to nullify questions of status in seating and to preclude private conversations. The wine was imported and plentiful. Jefferson's French chef was "his best ally in conciliating political opponents." Servants weren't allowed in the room — the president served out of a dumbwaiter near his chair — so the legislators felt free to speak in confidence. Jefferson wouldn't mix Federalists and Republicans, but he would use the dinners to cross over the boarding house factions in both parties.[53]

Congress has been most productive when both parties have been ideologically mixed and when the members have soothed political differences with social grace. "In the fifties and sixties, these guys hung out in the gym," said Gary Jacobson, a University of California, San Diego, political scientist. "They socialized at functions held by lobbyists, across parties. They hung out in Washington together, and they formed friendship on affinities that had nothing to do with politics. It reduced the level of conflict. Now they don't talk to anyone except for people in their own party . . . It's a very different world."

People living in like-minded communities don't regularly encounter political disagreement, observed Alan Rosenthal, a state legislative specialist at Rutgers University. Voters living in segregated neighborhoods and churches "are less likely to have any empathy with politics or legislatures, because fundamental to those politics and legislatures is disagreement. If you live in a homogeneous community, you think, 'Everyone agrees this is right, so why the hell don't they do it?' Well, they don't do it because there is another homogeneous community over there that thinks quite the opposite. And candidates who come up through that [community] may also have less appreciation for democratic politics."

And so may voters.

11

THE BIG SORT CAMPAIGN

THE EARLY RETURNS from exit polls on Election Day 2004 predicted that John Kerry would win. Kerry didn't win, of course, and the contrary findings of the exit polls launched a thousand conspiracies of stolen elections and monkeyed-with voting machines. The botched survey results were embarrassing, so the group that operates the exit polls investigated and eventually issued a long and quite detailed report on how the system had failed. To understand the findings, you have to know a little about how the polls were conducted. Interviewers set up at 1,480 polling places across the nation with instructions to interview a sample of voters. At some precincts, they were to interview, say, every fourth voter; at others, every other voter. Polling is meant to be exact, but there are always unexpected circumstances that can make obtaining a good sample difficult — even impossible. At some polls, for example, researchers are required to stand far away from the voting stations, which allows voters to escape questioning. At others, if it is pouring down rain, voters are disinclined to talk.

There were snafus throughout Election Day 2004, but a major problem with the exit polls turned out to be a human reaction: Republicans sometimes refused to answer the queries of polltakers. Bush supporters

were particularly unwilling to answer questions posed by young interviewers with graduate degrees. (No, polltakers weren't wearing their degrees on a badge. Although there was no overt display of educational
achievement, Bush voters avoided people with graduate degrees more
than the run-of-the-mill grungy college student.) The more educated or
the younger the researcher, the less likely Bush voters were to answer
questions. The official report came to no conclusion about why Republicans skirted the polltakers, except to note that "in this election voters
were less likely to complete questionnaires from younger interviewers."[1]
That factor alone caused an undercount of Bush votes. Kerry's supporters were inclined to talk with young, educated interviewers, and so
Kerry's vote was systematically overstated.

The pollsters also carried paperwork and notebooks bearing the logos
of the major news outlets sponsoring the survey. Republican voters may
have so mistrusted the major media that this association, too, led some
to avoid the polltakers. It's not a far-fetched conclusion. According to a
June 2004 survey by the Pew Research Center, "Republicans have become more distrustful of virtually all major media outlets over the past
four years."[2] A Fox News poll in late October 2006 found that Republicans were less likely to respond to exit poll questions asked on behalf of
"television networks."[3] The early, leaked exit poll results were wrong because they failed to account for this imbalance.

The exit poll failure remains a source of debate, fascination, and, for
some, paranoia.* But it appears that the poll was wrong not because of

---

*The conflict over the exit polls rolled on through 2005 and 2006. Mark Hertsgaard asked, "Is it
really so strange to imagine that Bush supporters — who tend to distrust the supposedly liberal
news media — might not answer questions from pollsters bearing the logos of CBS, CNN, and
the other news organizations financing the polling operation?" ("Was Ohio Stolen in 2004 or
Wasn't It?" *Mother Jones,* November/December 2005). Robert F. Kennedy Jr. devoted more than
14,000 words to this question in an article posted in June 2006 on *RollingStone.com* (http://
www.rollingstone.com/news/story/10432334/was_the_2004_election_stolen). Kennedy concluded that the discrepancies between the exit polls and the actual results indicated that the
2004 election had been stolen. Steven F. Freeman and Joel Bleifuss published a book titled *Was
the 2004 Presidential Election Stolen?* (2006). Michael Kinsley, in his review of the book in the
New York Times (November 5, 2006), wrote that "the whole stolen-election-2004 indictment has
that echo-chamber sound of people having soul-searching conversations with each other. Richard Hofstadter's 'paranoid style,' exhibited mainly on the right when he coined the term in the
1960's, seems to have been adopted by the left."

malfeasance or mechanical breakdown, but because of a malfunctioning culture. The poll was wrong because people avoided talking to those they thought had political leanings different from their own. In 2004, with the fractured, segmented, and segregated state of the nation thirty years in the making, Americans believed they could determine another's politics just by looking. And maybe they could.

By the time of the Kerry versus Bush contest, Americans were allergic to difference of opinion and were blind to compromise. That's why churches were homogeneous units and markets segmented — so that worshipers and consumers could be sure to get exactly the sermon and the product they desired. Politicians had resisted the techniques of the megachurch and the target marketers through the 2000 election, perhaps because candidates are always slow to innovate, but also because politicians had traditionally understood their job to be changing the minds of those with opposing beliefs. But by 2004, those techniques had caught up with politics. This was the first Big Sort election.

"We Don't See Them Anywhere"

Although both parties claimed to be concentrating on turnout in the '04 campaign, the two sides rarely crossed paths. To Democrats, the Republican campaign was invisible. "We have people looking hard, and we don't see them anywhere," a leader of the liberal activist group America Coming Together (ACT) told reporter Jeff Mapes of the *Portland Oregonian*.[4] Another ACT leader, in Ohio, said that a report lauding Republican organizing efforts was "a dream." The ACT leader told Matt Bai of the *New York Times,* "We've got the reality. They're wishing they had what we've got."[5] It was as if the parties were campaigning in parallel worlds.

Even after they'd lost, Democrats still didn't understand what had happened. The Bush campaign had been innovative in a number of ways, but it received the most attention for the sophisticated techniques it had used to identify voters.[6] The campaign compiled 182 pieces of information (according to one account) about each voter — the kind of consumer data that has been used for a generation to target customers for candy bars or computer gizmos. Then the sharp-pencil boys at Bush headquarters cross-referenced this data with political polls. With the resulting calculations, Republican organizers could tell (with a reported 85 to 90 percent accuracy) whether a person — any person — was a Republican or a Democrat.[7] "If you drive a Volvo and you do yoga, you are pretty much a Democrat," Bush campaign manager Ken Mehlman liked to say after the election. "If you drive a Lincoln or a BMW and you own a gun, you're voting for George Bush."*[8]

Democrats were convinced they had lost because they hadn't had the latest bit of technical expertise — in this case, the somewhat gray-haired technique of micro-targeting. Since the 2004 election, Democrats have been busy conducting polls and doing their own analysis of lifestyle data so that their candidates can better target and then pluck out individuals inclined to vote Democratic. But Democrats missed a big part of what happened in 2004 — because they never saw it.

Nationally, Democrats increased their votes by 8 million over 2000. Republicans, however, bumped up their votes by 11.5 million, and that was the election. The Republican increase came from turning out Republicans, not by persuading independent voters.[9] Kerry increased the Democratic Party's take of the independent vote over 2000, but his party still lost by more than 3 million votes. Micro-targeting probably helped increase Republican turnout, but Bush won because his campaign understood how communities and politics have changed over the past thirty years. His campaign knew that the way people organized their lives was more important than demographics. And the campaign realized that how people conceived of their communities was more impor-

---

*Marketers know that these kinds of databases are filled with problems — missing data fields, for example, or confusion over names and addresses. (In fact, one of the early contests of the 2008 presidential campaign will be over who controls the good lists that came out of 2006.) Of course, marketers don't care about accuracy, only results. In marketing terms, they are looking for "lift." So they constantly test their data, trying to improve its predictive power. That's exactly what the Republicans did during the campaign. In Portland, Oregon, Patrick Donaldson told me that his phone bank workers were told to ask two or three new questions each night. The answers were transmitted back to the main database. The next night, they asked another group of questions, so the party's information was being constantly improved. The party's ability to target voters improved daily.

tant than issues. The Republicans won because they understood the Big Sort and the Democrats did not.

A "Well-Slathered" Campaign

Matthew Dowd sat in a marshmallowy chair in an Austin coffee shop and explained to me in 2005 what had guided the Bush campaign in 2004. Dowd had been Bush's pollster in 2000 and the campaign's chief strategist in 2004. The 2000 campaign had been standard-issue, late-twentieth-century politics, Dowd said. The presumption then was that the key to winning rested largely with independents, the ticket splitters who floated in the mushy middle between the parties waiting to be persuaded. This had also been the 1996 model for campaigns, Matt Dowd said, and the 1992 model, and the model on down through the years, as candidates aimed 80 percent of their money and time at the confused clump of voters that could be swayed to one side or the other.

After the 2000 race, Dowd began to review records from the campaign and from recent political history. He found that the number of voters in the middle had shrunk to a nubbin. There were very few people who would listen to both sides of a political debate. In the 1980s, perhaps a fourth of the nation's voters were truly in the middle and available to be pulled or persuaded. But Dowd realized that the number of swing voters had since dropped by more than half, to less than 10 percent. Not only were there fewer people in the middle, but the 90 percent of Americans who had chosen sides were growing more adamant in their beliefs. Dowd studied polling results back to 1980 and saw that voters had become vastly more partisan. Democrats were more rigidly Democratic and Republicans more staunchly Republican. The key measure for Dowd was the gap in how Democrats and Republicans viewed the president. People were always more approving of presidents who came from their own party. But the gap between how Democrats and Republicans viewed the president had been growing: it was 36 percentage points for Richard Nixon in 1972, 42 percentage points for Jimmy Carter in 1980, 52 percentage points for Ronald Reagan in 1988, 55 percentage points for Bill Clinton in 1996, and 71 percentage points for George W.

Bush in 2004. By the time of the 2004 campaign, 90 percent of Republicans approved of the way Bush was doing his job; 81 percent of Democrats disapproved.*[10]

Dowd's insight was a genuine discovery. Political science textbooks were teaching students that voters "no longer strongly identify with one of the major parties as they once did." Journalists had written that the "most important phenomenon of American politics in the past quarter century has been the rise of independent voters."[11] Political scientists could see that members of Congress were becoming more partisan in the 1980s and 1990s, but they still contended that for voters, "the two major parties are no longer as central as they once were in tying people's everyday concerns to their choices in the political system."† In early 2000, Princeton University's Larry Bartels wrote the first academic paper challenging the notion that voters had lost interest in political parties, a view he called "both exaggerated and outdated." Americans' attachment to political parties had declined until the mid-1970s, Bartels wrote, but then the trend had reversed.[12] From the mid-1970s on, Americans had sorted themselves into political parties in the same way they had sorted themselves into like-minded communities, organizations, and churches. The middle of American politics dwindled, just like the middle of American religious life dwindled. When the Bush campaign strategists realized that the political middle consisted of a shallow pool of voters, they changed the way they planned for the 2004 election. The campaign wouldn't focus on persuading the undecided; instead, according to Dowd, Bush would spend 80 percent of his time and money motivating partisan Republicans to vote.

The Republican strategists seized on another insight, too — inspired by a mid-priced restaurant chain. Dowd saw that American communities were "becoming very homogeneous." He believed that to a large de-

---

*Even after what can be described only as a disastrous two years, 84 percent of self-described Republicans approved of Bush's handling of the presidency on Election Day 2006, according to House exit polls; only 18 percent of Democrats approved.

†Even Philip Converse, who tracked the decline in party allegiance to six months in the middle of 1965, didn't foresee the rebound in partisanship. In his 1976 book *The Dynamics of Party Support*, Converse projected only a modest restoration of support for political parties. His most extreme projections, in fact, fell far below the levels of partisanship Dowd found in 2000 (pp. 113–16).

gree, this clustering was defensive, the general reaction to a society, a country, and a world that were largely beyond an individual's control or understanding. For generations, people had used their clubs, their trust in a national government, and long-established religious denominations to make sense of the world. But those old institutions no longer provided a safe harbor. "What I think has happened," Dowd told me in the early summer of 2005, "is the general anxiety the country feels is building. We're no longer anchored."

No kidding. Unsurpassed prosperity had set people free — free to think, speak, move, and drift. Unsurpassed prosperity had enriched Americans — and it had loosened long-established social moorings. Americans were scrambling to find a secure place, to *make* a secure place. In the post-materialist culture that emerged after the 1950s, people weren't finding safety or a sense of self by obeying or abiding or even joining. There wasn't the same satisfaction to be found in learning a trade and attending noon lunches with the Lions. But if the post-materialist person couldn't find meaning in being a carpenter or a Mason, it became incumbent on him or her to create an identity. Most Americans have done that by seeking out (or perhaps just gravitating toward) those who share their lifeworlds — made up of old, fundamental differences such as race, class, gender, and age, but also, now more than ever, personal tastes, beliefs, styles, opinions, and values.

Americans joined communities, churches, and political parties in a manner that was almost tribal. "People were having a tendency to pick a team, and that team was having an effect up and down the ballot," Dowd said. People were siding with a party and then voting a straight ticket, from city council to president.* Political party affiliation had more to do with social identity than ideology. Choosing to be a Republican or a Democrat reflected a way of life.† Party membership shaped

---

*Pollster Neil Newhouse, with Public Opinion Strategies, told a conference at Princeton University in December 2004 that in a survey his firm had conducted in Arlington County, in northern Virginia, 20 percent of the voters said that they would vote for the Democratic candidate for county commissioner because they disapproved of President George W. Bush.

†Academics would confirm the Republicans' supposition. "Our interpretation emphasizes partisans' sense that they are part of a team," Donald Green, Bradley Palmquist, and Eric Schickler wrote in their book *Partisan Hearts and Minds* (New Haven, CT: Yale University Press, 2002, p. 219).

people's sense of reality. To Republicans, for example, the 2000 election had been a clear victory. To Democrats, it had been pure theft. People saw the world differently depending on their party affiliation, much as sports fans on opposite sides either cheer or boo a close call by a referee. Republicans understood that the 2004 contest would be driven by these tribal allegiances.

Dowd described for me people who had lost attachment to their employers. "People no longer work in jobs for twenty years," he said. "We no longer have our pensions, and that has created a great anxiety." Americans worry about health care and a shifting morality, and they see a world that appears particularly dangerous and fragmented. In urban America, the commercial response to this sense of apprehension and isolation is Starbucks. "Starbucks has nothing to do with coffee," Dowd said. "It has to do with people who want to come to a place where they can be around people and not be isolated." The suburban equivalent to Starbucks is Applebee's, the low-slung eatery found in every exurban settlement. Applebee's, Dowd said, provided the social organizing strategy for the 2004 campaign.

Dowd wasn't attracted by the food or the restaurant's design. Every Applebee's is like every other Applebee's in menu and architecture. (The food was characterized in one review as being "well-slathered.")[13] But each Applebee's is uniquely decorated in one way: it has a "neighborhood wall" just inside the front door. The wall is adorned with local photos, often from the region's agrarian past. There are bleached-out pictures of bonneted founding mothers and pioneer farmers wearing tall boots and droopy mustaches. Those links to the soil (the soil now covered by a Circuit City, the high school football stadium, and Applebee's own parking lot) are paired with present-day emblems of community: a yellow rubber jacket autographed by all the members of the volunteer fire department, photos of local sports heroes, a banner from the nearby high school. This is target nostalgia or micro-mythmaking, and it works because it reflects the real identities of the people hunkered down in the nearby booths. The business concept is to deliver a local experience along with Thousand Island dressing, to create a place where "our kind of people" take their dinner. Applebee's is "selling community" to the people enjoying the slathered entrées and the sepia photos.[14]

"It's not just nostalgia," Dowd protested. And then he said something that makes sense only in a country where the same set-piece psychology can evoke community in both a glassy stack of "riblets" and a Republican presidential candidate. What people are looking for, he said, is "a present-tense desire to recapture something that was lost."

In a sense, Applebee's applied the church growth techniques of Donald McGavran to restaurants. McGavran had learned as a missionary in India during the 1930s that trying to convince individuals to come to church one by one was infinitely slow. It was quicker to recruit whole villages or castes — "peoples," McGavran said — to enter a church as a "homogeneous unit." McGavran taught several generations of preachers that people wouldn't go to a church where services were conducted in languages they didn't understand or where members wore better clothes, were "obviously of a different sort," or ate strange foods. The trick to building larger congregations was to make the passage from community to church seamless and untroubled. The preachers who took McGavran's advice built suburban megachurches precisely to comfort the new communities Americans were moving to outside the cities. They removed the anxiety of coming to church by making church a piece of the community.

That was exactly Applebee's strategy. To be successful, you don't entice individuals to a restaurant. You bring in entire communities by breaking down barriers between your establishment and the "village." You don't serve strange foods; you serve foods that are comfortable — well slathered. It worked in the same way the megachurches worked. Indeed, said Applebee's CEO Lloyd Hill, "there's something evangelistic about what we do."[15] By the time of the 2004 presidential campaign, Applebee's was the largest sit-down food chain in the country.

The Republicans took the Applebee's marketing concept — and, by extension, the tactics of the megachurch — and applied both to a political campaign. It was a marketing question, really. How do you build a following of the faithful in an age of increasing partisanship, widespread distrust, and homogeneous communities? How can a campaign for president use community as a political asset? The answer, the Bush campaign decided, was to create a tribe of Bush voters. The decision was to take Applebee's technique of adopting a trusted community and, Dowd said, "re-create that politically."*

Savage Republicans

"The [Bush] strategy, which we took, we actually implemented it exactly the way they said that we should," said Robert Thibodeaux. Thibodeaux sat in a booth at one of a jillion Caribou Coffee shops in overwhelmingly Republican Scott County, Minnesota. He always wears outrageous Hawaiian shirts. Thibodeaux had spoken several times at a state Republican Party convention, and people remembered his voluble nature and garish wear. So even though he had moved to Scott County only six years earlier, the party picked him to chair the local Bush campaign in 2004.

Thibodeaux runs with a group of Republican activists from the little town of Savage. They are both geographically and ideologically Savage Republicans. A confidential briefing book put together by the Bush campaign in 2004 listed several "potential weaknesses" in Scott County. For one, the boys over in Savage were a little bit *too* Republican. "There is a significant number of ultra conservatives in the county, some of whom are disenchanted with some fiscal policies," the report said. For one thing, Thibodeaux and his group were hounding the party about Bush's ever-inflating budget, and it wasn't long before the state Republican Party had dubbed them the "Savage Mafia." But if being "ultra conservative" was a disadvantage in Scott County, you couldn't tell it from the vote in 2004. The Savage Mafia put together a campaign that won Bush more than 60 percent of the county vote. And, as Thibodeaux said, they did it all according to Dowd's plan.

After Matt Dowd realized that the number of undecided voters was both small and dwindling, he and the rest of the Bush campaign adopted a strategy that bypassed independents and concentrated on turnout. They collected methods thought to boost the number of voters (those

---

*To read more about Dowd's ideas, see Douglas B. Sosnik, Matthew J. Dowd, and Ron Fournier, *Applebee's America: How Successful Political, Business, and Religious Leaders Connect with the New American Community* (2006).

noxious computer-generated telephone calls, for example) and tested them in the 2002 off-year elections.

In 2000, Donald Green and Alan Gerber at Yale University had published research measuring the effects of different get-out-the-vote techniques. The political scientists had conducted a test during a 1998 election in New Haven, Connecticut. Some residents had received a piece of mail asking them to vote. Paid solicitors had made the same pitch over the phone to another group of people. And a third group of residents had received a visit from a paid canvasser. When Gerber and Green checked who actually voted, they discovered that direct mail and, especially, phone calls had had little effect. But face-to-face canvassing had raised turnout rates from 44 percent of registered voters to 53 percent. In a subsequent experiment, the researchers found that for every twelve front-door contacts, one additional person voted.[16] In the electoral world confronting both parties, these were huge increases. The four presidential elections from 1988 to 2000 were, on average, closer than in any comparable period over the past century. An increase of a fraction of a percent could win an election.

Both parties were familiar with Gerber and Green's research. The left-leaning ACT hired thousands of young people to canvass neighborhoods based on the face-to-face trial conducted in New Haven.[17] But the Republicans learned from their 2002 experiments that door-to-door canvassing came with an asterisk. The more closely tied the person making the appeal was to the neighborhood, the more likely it was that the appeal would result in an additional vote. A friend worked best, but if the person coming to the door was clearly from the community, that also worked well. "There was like a four times higher likelihood that voters would respond if they were contacted by somebody they knew, or if it was somebody from the neighborhood," Dowd told me in reference to his party's 2002 tests. This was an old principle of marketing. Insurance salesmen had known since the 1960s that the more they resembled a prospective customer — in age, income, and especially political outlook — the better chance they had of making a sale. Similarly, evangelists would make sure that the newly converted were first met at the altar by people of the same sex, age, and race. In 2004, Republicans rediscov-

ered the recruiting technique that had been refined by insurance salesmen and revivalists.*

Republican strategists had also come to understand why it was important in these times to have somebody from the neighborhood make
the appeal for Bush. Religious historian Robert Wuthnow had found a
"search for connections" in America. In earlier times, Wuthnow wrote in
1998, people identified their faith by membership in a larger church.
Now they were seeking kinship within smaller groups and communities.[18] Similarly, the marketing director of McDonald's had said that the
country had transformed from the "me decade" to the "age of I . . . And
by that [I] mean: I am an individual, but I don't want to feel alone. To
what group do I belong?"[19] Americans were seeking the company of others — albeit, others who were very much like themselves. J. Walker
Smith of Yankelovich Partners described Americans as "hiving." Their
reaction to the anxiety of the world — the uncertainty of work and
health and the volatility of global politics — was to seek "the embrace of
others in a safe setting abuzz with engagement and activity." They were
devising personalized environments. "People want to live where they can
enjoy the comforts of family, friends and neighbors," Smith told his clients. Americans were "finding comfort through connection," and the
strongest connections were with people like themselves.[20] "This self-
selection is incredibly important," Republican political consultant Bill
Greener told me in 2005. Greener lives in a heavily Democratic suburb
of Washington, D.C., and has been struck by the way Americans are
clustering in like-minded neighborhoods. We live in an "age of invisibil-
ity," Greener said, and people have a "constant sense that everything is a
hassle, where stress surrounds everything, whether it's driving to work or
trying to get something accomplished in public policy. When it comes
time to go home or it comes time to go to church or comes time to enjoy
other social endeavors at some level, there is the thought that 'I don't

---

*When asked to explain his approach to politics, Karl Rove quoted from a letter written by
Abraham Lincoln to his Whig Party campaign committee: "Keep a constant watch on the
doubtful voters, and from time to time have them talked to by those in whom they have the
most confidence." Former Bush speechwriter Michael Gerson wrote that Rove's contribution to
twenty-first-century campaigns was to "bring this peer-to-peer politics to a continental scale"
("What History Taught Karl Rove," *Washington Post*, August 17, 2007).

want to have to listen to all that shit' [from those with different opinions]. And that translates into what we're observing."

One person's social comfort, of course, is another's social prison, and as people seek the best place to live, they create a jagged cultural landscape. Places that are economically vibrant — that produce more technology and discover more marketable ideas — generally have looser social connections. People there are less likely to join clubs, volunteer, or attend church. These places, on average, vote Democratic.* Other people seem to prefer places with tighter social ties. Residents of these communities volunteer, join, and stay closer to their families. They largely vote Republican. This cultural difference had economic advantages for Democratic areas in 2004, but when it came time to build a grassroots political organization around community networks — the Applebee's strategy — the closer ties in Republican areas perfectly matched the Bush campaign strategy.†

Put simply, Republicans had more social networks to tap. In Republican landslide counties, 20 percent of the residents went to church more than once a week. In Democratic landslide counties, 8 percent did. In addition, 45 percent of the people in Republican landslide counties belonged to a Bible study or prayer group.[21] Those connections naturally transferred to politics. I visited with the Savage Republicans at a pizza party they held at the Tin Shed restaurant in town. I met Bob Stapleton, a commercial pilot. Stapleton had a deep interest in education and had become involved with the conservative group EdWatch, which opposes things such as "school-to-work" programs and other "European" innovations. He had also joined a Bible study group that included Randy Penrod, the chair of the Scott County Republican Party. Penrod had recruited Stapleton into the party, and soon Stapleton had

---

*There are notable exceptions, however, such as the Texas cities of Houston and Dallas — high-tech metro areas that are staunchly Republican.

†A study by University of California, Irvine, economist Jan Brueckner found that for every 10 percent decline in population density, the chances that people would talk to their neighbors at least once a week increased by 10 percent. The suburbs didn't destroy social networks; in fact, contact between homogeneous neighbors increased as places became more Republican. (See Roy Rivenburg, "Where to Hear 'Hi, Neighbor!': In the Suburbs," Los Angeles Times, November 27, 2006.) The Bush campaign devised by Dowd and Mehlman tapped into this strong social network.

become the education policy person on the party's county executive committee. "There's a synergism," Penrod explained. "Because Bob is involved with EdWatch, I asked him to sit on the executive committee. And I met him at Bible study."

Contrary to what the Democrats thought, the Republicans didn't convince preachers to organize parishioners and march them to the polls in 2004. Four years earlier, the Bush campaign *had* tried to recruit preachers, and the effort had flopped.* "What we learned in 2000 is that if you want something to happen on the ground, you have to have people on the ground," Bush's Portland, Oregon, campaign leader Patrick Donaldson told me. "The pastor is not on the ground in most cases. They are spiritual leaders, and they are reluctant to use the pulpit" in political campaigns.† So in 2004, the Bush campaign went after something more powerful than the minister. The campaign recruited churches' social networks. Bush workers collected rosters of church members, just as they collected the membership lists of organizations such as Ducks Unlimited (a hunters' group), the names of people who had signed petitions seeking to outlaw gay marriage, and the names of conservative homeschoolers. (Republicans were exact: they asked Donaldson to retrieve membership lists from precisely 149 congregations in the Portland area.) As the Bush campaign compiled names, it was simultaneously discovering the social networks that would become the campaign's delivery system — how the Republicans would build a local organization of volunteers and spread the word about Bush.

The Bush reelection campaign ideal would have neighbors contacting neighbors. This was the Applebee's model, the megachurch model. The campaign couldn't hire canvassers, as ACT and the Democrats were doing. The Republicans couldn't bus in campaign workers from other communities. People would notice right away if the person go-

---

*The religious right was officially left for dead by the media in 2000. Michael Kelly wrote in his *Washington Post* column on March 1, 2000, "The hour of the Christian right is well past." On February 16, 2000, Hana Rosin wrote about the religious right in the *Washington Post* under the headline "Christian Right's Fervor Has Fizzled." Similar columns and stories were written after the Republican defeat in 2006.

†Preachers aren't necessarily the best canvassers even for their own churches. Ed Stetzer, in *Planting New Churches in a Postmodern Age,* told of a study that found that ministers who made followup visits to newcomers were only half as effective at bringing these people into the church as lay members.

ing door-to-door came from a strange tribe, a different hive. Patrick Donaldson in Portland said that the young ACT and MoveOn.org canvassers coming to his door would talk about the future of "Or-e-gone," a pronunciation that grates on natives. ("It's Or-e-*gun*," Donaldson emphasized.) Oregon pollster Tim Hibbitts watched the waves of ACT and MoveOn.org canvassers crash over the state's neighborhoods and concluded that they were "absolutely worthless. At best they did nothing."*

The Republican campaign also recruited what it called "navigators," people trusted in particular communities who could be the personal representatives of George W. Bush. This was a strategy taken straight from the marketing world that, again, worked best within homogeneous communities. Elmo Roper first proposed in the 1940s that 10 to 12 percent of the population consisted of opinion leaders, influencing others in their choice of goods, services, and, perhaps, presidents.† Companies have tried to identify these "influentials" and convince them to use their products in the belief that they would bring many other customers along. Procter & Gamble, for example, began its Tremor advertising unit in 2001. Tremor identified influential teens who, on average, had 170 friends. Companies would give these young people free stuff and ask for their thoughts about, say, a new shampoo or a movie trailer. The strategy was to get these teens talking, to generate a buzz. By 2004, Tremor had 280,000 teens in its network and a client list that included Sony, Valvoline, DreamWorks, and Coca-Cola.[22]

The Bush campaign identified its navigators with Applebee's in mind. One was Wes Mader, the rail-thin former mayor of Prior Lake, in Scott County, Minnesota. Mader had grown up in a thin-soil Wisconsin farming community. His mother had been orphaned at age five; his father had lived to be ninety and would never accept a senior citizen discount. Mader had made his own way, becoming president of an aerospace firm and raising a family that still lived nearby. "There's a sense in Prior Lake

---

*"The GOP promotes its causes through naturally occurring community groups of like-minded people . . . ," Columbia University sociologist Dana R. Fisher wrote. "Democrats, however, often outsource their politics, relying on artificial, virtual networks and professional canvassers to evangelize their message and build their party" ("Ending Rot in America's Grass Roots," *Christian Science Monitor*, October 30, 2006).

†According to Dowd, the Bush campaign relied on Jon Berry and Ed Keller's 2003 book *The Influentials,* which updated and expanded the original Roper findings.

and in Scott County that families are the fundamental building block of society," Mader told me as we sat in his lakeside house. "That's the attitude that's here, and it's an identifiable value of the Republican Party." The former mayor, successful businessman, and utterly trustworthy neighbor was, according to the GOP strategy, the Scott County incarnation of George W. Bush. He was one of thousands.

The campaign was particularly interested in how its canvassers approached people identified as likely Republicans. Those going door-to-door were asked simply to tell why they backed Bush — to, in effect, witness their support for the president. Patrick Donaldson, who led the Bush campaign in Multnomah County in Oregon, said that his organizers urged canvassers not to argue with voters. He told his volunteers, "You aren't trying to change the world. You aren't trying to convince anybody of anything. [You] are trying to talk to friends and neighbors and family, saying, 'Here's who I support and here are the reasons why.' If they don't support who you support and they give you the reasons why, that's wonderful. The discipline was we're not here to engage in any sort of disagreement at all. It's not going to happen." In Scott County, canvassers were given the same orders. The strategy wasn't to convince people to vote for Bush, but to build a Bush community. "We made it all social events, and that's why we were more successful," said Robert Thibodeaux. "As opposed to going to somebody's door and saying, 'Hi, will you support the president because of this, this, and this?' We said, 'Hey, we're having a party at somebody's house to watch a video about the president, have some drinks, and just talk about things in the nation and Scott County.' If they come to a party and they're in a room with thirty other people, they realize it's okay to talk."

"Friendship Evangelism" Finds a Campaign

The technique of seeking connection as a means to conversion is familiar to anyone involved with an Evangelical church. The generation of ministers who opened churches in the new suburbs realized that people couldn't be bludgeoned into the pews. People came to faith most often through a network of friends and family. Friendship came first and then conversion. These ministers practiced what became known as "friendship evangelism" or "lifestyle evangelism," which is based on the biblical command that Christians be "witnesses" (Acts 1:8).[23] Much of this church practice originated outside America, specifically with Pastor David Yonggi Cho, the Korean inventor of the cell system. Pastor Cho has said that his cells attract new members through friendship and service. These groups "select someone who's not a Christian, whom they can pray for, love, and serve." Pastor Cho said, "They bring meals, help sweep out the person's store — whatever it takes to show they really care for them . . . After three or four months of such love, the hardest soul softens up and surrenders to Christ." Instead of a preacher trying to hook one convert at a time, Cho cast the neighborhood cells as nets — a technique that has grown his Yoido Full Gospel Church by more than 140 new members a day.[24] Cho's practice transferred to the United States (Chicago-area megachurch preacher Bill Hybels writes about "contagious" Christianity) and eventually, in 2004, to the Bush campaign.

I asked campaign organizers if this had been a conscious application of religious proselytizing to political campaigning. "A lot of us are very active in Evangelical churches, the witnessing churches," Thibodeaux answered. "So it was kind of in our DNA anyway to talk about what you want to do and bring people together to a party. I go back and forth. A lot of this stuff used for evangelism and churches I use in politics, and [I use] stuff I learned in politics in churches." Patrick Donaldson said, "We weren't there to convince anybody. We were there to give testimony of why we were for George Bush. And that's very religious."

As the Savage Mafia followed the strategy prepared by Dowd and Karl Rove, it probably didn't hurt that the Democratic Party nominee in a state representative race in Scott County was also the co-chair of the Queer Student Cultural Center at the University of Minnesota. "Ashley Sierra was just the perfect thing from a political standpoint," Robert Thibodeaux said of the student who won the nomination from clueless Scott County Democrats. But the Savage Republicans didn't need the help. The Big Sort had made Scott County overwhelmingly Republican. The Bush campaign's organizing strategy was aimed at affirming the homogeneous community's sense of itself. The navigators linked the president directly to Scott County; the ability to micro-target individuals allowed the campaign to deliver messages tailored to individual concerns.[25] The campaign held parties and tapped into the existing networks of schools, kids' sports teams, and churches that threaded through the county. The vote in November wasn't so much the reelection of a president as an affirmation of a way of life.

The Democrats "Achieve" Edina

One of the older suburbs in Minneapolis, and certainly one of the richest, is Edina. Edina gave Barry Goldwater a landslide victory in 1964, favored Richard Nixon by 9,000 votes over former Minneapolis mayor Hubert Humphrey in 1968, and gave Ronald Reagan an 11,000-vote victory over Minnesota senator Walter Mondale in 1984. There's a locally famous Richard Guindon cartoon of a very proper mother telling her child, "Daddy and I weren't born in Edina, dear. We achieved Edina." That's the kind of place it was — rich, satisfied, and Republican — until 2004. That year, Edina voted for John Kerry. The headline in the *Minneapolis Star Tribune* the day after the election pretty much told the story: KERRY CARRIES EDINA — AND PIGS FLY, RIGHT?

Despite the presumption that Republicans ruled the suburbs, places like Edina had been turning away from the Republicans since 1992, and not just in the blue-leaning upper Midwest. Older suburbs in the South were becoming more Democratic, as were those in the North and the rest of the Midwest.[26] The shift surprised Republicans and Democrats alike in 2004. The Bush campaign was certain it would win Washington County, in suburban Portland, a community filled with executives at Intel and Nike — platinum-card-carrying members of Bush's investor class. But Kerry won there instead, by 6 percentage points, and a local Republican campaign official said that the results "flummoxed" the Washington, D.C., party headquarters. If Rove, Dowd, and Mehlman were bewildered by the vote in Washington County, Edina must have blown their minds.

Morningside, the eastern section of Edina, looks like my Democratic neighborhood in Austin. The houses are older and close together, and France Avenue, which runs along the edge of Morningside, has that lived-in city look. There's a bagel shop next door to a coffee joint, and

near the corner of France and Sunnyside, the Convention Grill special-
izes in fudge banana malts and burgers. "I love to talk about my neighborhood," said Joni Bennett as she spread out precinct lists and maps
that documented Kerry's victory. Bennett was forty-nine the year of the
election and a forever Democrat — her first campaign was for George
McGovern when she was in high school. She's also a Columbia law
school graduate, a mom, and one of those bright-eyed, short-haired
women who can carry a neighborhood on her back.

All of Edina didn't vote for Kerry, she explained. The neighborhood
west of Morningside, where the houses are larger and farther apart,
still supported Bush, though barely. The precincts in Morningside had
changed in recent years, Bennett said. There were "urban pioneers"
moving in because the neighborhood, next door to downtown Minneapolis, had a city feel. People who "support the vitality of urban life" were
coming here, she said. There was a lot of "self-selection" taking place.
The people attracted to Morningside were of a different tribe from those
settling in Scott County. Two gay couples had moved to her block in the
past few years. "If you have gay couples moving in, then it's different
than what it used to be," she said.

Back in Austin, Dowd explained to me, "As people make lifestyle
choices about where they live, it means whole neighborhoods adjust."
It's not a single issue that changes a community. Politics today isn't
about issues. It's about a place, a way of life, a species. So a community
doesn't shift three or four people at a time. When Dowd looked at the
suburban counties that switched from Republican to Democratic in the
2005 Virginia governor's election, neighborhoods tipped wholesale. Entire communities "shifted in groups" — or, in Donald McGavran's language, as "peoples." That's exactly what happened in Edina.

Morningside voted heavily for Kerry, but Edina turned Democratic
in 2004 because the entire town was tipping. Tim O'Brien was Democratic-Farmer-Labor Party chair in Edina during the early 1980s. Over
the last generation, he's seen "the old inner-ring suburbs going through
this metamorphosis, changing from being solidly Republican to, not
Democratic, but moderate," he told me. The old Edina residents were
largely self-employed businessmen, country club Babbitts. The newer
residents are professionals. They read the *New York Times*, he said, and

both husband and wife have been to college. They want a connection to urban Minneapolis. By contrast, voters in Scott County have "no association with the inner metropolitan area whatsoever," O'Brien said. "They read the story in the paper today about four kids arrested for murdering somebody, a horror story, and they are damn glad they are living out in Scott County."

What about the people who have moved into Morningside? I asked. These are people who want a "city lifestyle," he answered. "I think you could say that the people in Morningside wouldn't move to Scott County if you put a gun to their head," O'Brien concluded. "And vice versa."

Panda Democrats

Back in heavily Republican and rural Crook County, Oregon, the local Democratic Party meets monthly at the Panda Chinese restaurant in Prineville. The night I visited, party regulars numbered in the high single digits. They wore their colors — a Prius in the parking lot and a RELIGIOUS LEFT pin on a lapel — and they collected donations for future campaigns in a Folgers coffee can. (The cumulative offering that night was $414.13.) That Democrats gathered at all in Prineville was somewhat new. Regular meetings at the Panda had begun only after the election wars of 2000. The goal of Crook County's underdog party in 2004 was modest. According to county chair Steve Bucknum, the Panda Democrats set out to "make it just okay to be a Democrat, to not be laughed out of town."

The Crook County Democrats fought guerrilla style, and their weapon of choice was the political sign. "The Democratic Party for years here had been afraid to put up signs during campaigns," explained Bucknum. "This last election cycle, we made it our major focus just to get signs up, as many signs as we could." They planted signs, and when those signs were ripped up and left for mulch, the Democrats replaced them. They weren't trying to convince the Republicans of anything. The goal was only to survive.

In the heat of the 2004 race, the Panda Democrats staged a bold daylight attack in downtown Prineville. They festooned cars with Kerry/Edwards signs and PROUD TO BE A RURAL OREGON DEMOCRAT bumper stickers and then parked these IEDs (improvised electoral devices) on the street in front of the Republican headquarters. A Democrat loitering in a nearby store overheard an irate citizen dialing the Prineville police department. The Republican sympathizer expected the local constabulary to come right away and tow the vehicles. Another person stuck his head out a door and yelled that the Democrats should be put in an insane asylum. That was the prevailing attitude in Crook County, Bucknum said. If you were a Democrat, you belonged in either the pokey or a padded room.

Rural America defected en masse from the Democratic Party in 2000. Between the second Clinton election in 1996 and the first Bush election in 2000, 856 counties changed allegiance. Exactly 2 of those 856 counties switched from Republican to Democratic. Both were metro communities: Charles County, Maryland, in suburban Washington, D.C., and Orange County, Florida, otherwise know as Orlando. The 854 counties that switched from Democratic to Republican were mostly tiny places. Half of them had fewer than 8,300 votes. The wholesale shift of rural Americans to the Republican Party wasn't isolated to one region or even two. The entire country broke apart, rural versus urban.

Rural people have always seen things differently from folks in the cities. But with television, the Internet, and increasing levels of education nationwide, it originally seemed that those differences would diminish. Instead, rural and urban Americans have grown further apart, a split that was plain to see in the 2000 and 2004 elections. Among rural young people (ages eighteen to twenty-nine), the Republican vote jumped from 48 percent in 1996 to 69 percent in 2000. Rural voters with some college education were evenly split in 1996; in 2000, 68 percent of them voted Republican.[27] Rural America made its own political rules. The stereotype of the rural voter is a white male — undoubtedly toting a weapon.* Although rural white men did vote Republican in 2000 and 2004, the dramatic switch to the right after 1996 was among rural white women. Married white women in rural counties gave Bush a 30-point

*For good reason, much has been made of the Florida vote in 2000, but it's just as important that Bush carried West Virginia. The Bush campaign seemed to turn in West Virginia after Charlton Heston stirred a large crowd at an NRA rally in Beckley just a week before the election.

advantage in 2004. Seventy percent of white women without a college education living in rural communities voted for Bush. Democrats had enjoyed a large advantage among all women voters throughout the 1990s, but the steady 10-point gap was reduced to only 3 percentage points in 2004. The decline in the gender gap between the parties was due largely to rural women voting Republican.[28]

John Kerry's response to the cultural division between rural and urban America was to borrow some camouflage clothing one day and sacrifice four ducks to the gods of the Second Amendment. When he traveled to rural America (or the fast-growing exurbs), he was painfully out of place. The Kerry campaign thought that it could drum up votes in rural counties by talking about new roads and the term-paper-sounding Manufacturing Extension Partnership. "That an upper class Bostonian encountered difficulty in connecting at the human level with everyday, largely more conservative, rural voters ought not to surprise," wrote political consultants Anna Greenberg and Bill Greener in 2005.*[29] Crook County Democrat Steve Bucknum put it more bluntly: "The problem with the Democratic Party is elitism."

Meanwhile, the rural Republican vote engendered a hostile reaction from some urbanites. The editors of Seattle's alternative newspaper, the *Stranger,* published a widely distributed manifesto titled "The Urban Archipelago," which was the inevitable result — and unwitting proclamation — of Big Sort politics: "Liberals, progressives, and Democrats do not live in a country that stretches from the Atlantic to the Pacific, from Canada to Mexico. We live on a chain of islands. We are citizens of the Urban Archipelago, the United Cities of America. We live on islands of sanity, liberalism, and compassion . . . And we are the real Americans. They — rural, red-state voters, the denizens of the exurbs — are not real Americans. They are rubes, fools, and hate-mongers."[30]

Political scientist Seth McKee compared the rural and urban ballots over time. After the 2004 election, he found that "never before has the gap in the presidential vote choice of rural and urban voters been so wide."[31]

---

*The entire affect of the Kerry campaign put off rural voters. "I'll give you one example in the Kerry campaign," Oregon county commissioner Bill Bellamy told me. "His wife was an arrogant bitch."

2006: Different but the Same

We vote with a vengeance in my neighborhood, so when my wife and I marched to the polls in November 2006, there was a line out the door of the Congress Avenue Baptist Church, with people dawdling almost to the end of the building. We chatted with neighbors and took pictures of our polling place for an Internet site created to collect photos from every American precinct. I snapped a shot of a smiling brown Lab with voters waiting in the background. I asked the owner the dog's name. "Che," she answered.

It's not a scientific poll, but when a dog picked at random at a polling place has been named for a South American Marxist revolutionary, odds are that the precinct will have a liberal bent. This wasn't the only hint that my neighborhood hadn't changed much in the two years since the 2004 election. There were still the same worries circulating that the election would be stolen by devious voting machine companies or that campaign tricks would turn another sure Democratic win into a Republican theft. (My wife dubbed such elaborate explanations for transgressions not yet committed "pre-spiracies.") The neighborhood was still engaged in activities that wouldn't likely be happening in, say, southern Georgia. For example, some good citizens were spending several Saturdays that November improving the local middle school's feng shui. A rice blessing had already been performed in the principal's office — "Many amazing results are occurring on the campus as a result of these first two hours," the organizer of the project had announced — and on the Saturday after the election, volunteers would hang Music of the Spheres wind chimes in the school's courtyards. When the ballots were counted, I saw that my wonderful Che-remembering, rice-blessing neighborhood voted 45 percentage points more Democratic than Texas as a whole.

The 2006 midterm elections were in many ways an extension of 2004 — only this time issues intruded. The war in Iraq, corruption, sex scandals, Hurricane Katrina, stagnant middle-class wages, and torture pushed a small percentage of former supporters against President Bush. Initially, a number of political commentators wrote that the results signaled major changes in the U.S. electorate. The *Washington Post* reported a few days after the vote that the "'God gap' in American politics has narrowed substantially."[32] This was a bit premature. Seventy percent of white Evangelicals voted for Republicans in the House races, according to exit polls. In the House races two years earlier — back when it had seemed abundantly clear to everyone that white Evangelicals were taking over the country — Republican support among Evangelicals had reached 74 percent. White Evangelicals, supposedly disgruntled with Bush in the fall of 2006, voted for Democrats in the same proportion that gays and lesbians voted for Republicans (both at about 25 percent, according to the 2006 exit polls of those voting in congressional races).* The story of the election wasn't big changes, but small, across-the-board shifts. Democrats picked up 3 points, 5 points, 7 points in every group. Gallup found the vote to be a "rising Democratic tide that lifted support in almost all key subgroups."[33] There wasn't a surge of votes from any one group, no realignment or stunning desertion. There was just a general — perhaps even a momentary — change among a small percentage of the public.†

The country had sorted and polarized to such an extent that one political scientist observed that voters "approached the race more like British voters casting votes for a parliamentary majority than like Americans weighing the unique merits of individual candidates." In blue Rhode Island, 63 percent of the voters approved of the way Republican senator Lincoln Chafee had done his job. It didn't matter. They voted him out because Rhode Islanders disapproved of his party.[34] Chafee lost in a straight-ticket landslide. The number of people who voted a straight Democratic ticket in Rhode Island in 2006 jumped two-thirds over the number in 2002.[35] People were voting for party, up and down the ballot and all across the country.‡ Among the three-quarters of the electorate

---

*There was a similar boomlet of excitement about the Jewish vote. In 2004, nearly eight out of ten Jews had voted Democratic. In 2006, it was nine out of ten.

†Nor was there any increase in the number of true independents. Political scientist Gary Jacobson told Newsweek at the time of the election that only about 5 or 6 percent of voters were truly undecided. See Susanna Schrobsdorff, "A More Liberal Electorate? Not Yet," MSNBC.com/Newsweek, November 9, 2006, http://www.msnbc.msn.com/id/15643639/site/newsweek/print/1/displaymode/1098/.

‡New Hampshire voters defeated both incumbent Republican House members and switched the state legislature from Republican to Democratic majorities largely on the strength of straight-ticket voting. David Broder reported in the Washington Post (November 26, 2006) that

nationwide who claimed a party (unchanged from 2004), there was nearly pure allegiance: 93 percent of Democrats said that they voted for Democrats; 91 percent of Republicans said that they voted for Republicans.[36]

The Republican Party in Congress swung further to the ideological right because of the election. Nine out of the twenty most liberal Republican House members lost — and nineteen of the thirty-one seats that went to Democrats had been held by Republicans in the less conservative half of the caucus. John Fortier, with the American Enterprise Institute, reported that before the midterm elections, Republicans had held eighteen House seats in districts that John Kerry had won in 2004 — so-called split districts. After the 2006 elections, only eight remained Republican.* The geographic segregation of the parties continued, as New Englanders rejected most of their remaining Republican representatives. Voters in eleven northeastern congressional districts held by Republicans elected Democrats. Only one Republican from New England remained, Connecticut's Chris Shays, and he barely won. "After Tuesday," Fortier wrote, "if you get into a car in Manhattan and drive north out of the city, you would have to go nearly 200 miles until you reach territory represented by Republicans." The result of the election was to make the Republican House caucus even more ideologically homogeneous. Democrats, meanwhile, did elect some moderates, but only a third of the party's class of 2006 could be considered socially conservative.[37]

The Big Sort was at work even within congressional districts. In Louisville, Kentucky, John Yarmuth beat a five-term Republican without carrying a single precinct where Republicans had a majority in registra-

---

there were 80,000 straight-ticket Democratic voters in New Hampshire in 2006, twice the number of straight-ticket Republicans. Aaron Blake noted in the *Hill* (November 20, 2006) that an increase in straight-ticket voting by Democrats was evident in several House races. According to Blake, straight-ticket Democratic voting jumped by 41 percent over 2002 levels in two of the most populous counties in Iowa representative Jim Leach's district. Leach, a Republican, lost. Straight-ticket Democratic voting doubled in Wisconsin and Pennsylvania districts where Republicans lost.

*Republican representative Jim Leach opposed the war in Iraq and was the most liberal Republican in the House. But Leach's Iowa district had given Kerry the highest vote percentage of any Republican House district in 2004, and in a system that was aligning itself top to bottom, Leach lost in 2006 after spending thirty years in Congress.

tion. Louisville has a large black community, which Yarmuth easily carried. But the margins in these precincts were the same as in previous elections. Yarmuth won because white, liberal neighborhoods "got even more liberal," giving the Democrat "astounding" majorities, according to a former chair of the local Republican Party.[38] Democrat Claire McCaskill spent weeks campaigning in rural Missouri and, according to Jeffrey Goldberg in *The New Yorker*, had what for the magazine was a special ability to "speak in language familiar to, among others, the disaffected hog farmers of Missouri."[39] Was this enough to break through the stark division between rural and urban voters? No. McCaskill did no better in rural counties (even those with hog farmers, disaffected though they may have been) than had Democrat Jean Carnahan when she lost to Jim Talent in the 2002 election. McCaskill beat Talent by 42,000 votes because she piled up a 113,000-vote advantage in the cities. The same was true for organic lentil farmer Jon Tester, the flat-topped and butch-waxed Democrat who won the Montana Senate seat from Republican Conrad Burns. Tester lost rural Montana by 9 percentage points, but he won Montana's cities by 11 points. Because he did well in the metro areas, he became a U.S. senator. Fightin' Irishman and Democratic candidate Jim Webb lost rural Virginia by 11 points but pulled enough votes in the cities to beat incumbent Republican senator George Allen. The gap between rural and urban voters in these key states — a gap that didn't exist nationally three decades ago — continued despite Democratic candidates suitably spoken, coifed, and armed for the countryside.

Americans remained politically segregated. In the 2004 presidential race in Missouri, 41 percent of the state's voters lived in counties where the contest between Kerry and Bush was decided by 20 or more percentage points. The 2006 race between Talent and McCaskill was much closer, but 38 percent of the state's voters still lived in landslide communities. In Virginia in 2004, 43.7 percent of the state's voters lived in counties that were carried by a landslide in the presidential election. In 2006, the geographic segregation of Virginia's voters increased. In a Senate contest decided by just 7,000 votes out of more than 1.3 million cast, 45.5 percent of the state's voters lived in communities where the gap between Allen and Webb was more than 20 percentage points.

The ideological divisions remained, too. A poll taken by thirty universities asked voters about fourteen issues. Republicans and Democrats disagreed about all fourteen. When Emory political scientist Alan Abramowitz compiled the issues to construct a liberal-to-conservative scale, he found that 86 percent of Democrats were on the liberal end of the scale, while 80 percent of Republicans were on the conservative end. Only 10 percent of the voters were in the moderate middle.[40] In a March 2007 *New York Times*/CBS poll, 78 percent of Republicans wanted a candidate in 2008 who was at least as conservative as Bush.[41] Republicans in 2007 were more religious than they were twenty years earlier; Democrats were less so.[42]

"My fear is there will be more partisanship," moderate (and defeated) Ohio Republican senator Mike DeWine told National Public Radio a few days after the 2006 election. "You can find areas of common ground, even with people you disagree with on other things; you can find their passion," DeWine said, sounding as if 2005 had been the good old days of bipartisanship. "My fear is that's not going to happen as much as it should in the future."[43] In April 2007, DeWine's concerns were borne out. Only four Republicans in Congress bucked the party to vote for troop withdrawals from Iraq. Partisan Republicans saw "the war in Iraq in fundamentally different terms than Democrats and political independents," reported Jonathan Weissman in the *Washington Post,* and "neither side wants compromise."[44] "The whole thing is so polarized," Senator Evan Bayh, an Indiana Democrat, said in May 2007. "There is a canyon separating the bases of both parties."[45]

12

TO MARRY YOUR ENEMIES

Democracy always reveals who we are, never what we
will become.

— ROBERT WIEBE, *Self-Rule: A Cultural
History of American Democracy.*

Bluer

THE BASEMENT AT the Calvary Baptist church in downtown Minneapolis on a Sunday afternoon was filled with about fifty homeless guys
finishing a soup kitchen dinner while they watched the Vikings whomp
a hapless Brett Favre and the Packers. The television was rabbit-eared
and fuzzy. The room was humid; it had the look of an elementary school
auditorium, with a small stage in the front and an open area where the
fellows with their bedrolls were rooting on the Vikings. During the meal,
several Generation Y kids wearing T-shirts and soul patches were on the
stage wiring mikes, setting up a drum kit, and running the whole system
through an Apple laptop. "Five minutes, guys," a mop-wielding church
worker told the dinner crowd. When the game was finished, the homeless guys spilled out onto Twenty-sixth Street. Meanwhile, more young
people arrived. And within the hour, the basement was transformed
from shelter/sports bar to church/coffee house. The kids erected small
"prayer stations" in the corners, with cushions, candles, and mosaics
of Jesus. There were a few Communion tables with wine and bread.
Photos were projected onto two small screens on the stage: a figure be-

hind a diaphanous curtain; a fire-eater; a boy in handcuffs. The images were more evocative than religious, more contemplative than doctrinal. Taped voices sang, "This is not a performance . . . Not a concert . . . It is our worship."

The people who trickled in were mostly twentyish, but a few gray heads settled around the tables, cushions, and candles. The musicians took to the low stage — bass, guitar, drums, and a small keyboard and synthesizer rigged through the Apple. The music began with rockish praise songs, the kind of swaying, arm-waving, Eaglesque anthems popular in Evangelical youth services. There was a hint of psychedelia in the music, however, that swelled and gradually took over. After about twenty-five minutes, without a break or a pause, the group's leader, Dan Lukas, led his band into something that sounded less like "Already Gone" and more like the Grateful Dead's "Feedback." Verses turned into chants, and forty-five minutes after the band had begun, the music assumed a meditative drone. The images on the two screens turned more cosmic — lights, then the planets, the sun, the moon. The music had gone on for a full hour, nonstop, when John Musick, in black jeans and stocking feet, slid to the middle of the room and asked if anyone would like to take Communion. Some did. The music had put everyone in a semitrance. The drummer, a kid in a stocking cap, dislodged himself from his kit and headed to the table with the bread and wine. Nobody rushed. Musick talked about finding time to "turn off my inner dialogue" and to discover a "centering prayer." He asked everyone to pick a word, a mantra — his was "grace" — and we meditated for another ten or fifteen minutes.

So began the weekly church service at Bluer.

A century ago, the Social Gospel emerged in response to the brutality of a new industrial, urban nation. Beginning in the mid-1960s, the decline of mainline religious denominations and the rise of more fundamentalist faiths were a reaction against a church dedicated more to social uplift than to salvation. The megachurches and "like attracts like" congregations began forming in the 1970s, designed as cultural safe havens after the post-materialist culture shift and social upheaval of 1965 sparked a decline in social trust. But society doesn't stop changing, no matter how much our own time seems the end-all of knowledge and the be-all of experience. Bluer, and churches like it all over the country, are another generation's reaction to the "people like us" design of the modern suburban church — and the segregated political life of present-day America.

Musick perched on a stool and said he wanted to talk about the first piece of Scripture he had ever been required to memorize, the first three verses of Hebrews 12 — the "cloud of witnesses" passage. This Scripture would be the topic of Musick's sermon — if "sermon" can apply both to Musick's talk and the carefully measured three-point presentations delivered at the megachurches. Musick's homily wandered, more like a slow conversation than a revelation of the Word of God. Rick Warren, the founder of the huge Saddleback Church, urges ministers to look for ways to save time during services, to "improve the pace and flow." Warren regularly times each element of his service and then looks for ways to speed things up, knowing that his suburban Orange County parishioners are on tight schedules and get easily bored. Remember, Warren wrote in his guidebook for ministers, *The Purpose-Driven Church,* "visitors have already formed an opinion about your church within the first ten minutes after they arrive."[1] After my first ten minutes at Bluer, Lukas was just getting limbered up on his keyboard. And while Saddleback disperses its Saddleback Sams and Samanthas to the well-appointed parking lot after a stopwatched seventy minutes, the service at Bluer lasted for two hours — and afterward everyone moved upstairs for coffee, tea, and another hour or so of conversation.

The Opposite of the Megachurch

There are hundreds of Bluers around the country — Ecclesia in Houston, Levi's Table in St. Louis, and the no-market-testing-here Scum of the Earth Church in Denver, founded first as a Bible study group by the Christian rock band Five Iron Frenzy. Musick attends a regular convention of the "emerging church" each fall near Santa Fe, New Mexico. (The convention is called "The Gathering.") The emerging church is not to be confused with the trying-hard-to-be-hip youth services that megachurches hold on Saturday or Sunday evenings, although many emerging churches began as offshoots of existing churches. Consider this culinary comparison: The Saturday night youth service at a megachurch may brag that it serves Starbucks coffee. At Sojourn, a vibrant emerging church in Louisville, Kentucky, the fare is what the kids would buy if they had a few bucks to spend at a convenience store. After Sojourn's meeting, the congregation retires to the kitchen of the church they are borrowing, and a guy in a Spiderman T-shirt lays out a spread of Ding Dongs, Hostess Cup Cakes, Twinkies, and fireplug-size jugs of Big K cola.

Whatever the megachurch has come to be, the emerging church is the opposite. Churches such as Second Baptist in Houston are large. Bluer and Sojourn are small. (Most emerging churches split like amoebas when they reach the size of a moderate family reunion.) The megachurch style is to have a charismatic leader, a "strong pulpit." The services at emerging churches are centered on the congregation. The megachurch service and its faith are certain. The emerging church is full of questions and doubt; the attitude is purposely nonjudgmental. If the megachurch is brimming with "people like us," the emerging church is mixed company. "I don't need them to be carbon copies," Dan Lukas said of his fellow congregants at Bluer. That's not to say the emerging church is squishy on faith or the Bible, a kind of New Age Episcopalianism. The ministers at Sojourn were schooled at Louisville's Southern Baptist Theological Seminary. When I asked a young woman why she worshiped at Sojourn, she told me it was because the ministers there "preach straight from the Word."

John Musick, age thirty-nine in the summer of 2005, grew up in the fundamentalist hothouse of the Assemblies of God. He was a youth minister in Illinois before he had what he called a "reformation awakening." The Assemblies of God is a strict denomination, and its set-in-stone doctrine chafed Musick. "People loved me there and everything, but I was becoming much too liberal," he said. "And there was an anti-intellectual feeling there. You don't question things. You believe and trust what you're told, and that's how it is." Musick drifted to the Vineyard Church, a loose affiliation both Evangelical and charismatic, and he became a youth minister at a Vineyard congregation in Minneapolis. There Musick began the Saturday evening service called Bluer, but he was actually busy creating a megachurch following the "homogeneous unit principle." "We had a huge stage and a light show — fog machines and big screens," he recalled. "I like to say we did everything but shoot Jesus out of a cannon. We were trying to market and minister to a demographic, to young adults. Our thinking was we had the truth, so we must market it so it will be palatable to young adults. And once they took a bite of it, they would think like us. But the problem was, we would attract a decent crowd, but we didn't see much transformation. We had no community. There were very few relationships. And I became very tired of having to put on this performance, this sermon, and create this thing. I discovered that I was a pretty postmodern type of person who was trained to minister in a very modern, linear fashion."

"Postmodern" is how emerging church members describe their movement. The fight between the Social Gospel of Walter Rauschenbusch and Eugene Carson Blake and the evangelism of the great nineteenth-century Fundamentalist Dwight Moody and his descendants had been a modernist struggle. To cope with the nation's change from rural to urban, from an agricultural to an industrial society, the earlier religious movements had taken opposing positions. The two sides each had dominated for a time, and then, Musick explained, "just when the Evangelicals are really copping a good head of steam, that's when there is a birth of another shift. And the emerging church is the result, the church emerging as a response to Evangelicalism not working for groups of people."

Mike Cosper is a minister with Sojourn. He grew up in a Southern Baptist community in southern Indiana. His home church was so focused on fulfilling the Great Commission that, for Cosper, it sacrificed any sense of community. "You're very focused on the mission," Cosper said, describing the rigid, hierarchical demands of mainline Evangelicalism, "and the mission is lived out through the structure. But the structure destroys community. The whole point of Christian life, the whole point of church, is community, and that's weblike." The modern church, whether Social Gospel or Fundamentalist, pursued truth; the emerging church seeks mystery.

Cosper moved to the Highlands neighborhood on the edge of downtown Louisville, a dense community of old houses, coffee shops, and restaurants. He met other young people who had left more fundamentalist churches. They opened an art gallery, Aslan's How — named for the place where the great lion in C. S. Lewis's *The Chronicles of Narnia* was killed. "The idea of the art gallery was for it to be a way of building relationships with people who wouldn't walk into the front door of a church, a way to connect with them," Cosper explained. The art gallery led to concerts and to a series of small gatherings. "Our strategy was to meet in homes, in community groups," Cosper recalled. "We would come together. There was time to reflect, more of an open atmosphere of just sharing life." The idea was to build a church that was part of the city and the neighborhood — something very different from the island community of the megachurch. Sojourn meets in one of the most Democratic-leaning areas of Louisville, yet Cosper and the other ministers are decidedly apolitical. "The reality of fundamentalism is that if I come out guns blazing with my politics, you are going to come out guns blazing back," Cosper said over a cup of coffee at a Bardstown Road café. "Somebody is going to lose. And I don't want Christianity to lose. The question of politics is not what God wants. The question of politics is how do we live together, recognizing that other people are different from me."

For most people these days, the question of politics certainly isn't this one: how do people with vastly different beliefs and backgrounds learn to live together? In the first four national elections of this century, the questions have been how best to isolate voters with sophisticated target marketing — a strategy endorsed and financially supported by both the Republican establishment and Democratic bloggers — and how to demonize the other side in order to gain, at best, a teetering advantage in the House of Representatives, Senate, or White House. Politics has become the enemy of Cosper's idea of community.

Lessons from Robbers Cave: The Contact Hypothesis

One of the tenets of democratic faith has been that direct, face-to-face contact between groups on different sides of an issue defines a self-governing people. Alexander Hamilton wrote that a "jarring of parties" was essential for government. Deliberation among ideological opposites was what made a country democratic. "It's hardly possible to overstate the value, in the present state of human improvement, of placing human beings in contact with other persons dissimilar to themselves, and with modes of thought and action unlike those with which they are familiar," the democratic philosopher John Stuart Mill wrote in 1848. "Such communication has always been, and is peculiarly in the present age, one of the primary sources of progress."[2]

Research conducted during World War II appeared to support the belief that understanding and tolerance stemmed from contact among groups that were otherwise isolated. The demands of battle would sometimes force an otherwise racially segregated U.S. Army to integrate on the field. Researchers found that white soldiers who had fought alongside black troops held more positive racial attitudes than whites who hadn't. Similarly, as white merchant marines took more voyages with black sailors, the racial attitudes of whites grew more tolerant.[3] These findings supported a belief that prejudice resulted from ignorance and ignorance was the result of a lack of contact. If people could only get to know each other, went the theory, groups would see that they shared a common humanity. In the 1950s, followers of the "human relations movement" had an "almost mystical faith in 'getting to know one another' as a solvent of racial tensions."[4] They believed that simple contact between groups would work to reduce racial prejudice. It was a way of thinking so prevalent at the time that it became part of the reasoning used by the U.S. Supreme Court to desegregate public schools in 1954.[5]

When social psychologists began to study what happened when groups came in contact, however, the findings pointed to something less than the democratic ideal. People do gravitate toward others with similar opinions and ways of life, and they tend to minimize the differences within the groups to which they belong. For instance, my Democratic Travis Heights neighbors in Austin see much more uniformity in opinion within the precinct than there really is. At the same time, people maximize the differences between groups. Travis Heights exaggerates the (already large) differences between this neighborhood and, say, Amarillo. Thus, when two groups think of each other, they define themselves as "us" and "them." People enhance their social identities by viewing their own groups positively and seeing other groups negatively. This is how they derive a sense of themselves. It's the way teams coalesce, companies build identities, and political parties maintain loyalties. The price of identity is that despite what the human relations movement had hoped, differences aren't diminished when groups come together. Instead, as social psychologists found, differences are exacerbated.

In 1954, Muzafer Sherif selected twenty-two boys for an experiment in group interaction.[6] The boys were alike in all measurable ways. They all came from middle-class homes; Sherif even picked boys with similar IQs. The social psychologist arbitrarily divided the boys into two groups. Separate buses picked up the boys and drove them to a two-hundred-acre Boy Scout camp surrounded by Oklahoma's Robbers Cave State Park, where they were put in different camps. The two groups instinctively developed group identities: one group spontaneously began calling themselves the Rattlers, while the other adopted the moniker the Eagles. The two groups gradually became aware of each other, and the knowledge that another pack of boys was camped at Robbers Cave immediately created tension. One of the Eagles referred to the Rattlers as "nigger campers" only after hearing the Rattlers playing at a distant ball field.

Boys from both groups asked Sherif's staff to set up competitions between the Rattlers and Eagles. (Sherif himself watched the experiment disguised as a camp janitor.) The researchers set up a series of contests, but even before the games began, the Rattlers and Eagles fell into conflict. When they first met, the boys razzed each other and sang derogatory songs. As the competitions (ball games, tugs of war, treasure hunts) proceeded, relations between the two camps deteriorated. The Eagles burned the Rattlers' flag. The staff had to prevent fights at the mess hall. One night, the Rattlers raided the Eagles' camp, dumping over beds and ripping down mosquito netting.

The Robbers Cave experiment taught Sherif that two groups placed in competition would devolve into discrimination and conflict. But subsequent experiments showed that the mere act of division was enough to trigger prejudice. Researchers found that there didn't have to be any discernible dissimilarity between groups for "us" versus "them" conflict to arise. People adopted group identifications with only the flimsiest of pretexts. In the late 1960s, social psychologist Henri Tajfel divided schoolboys from a suburb of Bristol, England, into two groups.[7] Tajfel made the divisions randomly, but he told the boys he had based the groupings on real differences. In one case, he asked the fourteen- and fifteen-year-old boys to estimate how many dots appeared on a screen. The boys were told that some people consistently overestimate the number of dots, while others underestimate the number. Tajfel told the boys that overestimators had been placed in one group and underestimators in another. (In another iteration of the experiment, the boys were asked whether they preferred paintings by Wassily Kandinsky or Paul Klee, both identified only as "foreign painters." The boys were then placed in a Klee group or a Kandinsky group.) The groupings were totally arbitrary, but to the boys, the groups, nonsensical as they were, became sources of social identity. When they were then asked to assign monetary rewards and penalties, they discriminated. Klee group members gave other Klee group members more money and Kandinsky group members less. A boy gained no individual advantage by favoring others in his group, but he did so anyway. Tajfel's experiment worked time and again. The simple fact of assigning people to groups led to discrimination — even when the division had been based on totally meaningless criteria. There didn't need to be a history of conflict or an ongoing struggle to set off intergroup hostility. They discriminated simply because the division existed.*

The "Kumbaya" philosophy of the human relations movement — we would all get along if we just got to know one another — wasn't wrong. Knowing about other groups *did* reduce prejudice and increase tolerance, just as the World War II battlefield studies had shown. But simply putting two groups together didn't result in mutual respect. It often had just the opposite effect. Placing groups together around a campfire (or in a school auditorium, city hall, or any of a thousand forums put on by

---

*One of the more famous experiments regarding discrimination was conducted in a small Iowa town by a third-grade teacher after the assassination of Martin Luther King Jr. Jane Elliott told her all-white students that blue-eyed students were superior to brown-eyed students. The creation of these arbitrary groups quickly resulted in the most base kind of discrimination: students were excluded from play because of their eye color, and blue-eyed students asserted their superiority over brown-eyed students. Descriptions and videos of Elliott's experiment can be found at http://www.janeelliott.com/index.htm.

strife-torn communities) without taking some very specific precautions would likely result in *increased* tension and discrimination.

Back in Oklahoma, Sherif reversed his experiment at Robbers Cave just as it was becoming a real-life version of *Lord of the Flies*. The psychologist shifted the rules of engagement between the Rattlers and Eagles. His research team introduced a number of tasks requiring them to pool their efforts against a common enemy. As the two sides had to cooperate to bring a movie to the camp or to unplug the park's stopped-up water supply, relations between the groups changed. Instead of fighting, they began collaborating. When they faced a common problem, contact between the groups both reduced conflict and prejudice and increased tolerance and cooperation.

Social psychologists took the results from these experiments and devised the "contact hypothesis." Not all contact between groups helped reduce prejudice, psychologist Gordon Allport concluded in the mid-1950s. Based on the research into group relations, Allport described a number of conditions that were necessary to bring opposing groups constructively together. First, the social psychologist wrote, the groups had to see themselves as equals. Second, meetings between the groups should take place as a regular pursuit of an ordinary and shared goal. And above all, Allport wrote, meetings should "avoid artificiality." It was best, Allport wrote, if the groups worked as a team, since "the deeper and more genuine the association, the greater its effect."[8]

Discussion between groups with different opinions or beliefs was more difficult than the democratic theorists had realized. Contact between adverse groups *could* bring greater understanding and tolerance, but there was a lot working against such an outcome. When members of the same group discovered that they disagreed about something, the instinct was to come together, to talk about their differences. Friendship within the group might be strained by the dispute, but at least there would usually be discussion. When the disagreement occurred between members of different groups, however, the typical reaction was avoidance and silence. Opposites didn't attract; they repelled. Some social psychologists described opposing groups as believing they had different "essences." According to Dale Miller and Deborah Prentice, an argument between groups "is perceived as reflecting deep, immutable, group-based differences . . . People tend to be less optimistic that a difference can be resolved when it occurs between people from different groups."[9]

Hearing the Other Side

Americans like to talk about politics. According to University of Pennsylvania political scientist Diana Mutz, compared with others around the world, they are above average in the frequency with which their conversations stray into politics.[10] Americans talk politics more than the circumspect British or those living in the tidy republic of Singapore. But they are less likely to discuss politics than the Poles, Swedes, Greeks, or Israelis (the most politically conversant of all). If Americans are slightly above average when it comes to talking about politics, Mutz found that when it comes to talking about politics with those who might disagree with their opinions, Americans are exceptionally reluctant. In a comparison of citizens from twelve countries, Americans are the least likely to discuss politics with someone holding a different view. They love other people's confrontations in sports brawls, on badgering cable news shows, and on "you're fired" reality TV. But they avoid political confrontations personally — more so than people in any other country in this study. Despite institutionalized patter about diversity and free speech, Mutz found that only 23 percent of Americans report having regular discussions with people who disagree with them politically.

Education is presumed to nurture an appreciation of diversity: the more schooling, the greater the respect for works of literature and art, different cultures, and various types of music. Certainly, well-educated Americans see themselves as worldly, nuanced, and comfortable with difference. Education also should make us curious about — even eager to hear — different political points of view. But it doesn't. The more educated Americans become — and the richer — the less likely they are to discuss politics with those who have different points of view, Mutz wrote. Americans who are poor and nonwhite are more likely than those who are rich and white to be exposed to political disagreement. In the United States today, people who haven't graduated from high school have the most diverse groups of political discussion mates. Those who have suffered through graduate school have the most homogeneous political lives.[11]

The Polarization of Deliberation

Many Americans have choices in how they live, where they settle, what news they read, and whom they associate with. But that increasing opportunity to choose has had the perverse effect of decreasing contrary political discussion. There have been attempts to reintroduce debate and deliberation into American politics, to revive the face-to-face democracy of the town meeting. Political scientist James Fishkin has been tireless in running "deliberative polls," where groups of citizens are brought together for a day to learn about and discuss a public issue. He and his colleague Bruce Ackerman have even proposed a national holiday called Deliberation Day, a time before each national election when every citizen would receive a small stipend for attending a political discussion led by trained volunteers within a neighborhood. In the best tradition of American democracy, Deliberation Day would make voting truly an informed choice, as citizens would learn about the issues of the day and then debate with others across boundaries of social and political division.[12]

But what would happen on a real Deliberation Day in the segmented, isolated, and like-minded communities created by the Big Sort? In 2005, David Schkade and Cass Sunstein recruited sixty-three Colorado citizens ages twenty to seventy-five, half from Boulder and half from Colorado Springs.[13] In 2004, 67 percent of the people in Boulder County had voted for John Kerry. In the same election, 67 percent of the people in El Paso County (Colorado Springs) had voted for George W. Bush. Schkade and Sunstein screened participants — in order to pick liberals from Boulder and conservatives from Colorado Springs — and then measured the individual opinions of these citizens about three issues: global warming, gay marriage, and affirmative action. True to form, the Boulder citizens were initially more liberal on these issues than the participants from Colorado Springs. Schkade and Sunstein then divided the citizens from the two cities into batches of six — making ten groups, five from each city. The groups were then asked to discuss the three issues, to deliberate, and then to come to a consensus on the same questions each participant had been asked individually.

The results were not encouraging for those who look to rational community discussion as an antidote to polarization. The ten groups discussed the three issues and came to a consensus in twenty-five out of thirty cases. In nineteen of these twenty-five cases, however, the consensus opinion of the group was more extreme than the prediscussion opinions of the individuals in the group. The Boulder groups' consensus opinions were more liberal than the opinions they had expressed as individuals. The Colorado Springs groups' opinions were more conservative.* As the law of group polarization would predict, each like-minded collection of people became extreme after discussion. Moreover, the differences *within* the groups narrowed. Discussion didn't spark free-thinking. Instead, each homogeneous community concluded its deliberations with greater conformity. People who were already like-minded grew more alike.

Before the discussion, Schkade and Sunstein wrote, "there was considerable overlap between many individuals in the two different cities. After deliberation, the overlap was much smaller." The participants' initial beliefs had been amplified by their exposure to like-minded others, and they had grown more polarized after only two hours of discussion.[14]

How Moderns Think

Back at Bluer, John Musick and I left the church basement and walked past a hall where a Hispanic Pentecostal congregation was holding a service. The preacher was romping, stomping, and praising the Lord. "They really throw down, don't they?" Musick said with a smile. We went to a room upstairs and began talking about the church and politics with a dozen or so members of the Bluer congregation. Many of Bluer's members are refugees from strict fundamentalist congregations, and they rel-

---

*Schkade and Sunstein assigned a simple ten-point scale (ranging from very strongly agree to very strongly disagree) that participants marked in answering three questions, one each about affirmative action, global warming, and gay marriage. The difference between the answers given by the individuals from Colorado Springs and those given by the individuals from Boulder averaged 4.59 points before deliberation. After deliberation, the difference between the groups had grown to 6.24.

ish the open, apolitical atmosphere of their basement services. "I grew up in an Assemblies of God church, and it was rigid," said Anna. "People were telling me how to think, how to dress, how to vote. Here I can state my opinion and not have people jump down my throat." Jason has long blond hair and a beard. He grew up as a Baptist, but, he said, "they wouldn't have me now; I'm a rocker." (His band is Fastest Turbo Fire Engine.) The Baptists were good at telling him a lot of "thou shalts and thou shalt nots," Jason said, "but I was never taught how to have a relationship." You hear that word, "relationship," quite a bit from emerging church members. "A lot of our core people have been ruined to just going to church and listening to a message, having a shallow relationship with other people in the congregation, believing what they are told," Musick explained. "They are ruined to that sort of thing. The relationship trumps all."

The "Bible says" certainty of the megachurch and the stale rituals of traditional denominations have bred a deep questioning among emerging church members. "They are highly suspicious of institutional religion," said Eddie Gibbs, a professor at Fuller Theological Seminary and the author of a book about the emerging church. "They don't want celebrities or performers. They want engagement, involvement. They want participation. They see church not as a weekly gathering, but as a community to which you belong."[15] And they don't expect the church to be the source of answers about life, politics, or even faith. Church is a place to ask questions and explore. "I think there are people who just don't think like moderns think," Musick said. "A typical modern thing would be, 'You be good and you pray, and God will answer your prayers.' Now, people who have a more postmodern leaning say, 'Sometimes that may work, but you cannot say that is a rule.' We are no longer taking a formulaic approach to faith. The king has no clothes."

The emerging church has traded in the locked-down certainty of the conservative church — the modern church — for doubt. And that doubt extends to civic life. Mike Cosper at Sojourn in Louisville talked about how ambivalent his congregation feels about questions of politics and public policy — and about the century-old division between Public and Private Protestantism. "To be honest, we're in a place where we are struggling with how to do that," Cosper answered when I asked him about politics. "The whole thing with politics anymore is that it is so polarized. And it's extremely polarized within the church. It seems to me the two streams that exist are the socially conscious stream that says the Gospel is the good news to the poor and the downhearted. The political slant becomes liberal, to support welfare and all the programs. The other slant is more fundamentalist Christian that interprets everything through the lens of morality and family values and the world's going to hell in a handbasket and we need to hold on to these values as long as we can. And what bothers us is, when we look at it, the issues seem way more gray. When it comes to politics, they seem *extremely* gray and extremely complicated. And we're not at a place where we feel comfortable as pastors saying you need to think this or that, vote for this person or support that. Because the issues seem so complicated."

People who think that religion is far too certain and that it plays too much of a leading role in politics will no doubt be heartened by Musick's questioning and Cosper's caution. But neutrality has its own price. Cosper told me that Louisville had been roiled by a police shooting that killed a young man. Civil rights leaders planned a march through the city, and the religious community was asked to join the gathering. "We wrestled with marching," Cosper said. "But the choice we made was we didn't advocate it institutionally." There were people on both sides of the issue at Sojourn, Cosper said. More fundamentally, he added, on these kinds of political questions, "you can't come down on one side or another often because you don't have Scriptural warrant to . . . I'm exhausted by how complex it seems. I feel exhausted by the tendency toward polarization, by things getting heated and out of control. I personally feel like I lack the wisdom." One hundred years after the split between Public and Private Protestantism, there's a third option: questioning, watching, and waiting.

The Benefits of Apathy and the Paradox of Democracy

There is nothing meek or apathetic about Cosper, Musick, or the people who attend Sojourn and Bluer. But one consequence of seeing both sides of an issue is hesitancy. The price of moderation in politics can be passivity. This response runs counter to our ninth-grade civics version of American democracy: as citizens come to understand both sides of an issue, they're emboldened by knowledge and set off to engage in the exciting work of self-government. That's not the way it works. Cosper had it right: hearing both sides of an issue — and seeing the gray in most questions — is the ticket to withdrawal. Paul Lazarsfeld was one of the first to notice the connection between partisanship and participation when he studied two presidential elections in the 1940s from the vantage points of small towns in New York and Ohio.[16] He discovered that partisans voted with certainty and with enthusiasm, while those who were tugged by both sides were less likely to cast ballots. Political scientists have since found again and again that partisanship increases participation. Partisans are the ones who vote and who donate to and work on campaigns. Indeed, the "relationship between voter turnout and political partisanship is among the most robust findings in social science."[17]

Although high voter turnout had always been considered consummately good, Lazarsfeld discovered that the rigid partisanship that spurred more people to the polls was in truth a mixed blessing. "Extreme interest goes with extreme partisanship and might culminate in rigid fanaticism that could destroy democratic processes if generalized throughout the community," Lazarsfeld wrote. The political system required flexibility. It demanded both partisans to invigorate politics and moderates to heal the nation after a divisive struggle. The civics texts were right: the system needed those who felt strongly about politics. But Lazarsfeld believed that a "lack of interest by some people is not without its benefits, too." Having a good number of people who didn't care much about politics was just as vital to democratic government as having the voting booths filled with eager supporters of both sides. Indifferent citizens leavened the system, gave it suppleness, just what the partisan personality lacked. Apathy gave politicians room to maneuver, compromise, make deals, smother grease on the gears of representative democracy. Having people who didn't give a flip about politics helped hold society together and cushioned the nation from the shock of disagreement and change. A democratic government needed a variety of political appetites, Lazarsfeld concluded, a "balance between total political war between segments of the society and total political indifference to group interests of that society."[18]

Diana Mutz has described this standoff as the paradox of democracy. We want citizens who are both active and deliberative. We want voters who are partisan and a society that allows compromise and conciliation. Simply put, we want what doesn't exist: reasonable citizens who are willing to listen to the other side but who are also excited about politics. Mutz has weighed the relative benefits of participation and deliberation and come down firmly on the side of indifference. There is no discernible benefit to increasing the percentage of people who vote, she wrote. Despite the commonplace admonition that low levels of voting threaten democratic government, there has been no measurable good associated with high levels of voting. But there are clear benefits to increasing conversation across ideological divides. The good produced when people stop to hear the other side is tolerance.[19]

Lazarsfeld realized that the attributes of partisanship and indifference didn't coexist within the same person. For that reason it was politically healthy for a society to foster a mix of people. Nothing could be more destructive than a society filled with knowledgeable, active, and opinionated "ideal citizens," Lazarsfeld warned. "We need some people who are active in a certain respect, others in the middle, and still others passive."[20] The old sociologist was writing long before the Big Sort. Since the 1970s, we have been busy creating exactly the society Lazarsfeld cautioned against. More of us are partisan, and more of us are living in ever-smaller communities of interest, places that nurture our certainty and feed our extremism. Tolerance — and its progeny in the political world, compromise — were the victims of late-twentieth-century politics.

Just Enough to Win the Turkey

I was sitting in a restaurant in Washington, D.C., with reporters who had served time in Kentucky. We were all older, white, and male — of an age that we knew the same politicians who plied their trade in the state capital of Frankfort. We swapped stories, and when it was Bill Greider's turn, he began talking about Bert Combs. At one time, Greider was the assistant managing editor of the *Washington Post* and then became an author (*Secrets of the Temple*), but in the 1960s, he covered Frankfort for a now-defunct daily newspaper, the *Louisville Times*. Combs is a colossal figure in Kentucky political history. He was a squeaky-voiced lawyer born in the Kentucky mountains who was elected governor and, later, appointed by Lyndon Johnson to be a federal appeals court judge. Combs was an idealist, and he was a fixer. He built the first modern road into his beloved mountains, and he represented a coal company that ran a mine so recklessly that it exploded twice and killed twenty-six men. He shilled for industry, and he represented a group of poor schools, a case that ended with the state supreme court ordering the largest increase in spending on public education in Kentucky history. He was the classic mountain attorney, said one acquaintance: "He wants to make you cry from both eyes. One eye for the pain and the other eye on the merits."

As Greider told the story, Governor Combs was sending an aide to Washington, D.C., to secure money for the Appalachian Mountains of Kentucky. The emissary asked if the governor had any last-minute instructions, and Combs allowed that he did. The governor said, cryptically, "Show them just enough to win the turkey." The man confessed that he had no idea what Combs was talking about, so the governor explained. Combs said that on a yearly trade day in one mountain town, there would be a contest of sorts. The young men would trail off behind a Main Street building and open their trousers; the gentleman with the largest display of manhood would win a live turkey. One trade day, the contest proceeded as tradition dictated. The competition was undecided until the judges reached a young man who slowly revealed his entry. The man had made only a partial disclosure when the judges acclaimed him clearly to be the most prodigious of that year's lot. The man tucked the feathered and flapping prize under his arm and walked back onto Main Street. The contest was no secret, of course, and when the man's wife saw her husband with the telltale turkey, she shrieked. How could he have done such a thing? "Don't worry, hon," the young man answered. "I just showed them enough to win the turkey." So, Combs told the aide, don't tell those people in Washington everything.

We all laughed, which surprised Greider, who said he'd been telling the story for years at Georgetown dinner tables to listeners who were either mystified or offended, but never amused. We all appreciated Kentucky politics — or at least the culture that once defined Kentucky politics. And we all knew this was quintessential Combs, a man who revealed himself, like the man with the turkey, only as necessary, a little bit at a time.

When I was a young reporter, I covered the explosions at the Scotia mine in 1976 that killed those twenty-six men, and I wrote about Combs as he defended the negligent coal company. The former governor did everything in his considerable power to win, and during that time, I considered him a traitor to his legacy. With politicians like Combs, however, you needed to stick around for a time to get the full story. Combs took the coal company's money, and a short time later, he resurfaced as the pro bono attorney representing public schools so poor that some of them couldn't afford to stock their restrooms with toilet paper. Combs sued the state on behalf of the schools. He demanded that the children in the poor, mostly rural communities be treated the same as their richer city neighbors. He was more successful representing kids than the coal company, but in both cases he was the insider, the fixer. Some say Combs not only represented the schoolchildren but also wrote the court's opinion. Nobody doubted the story.

A week before Combs died — in 1991, he accidentally drove his car into a stream that had flooded the road leading to his mountain home — he called me out of the blue and began describing a case to be made before the U.S. Supreme Court. Combs thought that he could make a winning argument that would overturn the Court's ruling that states couldn't limit spending on political campaigns. There was too much money in politics, Combs creaked, and the law didn't fit the times. That was Combs, a man who bounced between amazing grace and the temptations of the purse, the middleman between the factions and economic interests that squabbled over the carcass of Kentucky.

Our politics used to be filled with these Januses of special interests

and public purpose — old pols, guys who were funny, flawed, and conflicted. America's best political novels have been about these two-tone
politicians. Huey Long became Willie Stark in Robert Penn Warren's *All
the King's Men*. Lyndon Johnson was the model for Arthur "Goddamn"
Fenstemaker in Billy Lee Brammer's *The Gay Place*. Both books (and
the multiple biographies of Long and LBJ) wrestled with the ambiguity
inherent in their protagonists' occupation, but the fictional Fenstemaker
said it best when he explained how things worked to a young, liberal politician — an idealist reluctant to raise the money from the "wrong people" for a statewide campaign: "Your job is to get elected and stay
elected. That's the first consideration. When that's assured, you get good
enough, mean enough, you learn enough to fend off the bill collectors.
They come around wanting the moon and you give 'em green cheese and
make 'em think that was what they were lookin' for all the time. *That's*
what you do. That's what a professional *has* to do."[21]

The political world revolved around Fenstemaker. Others — Brammer
and his liberal (post-materialist) friends — lost their balance and were
consumed by alcohol or despair. Fenstemaker was able to fend off the
bill collectors for a time, and he served as the connection between the
state's ideological factions. He was able to do some good. At the end of
The Gay Place, the governor's aide, Jay McGown, finds Fenstemaker
dead, in bed, having spent the night with a woman (or maybe two) who
was not his wife. McGown remembers what Fenstemaker told him during an earlier campaign. "This is what you have to watch out for, Jay," the
governor warned. "Remember it. You sit here in these carpets up to your
ankles with a fire crackling in a corner and these black men serve you
red wine and rare roast beef — and there's crepes suzettes comin' later
— and tell me, now. Can you get all wrought up about the poor folks?"[22]
McGown knew that with Fenstemaker dead, an important part of what
made self-government possible was gone.

In the mid-1950s, an English anthropologist made a breakthrough in
his discipline's understanding of politics. Max Gluckman realized that
people were always in dispute. Societies were successful and long-
standing so long as they could devise mechanisms that kept simple conflicts from becoming cataclysmic. Gluckman described the Nuer, a

herding society of the Upper Nile. When the Nuer would fall into a dispute, the tribe would turn to a class of arbitrators known as the "men of the earth." The men of the earth had no formal powers, but they had cultural authority. When a person was killed in a village argument, a man of the earth would adjudicate compensation. When two groups of Nuer began fighting, a man of the earth could bring the factions to peace by rushing between the combatants and hoeing the soil. In modern democratic politics, Gluckman noted, we elect our men of the earth, politicians who are called upon to represent opposing factions and pressure groups.[23]

At one time, the politician's profession was to have divided loyalties. The conflicting desires and interests of a community were reconciled through the pol, the ward heeler. Politicians such as Combs and Lyndon Johnson were specialists in the art of showing just enough to win the turkey. With discretion and sometimes duplicity, they represented the diverse and conflicting factions within a county or a state, and through them disputes were mediated. Everyone would get angry with them, and everyone would also benefit from their work. Without them, the system, flawed as it is, has no way to reach the compromises that are fundamental to representative government.

Gluckman learned in Africa that people needed "cross-cutting" relationships to survive. Successful societies evolved so that friends and enemies would often change places: opponents at one time would be friends later. This dynamic mixing of interests gave a tribe stability and protected it from internal warfare. Gluckman, an anthropologist specializing in Africa, was a contemporary of the missionary Donald McGavran, but as a social theorist, Gluckman was, in a sense, McGavran's opposite. McGavran said, over and over, "Men do not join churches where services are conducted in a language they do not understand, or where members have a noticeably higher degree of education, wear better clothes, and are obviously of a different sort."[24] Whereas McGavran was interested in the attractive power of conformity, Gluckman studied the nature of conflict and its resolution. From his research into human discord, Gluckman came to see that normal conflict didn't escalate when people were connected to others in multiple ways, when the ties among the members of a tribe were conflicted. Societies that controlled disputes "are so organized into a series of groups and relationships, that people who are friends on one basis are enemies on another," Gluckman wrote.*[25]

Among the Nuer, Gluckman discovered, it not only ran against custom to marry within the family — a prohibition common in many cultures — but the tribe's rules "forbid, under penalty of disease, accident, and death, a man to marry any woman of his clan, or any woman to whom relationship can be traced in any line up to six generations." The rules forced marriages to be spread widely, with the result that all portions of the larger nation of Nuer were connected. The various clans had to remain friendly, if for no other reason than to avoid the risk of suffering a depressing decline in the number of available marriage partners. Marriage itself widened the web of friendship, or at least association. It was hard for there to be much internecine warfare, because no matter the configuration of warring parties, a Nuer would have to battle his (or his wife's) present or future in-laws. The saying, therefore, among some African peoples was "They are our enemies; we marry them."[26]

When political scientist Robert Dahl sought to explain the underlying stability of the American political system, he credited a "pattern of cleavages." America was divided by race, by faith, by geography, and by class, Dahl wrote. As long as those cleavages were mixed up in the country's politics — as long as groups weren't always friends or always foes — the heated conflicts that periodically arose would not boil over. However, Dahl wrote, "if all the cleavages occur along the same lines, if the same people hold opposing positions in one dispute after another, then the severity of conflicts is likely to increase. The man on the other side is not just an opponent; he soon becomes an enemy."[27]

The Big Sort, ironically, has given contemporary Americans a life simpler in important ways than the existence of Nuer herdsmen. Communities, churches, and volunteer groups are less likely now to be sources of those sometimes abrasive and troublesome cross-cutting relationships. Americans have used wealth and technology to invent and se-

---

*Gluckman quoted T. S. Eliot's observation on the need for overlapping and conflicting connections: "Indeed, the more the better: so that everyone should be an ally of everyone else in some respects, and an opponent in several others, and no one conflict, envy or fear will predominate" (quoted in Gluckman, *Custom and Conflict in Africa*, p. 2).

cure places of minimal conflict. They spend more time with people like themselves. Politicians are sharply partisan, mirroring the homogeneity of the electorate. The "men of the earth" are near extinction, and, most definitely, Americans are less likely to marry their enemies.*

Americans have been polarized before, of course, and these divisions have been cured by the eventual (some political scientists say inevitable) rise of cross-cutting issues. Although the two parties emerged from the 2006 midterm elections as polarized as at any time since the end of World War II, this kind of rigid partisanship can't last. Or at least it hasn't lasted in the past. Maybe the struggle to provide everyone with medical care will become one of those cross-cutting issues, urgent enough to put Republicans and Democrats in mixed company again. Already, an unlikely coalition including Wal-Mart, Intel, Kelly Services, and the Service Employees International Union is calling for a new American health care system by 2012.[28] Similar combinations of old enemies and new friends can be seen forming in debates surrounding immigration.

But the Big Sort has not been simply a difference of political opinion. The communities of interest — and the growing economic disparities among regions — won't disappear with a change in Congress or a new president. Moreover, it's wishful thinking to predict that a Generation Y LBJ will emerge to become a twenty-first-century "man of the earth," some kind of web-based "deus ex MySpace" politician who could forge a national consensus out of our disparate communities.† Presidential candidates and op-ed writers often lament the lack of leaders, as if entire generations of Americans were born without the skills of a Johnson, a Franklin D. Roosevelt, or a Dwight D. Eisenhower. There are, of course, just as many leaders as there have always been. What the coun-

---

*"The correlation between spouses' ideological orientations is strong," wrote political scientists Melissa Marschall and Wendy Rahn. These researchers also have found that online dating services specifically match clients with similar political views, a technological feat that "makes assortive mating ever more convenient." See "Birds of a Political Feather: Ideology, Partisanship, and Geographic Sorting in the American Electorate" (paper prepared for the annual meeting of the Midwest Political Science Association, April 21, 2006, pp. 6–7).

†Illinois senator Barack Obama presented himself early in the 2008 campaign as the man of the earth candidate, the politician able and eager to speak to — and listen to — all sides.

try is missing is old-fashioned followers. The generations that emerged in the second half of the twentieth century lost trust in every vestige of hierarchical authority, from the edicts of Catholic bishops to the degrees of Free Masons to the stature of federal representatives. There haven't been any new LBJs because the whole notion of leadership has changed — and the whole shape of democracy is changing.

Caffeinated Federalism and the End of Consensus

As people gather in like-minded places, their homogeneity will be reflected in the decisive actions of local governments. New Hampshire allowed civil unions in 2007, and New York governor Eliot Spitzer soon after introduced a bill that would legalize gay marriage. Meanwhile, the Texas legislature passed a bill in 2007 to protect religious "speech" in schools. Thanks to the Big Sort, the country will soon be awash in democratic experiments.

Meanwhile, those with the means will take more direct action.* The rich have always bought candidates, but now they will create their own political climates. In April 2007, two of the country's richest men, Bill Gates and Eli Broad, announced that they would spend $60 million to force candidates to address education in the 2008 presidential election. Two months later, U2 frontman Bono announced a $30 million public lobbying campaign to force presidential candidates to address Third World poverty, an effort that included actors Matt Damon and Ben Affleck, quarterback Tom Brady, and a celebrity bus tour through the early-primary states.[29] Tour de France winner and cancer survivor Lance Armstrong organized two forums in Iowa in mid-2007 so that Americans could hear what the presidential candidates intended to do about cancer, and the candidates answered the cyclist's call.[30]

The continued distrust of government, however, has reduced the size

---

*In a bizarre arrangement, private equity firms attempting to buy the huge Texas utility TXU offered Austin $30 million to help fund a pollution reduction plan for central Texas. The offer, however, came with a catch: local officials had to agree not to oppose TXU's plans to build a series of coal-fired power plants. See Claudia Grisales, "TXU Offer: $30 Million to Smooth Plant Deal," *Austin American-Statesman*, June 8, 2007, p. A1.

and scope of public life. Democracy has become so balky that the normal processes of representative government are being replaced by systems of issue brokering that are only quasi-representative. In Austin, public policy is often negotiated among interest groups, with government only ratifying decisions made behind the scenes.[31] Or decisions once regularly made by government are offloaded entirely to utility districts, homeowners associations, and water or road authorities. Representation of the whole is avoided, replaced by negotiations among tribes. Silicon Valley economist Doug Henton describes the coalition of businesses, government officials, and interest groups that manages his region as a "network governance" model.[32] In Austin and Silicon Valley, a democratically elected assembly is simply a single node on a crowded organizational chart.

A patchwork democracy is emerging: caffeinated federalism, representation by interest groups, decision making by nonelected officials, and, for those who are financially able, philanthropy as direct action to promote a social outcome. Americans are adopting an ad hoc style of governance, a niche democracy that tries to reconcile the demands of citizens today with laws and customs created over two centuries by people with very different ways of life.

Political life may have been emaciated over the past thirty years, but the Big Sort has served other institutions well. An economy built on loose social structures and the proliferation of new ideas has sorted people according to talents and education. Businesses and marketers have learned to segment products and target individual customers. Churches, communities, and volunteer groups cater to "people like us." All these institutions have nimbly shifted and adapted. They've changed, sometimes without even knowing it. For example, it's true that people choose their news based on ideology — conservatives pick Fox, liberals prefer CNN — but the news business may be even more finely altered by increasingly like-minded communities. Two University of Chicago economists measured "slant" in 377 newspapers representing 70 percent of the country's daily circulation. They found that editorial content skewed liberal or conservative based on the political leanings of readers. Newspapers in highly Republican Zip Codes (based on the 2004 vote) had a conservative slant. Newspapers in those communities used Republican catch phrases, such as "death tax," "war on terror," and "tax relief," more often than papers in Democratic Zip Codes. Those living in Democratic neighborhoods, meanwhile, were likely to have received a paper that skewed to the left. Ownership of the paper had little effect on the politics of the news. Without any specific command or strategy, the papers adopted the language preferred by their readers. The economists' explanation was that the newspapers were making subtle adjustments to satisfy "consumer demand."[33] That would be the market explanation. Another possibility is that a like-minded community has the power to mold its source for news so that it reflects readers' preexisting beliefs.

A friend asked the other evening, "Is it possible now to have a national consensus?" Perhaps not. Maybe the logic of the Big Sort is that there's no longer a national narrative to follow, no longer a communal path to unanimity. (Americans have so little in common that even television quiz shows are having a hard time coming up with questions that make sense to contestants and a broad audience.[34]) Baby Boomers, right and left, have tried to imprint on others their versions of the American story and will apparently battle to their graves to impose their will on the country. Think Peggy Noonan, Al Gore, James Dobson, Newt Gingrich, Cindy Sheehan, Martin Sheen, Al Sharpton, Roger Ailes, and Paul Krugman.

The kids at Bluer and Sojourn are less enticed by struggles over America's grand narrative. They are more interested in means, not ends, and don't believe that such an all-encompassing narrative does, or even should, exist.[35] "We don't know it all; it's hard to make judgments," said Dan Lukas, the Bluer musician. "We're in touch with others around the world — different languages and ways of thought. We can respond in two ways: we're right and they're wrong, or we can talk to one another." These young people are busy reshaping their churches now. Democracy may come later. Generational change — which created the Big Sort to begin with — is the force most likely to break down the divisions created over the past forty years. There are cracks already. Applebee's restaurant sales since the 2004 election have followed the same downward trajectory as George W. Bush's approval ratings. Applebee's was overtaken by hipper chains with less well-slathered food (for people who grew up with cooking shows on television) and free Internet connections. The company even considered redesigning its neighborhood wall — and then the chain was purchased by the International House of Pancakes.[36]

Meanwhile, national institutions have splintered. The idea of community has been "miniaturized," observed Francis Fukuyama. "Rather than seeking authoritative values in the national church that once shaped society's culture, people are picking and choosing their values on an individual basis, in ways that link them with smaller communities of like-minded folk."[37] That ability is both liberating and exciting. In this new world, there will be greater differences nationally among communities but fewer differences within the smaller groups — schools, neighborhoods, clubs, college dormitories, churches — where we actually live. There will be both more diversity and more conformity. But missing will be any sense of the whole. "I think we're going to see more isolation at the community or even [the] neighborhood level," Yankelovich Partners' J. Walker Smith told me. "We're going to have a nation of self-focused collectives. And the only universally shared American value is going to be the willingness to let other people live in their collectives in the ways they want to live. I worry that the traditional democratic notion of accommodating differences through compromise in order to sustain a shared way of life is going to fade away."

Beginning nearly thirty years ago, the people of this country unwittingly began a social experiment. Finding cultural comfort in "people like us," we have migrated into ever-narrower communities and churches and political groups. We have created, and are creating, new institutions distinguished by their isolation and single-mindedness. We have replaced a belief in a nation with a trust in ourselves and our carefully chosen surroundings. And we have worked quietly and hard to remove any trace of the "constant clashing of opinions" from daily life. It was a social revolution, one that was both profound and, because it consisted of people simply going about their lives, entirely unnoticed.[38] In this time, we have reshaped our economies, transformed our businesses, both created and decimated our cities, and altered institutions of faith and fellowship that have withstood centuries. Now more isolated than ever in our private lives, cocooned with our fellows, we approach public life with the sensibility of customers who are always right. "Tailor-made" has worked so well for industry and social networking sites, for subdivisions and churches, we expect it from our government, too. But democracy doesn't seem to work that way.

AFTERWORD

In 2008, Barack Obama and John McCain pictured themselves as post-partisan candidates, politicians who could reach beyond red and blue division. Obama wowed the nation with his speech at the 2004 Democratic National Convention when he disparaged those who "like to slice and dice our country into red states and blue states. . ." McCain was the "maverick" that no party or color could corral. Both believed they transcended the Big Sort.

They were wrong. America came out of the recent presidential election more divided than it had been in November of 2004. Nationally, political differences from county to county increased in '08, continuing the movement toward a more politically segregated country that began in the mid-1970s. Within seven out of ten states, divisions among counties widened. In 2004, 48.3 percent of all voters lived in counties where either George Bush or John Kerry won by 20 points or more. In this election, it was 47.6 percent. Several of the landslide counties changed, of course, as a widespread shift of voters toward Obama made most red communities slightly less vibrant and turned most blue counties darker. Not many changed colors entirely, however. Only 12 percent of the nation's counties switched parties from 2004 to 2008.

States grew more divided in 2008. In 1976, the average winning margin in the 50 states and Washington, D.C., was 10 percentage points. In 2004, 16 points. In 2008, the average winning margin for the 50 states and D.C. was 17.4 percentage points. The number of states where a candidate won by more than 10 points increased, from 19 states in '76 to 29 in 2004 to 36 in '08. And there were fewer states where the vote between Democrats and Republicans was at all close (less than five points) — 20 states in 1976, 11 in 2004, 7 in '08. The gap between how rural and urban residents voted also widened between 2004 and 2008. "There may be only one United States of America, as senator Obama says," Emory University's Alan Abramowitz observed in late 2008, "but the divide between red states and blue states is deeper than at any time in the past sixty years."

If we've learned anything since the publication of *The Big Sort* in the spring of 2008, it's that these geographic divisions are based first on the way people live and only secondarily by political party. For example, on a one-hour talk radio show in Minneapolis, three people called in to say they realized they were living in communities where they didn't belong. Could they tell by yard signs or political bumper stickers? No, they knew they were out of sorts with their community when they saw neighbors using lawn chemicals. These are the kinds of differences that are political in America today. People don't see themselves as members of demographic groups — a white working-class man, a college-educated woman. Like the woman in California who described herself to us as an "ocean-oriented person," Americans define themselves by their interests: the bands they listen to, the foods they eat, the sports they follow, the spiritual beliefs they adopt.

Most Americans have a kind of cultural literacy that allows them to pick up the clues that tell them when they are among their kind of people. We find the place that fits our style and, if we have the choice, that's where we settle. The *Salt Lake City Tribune* reported in mid-2008 that the total population of Mormons in Salt Lake City had declined by 5,000 over the previous five years.[1] There weren't fewer Mormons in the region, just fewer living in downtown Salt Lake. Mormons were leaving the city and resettling in more homogenous suburban developments outside the city. One of these new settlements was named Bountiful.

"There are twenty-eight children under twelve within nine houses on our cul-de-sac," a Bountiful resident told the *Tribune*. "We are all stay-at-home moms and all Mormons. It's great."

Lifestyle preferences are closely related to political preferences. After all, does anyone have a doubt about the political loyalties of the organic-minded Minnesotans who abhorred lawns by Monsanto? Meanwhile, in Salt Lake City, Mormons are abandoning downtown neighborhoods that have been growing more religiously diverse and politically Democratic, and they are moving to be among more like-minded neighborhoods in the increasingly Republican exurbs.

Family foretells political choice across the country, not just in Utah. In Chapter 9, we told of demographer Ron Lesthaeghe's research into what he calls the "second demographic transition." Lesthaeghe has tracked the increasing number of people who are adopting nontraditional approaches to family life. Women are postponing both marriage and childbearing, and more couples are living together without being married. Lesthaeghe created an index of these demographic tendencies and found that they were more pronounced in some parts of the United States than in others. Lesthaeghe calculated that states with high percentages of nontraditional families were more likely to vote for John Kerry in 2004. States with more traditional families sided with George Bush. After the 2008 election, Lesthaeghe ran his computations again. He discovered that the correlation between family formation and the vote had grown even stronger in the contest between Obama and McCain.

An election doesn't have to be between a Republican and a Democrat to find the Big Sort at work. In the long 2008 Democratic primary season, Obama and senator Hillary Clinton split the vote. But in a dead even contest between two ideologically similar candidates, half the voters lived in counties where either Obama or Clinton won by landslides — a greater percentage than in the 2004 general election between Kerry and Bush. In the Virginia Democratic primary, 72 percent of voters lived in a county where either Clinton or Obama won by 20 percentage points or more. Senator Clinton won 49 of Pennsylvania's 67 counties in landslides. The two Democrats had nearly identical voting records in the Senate, but their support came from two different Americas.

As we looked more closely at the results from the 2008 general election, we found that communities had grown increasingly unequal economically, educationally, and politically. People with higher incomes and more education were congregating in some communities. These places, on average, were growing more Democratic. Those with less income and fewer years of schooling were collecting in other counties. These communities were growing more Republican.

There were 605 counties (out of more than 3,100) that voted for George W. Bush in 2004 and then grew more Republican in the 2008 election. The average yearly household income in those counties was about $42,800, according to the Internal Revenue Service. ("Household income" here is defined as the total adjusted gross income reported on all individual tax returns in a county for the years 2003 through 2007, divided by the number of returns.) In contrast, for those 500-plus counties that were Democratic in 2004 and then voted more heavily Democratic in 2008, the average household income was $59,400, a nearly 40 percent difference.

We found these disparities across the board. Rural counties siding with Obama had higher average incomes than rural counties that went for McCain. Households in counties that flipped from Republican in 2004 to Democrat in 2008 had incomes that averaged 40 percent higher than those in counties that flipped from Democrat to Republican. The income differences carried over to the state level: all but 2 of the 18 states with incomes higher than the national average voted Democratic in '08.

Migration was reinforcing — perhaps creating — this geographic income inequality as poorer people moved into the counties trending Republican. Again using IRS data from 2003 through 2007, we found households that moved into those counties shifting Republican had average incomes of $38,200. Those who moved since the last election into counties that shifted Democratic had average household incomes of $49,100.

Places divided by income were also separated by education. In landslide Democratic counties, 32.7 percent of the adult population had a bachelor's degree or better. In counties where McCain won by 20 points or more, 20.4 percent of adults had finished college.

People with fewer moneymaking skills moved into one set of communities, and those places voted more Republican. Those with higher incomes (and more education) migrated to a separate set of counties, and those places voted more Democratic. The more lopsided the local political victory, the greater the differences in income and education.

We kept sorting economically, educationally, and politically — by our choice in religion and by the age when we decide to have children. And as Americans separated into their like-minded communities, political misunderstanding continued. In mid-October, just a few weeks before the election, pollster Peter Hart found that more than a third of each candidate's supporters reported that they had grown to "detest" their opponent. "How do you knit a nation back together with this kind of animosity?" Hart asked.[2] There was a belief after the 2006 midterm election that the success of "red state" Democrats, such as North Carolina congressman Heath Shuler and Montana senator Jon Tester, heralded the return of moderation to Congress. The cover of *Time* magazine announced, "Why the Center Is the New Place to Be."[3] The center's popularity was vastly overstated. In Chapter 10, we included Keith Poole's chart tracking the disappearance of political moderates in the House and Senate since the mid-1970s. Instead of a return to the center after the 2006 elections, Poole reports that the gap between the parties widened in the 110th Congress. The House in 2008 was the most polarized in its history. The Senate broke its record for polarization, one set in 1867.

Barack Obama may yet be able to reach some post-partisan happy hunting ground in his presidency. But his campaign segmented and targeted voters with all the polarizing effectiveness of George W. Bush. ("For a campaign that says it wants to end the politics of the Bush-Cheney years," Republican Karl Rove wrote, "the Obama for President effort has cribbed an awful lot from the Bush-Cheney playbooks of 2000 and 2004."[4]) Obama built what his campaign manager described as an "army of persuasion," the kind of neighbor-to-neighbor organizing scheme Bush used four years earlier. (See Chapter 11.) At "Obama Organizing Fellows" training sessions, campaign workers were encouraged to recruit voters by telling personal stories of their decision to support the Democrat. This is exactly the recruiting technique employed by Christian evangelicals and then by the Bush campaign in '04. (See

"'Friendship Evangelism' Finds a Campaign" in Chapter 11.) The goal wasn't to change minds, but to give voters constant reinforcement, to focus more on what people believed already than to have them think more broadly — to, perhaps, think of others.

Missouri senator Claire McCaskill told Democratic campaign workers, "The message you've got to send, more than any other message, is that Barack Obama is just like us."[5] In a country that is dividing by economic prospects, by years of education, by the look and feel of what constitutes a family, and by political persuasion, we continue to believe there might be a more important message we all need to hear. The message people living in a democracy must understand, more than any other message, is that there are Americans who aren't just like you. They don't live like you, they don't have families like yours, and they don't think like you. They may not live in your neighborhood, but this is their country, too.

Bill Bishop
Robert G. Cushing
January 2009
Austin, Texas

ACKNOWLEDGMENTS

THERE MAY NOT be an end to the number of people who contributed to the making of this book, but there are two people who were at the beginning: Tom and Pat Gish. Tom and Pat have owned and operated the *Mountain Eagle,* a weekly newspaper in the mountains of Eastern Kentucky, for the past half century. Before bloggers or citizen journalists or the Web 2.0, the Gishes practiced a tough, inclusive, honest, and ultimately democratic style of journalism that has guided me since I arrived on their doorstep in 1975. Tom and Pat have shown a respect for the people of Letcher County that is unusual in journalism and almost entirely missing from public life.

The Big Sort would have remained undiscovered without Bob Cushing. We met by chance, and it was due to his skill as a statistician and his curiosity as a scholar that we found the relationship between the economy, the culture, politics, and geography. Bob is a good scientist, and so, from the start, he let the facts, not ideological preference, lead his inquiry. (It also helped that Frances Cushing supported in all ways this very time-consuming project.) When I proposed to my editors at the *Austin American-Statesman* that Bob and I embark on an entirely speculative course of inquiry, they didn't blink. Rich Oppel and Fred Zipp decided that a midsize daily could conduct complicated social science research, and they sponsored this unusual project over three years. Maria Henson was a great editor on these stories in Austin, and she's been a better friend since we first met in Kentucky years ago. David Pasztor picked up editing chores when Maria moved on to California and quickly caught on to the spirit of the project.

Our research into city economies was helped immeasurably by an ad hoc research consortium. We found a group of scholars all studying the dynamics of city growth, and every few weeks throughout most of 2002, Bob and I would get on the phone with Richard Florida, Gary Gates, Terry Nichols Clark, Kevin Stolarick, and, at times, Joe Cortright. Florida, Stolarick, and Gates were busy with the research that would appear in Florida's book *The Rise of the Creative Class*. (Gates, then at the Urban Institute, was also in the middle of his work on the demography of gay America.) Clark, at the University of Chicago, was investigating how and why certain cities were attracting skilled workers. Cortright, a Portland, Oregon, economist, was deep into his own research on the connection between culture, demography, and economic growth. We shared information, thoughts, and problems in the most collaborative of relationships.

We sought help over the years from a number of people, and everyone we asked gave generously of their time and experience. Political scientists Jim Gimpel, Nate Persily, Mark Brewer, and Eric Schickler all advised us on the proper way to count and compare votes. Alan Abramowitz, Diana Mutz, and Peter Francia shared their research and their time. Social psychologist Dave Myers helped me understand the dynamics of group polarization. John Musick at Bluer and Mike Cosper at Sojourn were thoughtful guides into the emerging church. Joe Cortright and Ethan Seltzer showed me the Portland, Oregon, economy, and Anina Bennett introduced me to the wonderful artists in that town's comic book community. The Reverend Marvin Horan welcomed a complete stranger and honestly and eloquently explained the 1974 textbook battle in Kanawha County, West Virginia. Robert Gipe and Joan Robinett showed me how deeply the OxyContin plague had tortured Harlan County, Kentucky. Paul Stekler was a supportive, knowledgeable, and constructive reader.

That *The Big Sort* has been published at all is largely a matter of dumb luck. Tom Ashbrook of WBUR radio's *On Point* was kind enough to have me on his show in 2004. Anton Mueller, a Houghton Mifflin editor, was listening, and the next week he called with the suggestion that we turn our newspaper research into a book. Without his curiosity and willingness to take a chance, our explorations would have ended years ago. Thanks also to crack copy editors Barbara Jatkola and Beth Fuller.

We have benefited from the generosity of strangers throughout. I met Yankelovich Partners' Walker Smith in 2003 and have been peppering him with questions since. He's always answered with the knowledge of a marketing expert and the soul of a democratic citizen. Mickey Edwards was an eager reader of our stories in the *Austin American-Statesman* and organized a conference at Princeton University on political polarization after reading our series. (We've received advice since that conference from Princeton's Fred Greenstein and Larry Bartels.) Similarly, Robert Wright took an interest in our research and introduced me to his agent, Rafe Sagalyn, who not only navigated the business end of this endeavor but also helped shape an idea into a book.

Closer to home, this book is a celebration of a thirty-year adventure I've shared with Julie Ardery. We've done a lot together, but fundamental to my understanding of the Big Sort was our decision twenty-five years ago to buy a little newspaper in Smithville, Texas. Over several years of publishing the weekly in that wonderful town, the people there taught us how a decidedly unhomogeneous unit could exist as a community. We left Smithville a long time ago, but what we learned together there is a big part of this book. So, too, is Julie. She contributed her knowledge of social theory and her considerable skills as a writer. If this book is honest — and if you can understand what we are saying — it's due largely to her.

NOTES

Introduction

1. Unless otherwise noted, quotations in this book come from interviews conducted by the author.
2. James G. Gimpel and Jason E. Schuknecht, *Patchwork Nation: Sectionalism and Political Change in American Politics* (Ann Arbor: University of Michigan Press, 2003), pp. 27–28.
3. Richard Florida, *The Rise of the Creative Class* (New York: Basic Books, 2002).
4. Excluding third-party candidates was a common suggestion of the political scientists with whom we consulted. Eric Schickler, University of California, Berkeley; Nathaniel Persily, University of Pennsylvania; and James Gimpel, University of Maryland, were essential in setting the ground rules for this study. We found that including third parties changed the statistical details but not the substance of our studies.
5. Alaska votes by districts, which were not stable over this period, so the state was included as a whole.
6. In this calculation, Cushing and Logan used the "segregation index." Cushing used several measures, which showed the same pattern of change. Berkeley's Eric Schickler recommended measuring the change in standard deviation, weighted for the population of the county. The weighted standard deviation of the vote increased by 49 percent between 1976 and 2004.
7. For example, when we first began studying local election results, no academic institution kept county-by-county voting records for U.S. presidential elections. We found the results on a wonderful website (www.uselectionatlas.org)

maintained by Dave Leip, who began collecting election data as a hobby while he was a graduate student in engineering at MIT.

8. Gimpel and Schuknecht, *Patchwork Nation;* James G. Gimpel. *Separate Destinations: Migration, Immigration, and the Politics of Places* (Ann Arbor: University of Michigan Press, 1999).

9. J. Walker Smith, Ann Clurman, and Craig Wood, *Coming to Concurrence: Addressable Attitudes and the New Model for Marketing Productivity* (Evanston, IL: Racom Communications, 2005), p. 83.

1. The Age of Political Segregation

1. "Political Opinions Take a Violent Turn in Florida," *Seattle Times,* October 29, 2004, p. A8.

2. Akilah Johnson, "Police: Man Beats Woman About Vote," *South Florida Sun-Sentinel,* October 28, 2004, p. B5.

3. Lee Mueller, "Quarrel Between Friends Ends in Shooting in Floyd," *Lexington (KY) Herald-Leader,* August 6, 2005, p. A1.

4. Claire Taylor, "Vandals Target Democrats' Office for Second Time," *Lafayette (LA) Daily Advertiser,* September 17, 2004.

5. *Huntsville (AL) Times,* November 2, 2004.

6. Bill Bishop, "The Incredible Shrinking Middle Ground," *Austin American-Statesman,* August 29, 2004, p. A1.

7. Rick Lyman, "In Exurbs, Life Framed by Hours Spent in the Car," *New York Times,* December 18, 2006, p. 29.

8. "Political Parties and Partisanship: A Look at the American Electorate" (briefing, Brookings Institution/Princeton University, September 17, 2004), p. 17.

9. See Nolan McCarty, Keith T. Poole, and Howard Rosenthal, *Polarized America: The Dance of Ideology and Unequal Riches* (Cambridge, MA: MIT Press, 2006); see also Poole's website, www.voteview.com.

10. Alan Abramowitz, "Redistricting, Competition, and the Rise of Polarization in the U.S. House of Representatives" (paper presented at the annual meeting of the American Political Science Association, September 3, 2006).

11. Dana Milbank and David Broder, "Hopes for Civility in Washington Are Dashed," *Washington Post,* January 18, 2004, p. A1.

12. Hamilton College political scientist Philip Klinkner has argued that today's segregation is, in the long stretch of things, nothing unusual. See his article "Red and Blue Scare: The Continuing Diversity of the American Political Landscape," *Forum* 2, no. 2 (2004). See also Edward Glaeser and Bryce Ward, "Myths and Realities of American Political Geography" (Harvard Institute of Economic Research Discussion Paper 2100, January 2006).

13. Morris P. Fiorina, with Samuel J. Abrams and Jeremy C. Pope, *Culture War? The Myth of a Polarized America,* 2d ed. (New York: Pearson Longman, 2006), pp. xiii–xiv.

14. Ibid., pp. 21–22.

15. Morris P. Fiorina, with Samuel J. Abrams and Jeremy C. Pope, *Culture War? The Myth of a Polarized America* (New York: Pearson Longman, 2005), p. 5.

16. Jonathan Rauch, "Bipolar Disorder," *Atlantic,* January/February 2005, p. 102–10.

17. Joe Klein, "America Divided? It's Only the Blabocrats," *Time,* August 8, 2004, http://www.time.com/time/election2004/columnist/klein/article/0,18471,678593,00.html.

18. Robert Kuttner, "Red vs. Blue? Not True," *Boston Globe,* August 10, 2005, p. A15.

19. William Beaman, "A Fractured America?" *Reader's Digest,* November 2005.

20. E. J. Dionne Jr., "Why the Culture War Is the Wrong War," *Atlantic,* January/February 2006, p. 131.

21. Alan I. Abramowitz and Kyle L. Sanders, "Is Polarization a Myth?" (paper presented at the annual meeting of the Southern Political Science Association, January 5, 2006).

22. Alan Abramowitz and Bill Bishop, "The Myth of the Middle," *Washington Post,* March 1, 2007, p. A17. The data come from the Cooperative Congressional Election Study, which surveyed 24,000 people who voted in 2006.

23. Zachary Goldfarb, "How Many Wins Make Up a 'Wave'?" *Washington Post,* November 13, 2006; Rhodes Cook, "Democrats Made Gains in All Regions of the Country" (special to Pew Research Center, November 14, 2006).

24. Alan Abramowitz, Brad Alexander, and Matthew Gunning, "Don't Blame Redistricting for Uncompetitive Elections," *PS: Political Science and Politics* 39 (January 2006): 88. Also available at http://www.centerforpolitics.org/crystalball/article/php?id=AIA2005052601.

25. Jeanne Cummings, "Redistricting: Home to Roost," *Wall Street Journal,* November 10, 2006, p. A6.

26. Abramowitz, Alexander, and Gunning, "Don't Blame Redistricting," p. 88.

27. Bruce Oppenheimer, "Deep Red and Blue Congressional Districts," in *Congress Reconsidered,* ed. Lawrence C. Dodd and Bruce Oppenheimer, 8th ed., pp. 135–57 (Washington, DC: Congressional Quarterly Press, 2005).

28. Bill Bradley, "A Party Inverted," *New York Times,* March 30, 2005.

29. Lewis H. Lapham, "Tentacles of Rage: The Republican Propaganda Mill, a Brief History," *Harper's Magazine,* September 2004.

30. Jerome Armstrong and Markos Moulitsas Zuniga, *Crashing the Gate: Netroots, Grassroots, and the Rise of People-Powered Politics* (White River Junction, VT: Chelsea Green, 2006), pp. 26–27.

31. Mark Schmitt, "The Legend of the Powell Memo," *American Prospect,* April 27, 2005, http://www.prospect.org/cs/articles?articleId=9606.

32. John Micklethwait and Adrian Wooldridge, *The Right Nation: Conservative Power in America* (New York: Penguin Press, 2004), pp. 77–78.

33. Schmitt, "The Legend of the Powell Memo."

34. James Piereson, "Investing in the Right Ideas," *WSJ.com Opinion Journal,* May 27, 2005, http://www.opinionjournal.com/extra/?id=110006723.

35. Schmitt, "The Legend of the Powell Memo."

36. Abramowitz, Alexander, and Gunning, "Don't Blame Redistricting," p. 88.

37. Oppenheimer, "Deep Red and Blue Congressional Districts," pp. 152–53.

38. Gimpel was one of the first to see the growing geographic concentration of like-minded voters by community, writing about the phenomenon in James G. Gimpel and Jason E. Schuknecht, *Patchwork Nation: Sectionalism and Politi-*

cal Change in American Politics (Ann Arbor: University of Michigan Press, 2003).

39. John H. Fenton, *Midwest Politics* (New York: Holt, Rinehart & Winston, 1966), pp. 150–52.
40. Thomas Frank, *What's the Matter with Kansas? How Conservatives Won the Heart of America* (New York: Metropolitan Books, 2004).
41. Mark Blumenthal, "State of the Union Reaction," Pollster.com, January 24, 2007, http://www.pollster.com/blogs/state_of_the_union_reaction.php.

2. The Politics of Migration

1. David Myers, e-mail to author, 2004.
2. In this test, we simply measured the change in political segregation in the counties in each census region. We used the index of dissimilarity for this calculation.
3. Alan I. Abramowitz and Kyle L. Sanders, "Is Polarization a Myth?" (paper presented at the annual meeting of the Southern Political Science Association, January 5, 2006).
4. There were 19 surveys in this database and more than 31,000 interviews.
5. Scott Keeter of the Pew Research Center provided this analysis to the author. In one difference from Bob Cushing's analysis, Keeter slightly changed the dividing line for a strong partisan county. Instead of a 10-point difference, Keeter designated "landslide" counties as those with 20-point margins. Just under half the voters in 2004 lived in one of these counties.
6. Phillip Longman, "The Liberal Baby Bust," *USA Today,* March 14, 2006; David Brooks, "The New Red-Diaper Babies," *New York Times,* December 7, 2004; Joel Kotkin and William Frey, "Parent Trap," *New Republic,* December 2, 2004, http://www.joelkotkin.com/Politics/NR%20Parent_Trap.htm.
7. Ronald Brownstein, "As Democrats Look West, Colorado Budges," *Los Angeles Times,* September 28, 2006.
8. Bob Cushing used county-to-county migration data provided by the IRS to do this analysis.

3. The Psychology of the Tribe

1. James Sterling Young, *The Washington Community* (New York: Harcourt, Brace & World, 1966), pp. 17–18, 42–43, 56. As with much of history, some find fault with Young's analysis. See Allan G. Bogue and Mark Paul Marlaire, "Of Mess and Men: The Boardinghouse and Congressional Voting, 1821–1842, *American Journal of Political Science* 19, no. 2 (May 1975): 207–30.
2. Ibid., pp. 76–77, 81–82.
3. Ibid., p. 98.
4. Ibid., p. 102.
5. Ibid., pp. 102–4.
6. Ibid., p. 100.
7. Ibid., p. 105.

8. Ibid., p. 96.

9. "Walgren Slammed in Opponent's Spots for Living in McLean," *Roll Call*, November 5, 1990.

10. "The Polarization of American Politics: Myth or Reality" (transcript, Princeton University conference, panel 3, December 3–4, 2004), http://www.princeton.edu/~csdp/events/polarization.htm.

11. Mark Leibovich, "Taking Power, Sharing Cereal," *New York Times*, January 18, 2007, p. D1. See also Johanna Neuman, "At This 'Animal House,' the Party Is Democratic," *Los Angeles Times*, July 25, 2005.

12. Matt Stearns, "100 Block of D Street SE Embodies the Story of the GOP's Undoing," McClatchy Newspapers, November 16, 2006.

13. "The Polarization of American Politics."

14. Nelson W. Polsby, *How Congress Evolves: Social Bases of Institutional Change* (New York: Oxford University Press, 2004), pp. 125–26.

15. "The Polarization of American Politics."

16. Norman Triplett, "The Dynamogenic Factors in Pacemaking and Competition," *American Journal of Psychology* 9 (1897): 507–33. See also Michael A. Hogg and Joel Cooper, eds., *The Sage Handbook of Social Psychology* (London: Sage, 2003), pp. 3–23.

17. Muzafer Sherif, "A Study of Some Social Factors in Perception," *Archives of Psychology* 187 (July 1935): 47.

18. Ibid., pp. 48–53.

19. Stanley Schachter, "Deviation, Rejection, and Communication," *Journal of Abnormal and Social Psychology* 46 (1951): 190–207.

20. David Myers and Helmut Lamm, "The Group Polarization Phenomenon," *Psychological Bulletin* 83, no. 4 (1976): 602–3.

21. Serge Moscovici and Marisa Zavalloni, "The Group as a Polarizer of Attitudes," *Journal of Personality and Social Psychology* 1, no. 2 (1969): 125–35.

22. David G. Myers, *Social Psychology* (New York: McGraw-Hill Educational, 2004), pp. 308–24.

23. Cass R. Sunstein, *Why Societies Need Dissent* (Cambridge, MA: Harvard University Press, 2003), pp. 166–78; Cass R. Sunstein and David A. Schkade, "Judging by Where You Sit," *New York Times*, June 11, 2003, p. A31.

24. Myers, *Social Psychology*, pp. 313–16.

25. Robert Baron, interview with author, 2004. See also R. Baron, S. I. Hoppe, C. F. Kao, B. Brunsman, B. Linneweh, and D. Rogers, "Social Corroboration and Opinion Extremity," *Journal of Experimental Social Psychology* 321 (1996): 537–60.

26. Galatians 1:13–14.

27. Michael Schudson, *The Good Citizen: A History of American Civic Life* (New York: Free Press, 1998), pp. 82–83.

28. Federalist No. 37, *The Federalist Papers*, ed. Clinton Rossiter (New York: Mentor, 1961), p. 231.

29. "Brutus," quoted in Sunstein, *Why Societies Need Dissent*, p. 146.

30. Alexander Hamilton, quoted in Colleen A. Sheehan, "Madison v. Hamilton: The Battle over Republicanism and the Role of Public Opinion," *American Political Science Review* 98 (2004): 411.

31. Sheehan, "Madison v. Hamilton," p. 418.

32. Sunstein, *Why Societies Need Dissent,* p. 161.

33. Schudson, *The Good Citizen,* pp. 83–85.

34. Roger Sherman, quoted in Sunstein, *Why Societies Need Dissent,* pp. 151–52.

35. Federalist No. 70, *The Federalist Papers,* ed. Clinton Rossiter (New York: Mentor, 1961), pp. 426–27.

36. Warren Miller, "One-Party Politics and the Voter," *American Political Science Review* 50, no. 3 (September 1956): 707–25.

37. David E. Campbell, "What You Do Depends on Where You Are: Community Heterogeneity and Participation" (paper prepared for the annual meeting of the Midwest Political Science Association, April 15, 2004). See also David Campbell, *Why We Vote: How Schools and Communities Shape Our Civic Life* (Princeton, NJ: Princeton University Press, 2006).

38. Robert Huckfeldt, Edward G. Carmines, Jeffery J. Mondak, and Carl Palmer, "Blue States, Red States, and the Problem of Polarization in the American Electorate" (paper prepared for the annual meeting of the American Political Science Association, Washington, DC, September 2005), p. 25.

39. James L. Gibson, "The Political Consequences of Intolerance: Cultural Conformity and Political Freedom," *American Political Science Review* 86, no. 2 (June 1992): 344.

40. Shanto Iyengar and Richard Morin, "Red Media, Blue Media: Evidence for a Political Litmus Test in Online News Readership," *Washington Post,* May 3, 2006. The Pew Research Center found a similar polarization in news habits of Republicans and Democrats in 2004. See Pew Research Center for the People and the Press, "News Audiences Increasingly Politicized: Online News Audience Larger, More Diverse," June 8, 2004.

41. Drew Westen, quoted in Michael Shermer, "The Political Brain," *ScientificAmerican.com,* June 26, 2006, http://www.sciam.com/article.cfm?chanID=sa006&colID=13&articleID=000CE155-1061-1493-906183414B7F0162.

42. Paul F. Lazarsfeld, Bernard Berelson, and Hazel Gaudet, *The People's Choice: How the Voter Makes Up His Mind in a Presidential Campaign* (New York: Duell, Sloan & Pearce, 1944), pp. 82, 89, 90–91.

43. Matthew Dowd, chief strategist for the Bush campaign in 2004, interview with author, 2005.

44. Susanna Schrobsdorff, "A More Liberal Electorate? Not Yet," MSNBC.com/Newsweek, November 9, 2006, http://www.msnbc.msn.com/id/15643639/site/newsweek/print/1/displaymode/1098/.

4. Culture Shift: The 1965 Unraveling

1. Paul Tillich, quoted in Alan Ehrenhalt, "How the Yes Man Learned to Say No," *New York Times,* November 26, 2006.

2. Thomas Frank, *The Conquest of Cool* (Chicago: University of Chicago Press, 1997), p. 10.

3. C. Wright Mills, quoted in Michael Schudson, *The Good Citizen: A History of American Civic Life* (New York: Free Press, 1998), pp. 155, 365.

4. Arthur Schlesinger, quoted in Robert H. Wiebe, *Self-Rule: A Cultural History of American Democracy* (Chicago: University of Chicago Press, 1995), p. 219.

5. Wiebe, *Self-Rule,* p. 218.
6. David O. Sears, "Political Behavior," in *The Handbook of Social Psychology,* vol. 5, ed. Gardner Lindzey and Elliot Aronson (Reading, MA: Addison-Wesley, 1969), pp. 324–34.
7. Robert Wiebe, *The Segmented Society: An Introduction to the Meaning of America* (New York: Oxford University Press, 1975), p. 6.
8. Sears, "Political Behavior," p. 423.
9. V. O. Key Jr., *Southern Politics in State and Nation* (Knoxville: University of Tennessee Press, 1984), p. 37.
10. David W. Brady, Hahrie Han, and Doug McAdam, "Party Polarization in the Post WWII Era: A Two Period Electoral Interpretation" (paper prepared for the Midwest Political Science Association, April 2003).
11. "Toward a More Responsible Two-Party System: A Report of the Committee on Political Parties," pt. 2, *American Political Science Review* 44, no. 3 (1950): S18.
12. Ronald Inglehart and Christian Welzel, *Modernization, Cultural Change, and Democracy: The Human Development Sequence* (New York: Cambridge University Press, 2005), pp. 2–4.
13. Abraham Maslow, "A Theory of Human Motivation," *Psychological Review* 50 (1943): 370–96. See also Ronald Inglehart, *Culture Shift in Advanced Industrial Society* (Princeton, NJ: Princeton University Press, 1990), pp. 152–53.
14. Ronald Inglehart, *Modernization and Postmodernization: Cultural, Economic, and Political Change in 43 Societies* (Princeton, NJ: Princeton University Press, 1997), p. 8. See also Ronald Inglehart and Wayne Baker, "Modernization, Cultural Change, and the Persistence of Traditional Values," *American Sociological Review* 65 (February 2000): 21.
15. Ibid., pp. 115–18.
16. Ronald Inglehart, *The Silent Revolution: Changing Values and Political Styles in Advanced Industrial Society* (Princeton, NJ: Princeton University Press, 1977).
17. Inglehart, *Modernization and Postmodernization,* p. 295.
18. Inglehart and Welzel, *Modernization, Cultural Change, and Democracy,* pp. 57–58.
19. Pew Research Center for the People and the Press, "Trends in Political Beliefs and Core Attitudes: 1987–2007," March 22, 2007, pp. 28–37.
20. Ibid., p. 51.
21. See Inglehart, *Modernization and Postmodernization,* and Inglehart and Baker, "Modernization, Cultural Change, and the Persistence of Traditional Values," pp. 19–51.
22. Pew Research Center, "Trends in Political Values and Core Attitudes."
23. Philip E. Converse, *The Dynamics of Party Support* (Beverly Hills, CA: Sage, 1976), pp. 7, 32, 71–72.
24. Ibid., p. 69.
25. Robert D. Putnam, *Bowling Alone: The Collapse and Revival of American Community* (New York: Simon & Schuster, 2000), pp. 54–55, 112–13.
26. Anthony Bianco, "The Vanishing Mass Market," *BusinessWeek,* July 12, 2004, p. 65.
27. Francis Fukuyama, *The Great Disruption: Human Nature and the Reconstitution of Social Order* (New York: Touchstone, 2000), p. 27.

28. Martin Marty, foreword in *Understanding Church Growth and Decline: 1950–1978*, ed. Dean R. Hoge and David A. Roozen (New York: Pilgrim Press, 1979), p. 11.

29. Robert Wuthnow, "The Moral Minority: Where Have All the Liberal Protestants Gone?" *American Prospect*, May 22, 2000, p. 31.

30. David Roozen and Jackson Carroll, "Recent Trends in Church Membership and Participation: An Introduction," in *Understanding Church Growth and Decline: 1950–1978*, ed. Dean R. Hoge and David A. Roozen (New York: Pilgrim Press, 1979), pp. 11, 22–23.

31. Jerry Falwell, quoted in Geoffrey Layman, *The Great Divide: Religious and Cultural Conflict in American Party Politics* (New York: Columbia University Press, 2001), p. 10.

32. See Marc Hetherington and Thomas J. Rudolph, "Priming, Performance, and the Dynamics of Political Trust" (unpublished paper, n.d.).

33. See ibid. and Seymour Martin Lipset and William Schneider, *The Confidence Gap: Business, Labor, and Government in the Public Mind* (Baltimore: Johns Hopkins University Press, 1987), p. 15.

34. Lipset and Schneider, *The Confidence Gap*, pp. 15–16.

35. Joseph S. Nye Jr., Philip D. Zelikov, and David C. King, *Why People Don't Trust Government* (Cambridge, MA: Harvard University Press, 1997), pp. 1–4, 81, 111–13.

36. Everett Carll Ladd Jr., "Liberalism Upside Down: The Inversion of the New Deal Order, *Political Science Quarterly* 91, no. 4 (Winter 1976–1977): 593.

37. Converse, *The Dynamics of Party Support*, p. 106.

38. *New York Times*, January 9, 1965; January 10, 1965; March 3, 1965; August 7; 1965; Gene Roberts, "Mass Integration Is Quiet in South," *New York Times*, August 31, 1965.

39. *New York Times*, January 26, 1965.

40. Julia S. Ardery, *The Temptation: Edgar Tolson and the Genesis of Twentieth-Century Folk Art* (Chapel Hill, University of North Carolina Press, 1998), p. 145.

41. Jack Raymond, "Americans Called Ready to Assume Main Burden of War on Vietcong," *New York Times*, July 12, 1965.

42. *New York Times*, June 3, 1965.

43. Charles Mohr, "Village Burnings Disturb Marines," *New York Times*, August 9, 1965.

44. Austin C. Wehrwein, "U.S. Investigates Antidraft Groups," *New York Times*, October 18, 1965.

45. Edward C. Burns, "Buckley Assails Vietnam Protest," *New York Times*, October 22, 1965.

46. *New York Times*, November 15, 1965.

47. *New York Times*, November 25 and 28, 1965.

48. *New York Times*, March 27, 1965.

49. *New York Times*, August 15, 1965.

50. Gene Roberts, "Negroes Still Angry and Jobless Three Months After Watts Riot," *New York Times*, November 7, 1965.

51. Lawrence C. Davies, "California Issue for '66 Emerges," *New York Times*, August 16, 1965.

52. Todd Gitlin, *The Sixties: Years of Hope, Days of Rage* (New York: Bantam Books, 1993), p. 168.
53. Walter Dean Burnham, *The Current Crisis in American Politics* (New York: Oxford University Press, 1982), p. 295.
54. Lipset and Schneider, *The Confidence Gap,* p. 410.
55. Russell J. Dalton, "The Social Transformation of Trust in Government," *International Review of Sociology* 15, no. 1 (March 2005): 133–54.
56. Virginia A. Chanley, Thomas J. Rudolph, and Wendy M. Rahn, "The Origins and Consequences of Public Trust in Government," *Public Opinion Quarterly* 64 (2000): 239–56.
57. Lipset and Schneider, *The Confidence Gap,* p. 400.
58. Dalton, "The Social Transformation of Trust," pp. 135–38.
59. Jimmy Carter, quoted in Lipset and Schneider, *The Confidence Gap,* p. 13.
60. Ivor Crewe, quoted in Dalton, "The Social Transformation of Trust," p. 134.
61. Marc J. Hetherington, *Why Trust Matters: Declining Political Trust and the Demise of American Liberalism* (Princeton, NJ: Princeton University Press, 2005), p. 8.
62. Ibid., p. 36.
63. Ruth Marcus, "A Slide Toward Segregation," *Washington Post,* November 29, 2006, p. A23.
64. Hetherington, *Why Trust Matters,* pp. 101–3.
65. Harold L. Wilensky, *Rich Democracies: Political Economy, Public Policy, and Performance* (Berkeley: University of California Press, 2002), p. 205.
66. Terry Nichols Clark and Vincent Hoffmann-Martinot, eds., *The New Political Culture* (Boulder, CO: Westview Press, 1998).
67. Paul H. Ray and Sherry Ruth Anderson, *The Cultural Creatives: How 50 Million People Are Changing the World* (New York: Harmony Books, 2000).
68. Ruy Teixeira and John Judis, *The Emerging Democratic Majority* (New York: Scribner, 2002), p. 35.
69. Ray and Anderson, *The Cultural Creatives,* p. 23.
70. "American Piety in the 21st Century: New Insight to the Depth and Complexity of Religion in the U.S." (selected findings, Baylor Religion Survey, September 2006), pp. 7, 19, http://www.baylor.edu/content/services/document.php/33304.pdf.
71. Eileen E. Flynn, "Many in U.S. Pick Christ, Not Label," *Austin American-Statesman,* September 12, 2006, p. A1.
72. Clifford Krauss, "Canada Steers Closer to Europe Than the U.S. on Social Issues," *New York Times,* December 2, 2003, p. A1.
73. Adam Clymer, "College Students Not Drawn to Voting or Politics, Poll Shows," *New York Times,* January 13, 2000, p. A14.
74. Howard W. French, "As Japan's Women Move Up, Many Are Moving Out," *New York Times,* March 25, 2003, p. A3.
75. Denise Grady, "Scientists Say Herbs Need More Regulation," *New York Times,* March 7, 2000.
76. "Swiss Back Ban on Modified Crops," *International Herald Tribune,* November 27, 2005.
77. Inglehart, *Modernization and Postmodernization,* pp. 365–87; Krauss, "Canada Steers Closer to Europe," p. A1.

78. Justin Blum, "'Blue' States Tackling Energy on Their Own," *Washington Post,* January 22, 2006, p. A1.
79. Diana Jean Schemo, "In Small Town, 'Grease' Ignites a Culture War," *New York Times,* February 11, 2006, p. A1.
80. Jack Citrin, "Comment: The Political Relevance of Trust in Government," *American Political Science Review* 68 (1974): 973–74.
81. Burnham, *The Current Crisis in American Politics,* pp. 295–96.
82. Nye, Zelikov, and King, *Why People Don't Trust Government,* p. 97.
83. David Broder, "Victory Doubted by G.O.P. Leaders," *New York Times,* November 21, 1965, p. A1.
84. James L. Sundquist, *Dynamics of the Party System* (Washington, DC: Brookings Institution Press, 1983), p. 401.
85. Hetherington, *Why Trust Matters,* p. 142.
86. Sundquist, *Dynamics of the Party System,* pp. 376, 340.
87. Anna Greenberg, "Why Men Leave: Gender and Partisanship in the 1990s" (paper prepared for the annual meeting of the American Political Science Association, 2000).
88. Sundquist, *Dynamics of the Party System,* pp. 397–98.
89. Norman H. Nie, Sidney Verba, and John R. Petrocik, *The Changing American Voter* (Cambridge, MA: Harvard University Press, 1999).
90. See the various measures of congressional voting devised by Nolan McCarty, Keith Poole, and Howard Rosenthal, including their unpublished paper "Political Polarization and Income Inequality" (January 27, 2003), p. 3, http://www.wws.princeton.edu/research/papers/01_03_nm.pdf.

5. The Beginning of Division: Beauty and Salvation in 1974

1. Alice Moore, quoted in Catherine Candor, "A History of the Kanawha County Textbook Controversy" (PhD diss., Virginia Tech University, March 1976), p. 54.
2. Marvin Horan, quoted in Don J. Goode, "A Study of Values and Attitudes in a Textbook Controversy in Kanawha County, West Virginia: An Overt Act of Opposition to Schools" (PhD diss., Michigan State University, 1984), p. 95.
3. Goode, "A Study of Values and Attitudes." The following discussion is based on this source.
4. Geoffrey C. Layman and Edward G. Carmines, "Cultural Conflict in American Politics: Religious Traditionalism, Postmaterialism, and U.S. Political Behavior," *Journal of Politics* 59, no. 3 (August 1997): 751–77.
5. Rodney Stark, "Secularization, R.I.P.," *Sociology of Religion* 60, no. 3 (Autumn 1999): 249–50.
6. Peter Berger, quoted ibid., p. 250.
7. Pippa Norris and Ronald Inglehart, "God, Guns and Gays: Religion and Politics in the US and Western Europe" (paper presented at the John F. Kennedy School of Government, Harvard University, September 6, 2004), p. 2. Emphasis in original.
8. Martin E. Marty, *Righteous Empire: The Protestant Experience in America* (New York: Dial Press, 1970), pp. 177–80.

9. Ibid., p. 184.
10. Ibid., pp. 177, 179.
11. Walter Rauschenbusch, quoted in Robert William Fogel, *The Fourth Great Awakening and the Future of Egalitarianism* (Chicago: University of Chicago Press, 2000), p. 120.
12. Walter Rauschenbusch, *Christianity and the Social Crisis* (New York: Macmillan, 1908), pp. 230–86.
13. Fogel, *The Fourth Great Awakening*, pp. 124–25.
14. Marty, *Righteous Empire*, pp. 218–19.
15. Ibid.
16. Jerry Falwell, ed., *The Fundamentalist Phenomenon: The Resurgence of Conservative Christianity* (New York: Doubleday, 1981), pp. 79–80.
17. Ibid., p. 107.
18. Sara Diamond, *Roads to Dominion: Right Wing Movements and Political Power in the United States* (New York: Guilford Press, 1995), pp. 162–63.
19. Marty, *Righteous Empire*, pp. 203, 250.
20. John C. Green, James L. Guth, Corwin E. Smidt, and Lyman A. Kellstedt, *Religion and the Culture Wars: Dispatches from the Front* (Lanham, MD: Rowman & Littlefield, 1996), p. 270.
21. Diamond, *Roads to Dominion*, p. 25.
22. Robert Wuthnow, *After Heaven: Spirituality in America Since the 1950s* (Berkeley: University of California Press, 1998), pp. 90–93.
23. Ibid., pp. 149, 167, 161.
24. Ibid., p. 227.
25. Ibid., p. 181.
26. Diamond, *Roads to Dominion*, pp. 26–35.
27. Marty, *Righteous Empire*, p. 250.
28. Louis Menand, "Breaking Away: Francis Fukuyama and the New Conservatives," *The New Yorker*, March 27, 2006, pp. 82–84.
29. Tim LaHaye and Jerry B. Jenkins, *Left Behind: A Novel of the Earth's Last Days* (Wheaton, IL: Tyndale House, 1995), p. 273.
30. McGirr, *Suburban Warriors: The Origins of the New American Right* (Princeton, NJ: Princeton University Press, 2001), p. 44.
31. Fogel, *The Fourth Great Awakening*, p. 129.
32. *Time*, May 26, 1961; Paul A. Crow Jr., "Eugene Carson Blake: Apostle of Christian Unity," *Ecumenical Review* 21 (1986): 228–36.
33. "Churchmen Call Parley on Selma," *New York Times*, March 11, 1965, p. A1.
34. "Christianity: The Servant Church," *Time*, December 25, 1964, pp. 45–49.
35. David A. Roozen, "Four Mega-Trends Changing America's Religious Landscape" (speech, annual conference of the Religion Newswriters Association, September 22, 2001).
36. "Christianity: The Servant Church," p. 47.
37. *Time*, April 8, 1966.
38. James Moffett, *Storm in the Mountains* (Carbondale: Southern Illinois University Press, 1988), p. 11.
39. Candor, "A History of the Kanawha County Textbook Controversy," p. 31.
40. Ibid., pp. 27–33.

41. James C. Hefley, *Textbooks on Trial* (Wheaton, IL: Victor Books, 1976), p. 159.
42. Candor, "A History of the Kanawha County Textbook Controversy," p. 32.
43. Ibid., pp. 52, 54.
44. Ibid., pp. 27, 87, 92.
45. Ibid., pp. 109–71.
46. Carol Mason, "An American Conflict: Representing the 1974 Kanawha County Textbook Controversy," *Appalachian Journal* 32, no. 3 (2005): 65–66.
47. Ibid., p. 66.
48. Hal Lindsey, *The Late Great Planet Earth* (Grand Rapids, MI: Zondervan, 1970), p. 185.
49. Mason, "An American Conflict," p. 58.
50. Everett Carll Ladd Jr., "Liberalism Upside Down: The Inversion of the New Deal Order," *Political Science Quarterly* 91, no. 4 (Winter 1976–1977): 577.
51. Larry M. Bartels, "What's the Matter with *What's the Matter with Kansas?*" (paper prepared for the annual meeting of the American Political Science Association, September 2004), http://www.princeton.edu/~bartels/kansas.pdf. See also Jeffrey M. Stonecash, Mark D. Brewer, and Mack D. Mariani, *Diverging Parties: Social Change, Realignment, and Party Polarization* (Boulder, CO: Westview Press, 2003), pp. 89–90.
52. Ladd, "Liberalism Upside Down," p. 584.
53. John Egerton, quoted in Candor, "A History of the Kanawha County Textbook Controversy," p. 24.
54. Bartels, "What's the Matter?" p. 14.
55. Ruy Teixeira, "It's the White Working Class, Stupid," Emerging Democratic-Majority.com, February 5, 2005, http://www.emergingdemocraticmajority weblog.com/donkeyrising/archives/001042.php. See also Ruy Teixeira, "Once Again on the White Working Class," DemocraticStrategist.org, May 7, 2005, http://www.thedemocraticstrategist.org/donkeyrising/2005/05/once_again_on_ the_white_workin.html.
56. Goode, "A Study of Values and Attitudes," pp. 117, 120.
57. Candor, "A History of the Kanawha County Textbook Controversy," p. 177.
58. Ibid., p. 133.
59. Mason, "Textual Reproduction of Ethnicity," p. 65.
60. Moffett, *Storm in the Mountains*, p. 41.
61. Candor, "A History of the Kanawha County Textbook Controversy," p. 132.
62. Moffett, *Storm in the Mountains*, p. 41.
63. Mason, "Textual Reproduction of Ethnicity," p. 18.
64. Candor, "A History of the Kanawha County Textbook Controversy," pp. 214, 187.
65. Edward B. Jenkinson, *Censors in the Classroom* (Carbondale: Southern Illinois University Press, 1979), p. 29.
66. Richard Viguerie, quoted in Diamond, *Roads to Dominion*, p. 176.
67. Diamond, *Roads to Dominion*, p. 174.
68. Peter Francia, Jonathan S. Morris, Carmine Scavo, and Jody C. Baumgartner, "America Divided? Re-examining the 'Myth' of the Polarized American Electorate" (paper presented at the annual meeting of the American Political Science Association, Washington, DC, September 1–4, 2005).

69. Ibid.
70. Ibid.
71. Pippa Norris and Ronald Inglehart, *Sacred and Secular: Religion and Politics Worldwide* (New York: Cambridge University Press, 2004), p. 201.
72. Norris and Inglehart, "God, Guns and Gays."
73. Norris and Inglehart, *Sacred and Secular,* pp. 201–12.

6. The Economics of the Big Sort: Culture and Growth in the 1990s

1. Dave Eggers, *A Heartbreaking Work of Staggering Genius* (New York: Vintage Books, 2001), p. 129.
2. See Bill Bishop and Mark Lisheron, "Cities of Ideas" (series), *Austin American-Statesman,* 2002, http://www.statesman.com/specialreports/content/special reports/citiesofideas/.
3. Edward L. Glaeser and Christopher R. Berry, "The Divergence of Human Capital Levels Across Cities" (Harvard Institute of Economic Research Discussion Paper 2091, August 2005), p. 10, http://www.economics.harvard.edu/hier/2005papers/HIER2091.pdf.
4. Richard Florida, "The World Is Spiky," *Atlantic,* October 2005, pp. 48–49.
5. Glaeser and Berry, "The Divergence of Human Capital," pp. 10–11.
6. Joe Cortright, "The Young and Restless in a Knowledge Economy" (report prepared for CEOs for Cities, December 2005), p. 30.
7. Edward Glaeser and Jesse M. Shapiro, "City Growth and the 2000 Census: Which Places Grew, and Why" (Center of Urban and Metropolitan Policy, Brookings Institution, May 2001), p. 9, http://www.brookings.edu/reports/2001/05demographics_edward-glaeser-and-jesse-m—shapiro.aspx.
8. Glaeser and Berry, "The Divergence of Human Capital," pp. 2–11. See also Michael E. Porter, "The Economic Performance of Regions," *Regional Studies* 37, nos. 6 & 7 (August/October 2003): 550–51.
9. Joe Cortright, "The Young and Restless," p. 10.
10. Ibid., p. 29.
11. Yolanda K. Kodrycki, "Migration of Recent College Graduates: Evidence from the National Longitudinal Survey of Youth," *New England Economic Review,* January/February 2001, p. 15.
12. Cortright, "The Young and Restless," p. 43.
13. Porter, "The Economic Performance of Regions," p. 553.
14. Ibid., p. 550.
15. Glaeser and Berry, "The Divergence of Human Capital," pp. 29–30.
16. Nolan McCarty, Keith T. Poole, and Howard Rosenthal, *Polarized America: The Dance of Ideology and Unequal Riches* (Cambridge, MA: MIT Press, 2006).
17. Paul Seabright, *The Company of Strangers: A Natural History of Economic Life* (Princeton, NJ: Princeton University Press, 2004), p. 198.
18. Richard Florida, *The Rise of the Creative Class* (New York: Basic Books, 2002), pp. 236–42.
19. William O'Hare and Bill Bishop, "U.S. Rural Soldiers Account for a Dispropor-

tionately High Share of Casualties in Iraq and Afghanistan" (fact sheet, Carsey Institute, Fall 2006).

20. "Enlistment Supply in the 1990s" (Defense Manpower Data Center Report No. 2000–015, April 2001).

21. Roger Alford, "Fedex Has No Plans to Resume Drug Deliveries," *Whitesburg (KY) Mountain Eagle*, March 2, 2005, p. B1.

22. Tom Lasseter, "A Familiar Story: From Miner to Drug User to Dealer," *Lexington Herald-Leader*, December 7, 2003, p. A1.

23. Charles B. Camp, "Millions Sold, Office by Office," *Lexington Herald-Leader*, August 17, 2003, p. A1.

24. "OxyContin Maker Pleads Guilty to Misleading Public on Risks," *Wall Street Journal*, May 10, 2007.

25. "Drug Overdose Numbs Appalachia," *Lexington Herald-Leader*, January 19, 2003, p. A8.

26. Laura Ungar, "Poverty Fuels Medical Crisis," *Louisville Courier-Journal*, September 25, 2005, p. A1.

27. See Richard Florida, Robert Cushing, and Gary Gates, "When Social Capital Stifles Innovation," *Harvard Business Review*, August 1, 2002; the Social Capital Community Benchmark Survey, on which we based our analysis, can be found at http://www.ropercenter.uconn.edu/data_access/data/datasets/social_capital _community_survey.html.

28. Professor Putnam has made the DDB Needham Life Style survey, conducted by the advertising firm DDB Worldwide of Chicago, available at http:// www.bowlingalone.com/data.htm.

29. Florida, *The Rise of the Creative Class*, pp. 273–76.

30. Edward L. Glaeser and Joshua D. Gottlieb, "Urban Resurgence and the Consumer City" (Harvard Institute of Economic Research Working Paper 2109, 2006), pp. 6–9.

31. Paul M. Romer, "Two Strategies for Economic Development: Using Ideas and Producing Ideas," in *Proceedings of the World Bank Annual Conference on Development Economics*, 1992, pp. 68–69.

32. Joe Cortright, "New Growth Theory, Technology and Learning: A Practitioner's Guide" (U.S. Department of Commerce Economic Development Administration, Reviews of Economic Development Literature and Practice, no. 4, 2001), http://cherry.iac.gatech.edu/REFS/TRP-Ref/cortright-ngt.pdf.

33. Ibid., p. 4.

34. Ibid., pp. 4–6.

35. Ibid., p. 2.

36. Jane Jacobs, *The Economy of Cities* (New York: Vintage Books, 1970), pp. 51–52.

37. Ibid., pp. 52–53.

38. Paul Romer, "Innovation: The New Pump of Growth," *Blueprint: Ideas for a New Century*, Winter 1998.

39. Jacobs, *The Economy of Cities*, pp. 85–121.

40. Robert E. Lucas Jr., "On the Mechanics of Economic Development," *Journal of Monetary Economics* 22 (1988): 38–39.

41. Mark S. Granovetter, "The Strength of Weak Ties," *American Journal of Sociology* 78, no. 6 (May 1973): 1360–80.

42. Peter Hall, *Cities in Civilization* (New York: Fromm International, 1998), p. 494.

43. Ibid., pp. 526–35.

44. AnnaLee Saxenian, *Regional Advantage: Culture and Competition in Silicon Valley and Route 128* (Cambridge, MA: Harvard University Press, 1994). See also AnnaLee Saxenian, "Lessons from Silicon Valley," *Technology Review,* July 1994, pp. 42–51.

45. Glaeser and Gottlieb, "Urban Resurgence and the Consumer City," p. 2.

46. Jung Won Sonn and Michael Storper, "The Increasing Importance of Geographic Proximity in Technological Innovation: An Analysis of U.S. Patent Citations, 1975–1997" (paper prepared for the conference "What Do We Know About Innovation?" November 2003).

47. Randall Stross, "It's Not Who You Know. It's Where You Are," *New York Times,* October 22, 2006.

48. Sam Roberts, "Tech-Drive Metro Areas Renew Their Population Gains," *New York Times,* April 5, 2007, p. A11.

49. Glaeser and Gottlieb, "Urban Resurgence and the Consumer City," p. 13.

50. Cortright, "The Young and Restless," p. 10.

51. N. C. Aizenman, "D.C. May Be Losing Status as a Majority-Black City," *Washington Post,* May 17, 2007, p. A1.

52. Glaeser and Gottlieb, "Urban Resurgence and the Consumer City," pp. 13–15.

53. Joseph Gyourko, Christopher Mayer, and Todd Sinai, "Superstar Cities" (National Bureau of Economic Research Working Paper No. 12355, July 2006).

54. Glaeser and Gottlieb, "Urban Resurgence and the Consumer City."

55. Richard Florida, "Cities and the Creative Class," *City and Community,* March 2003, pp. 3–19.

56. Terry Nichols Clark, *The City as Entertainment Machine* (Oxford: Elsevier, 2004).

57. Gyourko, Mayer, and Sinai, "Superstar Cities," p. 2.

58. Data collected by the Bus Project in Portland, Oregon, and provided to the author.

7. Religion: The Missionary and the Megachurch

1. Brad Stone, "Social Networking's Next Phase," *New York Times,* March 3, 2007, p. B1.

2. Rick Warren, *The Purpose-Driven Church: Growth Without Compromising Your Message and Mission* (Grand Rapids, MI: Zondervan, 1995), pp. 29–30.

3. Donald McGavran, quoted in a presentation by Robert Shuster to Wheaton College alumni, May 11, 2002, Billy Graham Archives, Wheaton College, http://www.wheaton.edu/bgc/archives/treasure/tr02/tr02.html.

4. C. Peter Wagner, ed., *Church Growth: State of the Art* (Wheaton, IL: Tyndale House, 1986), p. 9.

5. Donald McGavran, *The Bridges of God* (New York: Friendship Press, 1968), pp. 44, 59.

6. Ibid., p. 66.
7. J. Waskom Pickett, *Christian Mass Movements in India* (New York: Abingdon Press, 1933), p. 43.
8. Ibid., pp. 43–45.
9. Wagner, *Church Growth*, pp. 41–42.
10. Donald McGavran, quoted in Wagner, *Church Growth*, p. 9.
11. McGavran, *The Bridges of God*, pp. 44–45.
12. Donald McGavran, *Understanding Church Growth* (Grand Rapids, MI: Eerdmans, 1970), p. 107.
13. Ibid., pp. 190, 198, 271.
14. Dean R. Hoge and David A. Roozen, eds., *Understanding Church Growth and Decline: 1950–1978* (New York: Pilgrim Press, 1979), pp. 70–80.
15. Eddie Gibbs, Donald A. McGavran Professor of Church Growth, Fuller Theological Seminary, interview with author, 2005.
16. Ibid.
17. Michael Luo, "Religion: With Expansion Stalled, Some Consider Steps Such as Replacing Pews with Tables and Chairs to Draw Young Congregants," *Los Angeles Times,* June 7, 1999.
18. Scott Thumma, Dave Travis, and Warren Bird, "Megachurches Today 2005: Summary of Research Findings" (paper prepared for the Hartford Institute for Religion Research, 2005), p. 13, http://hirr.hartsem.edu/megachurch/megastoday2005_summaryreport.html.
19. Malcolm Gladwell, "The Cellular Church: How Rick Warren's Congregation Grew," *The New Yorker*, September 12, 2005, pp. 60–67.
20. Joel Comiskey, "Cell-Based Ministry: A Positive Factor for Church Growth in Latin America" (PhD diss., Fuller Theological Seminary, June 1997), pp. 61–69.
21. Dean Kelley, quoted in Hoge and Roozen, *Understanding Church Growth and Decline,* p. 70.
22. C. Peter Wagner, "Church Growth Research: The Paradigm and Its Applications," in *Understanding Church Growth and Decline: 1950–1978,* ed. Dean R. Hoge and David A. Roozen (New York: Pilgrim Press, 1979), p. 282.
23. Martin Marty, foreword in "Church Growth Research: The Paradigm and Its Applications," in *Understanding Church Growth and Decline: 1950–1978,* ed. Dean R. Hoge and David A. Roozen (New York: Pilgrim Press, 1979), pp. 12–13.
24. David A. Roozen, "Oldline Protestantism: Pockets of Vitality Within a Continuing Stream of Decline" (Hartford Institute for Religion Research Working Paper 1104.1, 2004).
25. Marty, foreword, p. 13.
26. George M. Marsden, *Reforming Fundamentalism* (Grand Rapids, MI: Eerdmans, 1987), p. 243.
27. McGavran, *The Bridges of God*, p. 8.
28. Robert Evans, "Recovering the Church's Transforming Middle: Theological Reflections on the Balance Between Faithfulness and Effectiveness," in *Understanding Church Growth and Decline: 1950 1978,* ed. Dean R. Hoge and David A. Roozen (New York: Pilgrim Press, 1979), pp. 293, 304.
29. James H. Smylie, "Church Growth and Decline in Historical Perspective:

Protestant Quest for Identity, Leadership, and Meaning," in *Understanding Church Growth and Decline: 1950–1978*, ed. Dean R. Hoge and David A. Roozen (New York: Pilgrim Press, 1979), p. 79.

30. Warren, *The Purpose-Driven Church*, pp. 155–72. The following discussion is from this source.

31. Diana C. Mutz and Jeffery Mondak, "The Workplace as a Context for Cross-Cutting Political Discourse," *Journal of Politics* 68, no. 1 (February 2006): 140–55.

32. John Green, "The American Political Landscape and Political Attitudes: A Baseline for 2004," Pew Forum on Religion and Public Life, September 9, 2004, http://pewforum.org/publications/surveys/green-full.pdf.

33. "The 2000 Bum Steer Awards," *Texas Monthly*, January 2000, p. 84.

34. James Guth, "Southern Baptist Clergy, the Christian Right, and Political Activism in the South," in *Politics and Religion in the White South*, ed. Glenn Feldman (Lexington: University Press of Kentucky, 2005), p. 191.

35. Green, "The American Political Landscape," p. 3.

36. Thumma, Travis, and Bird, "Megachurches Today," p. 6.

37. Pew Forum on Religion and Public Life, "Myths of the Modern Mega-Church" (transcript, May 23, 2005).

38. John Green, "Religious Groups and the 2004 Election: Spring 2004 Baseline," p. 10.

39. Scott Keeter of the Pew Research Center provided this analysis to the author.

40. Andy Newman, "At Crusade, Spirit Meets Science in the Altar Call," *New York Times*, June 25, 2005, p. A1.

8. Advertising: Grace Slick, Tricia Nixon, and You

1. John E. O'Toole, "Are Grace Slick and Tricia Nixon Cox the Same Person?" *Journal of Advertising* 2, no. 2 (1973): 32–34.

2. Richard Jensen, *The Winning of the Midwest* (Chicago: University of Chicago Press, 1971), pp. 165–66.

3. Ibid., p. 173.

4. Daniel Pope, *The Making of Modern Advertising* (New York: Basic Books, 1983), p. 63.

5. Michael J. Piore and Charles F. Sabel, *The Second Industrial Divide* (New York: Basic Books, 1984), p. 57.

6. Ibid., p. 50.

7. Robert H. Wiebe, *Self-Rule: A Cultural History of American Democracy* (Chicago: University of Chicago Press, 1995), p. 134.

8. Richard B. Westbrook, "Politics as Consumption: Managing the Modern American Election," in *The Culture of Consumption: Critical Essays in American History, 1880–1980*, ed. Richard Wightman Fox and T. J. Jackson Lears (New York: Pantheon Books, 1983), p. 155.

9. Wendell Smith, "Product Differentiation and Market Segmentation as Alternative Marketing Strategies," *Journal of Marketing* 21, no. 1 (July 1956): 3–8.

See also Lizabeth Cohen, *A Consumers' Republic: The Politics of Mass Consumption in Postwar America* (New York: Knopf, 2003), chap. 7.

10. Smith, "Product Differentiation," p. 6.
11. Albert Lasker, quoted in Pope, *The Making of Modern Advertising*, p. 258.
12. Pierre Martineau, "Social Classes and Spending Behavior," *Journal of Marketing* 23, no. 2 (October 1958): 122–23.
13. Ibid., p. 127.
14. Pierre Martineau, quoted in Cohen, *A Consumers' Republic*, p. 297.
15. Ibid., p. 300.
16. Daniel Yankelovich, "New Criteria for Market Segmentation," *Harvard Business Review*, March/April 1964, pp. 83–90.
17. Richard Tedlow, *New and Improved: The Story of Mass Marketing in America* (Cambridge, MA: Harvard Business School Press, 1996), p. 23.
18. Ibid., pp. xxiii–xxvii.
19. Don Peppers and Martha Rogers, *The One to One Future: Building Relationships One Customer at a Time* (New York: Currency/Doubleday, 1993), pp. 174, 386–87.
20. Ibid., p. 132.
21. Joseph Turow, *Breaking Up America: Advertisers and the New Media World* (Chicago: University of Chicago Press, 1997), p. 192.
22. Vance Packard, *The Hidden Persuaders* (New York: McKay, 1957), pp. 3–4, 266.
23. Turow, *Breaking Up America*, pp. 3, 108, 126.
24. Robert Wiebe, *The Segmented Society: An Introduction to the Meaning of America* (New York: Oxford University Press, 1975), pp. 8–9.
25. Emanuel Rosen, *The Anatomy of Buzz* (New York: Doubleday, 2000), pp. 60–61.
26. William H. Whyte Jr., "The Web of Word of Mouth," *Fortune*, November 1954.
27. Mark Grinblatt, Matti Keloharju, and Seppo Ikaheimo, "Interpersonal Effects in Consumption: Evidence from the Automobile Purchases of Neighbors" (Yale International Center for Finance Working Paper No. 04-10, September 2004), http://ssm.com/abstract=513945.
28. Whyte, "The Web," p. 143.
29. George G. Hunter III, "The Bridges of Contagious Evangelism: Social Networks," in *Church Growth: State of the Art*, ed. C. Peter Wagner (Wheaton, IL: Tyndale House, 1986), pp. 69–81.
30. Rosen, *The Anatomy of Buzz*, p. 70.
31. F. B. Evans, "Selling as a Dyadic Relationship: A New Approach," *American Behavioral Scientist* 6, no. 9 (May 1963): 76–79.
32. David A. Roozen, "Oldline Protestantism: Pockets of Vitality Within a Continuing Stream of Decline" (Hartford Institute for Religion Research Working Paper 1104.1, 2004).
33. Cohen, *A Consumers' Republic*, p. 342.

9. Lifestyle: "Books, Beer, Bikes, and Birkenstocks"

1. Alfred Marshall, quoted in Joe Cortright, "Making Sense of Clusters" (paper prepared for the Brookings Institution, August 29, 2005).

2. Gwenda Richards Oshiro, "The Evolution of Dark Horse Comics," *Portland Oregonian,* July 6, 2006.

3. George Gene Gustines, "A Quirky Superhero of the Comics Trade," *New York Times,* November 12, 2006.

4. Joe Cortright, "The Economic Importance of Being Different: Regional Variations in Taste, Increasing Returns and the Dynamics of Development," *Economic Development Quarterly* 16, no. 1 (February 2002): 3–16.

5. Charles Tiebout, "A Pure Theory of Local Expenditures," *Journal of Political Economy* 64, no. 5 (October 1956): 416–24.

6. Ari L. Goldman, "The Catskills Come of 'New Age'; New Life for the Old Hotels, Though Not for the Tax Rolls," *New York Times,* August 14, 1992.

7. Tim Hibbitts, Oregon pollster, interview with author, 2005.

8. James Mayer, "Think the Commute's Bad Now? More Jobs May Mean More Jams," *Portland Oregonian,* October 2, 2005, p. A1.

9. Ronald Brownstein and Richard Rainey, "GOP Plants Flag on New Voting Frontier," *Los Angeles Times,* November 22, 2004.

10. Alan Berube, Audrey Singer, Jill H. Wilson, and William H. Frey, "Finding Exurbia: America's Fast-Growing Communities at the Metropolitan Fringe" (Brookings Institution, October 2006), p. 7, http://www.brookings.edu/reports/2006/10metropolitanpolicy_berube.aspx.

11. Michael Harrington, "Democrats Should Try Appealing to More Married Voters," *Christian Science Monitor,* May 25, 2006.

12. Robert E. Lang and Thomas W. Sanchez, "The New Metro Politics: Interpreting Recent Presidential Elections Using a County-Based Regional Typology" (election brief, Metropolitan Institute at Virginia Tech, 2006).

13. George Lakoff, *Moral Politics: What Conservatives Know That Liberals Don't* (Chicago: University of Chicago Press, 1996), p. 12.

14. Marc J. Hetherington and Jonathan Weiler, "Authoritarian Values and Political Choice" (paper prepared for the annual meeting of the Midwest Political Science Association, 2005); Marc J. Hetherington and Jonathan Weiler, "Spare the Rod and Spoil the Nation?" (unpublished paper, n.d.).

15. Hetherington and Weiler, "Authoritarian Values and Political Choice."

16. Daniel J. Elazar, *The American Mosaic: The Impact of Space, Time and Culture on American Politics* (Boulder, CO: Westview Press, 1994), p. 97.

17. Robert H. Wiebe, *The Search for Order, 1877–1920* (New York: Hill & Wang, 1967), pp. 2–3.

18. Manuel Castells, quoted in Craig Calhoun, "Populist Politics, Communications Media and Large Scale Societal Integration," *Sociological Theory* 6, no. 2 (Autumn 1988): 224.

19. Ibid., p. 226.

20. Stephanie McCrummen, "Redefining Property Values," *Washington Post,* April 16, 2006, p. A1.

21. Sarah Schweitzer, "Like Recycling? Cooking? Then Welcome Home," *Boston Globe,* September 3, 2006.

22. Ron Lesthaeghe and Lisa Neidert, "The Political Significance of the 'Second Demographic Transition' in the US: A Spatial Analysis" (paper prepared for the annual meeting of the Population Association of America, March 28–30,

2007). See also Ron Lesthaeghe and Lisa Neidert, "The Second Demographic Transition in the United States: Exception or Textbook Example?" *Population and Development Review* 32, no. 4 (December 2006): 669–98.

23. Émile Durkheim, *Selected Writings,* ed. Anthony Giddens (Cambridge: Cambridge University Press, 1972), pp. 142–44.
24. Ibid., pp. 186–88.
25. Ibid., p. 175.
26. Daniel Bell, *The Coming of Post-Industrial Society* (New York: Basic Books, 1999), pp. 287–88.

10. Choosing a Side

1. Alan Greenblatt, "What Makes ALEC Smart?" *Governing,* October 2003; Pauline Vu, "How ALEC, CPA Help Shape State Laws," *Stateline.org,* June 7, 2005, http://www.stateline.org/live/ViewPage.action?siteNodeId=136&languageId=1&contentId=35924.
2. Greenblatt, "What Makes ALEC Smart?"
3. Sarah A. Binder, "Elections and Congress's Governing Capacity," *Extensions: A Journal of the Carl Albert Congressional Research and Studies Center* (Fall 2005): 10–14.
4. Defenders of Wildlife and Natural Resources Defense Council, "Corporate America's Trojan Horse in the States: The Untold Story Behind the American Legislative Exchange Council," 2002, http://alecwatch.org/report.html.
5. People for the American Way and Defenders of Wildlife Action Fund, "ALEC and the Battle of the States," January 2003, http://www.pfaw.org/pfaw/dfiles/file_169.pdf.
6. Jason DeParle, "Goals Reached, Donor on Right Closes Up Shop," *New York Times,* May 29, 2005, p. A1.
7. Theda Skocpol, *Diminished Democracy: From Membership to Management in American Civic Life* (Norman: University of Oklahoma Press, 2003), p. 230.
8. James Piereson, "Investing in the Right Ideas," *WSJ.com Opinion Journal,* May 27, 2005, http://www.opinionjournal.com/extra/?id=110006723.
9. Skocpol, *Diminished Democracy,* pp. 135, 219.
10. Katrina vanden Heuvel, "Building to Win," *Nation,* July 9, 2001.
11. Michelle Goldberg, *Kingdom Coming: The Rise of Christian Nationalism* (New York: Norton, 2006), p. 206.
12. Jerome Armstrong and Markos Moulitsas Zuniga, *Crashing the Gate: Netroots, Grassroots, and the Rise of People-Powered Politics* (White River Junction, VT: Chelsea Green, 2006), pp. 95, 109.
13. Bill McKibben, "The Hope of the Web," *New York Review of Books* (April 27, 2006, p. 6.
14. Stephen Simon, "A Conservative's Answer to Wikipedia," *Los Angeles Times,* June 19, 2007.
15. Armstrong and Zuniga, *Crashing the Gate,* pp. 105–10. See also Matt Bai, "Wiring the Vast Left-Wing Conspiracy," *New York Times Magazine,* July 25, 2004.

16. Thomas B. Edsall, "Rich Liberals Vow to Fund Think Tanks; Aim Is to Compete with Conservatives," *Washington Post,* August 7, 2005, p. A1.

17. Carsey and Layman take up the issue of party identification in these pieces: Thomas M. Carsey and Geoffrey C. Layman, "Changing Sides or Changing Minds? Party Identification and Policy Preferences in the American Electorate," *American Journal of Political Science* 50, no. 2 (April 2006); Thomas M. Carsey and Geoffrey C. Layman, "Party Polarization and Party Structuring of Policy Attitudes: A Comparison of the 1972–1974–1976 and 1992–1994–1996 National Election Study Panels" (presentation at the Vanderbilt University Conference on Parties and Partisanship, October 25–27, 2001); Thomas M. Carsey, Geoffrey C. Layman, John Green, and Richard Herrera, "Party Polarization and 'Conflict Extension' in the United States: The Case of Party Activists" (paper presented at the annual meeting of the Southern Political Science Association, January 6–8, 2005).

18. Jacob S. Hacker and Paul Pierson, *Off Center: The Republican Revolution and the Erosion of American Democracy* (New Haven, CT: Yale University Press, 2005), p. 6.

19. Carsey and Layman, "Changing Sides or Changing Minds?" p. 470.

20. Ibid., p. 467.

21. Robert A. Dahl, *Democracy in the United States: Promise and Performance,* 2nd ed. (Chicago: Rand McNally, 1972), p. 372.

22. Sharon Waxman, "Two Americas of 'Fahrenheit' and 'Passion,'" *New York Times,* July 13, 2004, p. B1.

23. Brody Mullins, "Softball on the Mall Was Bipartisan Fun Until Politics Intruded," *Wall Street Journal,* April 24, 2006, p. A1.

24. Melissa Marschall and Wendy Rahn, "Birds of a Political Feather: Ideology, Partisanship, and Geographic Sorting in the American Electorate" (paper prepared for the annual meeting of the Midwest Political Science Association, April 21, 2006), p. 3.

25. Adam Nagourney and Michael Barbaro, "Eye on Election, Democrats Run as Wal-Mart Foe," *New York Times,* August 17, 2006.

26. Brian Czech and Rena Borkhataria, "The Relationship of Political Party Affiliation to Wildlife Conservation Attitudes," *Politics and the Life Sciences,* March 2001, pp. 3–12.

27. Pew Research Center for the People and the Press, "Two-in-Three Critical of Bush's Relief Efforts," September 8, 2005, http://people-press.org/reports/display.php3?ReportID=255.

28. *Newsweek* Poll, May 13, 2006, http://prnewswire.com/news/index_mail.shtml?ACCT=104&STORY=/www/story/05-13-2006/0004360839&EDATE=.

29. Janet Adamy and Richard Gibson, "Flak over 'Fast Food Nation,'" *Wall Street Journal,* May 18, 2006, p. B1.

30. Pew Research Center for the People and the Press, "Democrats and Republicans See Different Realities," November 6, 2006.

31. Laura McCallum, "Dean Johnson Defects to DFL," Minnesota Public Radio, January 12, 2000.

32. Kevin Featherty, "The Independent," *Minnesota Monthly,* October 2005, pp. 83–86.

33. Nelson W. Polsby, *How Congress Evolves: Social Bases of Institutional Change* (New York: Oxford University Press, 2004), p. 147.

34. Charles Babington, "One Party's Lawmaking Is Another's Electioneering," *Washington Post,* June 24, 2006, p. A1.

35. Donna Smith, "Congress Has Many Unfinished Tasks," *Boston Globe,* July 10, 2006.

36. Franklin Foer, "The Joy of Federalism," *New York Times Book Review,* March 6, 2005.

37. Marc Kaufman, "Plan B Battles Embroil States: Proposals Mirror Red-Blue Divide," *Washington Post,* February 27, 2006, p. A1.

38. Adam Liptak, "15 States Expand Right to Shoot in Self-Defense," *New York Times,* August 7, 2006.

39. David J. Lee, "ECISD Paves Way for Bible Elective," *Odessa (TX) American,* May 1, 2006.

40. Michael Janofsky, "Philadelphia Mandates Black History for Graduation," *New York Times,* June 25, 2005.

41. Blaine Harden, "Gore Film Sparks Anger in Washington School District," *Boston Globe,* January 26, 2007.

42. Juliet Eilperin, "Cities, States Aren't Waiting for U.S. Action on Climate," *Washington Post,* August 11, 2006, p. A1.

43. Anthony Faiola and Robin Shulman, "Cities Take Lead on Environment as Debate Drags at Federal Level," *Washington Post,* June 8, 2007, p. A1.

44. James Gimpel, "The Federalism Flip-Flop: Democrats Now Argue for States' Rights," *Boston Globe,* December 19, 2004.

45. Laura Mecoy, "Stem Cell Measure Takes Partisan Tone," *Monterey County (CA) Herald,* September 5, 2004.

46. Joanna Kempner, Clifford S. Perlis, and Jon F. Merz, "Forbidden Knowledge," *Science,* February 11, 2005, p. 854.

47. Ron Nissimov, "To the Republicans on City Council: Your Party Is Keeping an Eye on You," *Houston Chronicle,* February 24, 2005.

48. Keith T. Poole, "The Decline and Rise of Party Polarization in Congress During the Twentieth Century," *Extensions: A Journal of the Carl Albert Congressional Research and Studies Center* (Fall 2005): 6–9. See also Nolan McCarty, Keith T. Poole, and Howard Rosenthal, *Polarized America: The Dance of Ideology and Unequal Riches* (Cambridge, MA: MIT Press, 2006).

49. Alan I. Abramowitz, "Redistricting, Competition, and the Rise of Polarization in the U.S. House of Representatives" (paper prepared for the annual meeting of the American Political Science Association, Philadelphia, August 31–September 3, 2006), p. 3.

50. Keiko Ono, "Electoral Origins of Partisan Polarization in Congress: Debunking the Myth," *Extensions: A Journal of the Carl Albert Congressional Research and Studies Center* (Fall 2005): 16. See also Abramowitz, "Redistricting," p. 10.

51. McCarty, Poole, and Rosenthal, *Polarized America,* pp. 175–84.

52. Binder, "Elections and Congress's Governing Capacity."

53. James Sterling Young, *The Washington Community* (New York: Harcourt, Brace & World, 1966), pp. 168–70. See also Michael Barone, "Boardinghouse Rules," *U.S. News and World Report,* January 8, 2001, p. 21.

11. The Big Sort Campaign

1. "Evaluation of Edison/Mitofsky Election System 2004" (prepared by Edison Media Research and Mitofsky International for the National Election Pool, January 19, 2005), p. 43.
2. Pew Research Center for the People and the Press, "News Audiences Increasingly Politicized: Online News Audience Larger, More Diverse," June 8, 2004, p. 3.
3. Fox News/Opinion Dynamics Poll, October 26, 2006, http://www.foxnews.com/projects/pdf/FOX235_release_web.pdf.
4. Jeff Mapes, "GOP Works Behind Scenes in State," *Portland Oregonian,* September 12, 2004, p. B1.
5. Matt Bai, "Who Lost Ohio?" *New York Times Magazine,* November 21, 2004, p. 72.
6. See, among others, Peter Wallsten and Tom Hamburger, "The GOP Knows You Don't Like Anchovies," *Los Angeles Times,* June 25, 2006. See also Tom Hamburger and Peter Wallsten, *One Party Country: The Republican Plan for Dominance in the 21st Century* (Hoboken, NJ: John Wiley & Sons, 2006).
7. S. C. Gwynne, "Retail Politics," *Texas Monthly,* January 2006, p. 192.
8. Adam Nagourney, "Bush Campaign Manager Views the Electoral Divide," *New York Times,* November 19, 2004.
9. Michael Barone, "The 51 Percent Nation," *U.S. News and World Report,* November 15, 2004.
10. Alan I. Abramowitz and Kyle L. Sanders, "Is Polarization a Myth?" (paper presented at the annual meeting of the Southern Political Science Association, January 5, 2006).
11. Quoted in Larry M. Bartels, "Partisanship and Voting Behavior, 1952–1996," *American Journal of Political Science* 44, no. 1 (January 2000): 35.
12. Bartels, "Partisanship and Voting Behavior," p. 35.
13. Brendan I. Koerner, "The Big Applebee's," *Slate,* March 31, 2005, http://slate.com/id/2115997/.
14. Douglas B. Sosnik, Matthew J. Dowd, and Ron Fournier, *Applebee's America: How Successful Political, Business, and Religious Leaders Connect with the New American Community* (New York: Simon & Schuster, 2006), pp. 62–92.
15. Ibid., p. 62.
16. Alan S. Gerber and Donald P. Green, "The Effects of Canvassing, Telephone Calls, and Direct Mail on Voter Turnout: A Field Experiment," *American Political Science Review* 94, no. 3 (September 2000): 653–63; Donald P. Green, Alan S. Gerber, and David W. Nickerson, "Getting Out the Vote in Local Elections: Results from Six Door-to-Door Canvassing Experiments," *Journal of Politics* 65, no. 4 (November 2003): 1083–96.
17. Bai, "Who Lost Ohio?" p. 69.
18. Robert Wuthnow, *After Heaven: Spirituality in America Since the 1950s* (Berkeley: University of California Press, 1998), pp. 7–10.
19. J. Walker Smith, Ann Clurman, and Craig Wood, *Coming to Concurrence: Ad-*

dressable Attitudes and the New Model for Marketing Productivity (Evanston, IL: Racom Communications, 2005), p. 213; "Marketing in the 'Age of I'" (interview with Lawrence Light), *BusinessWeek,* July 12, 2004, http://www.businessweek.com/magazine/content/04_28/b3891011_mz001.htm.

20. Smith, Clurman, and Wood, *Coming to Concurrence,* pp. 211–12.

21. Scott Keeter of the Pew Research Center provided this analysis to the author.

22. Melanie Wells, "Kid Nabbing," *Forbes,* February 2, 2004.

23. C. Peter Wagner, ed., *Church Growth: State of the Art* (Wheaton, IL: Tyndale House, 1986), p. 51.

24. Joel Comiskey, "Cell-Based Ministry: A Positive Factor for Church Growth in Latin America" (PhD diss., Fuller Theological Seminary, June 1997), p. 66.

25. Daron Shaw, "Door to Door with the GOP," *Hoover Digest,* Fall 2004.

26. Seth C. McKee and Daron R. Shaw, "Suburban Voting in Presidential Elections," *Presidential Studies Quarterly* 33, no. 1 (March 2003).

27. Seth C. McKee, "The Matter with Kansas: Rural Republican Voting in Presidential Elections" (paper presented at the annual meeting of the Midwest Political Science Association, Chicago, April 2006).

28. Anna Greenberg and Bill Greener, "The 2004 Rural Vote Explained: Message from the Heartland" (memo, Greenberg Quinlan Rosner Research, Inc., and Greener and Hook, March 22, 2005), http://www.greenbergresearch.com/index.php?ID=1221.

29. Ibid.

30. "The Urban Archipelago," *Stranger,* November 11–17, 2006, http://www.urbanarchipelago.com/.

31. Seth McKee, "Rural Vote and the Polarization of American Presidential Elections" (unpublished paper, 2006).

32. Alan Cooperman, "Democrats Win Bigger Share of Religious Vote," *Washington Post,* November 11, 2006, p. A1.

33. Greg Sargent, "New Gallup Poll: Dems Made Gains Among Whites, Independents and Rural Voters," TalkingPointsMemo.com, November 9, 2006, http://tpmelectioncentral.com/2006/11/new_gallup_poll_dems_made_gains_among_whites_independents_and_rural_voters.php.

34. David W. Rohde, "Political Command and Control," *New York Times,* November 18, 2006.

35. Aaron Blake, "Straight-Party Voters' Support of Dems Draws Ire from Opposition," *Hill,* November 20, 2006.

36. Zachary Goldfarb, "How Many Wins Make Up a 'Wave'?" *Washington Post,* November 13, 2006; Rhodes Cook, "Democrats Made Gains in All Regions of the Country" (special to Pew Research Center, November 14, 2006).

37. John C. Fortier, "Elections May Divide Congress Even More," *Washingtonpost.com,* November 14, 2006, http://www.aei.org/publications/pubID.25136,filter.all/pub_detail.asp.

38. Kay Stewart, "Northup Lost Grip on Some Democrats," *Louisville (KY) Courier-Journal,* November 9, 2006.

39. Jeffrey Goldberg, "Central Casting," *The New Yorker,* May 29, 2006, p. 64.

40. Alan Abramowitz and Bill Bishop, "The Myth of the Middle," *Washington Post*, March 1, 2007, p. A17; the data come from the Cooperative Congressional Election Study, which surveyed 24,000 people who voted in 2006.

41. Adam Nagourney and Megan Thee, "G.O.P. Voters Voice Anxieties on Party's Fate," *New York Times*, March 13, 2007, p. A1.

42. Pew Research Center for the People and the Press, "Trends in Political Values and Core Attitudes: 1987–2007," March 22, 2007, p. 31.

43. Mike DeWine, interview, *All Things Considered*, National Public Radio, November 8, 2006.

44. Jonathan Weissman, "GOP's Base Helps Keep Unity on Iraq," *Washington Post*, April 30, 2007, p. A1.

45. Jeff Zeleny and Carl Hulse, "Democrats' Proposals Make Deal on an Iraq Bill Harder," *New York Times*, May 5, 2007, p. A5.

12. To Marry Your Enemies

1. Rick Warren, *The Purpose-Driven Church* (Grand Rapids, MI: Zondervan, 1995), p. 257.

2. John Stuart Mill, quoted in Diana C. Mutz and Jeffery Mondak, "The Workplace as a Context for Cross-Cutting Political Discourse," *Journal of Politics* 68, no. 1 (February 2006): 140.

3. John F. Dovidio, Samuel L. Gaertner, and Kerry Kawakami, "Intergroup Contact: The Past, Present, and the Future," *Group Process and Intergroup Relations* 6, no. 1 (2003): 6.

4. Thomas F. Pettigrew and Linda R. Tropp, "Does Intergroup Contact Reduce Prejudice? Recent Meta-Analytic Findings," in *Reducing Prejudice and Discrimination: The Claremont Symposium on Applied Social Psychology*, ed. Stuart Oskamp (Mahwah, NJ: Erlbaum, 2000), p. 93.

5. Michael Hogg and Dominic Abrams, "Intergroup Behavior and Social Identity," in *The Sage Handbook of Social Psychology*, ed. Michael Hogg and Joel Cooper (London: Sage, 2003), pp. 420–21.

6. Muzafer Sherif, O. J. Harvey, B. Jack White, William R. Hood, and Carolyn W. Sherif, *Intergroup Conflict and Cooperation: The Robbers Cave Experiment* (Norman, OK: University Book Exchange, 1961), http://psychclassics.yorku.ca/Sherif/.

7. Henri Tajfel, "Experiments in Intergroup Discrimination," *Scientific American*, November 1970, pp. 96–102.

8. Gordon Allport, quoted in Dovidio, Gaertner, and Kawakami, "Intergroup Contact," p. 6.

9. Dale T. Miller and Deborah A. Prentice, "Some Consequences of a Belief in Group Essence: The Category Divide Hypothesis," in *Cultural Divides: Understanding and Overcoming Group Conflict*, ed. Dale T. Miller and Deborah A. Prentice (New York: Russell Sage Foundation, 1999), pp. 216, 230.

10. Diana C. Mutz, *Hearing the Other Side: Deliberative Versus Participatory Democracy* (New York: Cambridge University Press, 2006).

11. Ibid., p. 31.

12. Bruce Ackerman and James S. Fishkin, *Deliberation Day* (New Haven, CT: Yale University Press, 2004).

13. David Schkade, Cass R. Sunstein, and Reid Hastie, "What Happened on Deliberation Day?" (AEI-Brookings Joint Center for Regulatory Studies Working Paper 06-19, July 2006), http://aei-brookings.org/admin/authorpdfs/redirect-safely.php?fname=../pdffiles/phpb7.pdf.

14. Ibid., p. 2.

15. See also Eddie Gibbs and Ryan K. Bolger, *Emerging Churches: Creating Christian Community in Postmodern Cultures* (Grand Rapids, MI: Baker Academic, 2005).

16. Mutz, *Hearing the Other Side,* p. 92.

17. Donald Green, Bradley Palmquist, and Eric Schickler, *Partisan Hearts and Minds* (New Haven, CT: Yale University Press, 2002), p. 49.

18. Paul Lazarsfeld, Bernard Berelson, and William McPhee, *Voting: A Study of Opinion Formation in a Presidential Campaign* (Chicago: University of Chicago Press, 1954), pp. 314-15, 320.

19. Mutz, *Hearing the Other Side,* pp. 141-51.

20. Paul F. Lazarsfeld, Bernard Berelson, and Hazel Gaudet, *The People's Choice: How the Voter Makes Up His Mind in a Presidential Campaign* (New York: Duell, Sloan & Pearce, 1944), p. 314.

21. Billy Lee Brammer, *The Gay Place* (1961; repr. Austin: University of Texas Press, 1995), pp. 332-33.

22. Ibid., p. 518.

23. Max Gluckman, *Custom and Conflict in Africa* (1956; repr. New York: Barnes & Noble Books, 1969), pp. 5-26.

24. Donald McGavran, *Understanding Church Growth* (Grand Rapids, MI: Eerdmans, 1970), p. 271.

25. Gluckman, *Custom and Conflict,* p. 4.

26. Ibid., pp. 12-13.

27. Robert A. Dahl, *Democracy in the United States: Promise and Performance* (Chicago: Rand McNally, 1972), p. 309.

28. Milt Freudenheim, "New Urgency in Debating Health Care," *New York Times,* April 6, 2007.

29. "Bono and Friends Open Bid to Make World Poverty a Focus of '08 Race," *Washington Post,* June 12, 2007, p. A6.

30. W. Gardner Selby, "Armstrong Rides into Political Fray with Two Cancer Forums," *Austin American-Statesman,* July 19, 2007, p. B1.

31. Bill Bishop, "Austin Wants to Be Austin," *Austin American-Statesman,* February 26, 2000).

32. Douglas Henton, "Lessons from Silicon Valley: Governance in a Global City-Region," in *Global City-Regions: Trends, Theory, Policy,* ed. Allen J. Scott (Oxford: Oxford University Press, 2002), p. 391.

33. Matthew Gentzko and Jesse M. Shapiro, "What Drives Media Slant? Evidence from U.S. Daily Newspapers" (University of Chicago and the National Bureau of Economic Research, October 17, 2006), http://faculty.chicagogsb.edu/matthew.gentzkow/research/biasmeas111306.pdf.

34. Mark Roth, "Smart and Dumber: Quiz Shows for the Best and Brightest Are in Jeopardy," *Pittsburgh Post-Gazette,* May 22, 2007, p. C-1.

35. Jean-Francois Lyotard, "The Postmodern Condition," in *Social Theory: The Multicultural and Classic Readings*, ed. Charles Lemert (Boulder, CO: Westview Press, 1993), pp. 510–13.

36. Janet Adams, "A Shift in Dining Scene Nicks a Once-Hot Chain," *Wall Street Journal*, June 29, 2007, p. A1.

37. Francis Fukuyama, *The Great Disruption: Human Nature and the Reconstitution of Social Order* (New York: Touchstone, 2000), p. 89.

38. See Ronald Inglehart, *The Silent Revolution: Changing Values and Political Styles in Advanced Industrial Society* (Princeton, NJ: Princeton University Press, 1977).

Afterword

1. Peggy Fletcher Stack, "More Mormons Exiting Salt Lake City and Moving to the Suburbs," *Salt Lake Tribune*, July 17, 2008.

2. Gerald F. Seib, "Hopes Quickly Fade for a Postpartisan Era," *Wall Street Journal*, October 14, 2008.

3. *Time*, November 20, 2006.

4. Karl Rove, "Barack's Brilliant Ground Game," *Wall Street Journal*, July 10, 2008.

5. Peter Slevin, "Obama Volunteers Share the Power of Personal Stories," *Washington Post*, July 26, 2008.

SELECTED BIBLIOGRAPHY

Abramowitz, Alan I. "Redistricting, Competition, and the Rise of Polarization in the U.S. House of Representatives." Paper presented at the annual meeting of the American Political Science Association, September 3, 2006.

Abramowitz, Alan, Brad Alexander, and Matthew Gunning. "Don't Blame Redistricting for Uncompetitive Elections." *PS: Political Science and Politics* 39 (January 2006). Also available at http://www.centerforpolitics.org/crystalball/article/php?id=AIA2005052601.

Abramowitz, Alan, and Bill Bishop. "The Myth of the Middle." *Washington Post,* March 1, 2007, p. A17.

Abramowitz, Alan I., and Kyle L. Sanders. "Is Polarization a Myth?" Paper presented at the annual meeting of the Southern Political Science Association, January 5, 2006.

Ackerman, Bruce, and James S. Fishkin. *Deliberation Day.* New Haven, CT: Yale University Press, 2004.

"American Piety in the 21st Century: New Insight to the Depth and Complexity of Religion in the U.S." Selected findings, Baylor Religion Survey, September 2006. http://www.baylor.edu/content/services/document.php/33304.pdf.

Ardery, Julia S. *The Temptation: Edgar Tolson and the Genesis of Twentieth-Century Folk Art.* Chapel Hill: University of North Carolina Press, 1998.

Armstrong, Jerome, and Markos Moulitsas Zúniga. *Crashing the Gate: Netroots, Grassroots, and the Rise of People-Powered Politics.* White River Junction, VT: Chelsea Green, 2006.

Bai, Matt. "Who Lost Ohio?" *New York Times Magazine,* November 21, 2004, pp. 67–74.

———. "Wiring the Vast Left-Wing Conspiracy." *New York Times Magazine,* July 25, 2004.

Baron, R., S. Hoppe, B. Linneweh, and D. Rogers. "Social Corroboration and Opinion Extremity." *Journal of Experimental Social Psychology* 321 (1996).

Barone, Michael. "The 51 Percent Nation." *U.S. News and World Report,* November 15, 2004.

Bartels, Larry M. "Partisanship and Voting Behavior, 1952–1996." *American Journal of Political Science* 44, no. 1 (January 2000): 35–50.

———. "What's the Matter with *What's the Matter with Kansas?*" Paper prepared for the annual meeting of the American Political Science Association, September 2004. http://www.princeton.edu/~bartels/kansas.pdf.

Bell, Daniel. *The Coming of Post-Industrial Society.* New York: Basic Books, 1999.

Berube, Alan, Audrey Singer, Jill H. Wilson, and William H. Frey. "Finding Exurbia: America's Fast-Growing Communities at the Metropolitan Fringe." Brookings Institution, October 2006. http://www.brookings.edu/reports/2006/10metropolitanpolicy_berube.aspx.

Bianco, Anthony. "The Vanishing Mass Market." *BusinessWeek,* July 12, 2004.

Binder, Sarah A. "Elections and Congress's Governing Capacity." *Extensions: A Journal of the Carl Albert Congressional Research and Studies Center* (Fall 2005): 10–14.

Bishop, Bill. "The Great Divide" (series). *Austin American-Statesman,* 2004. http://www.statesman.com/metrostate/content/specialreports/greatdivide/index.html.

Bishop, Bill, and Mark Lisheron. "Cities of Ideas" (series). *Austin American-Statesman,* 2002, http://www.statesman.com/specialreports/content/specialreports/citiesofideas/.

Black, Earl, and Merle Black. *Divided America: The Ferocious Power Struggle in American Politics.* New York: Simon & Schuster, 2007.

Brady, David W., Hahrie Han, and Doug McAdam. "Party Polarization in the Post WWII Era: A Two Period Electoral Interpretation." Paper prepared for the Midwest Political Science Association, April 2003.

Brammer, Billy Lee. *The Gay Place.* 1961. Reprint. Austin: University of Texas Press, 1995.

Brewer, Mark D. "A Divided Public? Party Images and Mass Polarization in the United States." Paper prepared for the annual meeting of the American Political Science Association, 2002.

Broder, David. *The Party's Over: The Failure of Politics in America.* New York: Harper & Row, 1972.

Brooks, David. "One Nation, Slightly Divisible." *Atlantic,* December 2001, pp. 53–65.

———. *On Paradise Drive: How We Live Now (and Always Have) in the Future Tense.* New York: Simon & Schuster, 2004.

Burnham, Walter Dean. *The Current Crisis in American Politics.* New York: Oxford University Press, 1982.

Calhoun, Craig. "Populist Politics, Communications Media and Large Scale Societal Integration." *Sociological Theory* 6, no. 2 (Autumn 1988): 219–41.

Campbell, David. *Why We Vote: How Schools and Communities Shape Our Civic Life.* Princeton, NJ: Princeton University Press, 2006.

Candor, Catherine. "A History of the Kanawha County Textbook Controversy." PhD diss., Virginia Tech University, March 1976.

Carsey, Thomas M., and Geoffrey C. Layman. "Changing Sides or Changing Minds? Party Identification and Policy Preferences in the American Electorate." *American Journal of Political Science* 50, no. 2 (April 2006).

———. "Party Polarization and Party Structuring of Policy Attitudes: A Comparison of the 1972–1974–1976 and 1992–1994–1996 National Election Study Panels." Presentation at the Vanderbilt University Conference on Parties and Partisanship, October 25–27, 2001.

Carsey, Thomas M., Geoffrey C. Layman, John Green, and Richard Herrera. "Party Polarization and 'Conflict Extension' in the United States: The Case of Party Activists." Paper presented at the annual meeting of the Southern Political Science Association, January 6–8, 2005.

Chanley, Virginia A., Thomas J. Rudolph, and Wendy M. Rahn. "The Origins and Consequences of Public Trust in Government." *Public Opinion Quarterly* 64 (2000): 239–56.

Citrin, Jack. "Comment: The Political Relevance of Trust in Government." *American Political Science Review* 68 (1974): 973–88

Clark, Terry Nichols, and Vincent Hoffmann-Martinot, eds. *The New Political Culture.* Boulder, CO: Westview Press, 1998.

Clark, Terry Nichols, and Seymour Martin Lipset, eds. *The Breakdown of Class Politics.* Washington, DC: Woodrow Wilson Center Press, 2001.

Cohen, Lizabeth. *A Consumers' Republic: The Politics of Mass Consumption in Postwar America.* New York: Knopf, 2003.

Converse, Philip E. *The Dynamics of Party Support.* Beverly Hills, CA: Sage, 1976.

———. "The Nature of Belief Systems in Mass Publics." In *Ideology and Discontent,* edited by David E. Apter, pp. 206–61. London: Free Press of Glencoe, 1964.

Cortright, Joe. "The Economic Importance of Being Different: Regional Variations in Taste, Increasing Returns and the Dynamics of Development." *Economic Development Quarterly* 16, no. 1 (February 2002): 3–16.

———. "New Growth Theory, Technology and Learning: A Practitioner's Guide." Paper prepared for the Economic Development Administration, 2001.

———. "The Young and Restless in a Knowledge Economy." Report prepared for CEOs for Cities, December 2005.

Crow, Paul A., Jr. "Eugene Carson Blake: Apostle of Christian Unity." *Ecumenical Review* 21 (1986): 228–36.

Dahl, Robert A. *Democracy in the United States: Promise and Performance.* 2nd ed. Chicago: Rand McNally, 1972.

Dalton, Russell J. "The Social Transformation of Trust in Government." *International Review of Sociology* 15, no. 1 (March 2005): 133–54.

Diamond, Sara. *Roads to Dominion: Right Wing Movements and Political Power in the United States.* New York: Guilford Press, 1995.

Dionne, E. J., Jr. *Why Americans Hate Politics.* New York: Simon & Schuster, 1991.

Dovidio, John F., Samuel L. Gaertner, and Kerry Kawakami. "Intergroup Contact: The Past, Present and the Future." *Group Process and Intergroup Relations* 6, no. 1 (2003): 5–21.

Durkheim, Émile. *Selected Writings*. Edited by Anthony Giddens. Cambridge: Cambridge University Press, 1972.

Elazar, Daniel J. *The American Mosaic: The Impact of Space, Time and Culture on American Politics*. Boulder, CO: Westview Press, 1994.

Evans, F. B. "Selling as a Dyadic Relationship: A New Approach." *American Behavioral Scientist* 6, no. 9 (May 1963): 76–79.

Falwell, Jerry, ed. *The Fundamentalist Phenomenon: The Resurgence of Conservative Christianity*. New York: Doubleday, 1981.

Feldman, Glenn, ed. *Politics and Religion in the White South*. Lexington: University Press of Kentucky, 2005.

Fenton, John H. *Midwest Politics*. New York: Holt, Rinehart & Winston, 1966.

Fiorina, Morris P., with Samuel J. Abrams and Jeremy C. Pope. *Culture War? The Myth of a Polarized America*. New York: Pearson Longman, 2006.

Florida, Richard. "Cities and the Creative Class." *City and Community*, March 2003, pp. 3–19.

———. "The Economic Geography of Talent." *Annals of the Association of American Geographers* 92, no. 4 (2002): 743–55.

———. *The Rise of the Creative Class*. New York: Basic Books, 2002.

———. "Where the Brains Are." *Atlantic,* October 2006.

———. "The World Is Spiky." *Atlantic,* October 2005.

Florida, Richard, Robert Cushing, and Gary Gates. "When Social Capital Stifles Innovation." *Harvard Business Review,* August 1, 2002.

Fogel, Robert William. *The Fourth Great Awakening and the Future of Egalitarianism*. Chicago: University of Chicago Press, 2000.

Fox, Richard Wightman, and T. J. Jackson Lears, eds. *The Culture of Consumption: Critical Essays in American History, 1880–1980*. New York: Pantheon Books, 1983.

Frank, Thomas. *The Conquest of Cool*. Chicago: University of Chicago Press, 1997.

———. *What's the Matter with Kansas?* New York: Metropolitan Books, 2004.

Frey, William H. "Emerging Demographic Balkanization: Toward One America or Two?" Research Report No. 97–410, Population Studies Center, University of Michigan.

Fukuyama, Francis. *The Great Disruption: Human Nature and the Reconstitution of Social Order*. New York: Touchstone, 2000.

Garreau, Joel. *The Nine Nations of North America*. New York: Avon Books, 1981.

Gentzko, Matthew, and Jesse M. Shapiro. "What Drives Media Slant? Evidence from U.S. Daily Newspapers." University of Chicago and the National Bureau of Economic Research, October 17, 2006. http://faculty.chicagogsb.edu/matthew.gentzkow/research/biasmeas111306.pdf.

Gerber, Alan S., and Donald P. Green. "The Effects of Canvassing, Telephone Calls, and Direct Mail on Voter Turnout: A Field Experiment." *American Political Science Review* 94, no. 3 (September 2000): 653–63.

Gibbs, Eddie, and Ryan K. Bolger. *Emerging Churches: Creating Christian Community in Postmodern Cultures*. Grand Rapids, MI: Baker Academic, 2005.

Gibson, James L. "The Political Consequences of Intolerance: Cultural Conformity and Political Freedom." *American Political Science Review* 86, no. 2 (June 1992).

Gimpel, James G. *Separate Destinations: Migration, Immigration, and the Politics of Places.* Ann Arbor: University of Michigan Press, 1999.

Gimpel, James G., J. Celeste Lay, and Jason E. Schuknecht. *Cultivating Democracy: Civic Environments and Political Socialization in America.* Washington, DC: Brookings Institution Press, 2003.

Gimpel, James G., and Jason E. Schuknecht. *Patchwork Nation: Sectionalism and Political Change in American Politics.* Ann Arbor: University of Michigan Press, 2003.

Gitlin, Todd. *The Sixties: Years of Hope, Days of Rage.* New York: Bantam Books, 1993.

Gladwell, Malcolm. "The Cellular Church: How Rick Warren's Congregation Grew." *The New Yorker,* September 12, 2005, pp. 60–67.

———. *The Tipping Point: How Little Things Can Make a Big Difference.* Boston: Little, Brown, 2000.

Glaeser, Edward. "The Future of Urban Research: Non-Market Interactions." Harvard University, September 9, 1999. http://www.economics.harvard.edu/faculty/glaeser/papers/1_00_paper.pdf.

Glaeser, Edward L., and Christopher R. Berry. "The Divergence of Human Capital Levels Across Cities." Harvard Institute of Economic Research Discussion Paper 2091, August 2005.

Glaeser, Edward L., and Joshua D. Gottlieb. "Urban Resurgence and the Consumer City." Harvard Institute of Economic Research Working Paper 2109, 2006.

Glaeser, Edward, and Jesse M. Shapiro. "City Growth and the 2000 Census: Which Places Grew, and Why." Center of Urban and Metropolitan Policy, Brookings Institution, May 2001. http://www.brookings.edu/reports/2001/05demographics_edward-glaeser-and-jesse-m—shapiro.aspx.

Glaeser, Edward L., and Bryce A. Ward. "Myths and Realities of American Political Geography." Harvard Institute of Economic Research Discussion Paper 2100, January 2006.

Gluckman, Max. *Custom and Conflict in Africa.* 1956. Reprint. New York: Barnes & Noble Books, 1969.

Goldberg, Jeffrey. "Central Casting." *The New Yorker,* May 29, 2006, pp. 62–71.

Goldberg, Michelle. *Kingdom Coming: The Rise of Christian Nationalism.* New York: Norton, 2006.

Goode, Don J. "A Study of Values and Attitudes in a Textbook Controversy in Kanawha County, West Virginia: An Overt Act of Opposition to Schools." PhD diss., Michigan State University, 1984.

Granovetter, Mark S. "The Strength of Weak Ties." *American Journal of Sociology* 78, no. 6 (May 1973): 1360–80.

Green, Donald P., Alan S. Gerber, and David W. Nickerson. "Getting Out the Vote in Local Elections: Results from Six Door-to-Door Canvassing Experiments." *Journal of Politics* 65, no. 4 (November 2003): 1083–96.

Green, Donald, Bradley Palmquist, and Eric Schickler. *Partisan Hearts and Minds.* New Haven, CT: Yale University Press, 2002.

Green, John C., James L. Guth, Corwin E. Smidt, and Lyman A. Kellstedt. *Religion and the Culture Wars: Dispatches from the Front.* Lanham, MD: Rowman & Littlefield, 1996.

Green, John C., Mark J. Rozell, and Clyde Wilcox. "Social Movements and Party Politics: The Case of the Christian Right." *Journal for the Scientific Study of Religion* 40, no. 3 (2001): 413–26.

Greenberg, Anna. "Why Men Leave: Gender and Partisanship in the 1990s." Paper prepared for the annual meeting of the American Political Science Association, 2000.

Greenberg, Anna, and Bill Greener. "The Message from the Heartland: The Rural Vote in 2004." Memo, Greenberg Quinlan Rosner Research, Inc., and Greener and Hook, March 22, 2005.

Greenberg, Stanley B. *The Two Americas: Our Current Political Deadlock and How to Break It.* New York: St. Martin's Press, 2004.

Gyourko, Joseph, Christopher Mayer, and Todd Sinai. "Superstar Cities." National Bureau of Economic Research. Working Paper No. 12355, July 2006.

Hacker, Jacob S., and Paul Pierson. *Off Center: The Republican Revolution and the Erosion of American Democracy.* New Haven, CT: Yale University Press, 2005.

Hall, Peter. *Cities in Civilization.* New York: Fromm International, 1998.

Hefley, James C. *Textbooks on Trial.* Wheaton, IL: Victor Books, 1976.

Hetherington, Marc J. *Why Trust Matters: Declining Political Trust and the Demise of American Liberalism.* Princeton, NJ: Princeton University Press, 2005.

Hetherington, Marc J., and Jonathan Weiler. "Authoritarian Values and Political Choice." Paper prepared for the annual meeting of the Midwest Political Science Association, 2005.

Hoge, Dean R., and David A. Roozen, eds. *Understanding Church Growth and Decline: 1950–1978.* New York: Pilgrim Press, 1979.

Hout, Michael, Andrew Greeley, and Melissa J. Wilde. "The Demographic Imperative in Religious Change in the United States." *American Journal of Sociology* 107, no. 2 (September 2001): 468–500.

Huckfeldt, Robert, Edward G. Carmines, Jeffery J. Mondak, and Carl Palmer. "Blue States, Red States, and the Problem of Polarization in the American Electorate." Paper prepared for the annual meeting of the American Political Science Association, Washington, DC, September 2005.

Hunter, James Davison. *American Evangelism.* New Brunswick, NJ: Rutgers University Press, 1983.

———. *Culture Wars: The Struggle to Define America.* New York: Basic Books, 1991.

Inglehart, Ronald. *Culture Shift in Advanced Industrial Society.* Princeton, NJ: Princeton University Press, 1990.

———. *Modernization and Postmodernization: Cultural, Economic, and Political Change in 43 Societies.* Princeton, NJ: Princeton University Press, 1997.

———. *The Silent Revolution: Changing Values and Political Styles in Advanced Industrial Society.* Princeton, NJ: Princeton University Press, 1977.

Inglehart, Ronald, and Wayne Baker. "Modernization, Cultural Change, and the Persistence of Traditional Values." *American Sociological Review* 65 (February 2000).

Inglehart, Ronald, and Christian Welzel. *Modernization, Cultural Change, and Democracy: The Human Development Sequence.* New York: Cambridge University Press, 2005.

Isenberg, Daniel J. "Group Polarization: A Critical Review and Meta-Analysis." *Journal of Personality and Social Psychology* 50, no. 6 (1986).

Jacobs, Jane. *Cities and the Wealth of Nations*. New York: Vintage Books, 1985.

———. *The Death and Life of Great American Cities*. New York: Random House, 1961.

———. *The Economy of Cities*. New York: Vintage Books, 1970.

Jacobson, Gary C. "Explaining the Ideological Polarization of the Congressional Parties Since the 1970s." Paper prepared for the annual meeting of the Midwest Political Science Association, 2004.

Jenkinson, Edward B. *Censors in the Classroom*. Carbondale: Southern Illinois University Press, 1979.

Jensen, Richard. "Religion, Morality, and American Politics." *Journal of Libertarian Studies* 6, nos. 3 & 4 (1982): 321–32.

———. *The Winning of the Midwest*. Chicago: University of Chicago Press, 1971.

Johnson, Benton, Dean R. Hoge, and Donald A. Luidens. "Mainline Churches: The Real Reason for Decline." *First Things*, no. 31 (March 1993): 13–18.

Kempner, Joanna, Clifford S. Perlis, and Jon F. Merz. "Forbidden Knowledge." *Science*, February 11, 2005, p. 854.

Key, V. O. "Secular Realignment and the Party System." *Journal of Politics* 21, no. 2 (May 1959): 198–210.

Kimball, David C. "A Decline in Ticket Splitting and the Increasing Salience of Party Labels." In *Models of Voting in Presidential Elections: The 2000 Elections*, edited by Herbert F. Weisber and Clyde Wilcox. Stanford, CA: Stanford Law and Politics, 2004.

Kleppner, Paul. *The Cross of Culture: A Social Analysis of Midwestern Politics, 1850–1900*. New York: Free Press, 1970.

Kodrycki, Yolanda K. "Migration of Recent College Graduates: Evidence from the National Longitudinal Survey of Youth." *New England Economic Review*, January/February 2001, pp. 13–34.

Ladd, Everett Carll, Jr. "Liberalism Upside Down: The Inversion of the New Deal Order." *Political Science Quarterly* 91, no. 4 (Winter 1976–1977): 577–600.

LaHaye, Tim, and Jerry B. Jenkins. *Left Behind: A Novel of the Earth's Last Days*. Wheaton, IL: Tyndale House, 1995.

Lakoff, George. *Moral Politics: What Conservatives Know That Liberals Don't*. Chicago: University of Chicago Press, 1996.

Lang, Robert E., and Thomas W. Sanchez. "The New Metro Politics: Interpreting Recent Presidential Elections Using a County-Based Regional Typology." Election brief, Metropolitan Institute at Virginia Tech, 2006.

Layman, Geoffrey. *The Great Divide: Religious and Cultural Conflict in American Party Politics*. New York: Columbia University Press, 2001.

Layman, Geoffrey C., and Edward G. Carmines. "Cultural Conflict in American Politics: Religious Traditionalism, Postmaterialism, and U.S. Political Behavior." *Journal of Politics* 59, no. 3 (August 1997): 751–77.

Lazarsfeld, Paul F., Bernard Berelson, and Hazel Gaudet. *The People's Choice: How the Voter Makes Up His Mind in a Presidential Campaign*. New York: Duell, Sloan & Pearce, 1944.

Lazarsfeld, Paul, Bernard Berelson, and William McPhee. *Voting: A Study of Opinion Formation in a Presidential Campaign.* Chicago: University of Chicago Press, 1954.

Lesthaeghe, Ron, and Lisa Neidert. "The Political Significance of the 'Second Demographic Transition' in the US: A Spatial Analysis." Paper prepared for the annual meeting of the Population Association of America, March 28–30, 2007.

———. "The Second Demographic Transition in the United States: Exception or Textbook Example?" *Population and Development Review* 32, no. 4 (December 2006): 669–98.

Lindsey, Hal. *The Late Great Planet Earth.* Grand Rapids, MI: Zondervan, 1970.

Lipset, Seymour Martin, and William Schneider. *The Confidence Gap: Business, Labor, and Government in the Public Mind.* Baltimore: Johns Hopkins University Press, 1987.

Lucas, Robert E., Jr. "On the Mechanics of Economic Development." *Journal of Monetary Economics* 22 (1988): 3–42.

Macedo, Stephen, ed. *Democracy at Risk: How Political Choices Undermine Citizen Participation, and What We Can Do About It.* Washington, DC: Brookings Institution Press, 2005.

Mann, Brian. *Welcome to the Homeland: A Journey to the Rural Heart of America's Conservative Revolution.* Hanover, NH: Steerforth Press, 2006.

Marsden, George M. *Reforming Fundamentalism.* Grand Rapids, MI: Eerdmans, 1987.

Marschall, Melissa, and Wendy Rahn. "Birds of a Political Feather: Ideology, Partisanship, and Geographic Sorting in the American Electorate." Paper prepared for the annual meeting of the Midwest Political Science Association, April 21, 2006.

Martineau, Pierre. "Social Classes and Spending Behavior." *Journal of Marketing* 23, no. 2 (October 1958): 121–30.

Marty, Martin E. *Righteous Empire: The Protestant Experience in America.* New York: Dial Press, 1970.

Maslow, Abraham. "A Theory of Human Motivation." *Psychological Review* 50 (1943): 370–96.

Mason, Carol. "An American Conflict: Representing the 1974 Kanawha County Textbook Controversy." *Appalachian Journal* 32, no. 3 (2005): 352–78.

———. "Textual Reproduction of Ethnicity in the Kanawha Valley: The 1974 Textbook Controversy Revisited." Unpublished research paper, 2002.

McCarty, Nolan, Keith T. Poole, and Howard Rosenthal. *Polarized America: The Dance of Ideology and Unequal Riches.* Cambridge, MA: MIT Press, 2006.

———. "Political Polarization and Income Inequality." Unpublished paper, January 27, 2003. http://www.wws.princeton.edu/research/papers/01_03_nm.pdf.

McGavran, Donald. *The Bridges of God.* New York: Friendship Press, 1968.

———. *Understanding Church Growth.* Grand Rapids, MI: Eerdmans, 1970.

McGavran, Donald, and Win Arn. *How to Grow a Church.* Glendale, CA: Gospel Light, 1973.

McGirr, Lisa. *Suburban Warriors: The Origins of the New American Right.* Princeton, NJ: Princeton University Press, 2001.

McKee, Seth C. "The Matter with Kansas: Rural Republican Voting in Presidential

Elections." Paper presented at the annual meeting of the Midwest Political Science Association, Chicago, April 2006.

———. "Rural Vote and the Polarization of American Presidential Elections." Unpublished paper, 2006.

McKee, Seth C., and Daron R. Shaw. "Suburban Voting in Presidential Elections." *Presidential Studies Quarterly* 33, no. 1 (March 2003).

McKibben, Bill. "The Hope of the Web." *New York Review of Books,* April 27, 2006, pp. 4–6.

McPherson, Miller, Lynn Smith-Lovin, and Matthew E. Brashears. "Social Isolation in America: Changes in Core Discussion Networks over Two Decades." *American Sociological Review* 71 (June 2006): 353–75.

McPherson, Miller, Lynn Smith-Lovin, and James M. Cook. "Birds of a Feather: Homophily in Social Networks." *Annual Review of Sociology* 27 (2001): 415–44.

Micklethwait, John, and Adrian Wooldridge. *The Right Nation: Conservative Power in America.* New York: Penguin Press, 2004.

Miller, Warren. "One-Party Politics and the Voter." *American Political Science Review* 50, no. 3 (September 1956).

Moffett, James. *Storm in the Mountains.* Carbondale: Southern Illinois University Press, 1988.

Morgan, Kevin. "The Exaggerated Death of Geography: Learning, Proximity and Territorial Innovation Systems." *Journal of Economic Geography* 4, no. 1 (2004): 3–21.

Moscovici, Serge, and Marisa Zavalloni. "The Group as a Polarizer of Attitudes." *Journal of Personality and Social Psychology* 1, no. 2 (1969).

Mutz, Diana C. *Hearing the Other Side: Deliberative Versus Participatory Democracy.* New York: Cambridge University Press, 2006.

———. *Impersonal Influence: How Perceptions of Mass Collectives Affect Political Attitudes.* Cambridge: Cambridge University Press, 1998.

Mutz, Diana C., and Jeffery Mondak. "The Workplace as a Context for Cross-Cutting Political Discourse." *Journal of Politics* 68, no. 1 (February 2006): 140–55.

Myers, David G. *Social Psychology.* New York: McGraw-Hill Educational, 2004.

Myers, David, and Helmut Lamm. "The Group Polarization Phenomenon." *Psychological Bulletin* 83, no. 4 (1976).

Nash, George H. *The Conservative Intellectual Movement in America Since 1945.* New York: Basic Books, 1976.

Nie, Norman H., Sidney Verba, and John R. Petrocik. *The Changing American Voter.* Cambridge, MA: Harvard University Press, 1999.

Norris, Pippa, and Ronald Inglehart. "God, Guns and Gays: Religion and Politics in the US and Western Europe." Paper presented at the John F. Kennedy School of Government, Harvard University, September 6, 2004.

———. *Sacred and Secular: Religion and Politics Worldwide.* New York: Cambridge University Press, 2004.

Nye, Joseph S., Jr., Philip D. Zelikov, and David C. King. *Why People Don't Trust Government.* Cambridge, MA: Harvard University Press, 1997.

O'Hare, William, and Bill Bishop. "U.S. Rural Soldiers Account for a Disproportionately High Share of Casualties in Iraq and Afghanistan." Fact sheet, Carsey Institute, Fall 2006.

Ono, Keiko. "Electoral Origins of Partisan Polarization in Congress: Debunking the Myth." *Extensions: A Journal of the Carl Albert Congressional Research and Studies Center* (Fall 2005).

Oppenheimer, Bruce. "Deep Red and Blue Congressional Districts." In *Congress Reconsidered,* edited by Lawrence C. Dodd and Bruce Oppenheimer. 8th ed. Washington, DC: Congressional Quarterly Press, 2005.

O'Toole, John E. "Are Grace Slick and Tricia Nixon Cox the Same Person?" *Journal of Advertising* 2, no. 2 (1973): 32–34.

Packard, Vance. *The Hidden Persuaders.* New York: McKay, 1957.

Peppers, Don, and Martha Rogers. *The One to One Future: Building Relationships One Customer at a Time.* New York: Currency/Doubleday, 1993.

Perlstein, Rick. *Before the Storm: Barry Goldwater and the Unmaking of the American Consensus.* New York: Hill & Wang, 2001.

Pew Research Center for the People and the Press. "News Audiences Increasingly Politicized: Online News Audience Larger, More Diverse," June 8, 2004.

———. "Trends in Political Beliefs and Core Attitudes: 1987–2007," March 22, 2007.

Pickett, J. Waskom. *Christian Mass Movements in India.* New York: Abingdon Press, 1933.

Piore, Michael J., and Charles F. Sabel. *The Second Industrial Divide.* New York: Basic Books, 1984.

Polsby, Nelson W. *How Congress Evolves: Social Bases of Institutional Change.* New York: Oxford University Press, 2004.

Poole, Keith T. "Changing Minds? Not in Congress." Unpublished paper, January 13, 2003.

———. "The Decline and Rise of Party Polarization in Congress During the Twentieth Century." *Extensions: A Journal of the Carl Albert Congressional Research and Studies Center* (Fall 2005): 6–9.

Pope, Daniel. *The Making of Modern Advertising.* New York: Basic Books, 1983.

Porter, Michael E. *The Competitive Advantage of Nations.* New York: Free Press, 1990.

———. "The Economic Performance of Regions." *Regional Studies* 37, nos. 6 & 7 (August/October 2003): 549–78.

Putnam, Robert D. *Bowling Alone: The Collapse and Revival of American Community.* New York: Simon & Schuster, 2000.

———. *Making Democracy Work: Civic Traditions in Modern Italy.* Princeton, NJ: Princeton University Press, 1993.

Rauschenbusch, Walter. *Christianity and the Social Crisis.* New York: Macmillan, 1908.

Ray, Paul H. "The New Political Compass: The New Progressives Are In-Front, Deep Green, Against Big Business and Globalization, and Beyond Left vs. Right." Discussion paper, version 7.3, April 2002. http://www.futurenet.org/pdf/newpoliticalcompassv73.pdf.

Ray, Paul H., and Sherry Ruth Anderson. *The Cultural Creatives: How 50 Million People Are Changing the World.* New York: Harmony Books, 2000.

Romer, Paul. "Innovation: The New Pump of Growth." *Blueprint: Ideas for a New Century,* Winter 1998.

———. "Two Strategies for Economic Development: Using Ideas and Producing

Ideas." In *Proceedings of the World Bank Annual Conference on Development Economics,* 1992.

Roozen, David A. "Four Mega-Trends Changing America's Religious Landscape." Speech, annual conference of the Religion Newswriters Association, September 22, 2001.

Roozen, David A. "Oldline Protestantism: Pockets of Vitality Within a Continuing Stream of Decline." Hartford Institute for Religion Research Working Paper 1104.1, 2004.

Rosen, Emanuel. *The Anatomy of Buzz.* New York: Doubleday, 2000.

Saxenian, AnnaLee. "Lessons from Silicon Valley." *Technology Review,* July 1994, pp. 42–51.

———. *Regional Advantage: Culture and Competition in Silicon Valley and Route 128.* Cambridge, MA: Harvard University Press, 1994.

Schachter, Stanley. "Deviation, Rejection, and Communication." *Journal of Abnormal and Social Psychology* 46 (1951).

Schkade, David, Cass R. Sunstein, and Reid Hastie. "What Happened on Deliberation Day?" AEI-Brookings Joint Center for Regulatory Studies Working Paper 06-19, July 2006. http://aei-brookings.org/admin/authorpdfs/redirect-safely .php?fname=../pdffiles/phpb7.pdf.

Schmitt, Mark. "The Legend of the Powell Memo." *American Prospect,* April 27, 2005. http://www.prospect.org/cs/articles?articleId=9606.

Schudson Michael. *The Good Citizen: A History of American Civic Life.* New York: Free Press, 1998.

Seabright, Paul. *The Company of Strangers: A Natural History of Economic Life.* Princeton, NJ: Princeton University Press, 2004.

Shaw, Daron. "Door to Door with the GOP." *Hoover Digest,* Fall 2004.

Sherif, Muzafer. "A Study of Some Social Factors in Perception." *Archives of Psychology* 187 (July 1935).

Sherif, Muzafer, O. J. Harvey, B. Jack White, William R. Hood, and Carolyn W. Sherif. *Intergroup Conflict and Cooperation: The Robbers Cave Experiment.* Norman, OK: University Book Exchange, 1961.

Skocpol, Theda. *Diminished Democracy: From Membership to Management in American Civic Life.* Norman: University of Oklahoma Press, 2003.

Smith, J. Walker, Ann Clurman, and Craig Wood. *Coming to Concurrence: Addressable Attitudes and the New Model for Marketing Productivity.* Evanston, IL: Racom Communications, 2005.

Smith, Wendell. "Product Differentiation and Market Segmentation as Alternative Marketing Strategies." *Journal of Marketing* 21, no. 1 (July 1956): 3–8.

Sonn, Jung Won, and Michael Storper. "The Increasing Importance of Geographic Proximity in Technological Innovation: An Analysis of U.S. Patent Citations, 1975–1997." Paper prepared for the conference "What Do We Know About Innovation?" November 2003.

Sosnik, Douglas B., Matthew J. Dowd, and Ron Fournier. *Applebee's America: How Successful Political, Business, and Religious Leaders Connect with the New American Community.* New York: Simon & Schuster, 2006.

Stark, Rodney. "Secularization, R.I.P." *Sociology of Religion* 60, no. 3 (Autumn 1999): 249–50.

Stetzer, Ed. *Planting New Churches in a Postmodern Age.* Nashville, TN: Broadman & Holman, 2003.

Stonecash, Jeffrey M., Mark D. Brewer, and Mack D. Mariani. *Diverging Parties: Social Change, Realignment, and Party Polarization.* Boulder, CO: Westview Press, 2003.

Sundquist, James L. *Dynamics of the Party System.* Washington, DC: Brookings Institution Press, 1983.

Sunstein, Cass R. *Designing Democracy: What Constitutions Do.* New York: Oxford University Press, 2001.

———. *Why Societies Need Dissent.* Cambridge: Harvard University Press, 2003.

Tajfel, Henri. "Experiments in Intergroup Discrimination." *Scientific American,* November 1970, pp. 96–102.

Tedlow, Richard. *New and Improved: The Story of Mass Marketing in America.* Cambridge, MA: Harvard Business School Press, 1996.

Teixeira, Ruy, and John Judis. *The Emerging Democratic Majority.* New York: Scribner, 2002.

Thumma, Scott, Dave Travis, and Warren Bird. "Megachurches Today 2005: Summary of Research Findings." Paper prepared for the Hartford Institute for Religion Research, 2005. http://hirr.hartsem.edu/megachurch/megastoday2005_summaryreport.html.

Tiebout, Charles. "A Pure Theory of Local Expenditures." *Journal of Political Economy* 64, no. 5 (October 1956): 416–24.

Toobin, Jeffrey. "The Great Election Grab." *The New Yorker,* December 8, 2003.

"Toward a More Responsible Two-Party System: A Report of the Committee on Political Parties." Pt. 2. *American Political Science Review* 44, no. 3 (1950, Suppl.).

Triplett, Norman. "The Dynamogenic Factors in Pacemaking and Competition." *American Journal of Psychology* 9 (1897): 507–33.

Turow, Joseph. *Breaking Up America: Advertisers and the New Media World.* Chicago: University of Chicago Press, 1997.

Urban, Glen. *Don't Just Relate — Advocate!* Upper Saddle River, NJ: Wharton School, 2005.

Wagner, C. Peter, ed. *Church Growth: State of the Art.* Wheaton, IL: Tyndale House, 1986.

Warren, Rick. *The Purpose-Driven Church: Growth Without Compromising Your Message and Mission.* Grand Rapids, MI: Zondervan, 1995.

Whyte, William H., Jr. "The Web of Word of Mouth." *Fortune,* November 1954.

Wiebe, Robert H. *The Segmented Society: An Introduction to the Meaning of America.* New York: Oxford University Press, 1975.

———. *Self-Rule: A Cultural History of American Democracy.* Chicago: University of Chicago Press, 1995.

Wilensky, Harold L. *Rich Democracies: Political Economy, Public Policy, and Performance.* Berkeley: University of California Press, 2002.

Wuthnow, Robert. *After Heaven: Spirituality in America Since the 1950s.* Berkeley: University of California Press, 1998.

———. *Loose Connections: Joining Together in America's Fragmented Communities.* Cambridge, MA: Harvard University Press, 1998.

————. "The Moral Minority: Where Have All the Liberal Protestants Gone?" *American Prospect,* May 22, 2000.

Yankelovich, Daniel. "New Criteria for Market Segmentation." *Harvard Business Review,* March/April 1964, pp. 83–90.

Young, James Sterling. *The Washington Community.* New York: Harcourt, Brace & World, 1966.

Zaller, John R. *The Nature and Origins of Mass Opinion.* Cambridge: Cambridge University Press, 1992.

INDEX